DATE DUE			
Jul 7'82			

PFANZAGL · THEORY OF MEASUREMENT

THEORY OF MEASUREMENT

BY

JOHANN PFANZAGL

in cooperation with

V. Baumann and H. Huber

2nd revised edition

reprint 1973

Physica-Verlag · Würzburg-Wien

1971

ISBN 3 7908 0016 3

Composed by: R. Oldenbourg, Graph. Betriebe GmbH, München.
Printed in Germany by: repro-druck „Journalfranz" Arnulf Liebing, Würzburg.

ISBN 3 7908 0016 3

Contents

Preface

Scope and Aim of the Book

At this stage of development of the theory of measurement it is too early to give a comprehensive presentation. The author, however, considers the time to be ripe for surveying the results obtained until now. The purpose of such a survey at this stage can only be to stimulate further research but not by any means to bring the theory to its final shape.

The student of this field is aware of the fact that almost every author has his own terminology; that seemingly unrelated topics such as latent structure analysis and intelligence testing do have a common basic model. Consequently, a further purpose of this book is to standardize terminology and trace seemingly different approaches back to their common roots. TORGERSON's book (1958) was a first important step towards the realization of these aims. The author hopes to have proceeded a step further.

The book aims at the methodological foundation of measurement. Nevertheless it is also concerned with specific applications such as measurement of pitch, simultaneous measurement of abilities of subjects and difficulties of tasks based on response, simultaneous measurement of utility and subjective probability based on risky choice and so on. A close relationship to applications is necessary, because otherwise the theory of measurement becomes rather fruitless, as clearly demonstrated by a book like that of ROSS (1964). However, even in discussing the problems of measurement for such specific instances the stress is always on the basic aspects (such as the existence and uniqueness of scales), never on workable techniques for practical performance. The reader interested in these aspects of measurement is referred to TORGERSON (1958) (The reader of TORGERSON's book will realize that there is a great number of procedures for computing scales for which no definition is available, except the one implicit in the computational procedure.).

The student who constructs a scale on the basis of empirical data, should always understand its methodological foundation in order to understand its meaning. There is no need for him to understand the computational procedures or computer programs. There is still another reason for completely neglecting computational procedures: Owing to the increasing use of computers, paper and pencil techniques, which were of overwhelming practical importance a few years ago, will become more and more unimportant. The ready access to computers might even influence the models themselves. The very restrictive model of classical factor analysis, for instance, will probably be substituted by the much more general model of a nonmetric factor analysis. (COOMBS and KAO (1955), SHEPARD (1965)). Of course the conceptual framework of nonmetric factor analysis might just as well have been developed a few decades ago. It was not so, however, until it resulted as a natural consequence of the enlarged computational facilities. I consider this example as typical: More general models usually require a greater amount of computations. The ability to perform this will raise the interest in more general models.

Stressing the foundational aspects of measurement naturally leads to some idealizations. In paired comparisons, for instance, we assume that $P(a_0, a_1)$ is known for each pair a_0, a_1. In practice we have only an estimate of the probability, based on a finite number of experiments, for a finite number of pairs a_0, a_1. This is, however, of no relevance for the theoretical foundation of the scale, because in principle we can always come arbitrarily close to the idealized assumption that $P(a_0, a_1)$ is known for any pair a_0, a_1. The question of how the scale is to be determined from a limited set of data is one of estimation and has nothing to do with the definition of the scale.

To illustrate the consequences of this approach let us consider the case of the so-called "ordered metric scales" (COOMBS (1964)). They do not exist in our theory: If distances can be compared for any pair a_0, a_1, this leads to an ordinary interval scale (see page 147). The fact that in practice the comparison can be performed only for a finite number of pairs poses the question, how the (uniquely determined) interval scale can be approximated from the data. It does not create a new type of scales. An attempt to build the inexactness of empirical operations into the theory is due to ADAMS (1965).

The reader will miss a very important subject in this book: Multidimensional Scaling. Though a number of computational procedures leading to successful applications are available (e. g. MESSICK (1956), SHEPARD (1962), B. KRUSKAL (1964a, 1964b), KÜNNAPAS, MÄLHAMMAR and SVENSON (1964)), a satisfactory theory was missing up to now. Recently, important results on this subject have been obtained by D. KRANTZ and others. They gave conditions under which the order between pairs of objects (according to "similarity") can be represented by the order of the intra-pair distances, if each object is assigned a point in a Euclidean space. These results are, however, yet unpublished. Furthermore, the forthcoming book of KRANTZ, LUCE, SUPPES and TVERSKY will treat multidimensional scaling in a competent and elaborate way. For this reason we decided to omit this subject completely.

In accordance with the theoretical orientation of the book applications are only dealt with as examples illustrating the theory. No attempt is made to give a comprehensive survey of the empirical work done in this field.

The reader will find that the applications are almost exclusively concerned with the behavioral sciences (including utility and subjective probability). The reason is that measurement in classical physics poses no problems comparable to those in the behavioral sciences. Except for temperature, all properties measured are of the additive type. The related problems were treated and solved in the paper of HELMHOLTZ (1887). Measurement in the behavioral sciences poses much more difficult and much more heterogeneous problems which justify the great emphasis placed upon them in this book. The problem of measurement in quantum physics are not dealt with. Some readers might ask for an explanation of this on the basis of the subject matter. There is only a pragmatic explanation for this omission: The author does not understand anything about quantum physics.

The level of mathematics used is a moderate one. The only parts of mathematics going beyond calculus are functional equations and a few elementary topological concepts. The reader who is familiar with calculus will find it easy and useful to make himself acquainted with the elements of functional equations from the excellent book of ACZÉL (1966). Both functional equations and topology are only used in the proofs. They are not necessary for understanding the results.

Style of Cooperation

Finally a few words concerning the cooperation of the author and his co-authors: The starting point for this book was the booklet

"Die axiomatischen Grundlagen einer allgemeinen Theorie des Messens". This booklet together with unpublished sketches of the author provided the material for this book. H. HUBER mainly cooperated in the preparation of chapters 3–9. All topics were thoroughly discussed with him, and he either prepared or rewrote many parts of these chapters. Many ideas only roughly sketched out by the author were elaborated by him. The author wishes to thank the Deutsche Forschungsgemeinschaft who enabled Mr. HUBER by a grant to concentrate on this subject for two years.

V. BAUMANN played an important role in the final formulation of chapters 1, 2, 12, section 6.6 and 9.5. Furthermore, the proof of Lemma 3.8.4 is due to him.

Acknowledgements

The author is further indebted to a great number of scholars for giving comments on talks on the theory of measurement as for instance at the Mathematisches Forschungsinstitut Oberwolfach, at the Econometric Research Program of Princeton University (Director O. MORGENSTERN), at the Congress on Methodology and Philosophy of Sciences, Stanford, at the Ford-Institute in Vienna (then directed by S. SAGOROFF) and at the Workshop on the Theory of Measurement, organized by COOMBS at the University of Michigan, Ann Arbor, in 1965. The discussions held on these occasions resulted in many valuable suggestions.

The discussions with M. LEVINE in Ann Arbor had a strong influence on chapters 10 and 11. The author wishes to thank Mr. LEVINE also for making unpublished material available to him.

He furthermore wishes to thank a great number of scholars who gave valuable comments on earlier drafts of the manuscript, among them J. ACZÉL, P. C. FISHBURN, R. D. LUCE, A. KUTZELNIGG, H. MÜNZNER (for the reference to ZERMELO's paper), H. SCHMERKOTTE, H. SCHNEEWEISS, S. S. STEVENS, A. TVERSKY and C. HIPP.

Finally the author wishes to thank K. LENHARD and R. MINTROP for their help in the preparation of chapters 10 to 12 and L. ROGGE who, in the very last stage of editing, eliminated a number of errors which were overlooked by both, the author and his coauthors.

Language

Readers might wonder why an author whose native language is German and who lives in a German-speaking country publishes a book in English only. The reasons are patent: He would miss most of his potential readers if the book were published in the German language only. He will not miss any potential reader if the book is published only in English. Let me close by expressing the hope that the reader will excuse all shortcomings in this text due to my insufficient command of the English language.

1. The Concept of Measurement

1.1 Properties and Manifestations

The subjects of measurement are properties. Weight, color, intelligence are typical examples to illustrate the sense in which the word "property" will be used here. If we speak of different *manifestations* of a property we mean e. g. red, blue, green... in the case of color, or different degrees of intelligence*).

Of course, properties exist only in connection with empirical objects such as physical bodies, electromagnetic waves, or persons. Electromagnetic waves, for example, are the objects carrying the property "color". Usually, one object shows various properties: a tone, for example, has the properties of loudness, pitch and timbre. In measuring one property, we neglect all the other properties the objects in question might have. In measuring weight, e. g., we neglect other properties of the bodies such as shape and color. In measuring hue we neglect brightness and saturation and the time and location where the color was perceived. Thus, quite different objects might become equivalent if consideration is restricted to one property: all bodies of identical weight, for example, are considered equivalent regardless of shape and color.

If we say that a property has a distinct structure we mean a structure determined by empirical relations between empirical objects.

*) We will not follow TORGERSON (1958) in using the term "attribute" for a measurable property and "magnitudes" for the manifestations of a measurable property, as there seems to be no necessity for a terminological distinction between properties in general and measurable properties in particular. We will also avoid the word "continuum" (as used, e. g., by S. S. STEVENS and TORGERSON) for the set of all possible manifestations of a given property, because this term suggests that there is a very large and connected set of manifestations. Though this holds true in most of the practical cases it is not true in general and should therefore not coin the general terminology. In conformity with this terminology we will also speak of metathetic and prothetic properties instead of metathetic and prothetic continua as STEVENS does.

This general formulation also covers the case of "empirical relations" being "statements of subjects on subjective relations between empirical objects". As an example let us consider the property "pitch". The simplest empirical relation between two tones concerning the structure of this property is the statement of a subject about which one of the two tones is of higher pitch. Furthermore, the subject can specify the pitch lying midway between two given pitches. Such relations give a specific structure to the property "pitch". Often the structure is even richer. Consider as another example the property "electrical resistance". By simple comparisons we can determine whether two rheostats have the same electrical resistances, and if not, which one has the greater electrical resistance. Furthermore we can switch rheostats in series. Such an operation gives a definite structure to the property "resistance" which is formally equivalent to addition.

Although we always start from relations between objects, it is the properties which are the concern of measurement, and not the objects themselves.

The reader interested in a further discussion of general problems of measurement is referred to TORGERSON (1958, chapters 1 and 2) and ADAMS (1966).

1.2 Representation of Properties by Language

In a prescientific stage only classificatory concepts are used in dealing with properties. In this situation it is not necessary to use numbers for an isomorphic representation of this very crude structure; words are wholly sufficient for this purpose. Our vocabulary for colors might be considered as a nominal scale for the property "hue". It is, however, not a nominal scale in the strict sense defined in 4.1, as a rather broad variety of easily distinguishable colors are denoted by the same word "green". Therefore the nominal scales for colors pertaining to two different languages are not necessarily in a $1-1$ relation to each other.

Language considered as a scale can even be used to form a very crude ordinal scale. In the Indoeuropean languages the order between two manifestations of a property can be expressed in a very systematic way by comparison of the adjective in question, such as warm, warmer. If language enables us to distinguish between a greater number of graduations, this is not achieved in a systematic way. Consider for instance the sequence hot – warm – tepid – cool – cold – icy. Nothing indicates that these words denote different manifestations of the same property and what the order relation is between them. Nevertheless the Indo-european languages show a high degree of abstraction insofar as they have a specific category of words for the expression of properties.

In more primitive languages it occurs that one and the same property is denoted by different expressions, depending on the object bearing this property. In Algonquian, for instance, "sū" is used to signify that an animate object is in state of heat or fire and "tä" to signify the same property for an inanimate object.

It is of obvious importance to describe the structure of a property in a more accurate and more systematic way than is achieved by language. The linguistic differentiation between various manifestations is too crude: a finer graduation is necessary for scientific analysis. In order to express even a simple law like "property *A* is monotone related to property *B*" we need some systematic manner of expressing the order between the different manifestations. Both aims, a finer graduation and a systematic expression of order, can be attained if we represent manifestations by real numbers rather than by words. Laws expressing more than a monotone relationship between properties require pictures of reality expressing structures of a more complicated type than just order (e. g. additivity or distance). For this purpose the practical advantage of taking numbers instead of words is unquestionable.

In prescientific stage we often observe that one and the same society uses different measures for the same property if it occurs in different contexts. The height of a tree e. g. is measured in feet, the distance between two villages in walkinghours. Though the property measured is the same, namely length, it obviously has different operational meaning and is therefore measured by different scales. The development of different scales for different societies often has deeper roots. A natural unit for areas is the area which can maintain one family. This area will be different for agricultural societies and hunting societies. Furthermore we observe that related scales (such as the scale for length and the scale for area) are defined independently (e. g. "walkinghours" for length and "area maintaining one family" for area).

The development of a coherent system of universally accepted scales is one of the first signs of transition to a scientific stage of the society.

1.3 Relational Systems

The situation exhibited by the examples given above can be described more formally as follows (SUPPES and ZINNES (1963)): We are dealing with a set A of empirical objects. Between the elements of A, a number of relations R_i ($i \in I$) is defined.

1.3.1 **Definition:** A set A together with a specified set of relations R_i ($i \in I$) on A will be called a relational system (r.s.) and symbolized by $\langle A; (R_i)_{i \in I} \rangle$, or, if $I = \{1, \ldots, n\}$, by $\langle A; R_1, \ldots, R_n \rangle$. If useful, the symbol $\mathbf{A}$ will be used as an abbreviation for $\langle A; (R_i)_{i \in I} \rangle$.

Simple examples of relational systems are: A is a set of tones, and R_1 is an (equivalence*)) relation to be denoted by $\approx$: The relation $\approx (a, b)$ (or $a \approx b$) holds iff**) the tones a, b have the same pitch. The pertaining relational system will be denoted by $\langle A; \approx \rangle$. In addition to equivalence, an order relation can be defined by: $\prec(a, b)$ (or $a \prec b$) holds iff tone a has a lower pitch than tone b. If besides equivalence order is considered, one is dealing with the relational system $\langle A; \approx, \prec \rangle$. In the examples considered hitherto, only binary (2-ary) relations occurred. An example of a quarternary (4-ary) relation is $D(a, b, c, d)$ which holds iff the distance between a and b equals the distance between c and d (see 9.1.7). An example of a unitary (1-ary) relation is, A being a set of persons, "a has been vaccinated" or "the surname of a is Miller".

In general, R_i will be a k_i-ary relation (i.e. a relation with k_i arguments), k_i being a positive integer.

1.3.2 **Definition**: If R_i is a k_i-ary relation on A, $(k_i)_{i \in I}$ is the *type* of the relational system $\langle A; (R_i)_{i \in I} \rangle$.

It is convenient to characterize a k-ary relation R by the set of those k-tuples $(a_1, \ldots, a_k) \in A^k$, for which $R(a_1, \ldots, a_k)$ holds, i.e.

$$R = \{(a_1, \ldots, a_k) \in A^k : R(a_1, \ldots, a_k) \text{ holds}\}.$$

For A being the set of real numbers, e.g., the relation $a \leqq b$ will be characterized by a certain half-plane (see p. 19).

We will denote by R the set in A^k characterizing the relation R, and by $R(a_1, \ldots, a_k)$ the value of the characteristic function of this set at the point $(a_1, \ldots, a_k)$.

---

*) see definition 1.4.1.

**) "iff" is the short form of "if and only if".

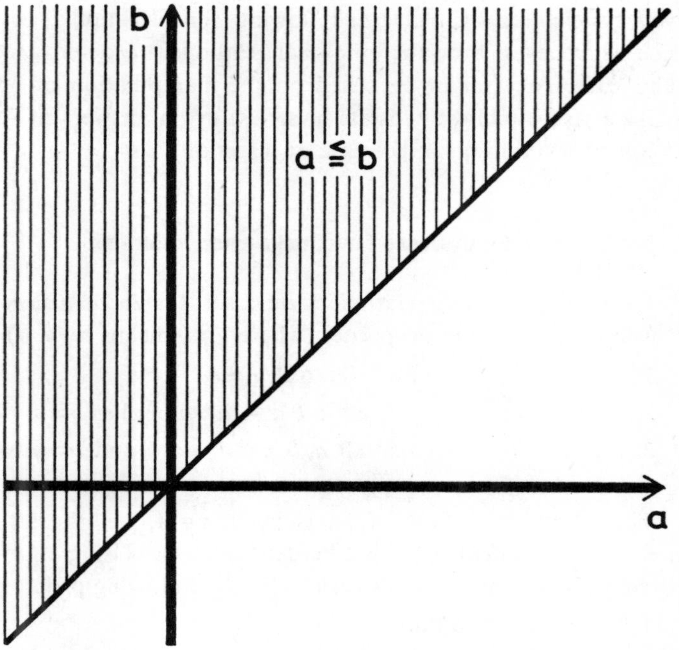

Thus $(a_1, \ldots, a_k) \in R$ and $R(a_1, \ldots, a_k) = 1$,

$(a_1, \ldots, a_k) \notin R$ and $R(a_1, \ldots, a_k) = 0$

are equivalent.

If $\langle A; (R_i)_{i \in I} \rangle$ is a r.s. and A_0 a subset of A, $\langle A_0; (R_i)_{i \in I} \rangle$ denotes the r.s. $\langle A_0; (R_i \cap A_0^{k_i})_{i \in I} \rangle$, i.e. the r.s. obtained from $\langle A; (R_i)_{i \in I} \rangle$ by restricting the relations R_i to A_0.

In a few of the examples, the structure of A was not only determined by relations, but also by operations, e.g. the operation of bisection or addition. If we have any operation $\circ$, assigning to each k-tuple $(a_1, \ldots, a_k) \in A^k$ a unique element $\circ(a_1, \ldots, a_k) \in A$, we can describe $\circ$ by the $(k+1)$-ary relation $R_\circ$ defined by

$$(a_1, \ldots, a_k, a_{k+1}) \in R_\circ \text{ iff } \circ(a_1, \ldots, a_k) = a_{k+1}.$$

1.3.3 **Definition:** The r.s. $\mathbf{A} = \langle A; (R_i)_{i \in I} \rangle$ is an *algebra* iff all relations R_i are operations. It is a (k-dimensional) *numerical relational system* (n.r.s.) iff $A = \mathbb{R}^k$, $\mathbb{R}$ being the set of real numbers.

If the set A consists of empirical objects and the relations R_i on A are empirically determined, $\langle A; (R_i)_{i \in I} \rangle$ will be called an *empirical relational system* (e.r.s.). For the following consideration it is of no relevance whatsoever, how the empirical relations are determined in a particular case. They might be based on the manipulation of physical objects (such as switching rheostats in series) or on answers of subjects based on introspection (as in the case of bisection).

1.4 Indifference, Equivalence and Congruence Relations

1.4.1 **Definition:** A binary relation $\approx$ on a set A is an *equivalence relation* iff it has the following properties (where $a \approx b$ means $\approx(a, b)=1$):

1. Reflexivity: For all $a \in A$, $a \approx a$.
2. Symmetry: For all $a, b \in A$, $a \approx b$ implies $b \approx a$.
3. Transitivity: For all $a, b, c \in A$, $a \approx b$ and $b \approx c$ together imply $a \approx c$.

The equivalence class of an element $a \in A$, i.e. the set of all elements of A equivalent to a, will be denoted by $\tilde{a}$. Using equivalence classes, equivalence can be characterized by the following properties:

1. For all $a \in A : a \in \tilde{a}$.
2. For all $a, b \in A$, we have either $\tilde{a} \cap \tilde{b} = \emptyset$ or $\tilde{a} = \tilde{b}$.

1.4.2 **Definition:** Let $\mathbf{A} = \langle A; (R_i)_{i \in I} \rangle$ be a r.s. An equivalence relation $\approx$ on A is a *congruence relation* for $\mathbf{A}$ iff it has the substitution property, i.e. iff for each $i \in I$, $(a_1, \ldots, a_{k_i}) \in A^{k_i}$, $(a'_1, \ldots, a'_{k_i}) \in A^{k_i}$, $a_j \approx a'_j$ for $j=1, \ldots, k_i$ together imply $R_i(a_1, \ldots, a_{k_i}) = R_i(a'_1, \ldots, a'_{k_i})$.

1.4.3 **Remark:** "For each $i \in I$, $(a_1, \ldots, a_{k_i}) \in A^{k_i}$, $j \in \{1, \ldots, k_i\}$ and $a \in A$, $a \approx a_j$ together imply $R_i(a_1, \ldots, a_{k_i}) = R_i(a_1, \ldots, a_{j-1}, a, a_{j+1}, \ldots, a_{k_i})$" is formally weaker than the substitution property, but implies it: Let be $a_j \approx a'_j$ for $j=1, \ldots, k_i$. Hence $R_i(a_1, a_2, \ldots, a_{k_i}) = R_i(a'_1, a_2, \ldots, a_{k_i}) = R_i(a'_1, a'_2, \ldots, a_{k_i}) = \ldots = R_i(a'_1, a'_2, \ldots, a'_{k_i})$.

Example of a congruence relation for the r.s. $\langle \mathbb{R}; R_1 \rangle$ with $R_1 = \{(x, y) : x^2 < y^2\}$: "$x \approx y$" iff $x=y$ or $x=-y$. Example for congruence relations for e.r.s.: In the measurement of weight, a body can be substituted by any other body of the same weight, regardless of shape, hardness, color etc. In the measurement of pitch, a tone can be substituted by any other tone of the same pitch regardless of loudness and color. If this were impossible, no such property as "pitch" would exist independently of loudness and color.

1.4.4 **Definition:** An equivalence relation $\approx_2$ is *coarser* than an equivalence relation $\approx_1$ iff $\approx_1 \subset \approx_2$, or equivalently, iff $a \approx_1 b$ implies $a \approx_2 b$.

1.4.5 **Theorem:** For every r.s. $\mathbf{A}=\langle A; (R_i)_{i\in I}\rangle$ there exists a (uniquely determined) coarsest congruence relation $\approx_{\mathbf{A}}$ (i.e. $\approx_{\mathbf{A}} \supset \approx$ for every congruence relation $\approx$ for $\mathbf{A}$).

Proof: We define: $a \approx_{\mathbf{A}} a'$ iff for all $i \in I, j = 1, \ldots, k_i$, and $a_1, \ldots, a_{j-1}, a_{j+1}, \ldots, a_{k_i} \in A$ we have

$$R_i(a_1, \ldots, a_{j-1}, a, a_{j+1}, \ldots, a_{k_i}) = R_i(a_1, \ldots, a_{j-1}, a', a_{j+1}, \ldots, a_{k_i}).$$

Obviously, $\approx_{\mathbf{A}}$ is an equivalence relation. Moreover it is a congruence relation for $\mathbf{A}$ because of the remark 1.4.3.

On the other hand, let $\approx$ be a congruence relation for $\mathbf{A}$, and let $a \approx a'$. Since $x \approx x$ for all $x \in A$, we obtain $a \approx_{\mathbf{A}} a'$.

Thus we can identify elements of A belonging to the same equivalence class with respect to $\approx_{\mathbf{A}}$: Using the given relations only, these elements are indistinguishable. On the other hand, elements belonging to different equivalence classes can be distinguished by means of the given relations: If $a \not\approx_{\mathbf{A}} a'$, there exists $i \in I$, $j \in \{1, \ldots, k_i\}$ and $a_1, \ldots, a_{j-1}, a_{j+1}, \ldots, a_{k_i} \in A$ such that $R_i(a_1, \ldots, a_{j-1}, a, a_{j+1}, \ldots, a_{k_i}) \neq R_i(a_1, \ldots, a_{j-1}, a', a_{j+1}, \ldots, a_{k_i})$.

If $\mathbf{A}=\langle A; (R_i)_{i\in I}\rangle$ is an e.r.s., the set A consists of empirical objects. From a strictly formal point of view, the property measured is defined by the empirical relations R_i $(i \in I)$. The equivalence classes induced by $\approx_{\mathbf{A}}$ correspond to the different distinguishable manifestations of this property.

Starting from a r.s. $\mathbf{A}=\langle A; (R_i)_{i\in I}\rangle$ and a congruence relation $\approx$ for $\mathbf{A}$ we can introduce the r.s. $\mathbf{A}/\approx\, = \langle \tilde{\tilde{A}}; (\tilde{\tilde{R}}_i)_{i\in I}\rangle$ which is of the same type: The elements of $\tilde{\tilde{A}}$ are the equivalence classes induced by $\approx$. The relations between the elements of $\tilde{\tilde{A}}$ are uniquely determined by the relations between the elements of A "representing" the classes:

$$\tilde{\tilde{R}}_i(\tilde{a}_1, \ldots, \tilde{a}_{k_i}) = R_i(a_1, \ldots, a_{k_i}) \text{ for } a_j \in \tilde{a}_j \ (j=1, \ldots, k_i).$$

1.4.6 **Definition:** The r.s. $\mathbf{A}/\approx$ is the "*quotient r.s. of* $\mathbf{A}$ *modulo* $\approx$".

As classes of empirical objects are empirical objects, $\mathbf{A}/\approx$ is an empirical r.s. together with $\mathbf{A}$.

1.4.7 **Definition:** A r.s. $\mathbf{A}$ will be called *irreducible* if $\approx_{\mathbf{A}}$ is the equality relation (i.e. if equality is the only congruence relation for $\mathbf{A}$).

1.4.8 **Theorem:** For any r.s. $\mathbf{A}$, $\tilde{\tilde{\mathbf{A}}}=\mathbf{A}/\approx_{\mathbf{A}}$ is irreducible. $\mathbf{A}/\approx_{\mathbf{A}}$ will be called the irreducible r.s. corresponding to $\mathbf{A}$.

Proof: Let $\sim$ be the coarsest congruence relation on $\tilde{\tilde{\mathbf{A}}}$ and $\tilde{a} \sim \tilde{a}'$. $\tilde{\tilde{R}}_i (\tilde{a}_1, \ldots, \tilde{a}_{j-1}, \tilde{a}, \tilde{a}_{j+1}, \ldots, \tilde{a}_{k_i}) = \tilde{\tilde{R}}_i (\tilde{a}_1, \ldots, \tilde{a}_{j-1}, \tilde{a}', \tilde{a}_{j+1}, \ldots, \tilde{a}_{k_i})$ for all $i \in I$, $j = 1, \ldots, k_i$ and $\tilde{a}_1, \ldots, \tilde{a}_{j-1}, \tilde{a}_{j+1}, \ldots, \tilde{a}_{k_i} \in \tilde{A}$. Hence $R_i (a_1, \ldots, a_{j-1}, a, a_{j+1}, \ldots, a_{k_i}) = R_i (a_1, \ldots, a_{j-1}, a', a_{j+1}, \ldots, a_{k_i})$ for all $i \in I$, $j = 1, \ldots k_i$ and $a_1, \ldots, a_{j-1}, a_{j+1}, \ldots, a_{k_i} \in A$. This however implies $a \approx_{\mathbf{A}} a'$, i.e. $\tilde{a} = \tilde{a}'$.

1.5 Maps, Homomorphisms and Isomorphisms

Let A and B be two arbitrary sets. A function m, assigning to each element $a \in A$ an element $m(a) \in B$ is called a *map* of A into B, symbolically $m: A \to B$. The element $m(a)$ is called the *value* of the function m at a, or the *picture* of a under m. For any subset A' of A, $m(A')$ is the set $\{m(a): a \in A'\}$. The set A is called the *domain* of m, the set B is called the *range* of m. In general $m(a)$ does not assume all values of B; there exist $b \in B$ which are not the picture of any a, i.e. $m(A)$ is a proper subset of B. If $m(A)=B$ the map is called *onto* (instead of into) B.

A map can be considered as a collection of pairs $(a, m(a))$, giving in the first place an element of A, in the second place the assigned element of B. If A consists of a finite number of elements $a_1, \ldots, a_n$, a map can be specified exhaustively by a table

a	$m(a)$
a_1	$m(a_1)$
a_2	$m(a_2)$
$\vdots$	$\vdots$
a_n	$m(a_n)$

As the map is single valued, no element $a \in A$ occurs with more than one value $m(a)$. The map is called $1-1$, if also the opposite is true: If each element of B occurs at most once as a picture of an element of A. In this case, to each element $b \in m(A)$ there corresponds one and only one element $a \in A$ such that $b=m(a)$.

If B' is any subset of B, by $m^{-1}(B')$ we will denote the set of all elements of A whose pictures are elements of B', i.e. $m^{-1}(B')=\{a \in A: m(a) \in B'\}$. The set $m^{-1}(B')$ is called the *inverse* of B'. Especially, $m^{-1}(\{b\})$ (or simply $m^{-1}(b)$) is the set of all elements of A having b as picture. If the map is into and not onto, $m^{-1}(b)$ will be empty for some elements of B. If the map is $1-1$, $m^{-1}(b)$ will consist of at most one element for each $b \in B$.

1.5.1 **Definition:** If we are given two r.s. of the same type, say $\mathbf{A}=\langle A; (R_i)_{i\in I}\rangle$ and $\mathbf{B}=\langle B; (S_i)_{i\in I}\rangle$, the map m of A into (onto) B is a *homomorphism of* $\mathbf{A}$ *into (onto)* $\mathbf{B}$ iff for each $i \in I$ and $(a_1, ..., a_{k_i}) \in A^{k_i}$

$$R_i(a_1, \ldots, a_{k_i}) = S_i(m(a_1), \ldots, m(a_{k_i})).$$

Let $m_{(k)}: A^k \to B^k$ be the map defined by $m_{(k)}(a_1, \ldots, a_k) = (m(a_1), \ldots, m(a_k))$. Then m is a homomorphism of $\mathbf{A}$ into $\mathbf{B}$ iff for all $i \in I$

$$R_i = m_{(k_i)}{}^{-1}(S_i) \; .$$

With this definition of homomorphism we follow Scott and Suppes (1958). Tarski (1954) and A. Robinson (1965) denote m as homomorphism iff

$$(*) \quad \begin{array}{l} R_i \subset m_{(k_i)}{}^{-1}(S_i) \text{ or, equivalently} \\ R_i(a_1, \ldots, a_{k_i}) = 1 \text{ implies } S_i(m(a_1), \ldots, m(a_{k_i})) = 1. \end{array}$$

As this notion is usual in algebra (see 1.3.3), we will denote maps m satisfying (*) as *algebraic homomorphisms.*

1.5.2 **Definition:** An *isomorphism of* $\mathbf{A}$ *to* $\mathbf{B}$ is a homomorphism of $\mathbf{A}$ onto $\mathbf{B}$ which is 1—1.

If m is an isomorphism of $\mathbf{A}$ to $\mathbf{B}$, m^{-1} is an isomorphism of $\mathbf{B}$ to $\mathbf{A}$. Thus it is meaningful to call a pair $\mathbf{A}$, $\mathbf{B}$ of r.s. *isomorphic* iff there is an isomorphism of $\mathbf{A}$ to $\mathbf{B}$.

A simple example of two isomorphic n.r.s. is the following: $\mathbf{A}=\langle \mathbb{R}; <, +\rangle$, $\mathbf{B}=\langle \mathbb{R}^+; <, \cdot\rangle$ where "$<$", "$+$" and $\cdot$ denote order, addition and multiplication of real numbers, respectively, in the usual sense. The map $m: \mathbb{R} \to \mathbb{R}^+ = \{r \in \mathbb{R}: r > 0\}$ defined by $m(x) = \exp x$ is an isomorphism, because it maps $1-1$ onto and

$$x < y \text{ iff } \exp x < \exp y \text{ and}$$
$$z = x + y \text{ iff } \exp z = \exp x \cdot \exp y.$$

1.5.3 **Definition:** An *automorphism* of $\mathbf{A}$ is an isomorphism of $\mathbf{A}$ to $\mathbf{A}$.

The identical map ($m(a) = a$ for all $a \in A$) is an automorphism of $\mathbf{A}$. Examples of nontrivial automorphisms will be given in 1.8.

1.5.4 **Definition:** Let A, B, C be sets, m a map of A into B, n a map of B into C. Then $n \circ m: A \to C$ denotes the map defined by $n \circ m(a) = n(m(a))$.

1.5.5 **Theorem:** Let **A**, **B**, **C** be relational systems. If m is a homomorphism of **A** into **B**, n a homomorphism of **B** into **C**, then $n \circ m$ is a homomorphism of **A** into **C**. If both, m and n, are isomorphisms, $n \circ m$ is an isomorphism.

Proof: The statement follows immediately from the definitions 1.5.1 to 1.5.4.

1.5.6 **Corollary:** The set of all automorphisms of a r.s. **A** constitute a group under $\circ$, the "group of automorphisms of **A**", say $\Gamma_{\mathbf{A}}$.

Proof: The identical map is the unit of the group. For any automorphism m, m^{-1} is an automorphism too and $m \circ m^{-1}$ = identity.

The following theorems deal with the relationship between homomorphisms and congruence relations.

1.5.7 **Theorem:** Let $\mathbf{A}=\langle A;(R_i)_{i\in I}\rangle$, $\mathbf{B}=\langle B;(S_i)_{i\in I}\rangle$ be r.s. of the same type and m a homomorphism of **A** into **B**. Then the binary relation $\approx$ defined by

(*) $a \approx a'$ iff $m(a)=m(a')$

is a congruence relation for **A** (called "the congruence relation induced by m").

Proof: Reflexivity, symmetry and transitivity of $\approx$ follow immediately from the corresponding properties of $=$. Thus $\approx$ is an equivalence relation. Let be $i \in I$, $a_{(k_i)} = (a_1, \ldots, a_{k_i}) \in A^{k_i}$, $a'_{(k_i)} = (a'_1, \ldots, a'_{k_i}) \in A^{k_i}$ such that $a_j \approx a'_j$ for all $j = 1, \ldots, k_i$. Hence $m_{(k_i)}(a_{(k_i)}) = m_{(k_i)}(a'_{(k_i)})$ by definition of $\approx$, and, m being a homomorphism

$$R_i(a_{(k_i)}) = S_i(m_{(k_i)}(a_{(k_i)})) = S_i(m_{(k_i)}(a'_{(k_i)})) = R_i(a'_{(k_i)}).$$

Therefore, $\approx$ is a congruence relation for **A**.

The converse of theorem 1.5.7 is the following.

1.5.8 **Theorem:** Let $\mathbf{A}=\langle A;(R_i)_{i\in I}\rangle$ be a r.s. and m a map of A into a set B. Suppose that the binary relation on A defined by 1.5.7 (*) is a congruence relation for **A**. Then there are relations S_i $(i \in I)$ on B, uniquely determined on $m_{(k_i)}(A^{k_i})$, such that m is a homomorphism of **A** into $\mathbf{B}=\langle B;(S_i)_{i\in I}\rangle$, namely

$$S_i := m_{(k_i)}(R_i).$$

Proof: Since the binary relation defined by 1.5.7 (*) is a congruence relation for **A**, $m_{(k_i)}^{-1}(m_{(k_i)}(a_1, \ldots, a_{k_i})) \subset R_i$ for every $i \in I$ and $(a_1, \ldots, a_{k_i}) \in R_i$. Thus $m_{(k_i)}^{-1}(m_{(k_i)}(R_i)) \subset R_i$. The inclusion $m_{(k_i)}^{-1}(m_{(k_i)}(R_i)) \supset R_i$ is obvious for any map. Hence $m_{(k_i)}^{-1}(m_{(k_i)}(R_i)) = R_i$, and according to the definition 1.5.1 m is a homomorphism of **A** into $\langle B; (m_{(k_i)}(R_i))_{i \in I}\rangle$. If, on the other hand, m is a homomorphism of **A** into $\langle B; (S_i)_{i \in I}\rangle$, we have $R_i = m_{(k_i)}^{-1}(S_i)$, $i \in I$; since $m_{(k_i)}$ maps A^{k_i} onto $m_{(k_i)}(A^{k_i})$, we obtain $S_i \cap m_{(k_i)}(A^{k_i}) = m_{(k_i)}(R_i)$, $i \in I$.

1.5.9 **Theorem:** Let $\mathbf{A}=\langle A; (R_i)_{i\in I}\rangle$ be a r.s. and $\approx$ a congruence relation for **A**.

(i) The map $h: a \to \tilde{a}$ is a homomorphism of **A** onto the quotient r.s. $\mathbf{A}_1 := \mathbf{A}/\approx$.

(ii) If, moreover, $\approx_1$ is a congruence relation for $\mathbf{A}_1$ then $\mathbf{A}_1/\approx_1$ is isomorphic to $\mathbf{A}/\approx_0$

where $\approx_0 = h^{-1}(\approx_1)$ or, equivalently, $a \approx_0 b$ iff $\tilde{a} \approx_1 \tilde{b}$.

Proof: (i) The map $m := h$ satisfies the assumption of 1.5.8. By 1.4.6, we have $\tilde{R}_i = h_{(k_i)}(R_i)$. Thus 1.5.8 implies that h is a homomorphism.

(ii)Let h_1 and h_0 be the homomorphisms corresponding to $\approx_1$ and $\approx_0$, respectively. By definition of $\approx_0$, $h_0 \circ h^{-1} \circ h_1^{-1}(c)$ consists of one element, say $m(c)$, for every $c \in \mathbf{A}_1/\approx_1$. Moreover, m is a 1—1-map of $\mathbf{A}_1/\approx_1$ onto $\mathbf{A}/\approx_0$. Since h_0 is a homomorphism, we get for every $i \in I$

$$m_{(k_i)}^{-1}(\tilde{\tilde{R}}_i^0) = h_{1\,(k_i)} \circ h_{(k_i)} \circ h_{0(k_i)}^{-1}(\tilde{\tilde{R}}_i^0) = h_{1\,(k_i)} \circ h_{(k_i)}(R_i).$$

By 1.4.6, the right-hand side is the i-th relation of the r.s. $\mathbf{A}_1/\approx_1$. Therefore m is a 1—1-homomorphism, and thus an isomorphism.

1.5.10 **Corollary:** Let **A** be an irreducible r.s. If m is a homomorphism of **A** into a r.s. **B**, then m maps 1—1.

Proof: Since the congruence relation induced by m has to be the equality, $m(a) = m(a')$ implies $a = a'$.

1.5.11 **Definition:** Let $\mathbf{A}=\langle A; (R_i)_{i\in I}\rangle$ be a r.s., $A_0 \subset A$. Then $\Gamma_{\mathbf{A}}(A_0)$ will denote the set of all 1—1 homomorphisms of $\langle A_0; (R_i)_{i\in I}\rangle$ into **A**. The elements of $\Gamma_{\mathbf{A}}(A_0)$ are called *partial endomorphisms* of **A** (defined on A_0).

If $\gamma \in \Gamma_{\mathbf{A}}$ and $A_0 \subset A$, then $\gamma \mid A_0$ (i.e. the restriction of γ to A_0) is an element of $\Gamma_{\mathbf{A}}(A_0)$. In general $\Gamma_{\mathbf{A}}(A)$ will contain elements which are not automorphisms of **A**. Furthermore $\Gamma_{\mathbf{A}}(A_0)$, $A_0 \subset A$, will contain elements which cannot be extended to automorphisms of **A**.

1.) Let $\mathbf{A}=(\mathbb{Z}; <)$, $\mathbb{Z}$ being the set of all integers and $<$ the usual order. Then α, defined by $\alpha(a)=2a$ for all $a \in A$, belongs to $\Gamma_{\mathbf{A}}(A)$, but not to $\Gamma_{\mathbf{A}}$.

2.) Let $\mathbf{A}$ be as in 1.) and let A_0 be the set of all even integers. Let α be defined by $\alpha(a)=1/2\, a$ for all $a \in A_0$. Then $\alpha \in \Gamma_{\mathbf{A}}(A_0)$; but α cannot be extended to an element of $\Gamma_{\mathbf{A}}$, because it maps onto $A=\mathbb{Z}$.

3.) Let be $\mathbf{A}=(\mathbb{R}^+; <)$, $A_0=\{r \in \mathbb{R}^+ : r<1\}$, $\alpha(r)=-\log(1-r)$ for $r \in A_0$. Then $\alpha \in \Gamma_{\mathbf{A}}(A_0)$; but as in 2.), α cannot be extended to an automorphism of $\mathbf{A}$.

1.5.12 **Theorem:** Let $\mathbf{A}=\langle A; (R_i)_{i \in I}\rangle$ be an irreducible r.s., $\mathbf{B}=\langle B; (S_i)_{i \in I}\rangle$ an arbitrary r.s. of same type, $\mathfrak{M}$ the set of all homomorphisms of $\mathbf{A}$ into $\mathbf{B}$, and m_0 an arbitrary element of $\mathfrak{M}$. Then $\mathfrak{M}=\{\gamma \circ m_0 : \gamma \in \Gamma_{\mathbf{B}}(m_0(A))\}$ and all elements of $\mathfrak{M}$ map $1-1$.

Proof: Because of corollary 1.5.10 all elements of $\mathfrak{M}$ map $1-1$. Thus m_0 is an isomorphism of $\mathbf{A}$ to $\langle m_0(A); (S_i)_{i \in I}\rangle$. For any $\gamma \in \Gamma_{\mathbf{B}}(m_0(A))$, the map $\gamma \circ m_0$ is a homomorphism of $\mathbf{A}$ to $\mathbf{B}$ according to theorem 1.5.5. For any $m \in \mathfrak{M}$, $m \circ m_0^{-1}$ is an isomorphism of $\langle m_0(A); (S_i)_{i \in I}\rangle$ to $\langle m(A); (S_i)_{i \in I}\rangle$; thus $m \circ m_0^{-1} \in \Gamma_{\mathbf{B}}(m_0(A))$ and $m = (m \circ m_0^{-1}) \circ m_0$.

1.6 Definition of Scales

By a *(k-dimensional) scale**) we mean a homomorphism m of an irreducible empirical r.s. $\mathbf{A}=\langle A; (R_i)_{i \in I}\rangle$ into a (k-dimensional) n.r.s. $\mathbf{B}=\langle \mathbb{R}^k; (S_i)_{i \in I}\rangle$. We have to use the more general concept of "homomorphisms into" (instead of "onto"), because the picture $m(A)$ will depend on m in general.

The pictures of the elements of A under this homomorphism will occasionally be referred to as "scale values". As the map is a homomorphism, we can draw conclusions from numerical relations between the scale values to empirical relations between empirical objects: The objects $a_1, \ldots, a_{k_i}$ are in relation R_i if and only if the corresponding scale values $m(a_1), \ldots, m(a_{k_i})$ are in relation S_i. Obviously, it is necessary to require "if and only if"; to require "if" only would mean that $R_i(a_1, \ldots, a_{k_i})$ might hold, that this fact might not, however, be recognizable from the scale values $m(a_1), \ldots, m(a_{k_i})$.

The more relations are taken into account in the definition of a scale, the more do the scale values tell us about reality. As we want the scales to be as informative as possible, we will require that in mapping A

---

*) In the terminology of MENGER (1959), maps whose domain consists of "extramathematical entities" are called *fluents*.

into $\mathbb{R}^k$ all known empirical relations should be taken into account. It would be a waste of information to construct a scale which is a homomorphism with respect to an order relation and to neglect, say, an additive relation, if one can be empirically defined.

The relations S_i $(i \in I)$ used in the definition of scale correspond to empirical relations. Is it meaningful to make use of numerical relations between scale values other than those used in the definition of the scale for statements about reality? This question will be dealt with in chapter 2.

Given an arbitrary e.r.s. $\mathbf{A}=\langle A; (R_i)_{i\in I}\rangle$ there exists a uniquely determined irreducible e.r.s. $\tilde{\tilde{\mathbf{A}}}=\langle \tilde{\tilde{A}}; (\tilde{\tilde{R}}_i)_{i\in I}\rangle$ corresponding to $\mathbf{A}$ (see 1.4.8 and the interpretation of $\tilde{\tilde{\mathbf{A}}}$ in 1.4). If m is a scale mapping $\tilde{\tilde{\mathbf{A}}}$ into a numerical r.s. $\mathbf{B}$, the map $\tilde{\tilde{m}}: a \to \tilde{\tilde{a}} \to m(\tilde{\tilde{a}})$ is a homomorphism of $\mathbf{A}$ into $\mathbf{B}$ because $a \to \tilde{\tilde{a}}$ is a homomorphism according to 1.5.9. Whenever the word "scale" is used in connection with a nonirreducible e.r.s., we mean such a map $\tilde{\tilde{m}}$ induced by a scale m of the corresponding irreducible e.r.s.

1.7 Uniqueness of Scales

By the requirement of homomorphism, the map $A \to \mathbb{R}^k$ is not uniquely determined. In general, a whole class of scales exists, mapping a given irreducible e.r.s. $\mathbf{A}$ homomorphically into a given n.r.s. $\mathbf{B}$. This class of scales will be denoted by $\mathfrak{M}(\mathbf{A}, \mathbf{B})$ or, in short by $\mathfrak{M}$, if no ambiguity arises. Occasionally the scales belonging to $\mathfrak{M}$ will be called *equivalent* and $\mathfrak{M}$ itself will be referred to as the "class of equivalent scales". As there is no criterion to select a single scale out of this class as *the* scale we have to face the fact that wherever we are talking about scales, we are in fact talking about classes of equivalent scales.

Given one scale m_0 belonging to $\mathfrak{M}(\mathbf{A}, \mathbf{B})$ we can characterize the whole class $\mathfrak{M}(\mathbf{A}, \mathbf{B})$ of scales by interior properties of $\mathbf{B}$, namely by partial endomorphisms of $\mathbf{B}$: According to theorem 1.5.12,

$$\mathfrak{M}(\mathbf{A}, \mathbf{B})=\{\gamma \circ m_0 : \gamma \in \Gamma_{\mathbf{B}}(m_0(A))\}.$$

Roughly speaking, this shows that two scales are equivalent iff there is a partial endomorphism of the n.r.s. transforming one scale into the other. The elements of the set $\Gamma_{\mathbf{B}}(m_0(A))$ of partial endomorphisms will be called "*admissible*" transformations of the scale m_0, because they take m_0 into equivalent scales. Not admissible transformations lead to maps which fail to be homomorphisms of **A** into **B** and which are therefore not scales in the sense defined above.

There is a second indefiniteness in the scale which is of a completely different nature. This indefiniteness is due to the fact that the numerical relational system itself is not uniquely determined. There might be different numerical relational systems into which a given empirical relational system can be mapped homomorphically. According to the example following definition 1.5.2 the n.r.s. $\langle \mathbb{R}; <, + \rangle$ and $\langle \mathbb{R}^+; <, \cdot \rangle$ are isomorphic. Thus, if an e.r.s. $\langle A; R_1, R_2 \rangle$ can be mapped homomorphically into $\langle \mathbb{R}; <, + \rangle$, it can also be mapped homomorphically into $\langle \mathbb{R}^+; <, \cdot \rangle$. Which one of these two n.r.s. is selected for the definition of the scale is merely a matter of convenience. If, for example, the two n.r.s. $\langle \mathbb{R}; <, + \rangle$ and $\langle \mathbb{R}^+; <, \cdot \rangle$ are in question, one will usually prefer the first one, as addition is more elementary than multiplication.

1.8 Some Types of Scales

A. Nominal Scales

The simplest e.r.s. is $\langle A; \approx \rangle$, based on an equivalence relation $\approx$. The equivalence relation itself is the coarsest congruence relation; the corresponding irreducible r.s. is $\langle \tilde{\tilde{A}}; = \rangle$, where $\tilde{\tilde{A}}$ is the set of equivalence classes of $\langle A; \approx \rangle$. A numerical scale mapping $\langle \tilde{\tilde{A}}; = \rangle$ into $\langle \mathbb{R}; = \rangle$ (or more generally $\langle \mathbb{R}^k; = \rangle$) exists iff the power of the set $\tilde{\tilde{A}}$ is at most that of the continuum. If a scale exists, it gives only information whether two elements $\tilde{\tilde{a}}_1, \tilde{\tilde{a}}_2 \in \tilde{\tilde{A}}$ are equal or not—or, considering the induced scale of A (see 1.6), whether two elements $a_1, a_2 \in A$ are equivalent or not.

1.8.1 **Definition:** A $1-1$ map of $\langle \tilde{\tilde{A}}; = \rangle$ into $\langle \mathbb{R}; = \rangle$ is called a *nominal scale.*

As a nominal scale gives only a minimum of information, there will be a great number of scales that will do: Given a nominal scale m_0, the scale $\gamma \circ m_0$ is a nominal scale again for any 1—1 map γ of $m_0(A)$ into $\mathbb{R}$ (see 1.5.12).

B. **Ordinal Scales**

In all cases of practical relevance, the e.r.s. **A** contains at least an equivalence and order relation such that the corresponding irreducible r.s. is an ordered set. For notational convenience assume that **A** itself is an ordered set, i.e. $\mathbf{A}=\langle A; <\rangle$ where $<$ is a binary relation satisfying the following conditions:

a) for all $a_1, a_2 \in A$: either $a_1=a_2$ or $a_1<a_2$ or $a_2<a_1$,

b) for all $a_1, a_2, a_3 \in A$: $a_1<a_2$ and $a_2<a_3$ together imply $a_1<a_3$ (such r.s. correspond to "ordinal systems" considered in 3.2). Especially $\mathbf{B}=\langle \mathbb{R}; <\rangle$, the set of real numbers with its natural order, is an ordered set. It might seem reasonable to use the term "ordinal scale" for a homomorphic (i.e. monotone and therefore $1-1$) map m of **A** into **B**, because the order of A is reflected by the order of $\mathbb{R}$. But this is achieved in an incomplete manner only: the topology on A defined by the order relation $<$ will not coincide with the relative topology of $m(A)$ induced by the natural topology of $\mathbb{R}$ (which coincides with its order topology). Since the general tools of "order topology" will be treated not before sections 3.4 and 3.5, we will define here the ordinal scale by the pertaining class of admissible transformations:

1.8.2 **Definition:** A scale $m: A\to\mathbb{R}$ is an *ordinal scale* iff it is unique up to monotone increasing and continuous maps of $m(A)$ into $\mathbb{R}$.

For a more detailed study of ordinal scales see the sections 4.2, 4.3.

C. **Scales Unique up to Groups of Linear Transformations**

The most important types of scales are the onedimensional scales ($B=\mathbb{R}$) which are unique up to certain linear transformations of $\mathbb{R}$. More precisely, there is a group Γ of linear transformations of $\mathbb{R}$ such that every $\gamma' \in \Gamma_{\mathbf{B}}(m(A))$ is the restriction to $m(A)$ of a uniquely determined element, and conversely. Therefore it is possible to describe $\Gamma_{\mathbf{B}}(m(A))$ by Γ.

1.8.3 **Definition:** The group Γ_p of "*positive linear*" transformations of $\mathbb{R}$ onto $\mathbb{R}$ consists of all transformations $\gamma_{\alpha,\beta}: x\to\alpha x+\beta$ with $\alpha\in\mathbb{R}^+$, $\beta\in\mathbb{R}$. $\Gamma_d=\{\gamma_{\alpha,0}:\alpha\in\mathbb{R}^+\}$ is the group of "*dilations*", $\Gamma_s=\{\gamma_{1,\beta}:\beta\in\mathbb{R}\}$ the group of "*shifts*". A scale is an *interval-*, *ratio-*, or *difference-scale**)

*) We will not use the misleading term cardinal scales.

if it is unique up to the positive linear transformations, dilations or shifts, respectively.

1.8.4 **Remark:** Γ_d is a subgroup of Γ_p, Γ_s a normal subgroup. The normal subgroups $\Gamma \neq \{\gamma_{1,0}\}$ of Γ_p are the groups

(*N*) $\Gamma = \{\gamma_{\alpha,\beta} : \alpha \in \mathbf{G}, \beta \in \mathbb{R}\}$

where $\mathbf{G}$ is a subgroup of the multiplicative group $\mathbb{R}^+$.

Proof: A group Γ is a normal subgroup of Γ_p iff $\gamma_{\alpha_0,\beta_0} \in \Gamma$ implies that

(*) $\gamma_{\alpha,\beta}\,\gamma_{\alpha_0,\beta_0}\,\gamma_{\alpha,\beta}^{-1} = \gamma_{\alpha_0,\alpha\beta_0+\beta(1-\alpha_0)} \in \Gamma$ for all $\alpha \in \mathbb{R}^+$, $\beta \in \mathbb{R}$.

Let Γ be a normal subgroup of Γ_p, $\Gamma \neq \{\gamma_{1,0}\}$. There is a pair $(\alpha_0, \beta_0) \neq (1, 0)$ such that $\gamma_{\alpha_0,\beta_0} \in \Gamma$. If $\alpha_0 \neq 1$, it follows immediately from (*) that

(**) $\{\gamma_{\alpha_0,\beta} : \beta \in \mathbb{R}\} \subset \Gamma$.

If $\alpha_0 = 1$, $\beta_0 \neq 0$ and Γ contains with γ_{1,β_0} the element $\gamma_{1,-\beta_0}$. By (*)

$\gamma_{1,+\beta_0\alpha} \in \Gamma$ and $\gamma_{1,-\beta_0\alpha} \in \Gamma$ for all $\alpha > 0$.

Thus (**) also holds for the case $\alpha_0 = 1$ whence Γ is of type (*N*). It is easy to verify by (*) that the groups (*N*) are normal.

Because in all practical cases we have an empirical order relation which is represented by the order of $\mathbb{R}$, scales unique up to the linear transformations $\Gamma_0 = \{\gamma_{\alpha,\beta} : \alpha \in \mathbb{R} - \{0\}, \beta \in \mathbb{R}\}$ are of no interest: the maps $\gamma_{\alpha,\beta}$ with $\alpha < 0$ do not preserve the order.

We have assumed that the linear transformation $\gamma \in \Gamma_p$, Γ_d or Γ_s is uniquely determined by the inducing transformation $\gamma' \in \Gamma_{\mathbf{B}}(m(A))$. Thus $m(A)$ has to contain at least one point for ratio- and difference-scales, and at least two points for interval scales.

1.9 Multidimensional Measurement

It almost never occurs in practice that we consider one property only, for it is the relations between properties which are of interest. Even if it makes sense to say that two coins have different weight, it makes no sense to say that the one coin is heavier than the other unless we "measure" a second (possibly qualitative) property which distinguishes between the coins. If we wish to test e.g. the law of BOYLE-MARIOTTE $pV = RT$ for the ideal gas, it is failing to measure first the pressure p of all objects, then the volume V and then the temperature T, for then we do not know which triples (p, V, T) belong to one object. Either we have to measure pressure p and name w of each object, then volume V and name w of each object and so on—then $((p, w), (V, w), (T, w))$ belongs to one object—or we measure p, V, T simultaneously for each object. In the first case we use twodimensional, in the second threedimensional scales. Since the "name" of the object is irrelevant for the law of BOYLE-MARIOTTE and since it may be impossible under certain circumstances to give other names to the objects than the triple (p, V, T)—e.g. if the experimenter has only one zylinder filled with gas—, the second way is more natural. The concept of measuring a n-tuple of properties simultaneously by onedimensional scales will be formalized as multidimensional measurement.

1.10 Fundamental and Derived Measurement

The distinction between fundamental and derived measurement was originally introduced by CAMPBELL (1928, p. 14). If we try to eliminate the too restrictive concept of fundamental measurement CAMPBELL actually held (see section 7.1), we can define fundamental measurement as the construction of scales by mapping an empirical relational system isomorphically into a numerical relational system. Derived measurement, on the other hand, derives a new scale from other given scales. (In this sense the concepts are used e.g. by HEMPEL (1952) and SUPPES and ZINNES (1963)). A typical example for derived measurement is the scale for density, derived from scales for mass and volume.

The author doubts whether it is reasonable to consider "derived measurement" as measurement at all. Of course, we can consider any meaningful function as a scale for a property which is defined by this scale. On the other hand, if the property allegedly measured by this derived scale has an empirical meaning by its own, it would also have its own fundamental scale. The function used to define the derived scale then becomes an empirical law stating the relation between fundamental scales. This can be illustrated by the equation of state of the ideal gas: Starting from the law of BOYLE-MARIOTTE, stating that the product pV is constant if temperature is held constant, pV can be used to *define* a scale for temperature. That such a definition makes sense follows from the fact that temperature thus defined is independent of the special type of gas used in the experiment (as long as the conditions are such that it behaves like an ideal gas). In a higher stage of development, however, temperature was defined by thermodynamic considerations, leading to an interval scale for temperature standing on its own feet. Thus, $pV=RT$ became an empirical law, relating pressure, volume and temperature of a gas under certain conditions.

The aim of science should always be to construct fundamental scales for properties with independent meaning and to state empirical laws rather than to be satisfied with derived scales.

The reader interested in a "general theory of derived measurement" is referred to SUPPES and ZINNES (1963), section 3*).

We speak of measurement by fiat, if the assignment of numbers is defined by some operational prescription which is neither based on homomorphic mapping of an empirical relational system into a numerical relational system (fundamental measurement) nor on the functional relationship to fundamental scales (derived measurement).

Measurement by fiat occurs if a prescientific concept turns out to be of great importance and no scaling procedure is available. Typical examples for measurement by fiat are socalled intelligence tests, scales for social status etc. The practical importance of scales like these is proved by their probation for predictions.

1.11 Practical Performance of Measurement

The question of how to perform measurement in practice is completely distinct from the question of how a scale is defined. Even a methodologist heavily concerned with foundational aspects of the theory of measurement will use a thermometer and not a CARNOT process if he wants to decide whether he should take his coat or not.

Generally speaking, measurement is in practice performed with the aid of instruments yielding numerical values. These instruments might be directly based on the empirical operations used for the definition of the scale, such as a beam balance. It might also be based on an empirical law connecting the property to be measured with another property, as the spring-balance using HOOKE's law to measure weight by means of the extension of a spring.

---

*) From this paper, the reader will also see that the concept of derived measurement is not very clear after all: Paired comparisons, considered in section 11.6 of this book as "fundamental measurement" are given as "examples of derived measurement" in section 5 of SUPPES and ZINNES.

In this sense, we also have to consider a phonometer together with a table for the conversion of decibels into tones as an instrument to measure subjective loudness. This instrument is based on a psychophysical law, relating objective and subjective loudness.

Of course, there are also instruments in use leading to ordinal scales only. An example of such an instrument is the procedure for the determination of hypostasis (see p. 76).

2. Meaningfulness

2.1 Meaningful Relations

Assume that two experimenters measure temperature under identical conditions using perfect mercury thermometers, one of the experimenters using centigrade, the other Fahrenheit. Comparing temperatures x_1, x_2 measured on different occasions, they will always agree whether $x_1 < x_2$ is true or false, but never whether $x_2 = 2x_1$, because $x_2 = 2x_1$ in centigrades implies $x_2 = 2x_1 - 32$ in Fahrenheit. Thus contrary to the relation $x_1 < x_2$, the relation $x_2 = 2x_1$ between the real numbers x_1, x_2 is meaningless without specification of the scale.

2.1.1 **Definition:** Let $\mathbf{A} = \langle A; (R_i)_{i \in I} \rangle$ be an irreducible e.r.s., $\mathbf{B} = \langle B; (S_i)_{i \in I} \rangle$ a n.r.s. of the same type such that there is at least one scale m of $\mathbf{A}$ into $\mathbf{B}$. Let S be a k-ary relation on B. S is called *meaningful* iff for all $m, m' \in \mathfrak{M}(\mathbf{A}, \mathbf{B})$ and $a_1, \ldots, a_k \in A$

$$S(m(a_1), \ldots, m(a_k)) = S(m'(a_1), \ldots, m'(a_k)),$$

or equivalently $m_{(k)}^{-1}(S) = m'^{-1}_{(k)}(S)$.

(For the definition of $m_{(k)}$ see 1.5.1.) According to 1.5.1 we can characterize meaningful relations by the following

2.1.2 **Criterion:** Let $\mathbf{A}, \mathbf{B}, S$ have the same meaning as in 2.1.1, and let m be an arbitrary fixed scale of $\mathbf{A}$ into $\mathbf{B}$. Then S is meaningful iff

$$(*) \qquad \mathfrak{M}(\mathbf{A}, \mathbf{B}) = \mathfrak{M}(\langle A; (R_i)_{i \in I}, m_{(k)}^{-1}(S) \rangle, \langle B; (S_i)_{i \in I}, S \rangle);$$

in other words: Every $1-1$ homomorphism of $\mathbf{A}$ into $\mathbf{B}$ is a $1-1$-homomorphism of the r.s. $\mathbf{A}$ enriched by the relation $m_{(k)}^{-1}(S)$ into the r.s. $\mathbf{B}$ enriched by the relation S.

Given $\mathbf{A}, \mathbf{B}, S, m$ as in 2.1.2, $R = m_{(k)}^{-1}(S)$ will be a uniquely determined k-ary relation on A. Thus a fixed scale m gives an "interpretation" R of S on A. In general $m_{(k)}^{-1}(S)$ will be different for equivalent scales m. The meaningful relations on B—and only these—"define" relations on A (in the ordinary sense that a definition is meaningful if it defines uniquely).

A different approach to the problem of meaningfulness is to consider as meaningful only relations S between the scale values which can be expressed in terms of the relations S_i $(i \in I)$ involved in the definition of the scale. For such relations, the corresponding relation R on A is uniquely determined (see 2.3.2) and can be expressed in terms of the empirical relations R_i $(i \in I)$. Thus, any such relation has an interpretation in terms of empirical relations. To consider only such relations as meaningful is e.g. proposed by WEITZENHOFFER (1951). The aim of this approach is obviously to guarantee that to any meaningful relation there corresponds an empirical relation. Whether this is true or not depends on the precise meaning given to the notion "expressed in terms of": Let $\langle A; <\rangle$ be a totally ordered r.s.; then the relation R defined by "$R(a, b)=1$ iff there exists $c \in A$ such that $a<c<b$" is expressed in terms of the relation $<$, namely by means of lower predicate calculus. One might, however, hesitate to call it "empirical".

We are, however, of the opinion that this concept of meaningfulness is too restrictive. If a property can be measured in an interval scale, it makes sense to compute the average of a number of manifestations, even though there might be no original empirical operation corresponding to "addition" (see 2.3.3). More general, accepting the procedure of measurement itself as "real", $S(m(a_1), \ldots, m(a_k))=1$ is a statement about reality, namely that the scale values of the k objects $a_1, \ldots, a_k$ are in relation S regardless to which specific scale is chosen out of the class of equivalent scales.

It follows immediately from 2.1.2 that the relations S_i, $i \in I$, constituting the n.r.s. $\mathbf{B}$, are meaningful. If $\mathfrak{M}(\mathbf{A}, \mathbf{B})$ consists of exactly one element, every relation on B is meaningful. If S is meaningful for $\mathbf{A}_0=\langle A; (R_i)_{i \in I_0}\rangle$ and $\mathbf{B}_0=\langle B; (S_i)_{i \in I_0}\rangle$ and $I_0 \subset I$, it is meaningful for $\mathbf{A}=\langle A; (R_i)_{i \in I}\rangle$ and $\mathbf{B}=\langle B; (S_i)_{i \in I}\rangle$, because every scale of $\mathbf{A}$ into $\mathbf{B}$ is a scale of $\mathbf{A}_0$ into $\mathbf{B}_0$. In the following chapter, we will give an intrinsic characterization of meaningful relations.

2.2 Invariant Relations

For any r.s. $\mathbf{A}=\langle A; (R_i)_{i \in I}\rangle$ and any subset A_0 of A we have defined the set $\Gamma_{\mathbf{A}}(A_0)$ of partial endomorphisms (1.5.11) and the group

$\Gamma_{\mathbf{A}}$ of automorphisms (1.5.6) as intrinsic systems of the r.s. **A**. We will use them to characterize meaningful relations and the empirical relations corresponding to them.

2.2.1 **Definition:** Let γ be a map of $A_0 \subset A$ into A, and R a k-ary relation on A. R is *γ-invariant* iff $R(a_1, \ldots, a_k) = R(\gamma(a_1), \ldots, \gamma(a_k))$ for all $(a_1, \ldots, a_k) \in A_0^k$ or, equivalently, iff $R \cap A_0^k = \gamma_{(k)}^{-1}(R)$.

Let Γ be a set of maps. R is *Γ-invariant,* iff it is γ-invariant for all $\gamma \in \Gamma$. R is *invariant* iff it is $\Gamma_{\mathbf{A}}$-invariant.

The relations R_i $(i \in I)$, for example, are invariant as well as $\Gamma_{\mathbf{A}}(A_0)$-invariant for all $A_0 \subset A$. If R is invariant, $R = \gamma_{(k)}^{-1}(R) = \gamma_{(k)}(R)$, since the automorphism γ maps A $(=A_0)$ $1-1$ onto A. As an immediate consequence of 2.2.1, 1.5.1, and 1.5.11 we obtain

2.2.2 **Proposition:** The relation R is $\Gamma_{\mathbf{A}}(A_0)$-invariant (resp. invariant) iff $\Gamma_{\mathbf{A}}(A_0) = \Gamma_{\mathbf{A}'}(A_0)$ (resp. $\Gamma_{\mathbf{A}} = \Gamma_{\mathbf{A}'}$) with $\mathbf{A}' = \langle A; (R_i)_{i \in I}, R \rangle$. In other words, every partial endomorphism defined on A_0 (resp. automorphism) is a partial endomorphism (resp. automorphism) of the r.s. **A** enriched by the relation R.

2.2.3 **Theorem:** Let $\mathbf{A} = \langle A; (R_i)_{i \in I} \rangle$ be an irreducible e.r.s., $\mathbf{B} = \langle B; (S_i)_{i \in I} \rangle$ a n.r.s. of the same type, m_0 an arbitrary fixed scale of **A** into **B**, and S a relation on B. Then S is meaningful iff it is $\Gamma_{\mathbf{B}}(m_0(A))$-invariant.

Proof: a) Let the k-ary relation S be $\Gamma_{\mathbf{B}}(m_0(A))$-invariant and $m \in \mathfrak{M}(\mathbf{A}, \mathbf{B})$. According to 1.5.12 there exists $\gamma \in \Gamma_{\mathbf{B}}(m_0(A))$ such that $m = \gamma \circ m_0$ and therefore $m_{(k)}^{-1}(S) = m_{0(k)}^{-1} \circ \gamma_{(k)}^{-1}(S)$. Since S is $\Gamma_{\mathbf{B}}(m_0(A))$-invariant and m_0 maps onto $m_0(A)$, we have $m_{0(k)}^{-1} \circ \gamma_{(k)}^{-1}(S) = m_{0(k)}^{-1}(S \cap m_0(A)^k) = m_{0(k)}^{-1}(S)$. Thus $m_{(k)}^{-1}(S) = m_{0(k)}^{-1}(S)$ for all $m \in \mathfrak{M}(\mathbf{A}, \mathbf{B})$.

b) Let S be meaningful and $\gamma \in \Gamma_{\mathbf{B}}(m_0(A))$. Then according to 1.5.12 $\gamma \circ m_0 \in \mathfrak{M}(\mathbf{A}, \mathbf{B})$ and therefore $m_{0(k)}^{-1}(S) = m_{0(k)}^{-1} \circ \gamma_{(k)}^{-1}(S)$. Since m_0 maps onto $m_0(A)$, we obtain $S \cap m_0(A)^k = \gamma_{(k)}^{-1}(S)$.

This theorem implies that meaningfulness essentially depends only on the invariance under partial endomorphisms of the n.r.s. **B**. We only need to know the picture $m(A)$ of A for *one* of the scales. If we know for instance that there exists a scale m with $m(A) = B$, the behavior of a relation S under the partial endomorphisms of B completely determines whether S is meaningful or not.

2.2.4 **Corollary:** Let **A**, **B** have the same meaning as in 2.2.3, and let S be a relation on B. Then S is $\Gamma_{\mathbf{B}}(m(A))$-invariant for all $m \in \mathfrak{M}(\mathbf{A}, \mathbf{B})$ if it is $\Gamma_{\mathbf{B}}(m_0(A))$-invariant for at least one $m_0 \in \mathfrak{M}(\mathbf{A}, \mathbf{B})$.

Proof: If S is $\Gamma_{\mathbf{B}}(m_0(A))$-invariant for one $m_0 \in \mathfrak{M}$, it is meaningful according 2.2.3. Given any other $m \in \mathfrak{M}(\mathbf{A}, \mathbf{B})$, it follows again by 2.2.3 that S is $\Gamma_{\mathbf{B}}(m(A))$-invariant.

An immediate consequence of 2.2.3 and 2.2.4 is the following important technical criterion for meaningfulness:

2.2.5 **Corollary:** Let $\mathbf{A}$, $\mathbf{B}$ have the same meaning as in 2.2.3 and suppose that there exists a scale $m_0 \in \mathfrak{M}(\mathbf{A}, \mathbf{B})$ such that every element of $\Gamma_{\mathbf{B}}(m_0(A))$ is the restriction of an element of $\Gamma_{\mathbf{B}}$, i.e. of an automorphism of $\mathbf{B}$. Then the following statements about a k-ary relation S on B are equivalent:

(i) S is meaningful,

(ii) there exists a scale $m \in \mathfrak{M}(\mathbf{A}, \mathbf{B})$ such that
(*) $S(\gamma(b_1), \dots, \gamma(b_k)) = S(b_1, \dots, b_k)$ for all $\gamma \in \Gamma_{\mathbf{B}}$ and all $(b_1, \dots, b_k) \in m(A)^k$,

(iii) (*) holds for all scales $m \in \mathfrak{M}(\mathbf{A}, \mathbf{B})$.

Proof: According to 2.2.3 and 2.2.4 we have only to show that (*) is equivalent to $\Gamma_{\mathbf{B}}(m(A))$-invariance of S. Let $\eta \in \Gamma_{\mathbf{B}}(m(A))$. Since m and $m_1 := \eta \circ m$ are scales, because of 1.5.12 and the assumption about m_0 there exist two automorphisms γ, γ_1 such that $m = \gamma \circ m_0$ and $m_1 = \gamma_1 \circ m_0$, and thus $\gamma_1 \circ m_0 = \eta \circ \gamma \circ m_0$. Hence η and $\gamma_1 \circ \gamma^{-1}$ coincide on $m(A)$. Therefore every element of $\Gamma_{\mathbf{B}}(m(A))$ is the restriction of an automorphism.

2.2.6 **Corollary:** Under the assumptions of 2.2.5 every invariant relation on B is meaningful.

2.2.7 **Remark:** A meaningful relation on B is not necessarily invariant, not even under the assumptions of 2.2.5, as can be seen from the following example.

Let $\mathbf{A}$ be the field of rational numbers, $\mathbf{B}$ the algebraic field over $\mathbf{A}$ in which $x^2 = 2$ is solvable (i.e. $B = \{r + s\sqrt{2} : r, s \text{ rational}\}$). The natural imbedding of $\mathbf{A}$ into $\mathbf{B}$ is the only $1-1$ homomorphism of $\mathbf{A}$ into $\mathbf{B}$. Thus any relation on B is meaningful, e.g. the 1-ary relation $x = \sqrt{2}$. But this relation is not invariant under the automorphism which maps $\sqrt{2}$ into $-\sqrt{2}$. The deeper source of this fact is that $\mathbf{B}$ is too great for measuring $\mathbf{A}$: $\sqrt{2}$ never occurs as a scale value.

As a consequence of 2.2.5 ((i) and (iii)) we obtain the following

2.2.8 **Corollary:** If under the assumptions of 2.2.5 for every $(b_1, \dots, b_k) \in B^k$ there exists a scale m such that $(b_1, \dots, b_k) \in m(A)^k$, i.e. if

$B^k = \cup \{m(A)^k : m \in \mathfrak{M}\}$, then every meaningful relation on B is invariant.

A meaningful relation S on B defines the *corresponding* relation $R := m_{(k)}^{-1}(S)$ on A independently of $m \in \mathfrak{M}(\mathbf{A}, \mathbf{B})$. As stated in 2.1.2, R is the uniquely determined relation such that $\mathbf{A}$ enriched by R and $\mathbf{B}$ enriched by S admit the same scales as $\mathbf{A}$ and $\mathbf{B}$.

Up to now we have tried to characterize meaningful relations on B by intrinsic properties of $\mathbf{B}$. The following attempt to characterize relations on A which correspond to meaningful relations on B by intrinsic properties of $\mathbf{A}$ is less satisfactory than the result 2.2.3, because it involves partial endomorphisms of $\mathbf{A}$ induced by pairs of scales and not only the picture of A for one arbitrary fixed scale.

2.2.9 **Theorem:** Let $\mathbf{A}$, $\mathbf{B}$ have the same meaning as in 2.2.3, let R be a k-ary relation on A and suppose that $\mathfrak{M}(\mathbf{A}, \mathbf{B}) \neq \emptyset$. Then R corresponds to a meaningful relation on B iff R is Γ-invariant where

$$\Gamma = \{m_1^{-1} \circ m_2 : \; m_1, m_2 \in \mathfrak{M}(\mathbf{A}, \mathbf{B})\}.$$

Proof: a) Suppose that R is Γ-invariant and define $S = \cup \{m_{(k)}(R) : m \in \mathfrak{M}(\mathbf{A}, \mathbf{B})\}$. As subset of B^k S is a k-ary relation on B and $m_{(k)}^{-1}(S) \supset m_{(k)}^{-1} m_{(k)}(R) = R$ for all $m \in \mathfrak{M}(\mathbf{A}, \mathbf{B})$. It remains to show that $m_{(k)}^{-1}(S) \subset R$. For $(a_1, \ldots, a_k) \in m_{(k)}^{-1}(S)$ there exists a scale m' and $(a_1', \ldots, a_k') \in R$ such that $(a_1, \ldots, a_k) = m_{(k)}^{-1} \circ m'_{(k)}(a_1', \ldots, a_k')$, i.e. $(a_1, \ldots, a_k) = \gamma_{(k)}(a_1', \ldots, a_k')$ with $\gamma = m^{-1} \circ m' \in \Gamma$. As R is Γ-invariant, $(a_1, \ldots, a_k) \in R$.

b) If the relation S on B is meaningful and R corresponds to S and $\gamma = m_1^{-1} \circ m_2 \in \Gamma$, then

$$R = m_{1(k)}^{-1}(S) \text{ implies } (m_1^{-1} \circ m_2)_{(k)}^{-1}(R) = m_{2(k)}^{-1} \circ m_{1(k)}(R)$$
$$= m_{2(k)}^{-1} \circ m_{1(k)} \circ m_{1(k)}^{-1}(S) = m_{2(k)}^{-1}(S \cap m_1(A)^k)$$
$$= m_{2(k)}^{-1}(S) \cap m_{2(k)}^{-1} \circ m_1(A)^k = m_{2(k)}^{-1}(S) \cap (m_2^{-1} \circ m_1(A))^k.$$

Since $m_{2(k)}^{-1}(S) = R$ and $m_2^{-1} \circ m_1(A)$ is the domain A_0 of γ, the last term equals $R \cap A_0^k$.

2.2.10 **Corollary:** Let $\mathbf{A}$, $\mathbf{B}$, R have the same meaning as in 2.2.9 and suppose that $m(A) = B$ for all $m \in \mathfrak{M}(\mathbf{A}, \mathbf{B}) \neq \emptyset$. Then R corresponds to a meaningful relation on B iff R is invariant.

Proof: As $m(A) = B$ for all $m \in \mathfrak{M}(\mathbf{A}, \mathbf{B})$, each element of Γ (defined in 2.2.9) is an automorphism of $\mathbf{A}$ and thus $\Gamma \subset \Gamma_{\mathbf{A}}$. If, conversely, $\gamma \in \Gamma_{\mathbf{A}}$ let m be an arbitrary element of the nonvoid set $\mathfrak{M}(\mathbf{A}, \mathbf{B})$. Then $\gamma = m_1^{-1} \circ m_2 \in \Gamma$ where $m_1 = m$ and $m_2 = m \circ \gamma$ and thus $\Gamma_{\mathbf{A}} \subset \Gamma$.

2.2.11 **Corollary:** Let **A**, **B**, Γ have the same meaning as in 2.2.9. Suppose that every $\gamma \in \Gamma$ is the restriction of an automorphism of **A**. Then each invariant relation on A corresponds to a meaningful relation on B.

2.2.12 **Remark:** Throughout chapter 2 it is assumed that **A** is irreducible. The measurement of a reducible r.s. **A** was reduced to the measurement of the irreducible $\bar{\bar{\mathbf{A}}}$ by the canonical map $\pi: \mathbf{A} \to \bar{\bar{\mathbf{A}}}$ (see 1.6). To every k-ary relation $\bar{\bar{R}}$ on $\bar{\bar{A}}$ there corresponds $R := \pi_{(k)}^{-1}(\bar{\bar{R}})$ on A. Obviously the coarsest congruence relation for $\mathbf{A} = \langle A; (R_i)_{i \in I} \rangle$, say $\approx_{\mathbf{A}}$, is a congruence relation for $\mathbf{A}' = \langle A; (R_i)_{i \in I}, R \rangle$; roughly speaking, the enrichment by R does not refine the coarsest congruence relation $\approx_{\mathbf{A}}$. Thus especially every relation on A which corresponds to a meaningful relation on B has this property in addition to certain invariance properties. As we attempt to characterize relations on A corresponding to meaningful relations on B by invariance properties, the question arises whether invariance of a relation R implies that R does not refine $\approx_{\mathbf{A}}$. A negative answer is given by the following example: $\mathbf{A} = \langle A; R_1 \rangle$ with $A = \{-1, 0, 1\}$ $R_1 = \{(0, 1), (0, -1)\} \subset A^2$. Then $\Gamma_{\mathbf{A}}$ consists of the two permutations

$$(-1, 0, 1) \to (-1, 0, 1)$$
$$(-1, 0, 1) \to (1, 0, -1)$$

and satisfies the assumption of 2.2.11 concerning Γ. The sets $\{0\}$ and $\{-1, 1\}$ are the congruence classes given by $\approx_{\mathbf{A}}$. The relation $R := \{(-1, -1), (1, 1)\}$ is invariant under $\Gamma_{\mathbf{A}}$. The set $\{-1, 1\}$ is, however, not a congruence class for $\langle A; R_1, R \rangle$, because $R(1, 1) \neq R(1, -1)$.

2.2.13 **Remark:** The results of the chapters 2.1 and 2.2 hold for infinitary relations too.

2.2.14 **Remark:** For technical reasons it might often be convenient to admit only a certain subset $\tilde{\mathfrak{M}}$ of $\mathfrak{M}$. Then the concept of meaningfulness can be weakened by substituting $\tilde{\mathfrak{M}}$ for $\mathfrak{M}$ in 2.1.1. This will change (*) in 2.1.2 into an inclusion: $\tilde{\mathfrak{M}}(\mathbf{A}, \mathbf{B}) \subset \mathfrak{M}(\ldots, \ldots)$. If we substitute

$$\Gamma_{\mathbf{B}}(m_0(A)) \text{ by } \tilde{\Gamma}_{\mathbf{B}}(m_0(A)) := \{\gamma = m_1 \circ m_0^{-1} : m_1 \in \tilde{\mathfrak{M}}\}$$

for $m_0 \in \tilde{\mathfrak{M}}$, the results remain valid in the $\sim$-version.

2.2.5 can be modified to "... such that $\tilde{\Gamma}_{\mathbf{B}}(m_0(A))$ consists of all restrictions of elements of $\tilde{\Gamma}_{\mathbf{B}}$, where $\tilde{\Gamma}_{\mathbf{B}}$ is an arbitrary fixed subgroup of $\Gamma_{\mathbf{B}}$ ..." and, substituting $\Gamma_{\mathbf{B}}$ in (*) by $\tilde{\Gamma}_{\mathbf{B}}$ 2.2.11 may be modified to "... Suppose that there is a subgroup $\tilde{\Gamma}_{\mathbf{A}}$ of $\Gamma_{\mathbf{A}}$ such that every $\gamma \in \Gamma$ is a restriction of an element of $\tilde{\Gamma}_{\mathbf{A}}$. Then ...". These modifications are of interest, because often such scales only out of $\mathfrak{M}$ are admitted which can be obtained from a fixed scale, say m_0, by application of transformations belonging to a certain subgroup $\tilde{\Gamma}$ of $\Gamma_{\mathbf{B}}$. In this case $\tilde{\mathfrak{M}} = \{\gamma \circ m_0 : \gamma \in \tilde{\Gamma}\}$.

2.3 Examples

2.3.1 **Example*):** We consider $\mathbf{A}$, $\mathbf{B} = \langle B; (S_i)_{i \in I}\rangle$ as in 2.1.1 and assume that $\mathfrak{M}$ $(\mathbf{A}, \mathbf{B})$ is not empty. Let L be a lower predicate calculus language the vocabulary of which consists of the relative symbols S_i $(i \in I)$ and object symbols b $(b \in B)$. $\mathbf{B}$ is a model of this language by the identity map. Let S be a welldefined formula of L which contains no object symbol and k free variables, say $x_1, \ldots, x_k$. This will be expressed by $S(x_1, \ldots, x_k)$. S is a predicate and defines a k-ary relation on B.

2.3.2 **Proposition:** S is meaningful.

Proof: Consider a fixed $m_0 \in \mathfrak{M}$ $(\mathbf{A}, \mathbf{B})$ and $\gamma \in \Gamma_{\mathbf{B}}(m_0(A))$. By definition, γ is an isomorphism of $\langle B_0 := m_0(A); (S_i)_{i \in I}\rangle$ onto $\langle B_1 := \gamma \circ m_0(A); (S_i)_{i \in I}\rangle$. Let $\mathscr{X}$ be the set of all sentences of L which contain only object symbols belonging to B_0. Substituting every $b \in B_0$ contained in X by γb, to every $X \in \mathscr{X}$ corresponds a uniquely determined sentence $X' \in L$. We show by induction on the rules of formation of sentences that

(*) X' holds in $\mathbf{B}$ iff X holds in $\mathbf{B}$.

a) The atomic formulas are $X = S_i(b_1, \ldots, b_{k_i})$. Since γ is an isomorphism, X' holds iff X holds.

b) Let be $X_1, X_2 \in \mathscr{X}$ and assume that (*) is proved for X_1, X_2. $X := X_1 \cap X_2$ holds in $\mathbf{B}$ iff X_1 and X_2 hold in $\mathbf{B}$. This is true iff X_1' and X_2' hold and thus $X_1' \cap X_2'$. For $X_1 \cup X_2$ (disjunction) and $X_1 \supset X_2$ (implication) this will be shown in the same manner.

c) Let $X(z)$ be a well-defined formula in which z and no other variable is free and which contains only object symbols belonging to B_0. Assume that (*) is proved for all $X(b)$ $(b \in B_0)$. Then $X_0 := \forall z\, X(z)$ holds iff all $X(b)$ $(b \in B_1)$ hold. This is true iff all $X'(\gamma(b))$ $(b \in B_1)$ hold and thus $X_0' = \forall z\, X'(z)$. From (*) it follows that $S(b_1, \ldots, b_k)$ holds iff $S(\gamma(b_1), \ldots, \gamma(b_k))$ hold for all $(b_1, \ldots, b_k) \in m_0(A)^k$, because S contains no object symbol. Application of 2.2.3 completes the proof.

---

*) For the logical concepts see for example A. Robinson (1965, 1.2 and 1.4).

2.3.3 **Example:** Let $x'_1, \ldots, x'_k, x''_1, \ldots, x''_k$ be $2k$ (not necessarily different) values belonging to the range of an interval scale and consider the $(2k)$-ary relation $S: \bar{x}' < \bar{x}''$ with

$$\bar{x}' = \frac{1}{k} \sum_{i=1}^{k} x'_i \text{ and } \bar{x}'' = \frac{1}{k} \sum_{i=1}^{k} x''_i .$$

Since $\Gamma_B = \{x \to ax + b : a \in \mathbb{R}^+, b \in \mathbb{R}\}$, S is Γ_B-invariant and therefore meaningful according to 2.2.6. But the relation $\bar{x}'' < 2\bar{x}'$ is not meaningful: For arbitrary $\bar{x}'$, $\bar{x}''$, we have $\bar{x}'' < 2\bar{x}' + b$ for sufficiently great b and $\bar{x}'' > 2\bar{x}' + b$ for sufficiently small b. Thus this relation is not meaningful according to 2.2.5 (ii).

2.4 Meaningful Statistics

By a statistic we mean a real function f depending on the scale values only (and involving no other variables such as "parameters"), or more formally, a map of B^n into $\mathbb{R}$. If, for example, $x = (x_1, \ldots, x_n)$ is an n-tuple of scale values $x_i \in B$, then the *mean*

$$\bar{x} = \frac{1}{n} \sum_{i=1}^{n} x_i$$

or the *standard deviation*

$$s = \left(\frac{1}{n-1} \sum_{i=1}^{n} (x_i - \bar{x})^2 \right)^{\frac{1}{2}}$$

are typical examples of statistics. If x is the quantity and p the price of a commodity, then xp is a statistic in the sense defined above: The scale values consist of all possible pairs (quantity, price) of the $\mathbb{R}^2$ and xp depends only on the two-dimensional scale value (x, p). These examples illustrate that the statistic may depend on several values of a single one-dimensional scale, e.g. $\bar{x}$, as well as on one or more values of a multi-dimensional scale.

As the scale values are only unique up to a set Γ of admissible transformations, the value of $f(m(a_1), \ldots, m(a_n))$ $(= f(m_{(n)}(a_{(n)}))$ for short), considered as a real function on A^n, will depend on which one of the equivalent scales m is chosen (see 1.7). Starting from the idea that the value of $f(m_{(n)}(a_{(n)}))$ may tell us something about reality, the question arises: How? Does $f(m_{(n)}(a_{(n)})) < 2$, $f(m_{(n)}(a_{(n)})) = f(m_{(n)}(a'_{(n)}))$,

$f(m_{(n)}(a_{(n)})) \leqq 2f(m_{(n)}(a'_{(n)}))$, tell us something about reality? This is the case if these relations between the values of the statistic determine relations between elements of A which are independent of the special scales $m \in \mathfrak{M}$. The *minimum requirement,* however, is that the equivalence relation on A^n induced by $f(m_{(n)}(a_{(n)})) = f(m_{(n)}(a'_{(n)}))$ is independent of m. If this were not the case, we would have

$f(m_{(n)}(a_{(n)})) = f(m_{(n)}(a'_{(n)}))$ for scale m but,

$f(m'_{(n)}(a_{(n)})) \neq f(m'_{(n)}(a'_{(n)}))$ for a certain other scale $m' \in \mathfrak{M}$.

This justifies the following.

2.4.1 **Definition:** Given a class $\mathfrak{M}(\mathbf{A}, \mathbf{B})$ of equivalent scales, a statistic f on B^n (B being the support of $\mathbf{B}$) is *meaningful* iff the equivalence relation on A^n defined by

$$a_{(n)} \approx a'_{(n)} \text{ iff } f(m_{(n)}(a_{(n)})) = f(m_{(n)}(a'_{(n)}))$$

is independent of $m \in \mathfrak{M}(\mathbf{A}, \mathbf{B})$.

Meaningfulness thus defined is called "comparison invariance" by ADAMS, FAGOT and ROBINSON (1964, p. 23 and 1965, (a) p. 106). Remarking that an equivalence relation on A^n is a $(2n)$-ary relation on A we obtain as an immediate consequence of 2.4.1, 2.1.1 and 2.2.3

2.4.2 **Proposition:** Let $\mathbf{A} = \langle A; (R_i)_{i \in I}\rangle$ be an irreducible e.r.s., $\mathbf{B} = \langle B; (S_i)_{i \in I}\rangle$ a n.r.s. and f a map of B^n into $\mathbb{R}$. Then the following statements are equivalent

(i) f is a meaningful statistic;

(ii) for an arbitrary fixed scale $m \in \mathfrak{M}(\mathbf{A}, \mathbf{B})$ the n-ary relation $f^{-1} \circ f(x_{(n)})$ on B is $\Gamma_{\mathbf{B}}(m(A))$-invariant for all $x_{(n)} \in B^n$;

(iii) the $(2n)$-ary relation $\{(x_{(n)}, x'_{(n)}) \in B^{2n} : f(x_{(n)}) = f(x'_{(n)})\}$ on B is meaningful.

2.4.3 **Remark:** Any $1-1$ real function of a meaningful statistic is itself a meaningful statistic.

Meaningfulness of f does not require that the value $f(x_{(n)})$ itself remains unchanged under admissible transformations, i.e. $f(\gamma_{(n)}(x_{(n)})) = f(x_{(n)})$ for all $\gamma \in \Gamma_{\mathbf{B}}(m(A))$. But for a meaningful statistic f each $\gamma \in \Gamma_{\mathbf{B}}(m(A))$ induces a $1-1$ transformation γ' of the range $f(m(A)^n)$ into $\mathbb{R}$ by

(*) $\gamma' : f(x_{(n)}) \to f(\gamma_{(n)}(x_{(n)}))$.

If $f(x_{(n)}) = f(x'_{(n)})$, $f(\gamma_{(n)}(x_n)) = f(\gamma_{(n)}(x'_n))$. Thus γ' is uniquely defined. $f(x_{(n)}) \neq f(x'_{(n)})$ implies $f(\gamma_{(n)}(x_n)) \neq f(\gamma_{(n)}(x'_n))$ and therefore γ' is a $1-1$ map. If, conversely, for a given statistic f each $\gamma \in \Gamma_{\mathbf{B}}(m(A))$ induces by (*) a $1-1$ map of $f(m(A)^n)$ into $\mathbb{R}$ then f is meaningful. Thus we obtain

2.4.4 **Theorem:** A statistic f is meaningful iff for each $\gamma \in \Gamma_{\mathbf{B}}(m(A))$, γ' defined by (*) is a $1-1$ map of $f(m(A)^n)$ into $\mathbb{R}$.

If especially $\Gamma_{\mathbf{B}}(m(A)) = \Gamma_{\mathbf{B}}$, the group of all automorphisms of **B**, each automorphism γ of **B** will induce a $1-1$ transformation γ' of $f(B^n)$ onto $f(B^n)$. The family of these induced transformations γ' is a group Γ' which is isomorphic to a factor group of $\Gamma_{\mathbf{B}}$; Γ' is isomorphic to $\Gamma_{\mathbf{B}}/\Gamma_0$ where $\Gamma_0 := \{\gamma \in \Gamma_{\mathbf{B}} : f(x_{(n)}) = f(\gamma_{(n)}(x_{(n)}))$ for all $x_{(n)} \in B^n\}$ is the normal subgroup of $\Gamma_{\mathbf{B}}$ leaving the range $f(B^n)$ of f pointwise unchanged. This includes the two extreme cases $\Gamma_0 = \Gamma_{\mathbf{B}}$ and $\Gamma_0 = \{\iota\}$, when ι is the identity transformation. In the first case, $\Gamma_{\mathbf{B}}/\Gamma_0 = \{\iota'\}$ and $f(\gamma_{(n)}(x_{(n)})) = f(x_{(n)})$ for all γ and $x_{(n)}$; in the second case $\Gamma_{\mathbf{B}}/\Gamma_0 = \Gamma_{\mathbf{B}}$, and there exists for each γ an element $x_{(n)} \in B^n$ with $f(\gamma_{(n)}(x_{(n)})) \neq f(x_{(n)})$. These two extreme cases correspond to the two cases considered by STEVENS (1959, p. 28), namely the "invariance of numerical value" and the "invariance of reference", respectively.

In general, meaningfulness of f does, however, not imply meaningfulness of the binary relation $f(x_{(n)}) < f(x'_{(n)})$ on B^n. This is shown by the following example:
Let $B := \{r : r \text{ rational and positive}\} \cup \{r\sqrt{2} : r \text{ rational and positive}\}$ and $\Gamma_{\mathbf{B}}$ the similarity transformations consisting of the same set, i.e. $\Gamma_{\mathbf{B}} = \{x \to sx : s \in B\}$. Then

$$f(x) = \begin{cases} 0 \text{ for } x \text{ rational} \\ 1 \text{ elsewhere} \end{cases} \text{ is a meaningful statistic}$$

on B if $\Gamma_{\mathbf{B}} = \Gamma_{\mathbf{B}}(m(A))$. However, $f(1) < f(\sqrt{2})$, whereas $f(\sqrt{2} \cdot 1) > f(\sqrt{2} \cdot \sqrt{2})$. (The example given by ADAMS, FAGOT, ROBINSON (1964, p. 119) is wrong, because this function $\mathscr{F}$ is not meaningful ("comparison invariant")).

2.4.5 **Theorem:** Let **A**, **B** and f be as in 2.4.2 and assume that there exists a scale $m \in \mathfrak{M}(\mathbf{A}, \mathbf{B})$ such that $\Gamma_{\mathbf{B}}(m(A))$ can be topologized by a topology such that

a) $\Gamma_{\mathbf{B}}(m(A))$ is connected,

b) the map $\gamma \to f(\gamma_{(n)}(x_{(n)}))$ of $\Gamma_{\mathbf{B}}(m(A))$ into $\mathbb{R}$ is continuous for each $x_{(n)} \in m(A)^n$.

Let, moreover, F be a continuous map of $\mathbb{R}^k$ into $\mathbb{R}$ such that the (kn)-ary relation S_0:

$$F(f(x^1_{(n)}), f(x^2_{(n)}), \ldots, f(x^k_{(n)}))=0$$

on B is meaningful. Then the relation S_1:

$$F(f(x^1_{(n)}), f(x^2_{(n)}), \ldots, f(x^k_{(n)}))>0$$

on B is meaningful.

Proof: Let $(x^1_{(n)}, x^2_{(n)}, \ldots, x^k_{(n)})$ be a fixed element of $m(A)^{nk}$ satisfying the relation S_1 and consider the map

$$\varphi: \gamma \to F(f(\gamma_{(n)}(x^1_{(n)}), \ldots, f(\gamma_{(n)}(x^k_{(n)})))$$

of $\Gamma_{\mathbf{B}}(m(A))$ into $\mathbb{R}$; then $\varphi(\iota) > 0$ by definition of S_1 (ι being the identity transformation). Since the relation S_0 is meaningful and therefore $\Gamma_{\mathbf{B}}(m(A))$-invariant according to 2.2.3, $\varphi(\iota) \neq 0$ implies

(*) $\quad \varphi(\gamma) \neq 0$ for all $\gamma \in \Gamma_{\mathbf{B}}(m(A))$.

Assume that there is an element $\gamma \in \Gamma_{\mathbf{B}}(m(A))$ with $\varphi(\gamma) < 0$. φ is continuous by assumption b) and the continuity of F. $\Gamma_{\mathbf{B}}(m(A))$ is connected by assumption a). Thus $\varphi(\Gamma_{\mathbf{B}}(m(A)))$ is connected (see 3.6.6). Hence $\varphi(\iota) > 0$ and $\varphi(\gamma) < 0$ imply that there exists an element $\gamma' \in \Gamma_{\mathbf{B}}(m(A))$ with $\varphi(\gamma') = 0$ in contradiction to (*). It follows that $\varphi(\gamma) > 0$ for all $\gamma \in \Gamma_{\mathbf{B}}(m(A))$, i.e. the relation S_1 is $\Gamma_{\mathbf{B}}(m(A))$-invariant and therefore meaningful.

2.4.6 **Corollary:** Let **A**, **B** and f be as in 2.4.2 and suppose that there is an $m \in \mathfrak{M}(\mathbf{A}, \mathbf{B})$ satisfying the conditions a) and b) of 2.4.5. Then the ($2n$)-ary relation $f(x_{(n)}) > f(x'_{(n)})$ on B is meaningful if the statistic f is meaningful.

Proof: The function $F(r_1, r_2) = r_1 - r_2$ on $\mathbb{R}^2$ into $\mathbb{R}$ is continuous and the relation $S: F(f(x^1_{(n)}), f(x^2_{(n)})) = f(x^1_{(n)}) - f(x^2_{(n)}) = 0$ is meaningful if f is meaningful (2.4.2 (iii)). It follows from 2.4.5 that $S_1: f(x^1_{(n)}) > f(x^2_{(n)})$ is meaningful.

This corollary is essentially theorem 16, p. 119, of Adams, Fagot, Robinson (1964).

2.4.7 **Remark:** The condition that $\Gamma_{\mathbf{B}}(m(A))$ is connected under the topology considered in 2.4.5 cannot be omitted in general as will be shown by the following example:

Let $B = \mathbb{R}$ and assume that the scale is unique up to linear $1-1$-transformations, i.e. $\Gamma_{\mathbf{B}}(m(A)) = \Gamma_{\mathbf{B}} = \{\gamma_{\alpha,\beta} : \alpha \in \mathbb{R} - \{0\}, \beta \in \mathbb{R}\}$ with $\gamma_{\alpha,\beta}$: $x \to \alpha x + \beta$. If $\Gamma_{\mathbf{B}}$ is topologized by the natural imbedding $\gamma_{\alpha,\beta} \to (\alpha, \beta) \in \mathbb{R}^2$

of Γ_B into the $\mathbb{R}^2$, Γ_B is not connected since Γ_B is union of the two disjoint open sets $\{\gamma_{\alpha,\beta}:\alpha>0, \beta\in\mathbb{R}\}$ and $\{\gamma_{\alpha,\beta}:\alpha<0, \beta\in\mathbb{R}\}$. The identical statistic $f: f(x)=x$ for all $x\in B$, is meaningful and satisfies condition b) of 2.4.5 with respect to the topology of Γ_B defined above. The relation $f(x)<f(x')$ on B, however, is not meaningful: $f(0)=0<1=f(1)$, whereas $f(\gamma_{\alpha,\beta}(0))=\beta>\alpha+\beta=f(\gamma_{\alpha,\beta}(1))$ for each $(\alpha,\beta)\in\mathbb{R}^2$ with $\alpha<0$.

2.5 Examples of Meaningful and Meaningless Statistics

For the definition of the scales considered in this section we refer the reader to section 1.8.

2.5.1 Ordinal Scales

Obviously, the *mean*

$$f(x_1,\ldots,x_n) = \frac{1}{n}\sum_{i=1}^{n} x_i$$

is not meaningful for ordinal scales, as the relation

$$\frac{1}{n}\sum_{i=1}^{n} x_i' = \frac{1}{n}\sum_{i=1}^{n} x_i''$$

will be destroyed if arbitrary monotone transformations are applied. A statistic meaningful even in this case is e.g. the *median*, i.e. the $(k+1)^{\text{th}}$ value if we order $n=2k+1$ values in ascending magnitude. This fact is occasionally neglected by experts in the field of measurement. If in bisection different experiments lead to different estimates of the tone midway (with respect to pitch, for instance) between two given tones, it is not uncommon to use the geometric mean of the frequencies of the tones to average over the estimates of different experiments.

If we assume that the estimates of different persons are randomly distributed around the true pitch of the mid-tone, the median would be a natural estimate of the true mid-tone. If we assume that the random errors are normally distributed in the subjective scale, the frequency of the mid-tone would have to be computed from the frequencies x_1, ..., x_n of the n estimates by

$$f^{-1}\left(\frac{f(x_1)+\ldots+f(x_n)}{n}\right),$$

where f is the function assigning to frequency x the corresponding value of pitch, $f(x)$. On the bases of this considerations, a geometric mean of the frequencies would be justified only if $f(x) = \log x$.

If the power law claimed by STEVENS really holds true, the adequate mean would be

$$\left(\frac{x_1^\beta + \ldots + x_n^\beta}{n}\right)^{\frac{1}{\beta}},$$

where β is the exponent depending on the special sensation (see also p. 128).

Unless the validity of a distinct law and the hypothesis of normal distribution of estimates in the subjective scale are well established, for practical purposes the median will be the best average, as it assumes no more than that the true mid-tone is over-estimated and under-estimated equally often.

2.5.2 Interval Scales

According to the remark 1.8.4 each statistic meaningful for interval scales is meaningful for ratio and difference scales, but not conversely.

a) Let us consider the sum $x_1 + x_2$. If $(x_1, x_2) \in \mathbb{R}^2$ is a value of two-dimensional scale such that x_1 and x_2 are measured in different ratio scales, i.e. if the set of admissible transformations is $\{(x_1, x_2) \to (\alpha_1 x_1, \alpha_2 x_2) : \alpha_1 > 0, \alpha_2 > 0\}$, then $x_1 + x_2$ is meaningless, because $x_1 + x_2 = x_1' + x_2'$ does not necessarily imply $\alpha_1 x_1 + \alpha_2 x_2 = \alpha_1 x_1' + \alpha_2 x_2'$. If, on the other hand, x_1 and x_2 are two values of the same one-dimensional interval scale, the sum $x_1 + x_2$ is meaningful, because $x_1 + x_2 = x_1' + x_2'$ implies $\alpha x_1 + \alpha x_2 + \beta = \alpha x'_1 + \alpha x'_2 + \beta$ for all $\alpha, \beta \in \mathbb{R}$.

b) Let us now consider the general case of meaningful statistics for interval scales, the linear functions,

$$f(x_1, x_2, \ldots, x_n) = \sum_{i=1}^{n} \lambda_i x_i + \lambda_0,$$

the λ_i being arbitrarily fixed real constants. The most important cases are $\lambda_0 = 0$, $\lambda_i = 1$ $(i = 1, \ldots, n)$ and

$$\lambda_0 = 0,\ \lambda_i = \frac{1}{n} (i = 1, \ldots, n),$$

the mean. f is meaningful for interval scales, because

$$(*)\qquad f(\alpha x_1+\beta,\ldots,\alpha x_n+\beta)=\alpha f(x_1,\ldots,x_n)+\beta\sum_{i=1}^{n}\lambda_i+(1-\alpha)\lambda_0\,.$$

Moreover, it follows from (*) that the group of transformations induced in the range space of f is, in general, isomorphic to the whole group of positive linear transformations (i.e. f is only "reference-invariant" in the sense of STEVENS (1959)). In the special case

$$\sum_{i=1}^{n}\lambda_i=0\,,$$

the group Γ' of induced transformations is the group Γ_d of dilations of $\mathbb{R}$.

c) As another example consider the statistic s:

$$s(x_1,\ldots,x_n)=\left(\frac{1}{n-1}\sum_{i=1}^{n}(x_i-\bar{x})^2\right)^{\frac{1}{2}},$$

where

$$\bar{x}=\frac{1}{n}\sum_{i=1}^{n}x_i$$

is the mean of $x_1,\ldots,x_n$. The statistic s is meaningful for interval scales, because $s\to\alpha s$ for $x_i\to\alpha x_i+\beta$. The statistic remains unchanged under shift transformations $x\to x+\beta$ only. The group Γ' of transformations induced in the range of s is the group Γ_d of dilations of $\mathbb{R}$.

d) Finally, we consider the statistic

$$q(x_1,\ldots,x_{2n})=\frac{s(x_1,\ldots,x_n)}{s(x_{n+1},\ldots,x_{2n})}$$

which is invariant under any linear transformation. Thus the group of transformations induced in the range of q consists of the identity transformation only. Therefore, the relations

$$s(x_1,\ldots,x_n)=\varrho s(x_{n+1},\ldots,x_{2n})\quad(\varrho>0)$$

are meaningful, whereas the relation

$$\bar{x}(x_1,\ldots,x_n)=\varrho\bar{x}(x_{n+1},\ldots,x_{2n})$$

is not (except $\varrho=1$ or the scale is unique up to dilations).

2.5.3 **Remark:** In the examples in 2.5.2 the subgroups Γ_0 of Γ_p leaving the values of the meaningful statistics unchanged were either Γ_p or Γ_s or

$\Gamma=\{\iota\}$. This is not surprising, because according to 1.8.4 these groups are normal subgroups of Γ_p and the examples do not specify nontrivial subgroups **G** of the multiplicative group $\mathbb{R}^+$. Hence the other normal subgroups of Γ_p do not appear. $\Gamma_0=\Gamma_d$ is impossible, since Γ_d is not a normal subgroup of Γ_p. For $\Gamma=\Gamma_s$ the group Γ' of induced automorphisms of the range space is algebraically isomorphic to Γ_p/Γ_s which is isomorphic to Γ_d, the group of dilations. It therefore follows immediately that Γ' is algebraically isomorphic to Γ_d.

This statement about isomorphism, however, does not necessarily imply that Γ' itself *is* the group of dilations of $\mathbb{R}$: The map $\varphi:\gamma_{\alpha,0}\to\gamma_{1,\log\alpha}$ is an algebraic isomorphism of Γ_d onto Γ_s. Hence the group Γ' is also isomorphic to Γ_s, the group of shifts. From the statement in examples b) and c) that Γ' *is* the group of dilations of $\mathbb{R}$, the question arises whether it may occur that, for certain meaningful statistics, Γ' *is* a group of shifts of $\mathbb{R}$. Except for the trivial case $\Gamma'=\{\iota\}$ this question will be answered negatively:

Let m be an interval scale and let $f:\mathbb{R}^n\to\mathbb{R}$ be a meaningful statistic for m. If there is a function $g:\mathbb{R}^+\times\mathbb{R}\to\mathbb{R}$ such that for all $(x_1,\ldots,x_n)\in m(A)^n$ and all $\alpha>0$, $\beta\in\mathbb{R}$

(*) $\quad f(\gamma_{\alpha,\beta}(x_1),\ldots,\gamma_{\alpha,\beta}(x_n))=f(x_1,\ldots,x_n)+g(\alpha,\beta),$

then $g(\alpha,\beta)=0$ for all α, β.

Proof: As $m(A)$ contains at least two points, we may assume without loss of generality that $0\in m(A)$ and $1\in m(A)$. For $x_1=x_2=\ldots=x_n=0$ we obtain from (*): For all $\alpha>0$, $\beta\in\mathbb{R}$

$f(\beta,\ldots,\beta)=f(0\cdot\alpha+\beta,\ldots,0\cdot\alpha+\beta)=f(0,\ldots,0)+g(\alpha,\beta)$. Hence

(**) $\quad g(\alpha,\beta)=g(1,\beta)=:h(\beta)$ for all $\alpha>0$, $\beta\in\mathbb{R}$.

For $x_1=x_2=\ldots=x_n=1$ we obtain from (*): For all $\alpha>\max(0,\beta)$, $\beta\in\mathbb{R}$: $f(1,\ldots,1)+g(\alpha,-\beta)=f(\alpha-\beta,\ldots,\alpha-\beta)=$ $f(1,\ldots,1)+g(\alpha-\beta,0)$. Given $\beta\in\mathbb{R}$, fix an arbitrary $\alpha>\max(0,\beta)$. Together with (**) the last equality implies

$$h(-\beta)=g(\alpha,-\beta)=g(\alpha-\beta,0)=h(0) \text{ for all } \beta\in\mathbb{R}.$$

Since $g(1,0)=0$ by (*), $h(0)=0$ by definition of h.

2.5.4 Ratio Scales

a) Though both $\bar{x}$ (see 2.5.2b) and s (2.5.2 c) are meaningful for interval scales, the "coefficient of variation" $s/\bar{x}$ would not be meaningful in this case as $s/\bar{x}=s'/\bar{x}'$ does not imply $\alpha s/(\alpha\bar{x}+\beta)=\alpha s'/(\alpha\bar{x}'+\beta)$ for all $\alpha>0$ and $\beta\in\mathbb{R}$. The coefficient of variation is, however, meaningful and even invariant for ratio scales.

b) A further example for meaningless statistics are certain price index formulas. A price index formula concerning n commodities may be considered as a statistic on $B_0\times B_1$ where $B_k=\mathbb{R}^n$ (k=0,1), and the ith component of B_k is the price of the commodity i at time k.

A typical example of a meaningless index-formula is

$$(*)\qquad f((p_1^{(0)},\ldots,p_n^{(0)}),(p_1^{(1)},\ldots,p_n^{(1)}))=\sum_{i=1}^{n}p_i^{(1)}/\sum_{i=1}^{n}p_i^{(0)}$$

due to Bradstreet and Dutot (see I. Fisher (1923) p. 40).

When the commodities are of a very different nature (such as foods, clothing and fuel, for instance) there is no natural common scale to measure the quantities. As the scale of each component is only unique up to dilations and no common unit of measurement exists, the dilations for different commodities might be independent. Thus the class of admissible transformations consists of the maps

$$(p_1,p_2,\ldots,p_n)\rightarrow(\alpha_1p_1,\alpha_2p_2,\ldots,\alpha_np_n),\quad \alpha_1,\alpha_2,\ldots,\alpha_n\in\mathbb{R}^+,$$

for which the index given by (*) is not meaningful. The example is the more useless as for economic reasons we have to require that the price index be not only meaningful but that its numerical value be invariant under admissible transformations, in other words: it ought to satisfy the so-called "commensurability-test" (see I. Fisher (1923) p. 420). An index formula which is independent of dilations is, e.g.

$$(**)\qquad \left(\prod_{i=1}^{n}p_i^{(1)}\Big/\prod_{i=1}^{n}p_i^{(0)}\right)^{1/n}$$

This example also illustrates that the concept of "meaningfulness" or of "invariance of numerical value" as introduced here has to be interpreted with the necessary care: If a statistic is meaningful or even numerical-invariant this does not necessarily imply that it is meaningful if interpreted in real terms: Formula (**) is "meaningful" (and numerical-invariant) in the sense defined above; it is however bare of any economic reason! Therefore, meaningfulness in the formal sense as used here is a necessary precondition, but not sufficient for being reasonable in real terms.

2.6 Meaningfully Parametrized Relations

It is easy to see that the concept of a meaningful relation is too restrictive for many practical purposes. Consider the case that all values obtained by measuring with a fixed scale m satisfy a certain k-ary relation T on B which is not meaningful in the sense of definition 2.1.1. But the fact that the scale values satisfy the relation T says something about reality: The measured objects satisfy the "empirical law" $T \circ m_{(k)}$. If we change the scale we must use a different relation T' on B to describe the same empirical law as T is not meaningful. Thus we have to each admissible scale m another k-ary relation T_m describing the empirical law; $(T_m)_{m \in \mathfrak{M}}$ is a family of relations which together with the parametrization give a statement about reality.

Let **A** be an irreducible e.r.s., **B** a n.r.s. of the same type. Let Θ be an arbitrary set such that to each $\vartheta \in \Theta$ there is a k-ary relation T_ϑ on B.

2.6.1 **Definition:** The family $(T_\vartheta)_{\vartheta \in \Theta}$ is *meaningfully parametrized* (m.p.) by the map φ of $\mathfrak{M}$ (**A**, **B**) into Θ iff for all $m, m' \in \mathfrak{M}$ (**A**, **B**)

$$T_{\varphi(m)} \circ m_{(k)} = T_{\varphi(m')} \circ m'_{(k)}.$$

If $T_{\varphi(m)}$ holds for the scale values measured by m, then a meaningful parametrization φ gives us the relation $T_{\varphi(m')}$ which describes the empirical relation $T_{\varphi(m)} \circ m_{(k)}$ under the scale m'.

Since the T_ϑ's with $\vartheta \in \varphi(\mathfrak{M})$ and only these are needed for describing the empirical relation for the different scales $m \in \mathfrak{M}$ (**A**, **B**), only "closed" families are of interest:

2.6.2 **Definition:** A m.p. family $(T_\vartheta)_{\vartheta \in \Theta}$ is *closed* iff $\varphi(\mathfrak{M}) = \Theta$.

As we could characterize meaningfulness of relations by their invariance (see 2.2) we can characterize the meaningfulness of parametrization by the admissible transformations:

2.6.3 **Theorem:** The family $(T_\vartheta)_{\vartheta \in \Theta}$ is m.p. by φ iff for any fixed $m_0 \in \mathfrak{M}$ (**A**, **B**) and for all $\gamma \in \Gamma_{\mathbf{B}}(m_0(A))$

$$T_{\varphi(m_0)} = T_{\psi(\gamma)} \circ \gamma_{(k)} \quad \text{on } (m_0(A))^k$$

where $\psi(\gamma) = \varphi(\gamma \circ m_0)$, or conversely, $\varphi(m) = \psi(m \circ m_0^{-1})$.

The proof follows immediately from

$$\mathfrak{M}(\mathbf{A}, \mathbf{B}) = \{\gamma \circ m_0 : \gamma \in \Gamma_{\mathbf{B}}(m_0(A))\} \quad \text{(see 1.5.12).}$$

As mentioned above meaningful parametrization means to imbed a relation T into a family (T_ϑ), expressing the same empirical relation for different scales. How this may be achieved is stated by

2.6.4 **Corollary:** If T_0 is a k-ary relation on B and $m_0 \in \mathfrak{M}$ **(A, B)** then the family $(T_\gamma)_{\gamma \in \Gamma_{\mathbf{B}}(m_0(A))}$:

$$T_\gamma = \begin{cases} T_0 \circ \gamma_{(k)}^{-1} & \text{on } (\gamma \circ m_0(A))^k \\ T_0 & \text{elsewhere} \end{cases}$$

is a closed family meaningfully parametrized by $\varphi(m) = m \circ m_0^{-1}$, such that $T_{\varphi(m_0)} = T_{\varphi(\iota)} = T_0$.

2.6.5 The definition of the family (T_γ) and the parametrization depend on m_0. Even if for $m_1 = \gamma_1 \circ m_0$ the map $\gamma \to \gamma\gamma_1$ is a $1-1$ map of $\Gamma_{\mathbf{B}}(m_1(A))$ onto $\Gamma_{\mathbf{B}}(m_0(A))$, the families $(T_\gamma)_{\gamma \in \Gamma_{\mathbf{B}}(m_0(A))}$ and $(T_\gamma)_{\gamma \in \Gamma_{\mathbf{B}}(m_1(A))}$ may be different. This is not surprising, since T_0 under m_0 reflects in general an empirical law different from T_0 under $m_1 \neq m_0$. If, however, $m_0(A) = B$ and $\Gamma_{\mathbf{B}}(m_0(A)) = \Gamma_{\mathbf{B}}$, the group of automorphisms of B, then the families coincide and the parametrization φ' with $T_{\varphi'(m_1)} = T_0$ can be obtained from the parametrization φ with $T_{\varphi(m_0)} = T_0$ by $\varphi'(m) = \varphi(m) \circ \gamma_1^{-1}$ where $m_1 = \gamma_1 \circ m_0$.

The notion $(T_\gamma)_{\gamma \in \Gamma}$ may not suggest that $T_{\gamma'} \neq T_\gamma$ for $\gamma' \neq \gamma$. The relations T_γ, for example, coincide for all $\gamma \in \Gamma_{\mathbf{B}}(m_0(A))$ iff T_0 is meaningful. The equivalence relation: $\gamma \approx \eta$ iff $T_\gamma = T_\eta$ defines equivalence classes which correspond uniquely to the *different* relations of the family $(T_\gamma)_{\gamma \in \Gamma}$.

If, moreover, $m_0(A) = B$ and $\Gamma_{\mathbf{B}}(m_0(A)) = \Gamma_{\mathbf{B}}$, the set $\Gamma_0 = \{\gamma : T_\gamma = T_0\}$ is a subgroup of $\Gamma_{\mathbf{B}}$: Since $T_{\gamma\eta} = T_0 \circ \eta_{(k)}^{-1} \circ \gamma_{(k)}^{-1} = (T_\eta)_\gamma$ we obtain for all $\gamma, \eta \in \Gamma_0$: $T_{\eta^{-1}} = (T_\eta)_{\eta^{-1}} = T_{\eta^{-1}\eta} = T_0$ and $T_{\gamma\eta} = (T_\eta)_\gamma = T_\gamma = T_0$. If $T_\gamma = T_{\gamma'}$ then $T_0 \circ \gamma_{(k)}^{-1} = T_0 \circ \gamma_{(k)}'^{-1}$ and thus $\gamma'^{-1} \circ \gamma \in \Gamma_0$, and conversely. Hence the equivalence classes of $\Gamma_{\mathbf{B}}$ in which T_γ is constant are the right cosets of $\Gamma_{\mathbf{B}}$ modulo $\Gamma_0 : \gamma\Gamma_0$.

If Γ_0 is a normal subgroup of Γ there is a $1-1$-correspondence between the cosets and the elements of the factor group Γ/Γ_0. In this case we can parametrize the families $\{T_\gamma\}_{\gamma \in \Gamma}$ by the (in general smaller) set Γ/Γ_0. We remark that Γ_0 is not normal in general: Let $B = \mathbb{R}$ and $\Gamma = \Gamma_p$, the group of positive linear transformations of $\mathbb{R}$. The 1-ary relation $T_0 : x = 0$ (i. e. $T_0(x) = 1$ iff $x = 0$) is only invariant under dilations; thus $\Gamma_0 = \Gamma_d$. But Γ_d is not normal in Γ_p (see 1.8.4).

2.7 Examples on Meaningful Parametrization

a) Let $B=\mathbb{R}^+\times\mathbb{R}^+$ and $\Gamma_B=\{\eta_{\alpha_1,\alpha_2}: (x_1, x_2)\to(\alpha_1 x_1, \alpha_2 x_2), \alpha_1, \alpha_2 \in \mathbb{R}^+\}$.

Assume furthermore that for a given scale m_0 the following relation holds:

$$T_0\,(x_1, x_2)=1 \text{ iff } x_2=2\,x_1^3.$$

According to 2.6.4 the m.p. family is given by

$$T_{\alpha_1,\alpha_2}(x_1,x_2)=1 \text{ iff } T_0\left(\frac{x_1}{\alpha_1}, \frac{x_2}{\alpha_2}\right)=1$$

which means

$$\frac{x_2}{\alpha_2}=2\frac{x_1^3}{\alpha_1^3}.$$

We have

$$T_{\alpha_1,\alpha_2}=T_0 \text{ iff } \frac{\alpha_2}{\alpha_1^3}=1$$

and therefore

$$T_{\alpha_1,\alpha_2}=T_{\alpha_1',\alpha_2'} \text{ iff } \frac{\alpha_2}{\alpha_1^3}=\frac{\alpha_2'}{\alpha_1'^3}.$$

Hence the set $\{T_{\alpha_1,\alpha_2}:\alpha_1,\alpha_2\in\mathbb{R}^+\}$ coincides with the set $\{T_\vartheta:\vartheta\in\mathbb{R}^+\}$ of relations where "$T_\vartheta\,(x_1, x_2)=1$ iff $x_2=2\,\vartheta x_1^3$". The meaningful parametrization for this family is given by

$$\psi\,(\eta_{\alpha_1,\alpha_2})=\frac{\alpha_2}{\alpha_1^3}\in\Theta=\mathbb{R}^+.$$

b) A typical example of a m.p. family of relations is the equation of state of the ideal gas: $pV=RT$. To write this relation in the general form, put $V=x_1$, $p=x_2$, $T=x_3$, $R=\vartheta$. Then $x_1x_2=\vartheta x_3$. If we assume that the transformations Γ are induced by a change of unit of length, Γ consists of the transformations γ_t: $(x_1, x_2, x_3)\to(t^3x_1, t^{-2}\,x_2, x_3)$. If for a fixed scale m_0 the relation holds with $\vartheta=\vartheta_0$, the meaningful parametrization is given by $\psi\,(\gamma_t)=t\vartheta_0$.

Obviously, such a family can only be meaningfully parametrized with a temperature scale unique up to dilations. If the zero point were not fixed, i.e. positive linear transformations $\gamma_{\alpha,\beta}: x_3\to\alpha x_3+\beta$ with $\alpha>0$ and $\beta\in\mathbb{R}$ were admissible, no corresponding function $\psi\,(\alpha, \beta)$ would exist such that $x_1x_2=\vartheta_0x_3$ implies

$$x_1 x_2 = \psi(\alpha, \beta)(\alpha x_3 + \beta).$$

(The existence of such a function ψ would imply

$$(\psi(\alpha, \beta)\alpha - \vartheta_0) x_3 + \psi(\alpha, \beta) \cdot \beta = 0 \text{ for all } x_3 \in \mathbb{R}.$$

But this functional equation is solvable only for $\beta = 0$.)

c) A parametric relationship which is not meaningful was proposed by WAUGH (1935, p. 395) for the relationship between amount of money M and subjective utility U of this amount.

$$U = \frac{\vartheta_1}{\operatorname{loglog} M - \operatorname{loglog} \vartheta_2}$$

where ϑ_1 and ϑ_2 are real parameters.

Obviously, this law is a modification of a law proposed by R. FRISCH

$$U = \frac{\vartheta_1}{\log M - \log \vartheta_2}.$$

If we take into account that M is only unique up to dilations, we find that FRISCH's law is meaningfully parametrizable whereas WAUGH's law is not: If WAUGH's law would hold with money expressed in dollars, it could not hold with money expressed in cents. To write the two laws in our general form, put $U = x_1$, $M = x_2$. Then,

$$x_1 = \frac{\vartheta_1}{\operatorname{loglog} x_2 - \operatorname{loglog} \vartheta_2}$$

and

$$x_1 = \frac{\vartheta_1}{\log x_2 - \log \vartheta_2}.$$

x_1 and x_2 are unique up to dilations; as both scales are independent, the admissible transformations are: $\eta_{t_1, t_2}: (x_1, x_2) \to (t_1 x_1, t_2 x_2)$. Does there exist a meaningful parametrization $\psi: (t_1, t_2) \to \Theta$? The answer is affirmative in the case of FRISCH's relation: $\psi(t_1, t_2) = (t_1 \vartheta_1, t_2 \vartheta_2)$ is a m.p. In the case of WAUGH's relation, however, no such parametrization exists: If this were so, we should have

$$\frac{\vartheta_1}{\operatorname{loglog} x_2 - \operatorname{loglog} \vartheta_2} = \frac{t_1 \psi_1(t_1, t_2)}{\operatorname{loglog}(t_2 x_2) - \operatorname{loglog} \psi_2(t_1, t_2)}$$

for all $x_2 > 0$ which would imply that loglog $(t_2 x_2)$ is a linear function of loglog x_2; but this holds only for $t_2 = 1$.

Another example of a meaningless law is the following modification of WEBER's law, proposed by MACDONALD and ROBERTSON (1930: I p. 830, II p. 1064) for loudness and sense of touch:

$$\Delta S = \frac{\alpha}{\log S}$$

where S is the physical intensity, ΔS the "just noticeable increase" of the physical intensity, α a parameter. To put this formula into standard form, let $S = x_1$, and let the intensity $S + \Delta S$, which is just noticeably stronger than x_1, be denoted by x_2. Finally, let $\alpha = \vartheta_0 \in \mathbb{R}^+$. Then

$$x_2 - x_1 = \frac{\vartheta_0}{\log x_1}.$$

Physical intensity is usually measured in a scale unique up to dilations. The transformation $(x_1, x_2) \to (tx_1, tx_2)$ cannot be compensated by a parametrization, as in this case we ought to have

$$\frac{\psi(t)}{\log tx_1} = \frac{t\vartheta_0}{\log x_1}$$

for all x_1, which is impossible (except for $t = 1$).

As in the foregoing example the meaningless relationship is the modification of a meaningful one, in this case of WEBER's law:

$$\Delta S = \frac{\vartheta_0}{S}$$

Here, to any transformation $\gamma_t: S \to tS$ a meaningful parametrization is given by $\psi(t) = t^2 \vartheta_0$.

e) The parameter space Θ in our general theory is completely arbitrary. Most examples of practical relevance involve a finite number of real parameters only. An example using a more general parameter space is the following:

Assume, e.g. that x_1 is a scale value of pitch and x_2 is a scale value of the latitude of the spot of maximal excitation (see STEVENS and VOLKMANN (1940)). Assume that the scale for pitch were only unique up to arbitrary monotone transformations. Then the only meaningful statement about relations between x_1 and x_2 would be that x_1 is a monotone increasing function of x_2: If the scales of x_1 and x_2 are fixed, there exists a monotone increasing function $u(.)$, such that $x_1 = u(x_2)$. By a change of the scale of x_1, the function u will be transformed into a different monotone increasing function. The parameter space in this case consists of all monotone increasing functions. If we restricted u, e.g., to linear functions: $u_{\vartheta_1, \vartheta_2}(x)=\vartheta_1 x+\vartheta_2$ we should be back to the case of real parameters: $x_1=\vartheta_1 x_2+\vartheta_2$. This family, $(\vartheta_1, \vartheta_2) \in \mathbb{R}^2$, of relations, stating that x_1 is a linear function of x_2 would, however, not be meaningfully parametrizable if the scale of x_1 would admit arbitrary monotone transformations, as an arbitrary change of the scale in x_1 could not be compensated by a change of the parameter values ϑ_1, ϑ_2. A relationship of this type could, however, be meaningfully parametrized if the scale of x_1 were unique up to linear transformations.

f) The presence of parameters (dimensional constants) depending on scales, a fact familiar to all physicists, seems to confuse psychologists. In this connection we should mention an interesting attempt of R. D. LUCE (1959), (1964) to determine all "possible" psychophysical laws by the following consideration: Let the scale values x_i be unique up to a set Γ_i of transformations $(i=1, \ldots, n+1)$ and f a map of B^n into B. The functional relation T on B^{n+1}:

$$(*) \qquad x_{n+1}=f(x_1, \ldots, x_n)$$

is "possible" iff for each $(\gamma_1, \ldots, \gamma_n) \in \Gamma_1 \times \Gamma_2 \times \ldots \times \Gamma_n$ there exists $\gamma_{n+1} \in \Gamma_{n+1}$ such that (*) implies

$$\gamma_{n+1}(x_{n+1})=f(\gamma_1(x_1), \ldots, \gamma_n(x_n)).$$

As an illustration let us consider the case $B=\mathbb{R}$, $n=1$ and $\Gamma_1=\Gamma_2=\Gamma_d$ (i.e. both scales are unique up to dilations).

Then to each $\alpha \in \mathbb{R}^+$ there ought to exist a value $\delta(\alpha) \in \mathbb{R}^+$ such that $x_2=f(x_1)$ iff $\delta(\alpha)=f(\alpha x_1)$. This is a functional equation for δ and f. If f is assumed to be continuous we obtain $f(x)=\varrho x^\tau$ and $\delta(\alpha)=\alpha^\tau$ where $\varrho, \tau \in \mathbb{R}$. Therefore, a "possible" functional relation connecting two scales unique up to dilations is necessarily of the type $x_2=\varrho x_1^\tau$.

Though the principle applied by LUCE for the determination of f seems to be reasonable at first sight, we object, that there are laws which can only be described by "impossible" functional relations; they cannot be expressed without parameters which are transformed together with the scales. The one-dimensional movement of a linearly braked body is described by the relation

$$x_2=-\tau e^{-\varrho x_1}+\sigma \quad (\tau, \varrho \in \mathbb{R}^+, \sigma \in \mathbb{R})$$

where x_1 denotes time, x_2 distance. Here a change of the unit of time cannot be compensated by a change of the unit of length if ϱ is fixed.

Besides these critical remarks on "possible" functions the theorems proved by LUCE (1964) are useful by another interpretation: They determine the real functions f on $\mathbb{R}^n$ or $(\mathbb{R}^+)^n$ such that the family $(T_\vartheta)_{\vartheta \in \mathbb{R}^2}$:

$$x_{n+1} = \vartheta_1 f(x_1, \ldots, x_n) + \vartheta_2$$

of relations can be meaningfully parametrized if $\Gamma_1, \ldots, \Gamma_n = \Gamma_d$ and

$$\text{(i) } \Gamma_{n+1} = \Gamma_d \quad \text{or} \quad \text{(ii) } \Gamma_{n+1} = \Gamma_p.$$

LUCE proves that for f being continuous

$$f(x_1, \ldots, x_n) = \varrho \prod_{i=1}^{n} x_i^{\tau_i}$$

in case (i),

$$= \varrho \prod_{i=1}^{n} x_i^{\tau_i} + \sigma \quad \text{or} \quad \sum_{i=1}^{n} \tau_i \log x_i + c$$

in case (ii).

g) Until now, meaningfulness of a statistic $f(x_{(n)})$ was connected with the meaningfulness of relations on B by (2.4.2) which is equivalent to the meaningfulness of the $(2n)$-ary relation $f(x_{(n)}) = f(x'_{(n)})$ on B. Introducing an artificial real parameter, a meaningful statistic can be interpreted as a m. p. family of n-ary relations: Let f be a statistic on B^n, $m_0 \in \mathfrak{M}(\mathbf{A}, \mathbf{B})$, $B_0 = \cup \{m(A) : m \in \mathfrak{M}(\mathbf{A}, \mathbf{B})\}$. Then f is meaningful iff for each $x_{(n)} \in m_0(A)^n$ the map $\psi(\gamma) = f(\gamma_{(n)}(x_{(n)}))$ on $\Gamma_{\mathbf{B}}(m_0(A))$ is a meaningful parametrization of the family $\{T_\vartheta\}_{\vartheta \in f(B_0{}^n)}$ where T_ϑ is the relation $f(x_{(n)}) - \vartheta = 0$.

3. Topology on Ordered Sets

3.1 Topological Spaces

3.1.1 **Definition:** A *topology* is a family $\mathscr{T}$ of sets which satisfies the following conditions:

(i) the empty set is a member of $\mathscr{T}$,

(ii) the intersection of any two members of $\mathscr{T}$ is a member of $\mathscr{T}$,

(iii) the union of each subfamily of $\mathscr{T}$ is a member of $\mathscr{T}$.

The set $A := \cup \{U : U \in \mathscr{T}\}$ is called the *space* of the topology $\mathscr{T}$. The pair $(A, \mathscr{T})$ is a *topological space*. The sets of the topology $\mathscr{T}$ are called *open* sets. The space A of the topology and the empty set are always open.

3.1.2 **Definition:** If $\mathscr{T}_1$ and $\mathscr{T}_2$ are topologies for A, $\mathscr{T}_1$ is *coarser* than $\mathscr{T}_2$ ($\mathscr{T}_2$ is *finer* than $\mathscr{T}_1$) iff $\mathscr{T}_1 \subset \mathscr{T}_2$.

3.1.3 **Definition:** A set U in a topological space $(A, \mathscr{T})$ is a *neighborhood* of an element a iff U is open and contains a. The *neighborhood system* of a point is the family of all neighborhoods of the point.

3.1.4 **Criterion:** A set is open iff it contains a neighborhood of each of its points.

Proof: See KELLEY (1955, p. 38).

3.1.5 **Definition:** A subfamily $\mathscr{T}_0 \subset \mathscr{T}$ is called a *base* for $\mathscr{T}$ iff each member of $\mathscr{T}$ is the union of members of $\mathscr{T}_0$. A subfamily $\mathscr{T}_1 \subset \mathscr{T}$ is called a *subbase* for $\mathscr{T}$ iff each member of $\mathscr{T}$ is the union of finite intersections of members of $\mathscr{T}_1$.

3.1.6 **Criterion:** A subfamily $\mathscr{T}_0 \subset \mathscr{T}$ is a base for $\mathscr{T}$ iff for each point a of the space and each neighborhood U of a there exists $V \in \mathscr{T}_0$ such that $a \in V \subset U$.

Proof: See KELLEY (1955, p. 46).

3.1.7 **Definition:** A space whose topology has a countable base is said to satisfy the *second axiom of countability.*

3.1.8 **Definition:** A *base for the neighborhood system* of a point a is a family of neighborhoods of a such that every neighborhood of a contains a member of this family.

3.1.9 **Definition:** A topological space satisfies the *first axiom of countability* iff the neighborhood system of every point has a countable base.

3.1.10 **Lemma:** A topological space which satisfies the second axiom of countability also satisfies the first.

Proof: See KELLEY (1955, p. 50).

3.1.11 **Definition:** A topological space is a *Hausdorff space* iff for any pair a, b of distinct points there exist disjoint neighborhoods.

3.1.12 **Definition:** The element a_0 is a *limit point* of the sequence $(a_n)_{n=1,2,\dots}$ iff to each neighborhood U of a_0 there exists $n(U)$ such that $a_n \in U$ for all $n \geqq n(U)$.

If a_0 is the unique limit point of the sequence $(a_n)_{n=1,2,\dots}$, we write: $a_0 = \lim\limits_{n\to\infty} a_n$.

3.1.13 **Lemma:** If a topological space is a Hausdorff space, each sequence has at most one limit point.

Proof: See KELLEY (1955, p. 67).

3.2 Order Relations

3.2.1 **Definition:** A relational system $\langle A; \approx, \prec\rangle$ is called an *order system* iff the following axioms are fulfilled:

3.2.2 **Order axioms:**

O1. For all $a, b \in A$, exactly one of the relations
$a \approx b$, $a \prec b$, $b \prec a$ holds

O2. "$\approx$" is an equivalence relation

O3. "$\prec$" is transitive.

A trivial example of an order system is $\langle \mathbb{R}; =, <\rangle$, the system of real numbers. Most empirical relational systems are order systems. If, for example, A are tones, "$\approx$" and "$\prec$" might be equivalence and order according to pitch.

As in section 1.4, we can consider $\tilde{\tilde{A}}$, the set of all equivalence classes and the relational system $\langle \tilde{\tilde{A}}; =, < \rangle$ defined as follows:

$\tilde{a} = \tilde{\tilde{b}}$, if the two classes consist of the same elements.

$\tilde{a} < \tilde{\tilde{b}}$, if $a \prec b$.

The last definition makes sense only if the order relation is the same regardless which elements of the equivalence classes are taken as representatives. In other words, we have to show that $a \prec b$, $a \approx a'$, $b \approx b'$ together imply $a' \prec b'$. This is established by the following lemma:

3.2.3 **Lemma:** In an order system, "$\approx$" is a congruence relation with respect to "$\prec$".

Proof: $a \approx b$ and $b \prec c$ together imply $a \prec c$: $a \approx c$ together with $a \approx b$ implies $b \approx c$, which contradicts $b \prec c$. Furthermore, $c \prec a$ together with $b \prec c$ implies $b \prec a$ which contradicts $a \approx b$. Similarly, we show that $a \prec b$ and $b \approx c$ together imply $a \prec c$. Therefore, $a \prec b$ and $a \approx a'$ together imply $a' \prec b$; together with $b \approx b'$, this implies $a' \prec b'$.

In dealing with empirical relational systems a question of practical relevance is the simultaneous occurrence of an *indifference* relation (reflexive and symmetric, but not transitive) and a transitive preference relation. Such a situation occurs, for example, if subjects are uncertain in the distinction of similar stimuli. They might be indifferent between a, b as well as indifferent between b, c, but might prefer a to c.

The question is whether it is possible to "refine" indifference to a transitive equivalence relation. One reasonable suggestion is to eliminate from $\tilde{a}$ (the set of all elements which are indifferent to a) all elements, which are indifferent to an element which is preferred or postponed to a and to consider these elements as preferred to a or postponed to a, respectively.

The following example shows that this does not lead to an order relation in general: Let A be a system of sets, interpret $a \prec b$ that a is a proper subset of b and interpret $a \sim b$ that neither $a \prec b$ nor $b \prec a$. If we would define a stronger preference relation $\prec_1$ in the way indicated above, we would have $a \prec_1 b$ as well as $b \prec_1 a$ in the following situation:

$$a = \{0, 1, 2\},\ b = \{1, 2, 4\},\ c = \{0, 1\},\ d = \{0, 1, 2, 3\}.$$

We have $b \sim a$ and $b \sim c$ but $c \prec a$; hence, $b \prec_1 a$. On the other hand, $b \sim a$ and $b \sim d$ but $a \prec d$; hence $a \prec_1 b$.

We must therefore require more than transitivity for the preference relation in order to be able to "refine" the indifference relation into a transitive equivalence relation. This can be done by starting from the following relational system $\langle A; \sim, \prec\rangle$:

3.2.4 1. For all $a, b \in A$ exactly one of the relations $a \sim b$, $a \prec b$, $b \prec a$ holds.

2. "$\sim$" is an indifference relation.

3. $a \prec b'$, $b' \sim b''$, $b'' \prec c$ together imply $a \prec c$.

Axiom 3 implies transitivity of order, if we identify b' and b'', (as "$\sim$" is reflexive).

3.2.5 **Theorem:** If 3.2.4 is fulfilled for a r.s. $\langle A; \sim, \prec\rangle$, an order system $\langle A; \approx, \prec_1\rangle$ can be derived.

Proof: Let P_a be the set of all elements preferred to a: $b \in P_a$ if, and only if, $a \prec b$. Then, for any two elements a, b we have either $P_a = P_b$ or $P_a \subsetneqq P_b$ or $P_b \subsetneqq P_a$. This can be seen as follows: Assume, that there exists c such that $c \in P_a$, $c \notin P_b$. We show that $P_b \subset P_a$ ($P_b \neq P_a$ is obvious from the existence of c). As $c \notin P_b$, we have either $c \sim b$ or $c \prec b$. Thus, we have for any $d \in P_b$: $a \prec c$; $c \sim b$ or $c \prec b$; $b \prec d$. In either case, we obtain $a \prec d$, i.e. $d \in P_a$. Therefore, we can define an order system $\langle A; \approx, \prec_1\rangle$ as follows: $a \approx b$ if $P_a = P_b$, $a \prec_1 b$ if $P_b \subsetneqq P_a$. The axioms O1, O2, O3 are fulfilled as can be seen easily.

3.3 Interval Topology

The purpose of this section is to present a number of topological theorems on ordered sets for further reference. We remind the reader that we always assume equality to be the only equivalence relation.

3.3.1 **Definition:** By an *open ray* in A we mean a set of the form

$$(\leftarrow, a) := \{x \in A : x < a\} \text{ or } (a, \rightarrow) := \{x \in A : a < x\},\ a \in A.$$

By a *closed ray* in A we mean a set of the form

$$(\leftarrow, a] := \{x \in A : x \leqq a\} \text{ or } [a, \rightarrow) := \{x \in A : a \leqq x\},\ a \in A.$$

It is convenient to consider A itself as well as the empty set as rays which are open and closed at the same time.

3.3.2 **Definition:** By an $\left\{\begin{matrix}\textit{open}\\ \textit{closed}\end{matrix}\right.$ *interval* we mean a set which is either an $\left\{\begin{matrix}\text{open}\\ \text{closed}\end{matrix}\right.$ ray or is of the form

$$\left\{\begin{matrix}(a, b) := \{x \in A : a < x < b\}\\ [a, b] := \{x \in A : a \leqq x \leqq b\}\end{matrix}\right. \qquad a, b \in A.$$

The set of open (closed) intervals is the smallest system of subsets of A closed under finite intersections and containing all open (closed) rays.

3.3.3 **Definition:** By an *interval* in A we mean a set which is an open interval or a closed interval or is of the form

$$\left.\begin{array}{l}[a, b) := \{x \in A : a \leqq x < b\} \\ (a, b] := \{x \in A : a < x \leqq b\}\end{array}\right. \quad a, b \in A.$$

3.3.4 **Definition:** The *interval topology* $\mathscr{I}$ is the smallest system of subsets of A, closed under finite intersections and arbitrary unions, containing all open rays. Equivalently, $\mathscr{I}$ is the smallest system of subsets of A, closed under arbitrary unions, containing all open intervals. Thus each set of $\mathscr{I}$ is the union of open intervals. Therefore the system of all open intervals is a base for $\mathscr{I}$, the system of all open rays is a subbase.

3.3.5 **Criterion:** A set $B \subset A$ belongs to the interval topology $\mathscr{I}$ iff each of its points is contained in an open interval contained in B.

Proof: Follows immediately from 3.1.4.

3.3.6 **Criterion:** A subfamily $\mathscr{I}_0 \subset \mathscr{I}$ is a base for $\mathscr{I}$, iff for each open interval I and each $x \in I$ there exists a set $I_0 \in \mathscr{I}_0$ such that $x \in I_0 \subset I$.

Proof: Follows immediately from 3.1.6.

3.3.7 **Definition:** A set $B \subset A$ is a *segment* iff $a < x < b$ and $a, b \in B$ together imply $x \in B$.

Obviously any interval is a segment but not vice versa.

3.3.8 **Example:** If A is the union of all negative and all positive real numbers, the subset consisting of all positive numbers is a segment, but not an interval.

We remark that the interval topology is a HAUSDORFF topology: Let $a, b \in A$ with $a < b$. If there exists $c \in (a, b)$, then $(\leftarrow, c)$ and $(c, \rightarrow)$ are disjoint open intervals containing a and b, respectively. If (a, b) is empty, $(\leftarrow, b)$ and $(a, \rightarrow)$ are disjoint open intervals containing a and b, respectively.

As the interval topology is HAUSDORFF, each sequence has at most one limit point.

3.4 Relative Topology and Interval Topology

If B is a subset of an ordered set A, we have to distinguish between two topologies:

(i) The interval topology of $\langle B; =, < \rangle$, denoted by $\mathscr{I}_B$.

(ii) The relative topology induced in B by $\mathscr{I}_A$: $B \cap \mathscr{I}_A$. (Open sets in the relative topology are intersections of sets of $\mathscr{I}_A$ with B.)

We have $\mathscr{I}_B \subset B \cap \mathscr{I}_A$: This follows immediately from the fact that any open ray of $\langle B; =, < \rangle$ is the intersection of an open ray of $\langle A; =, < \rangle$ with B. In general, the two topologies are *not* identical. Examples of divergence will become clear from Lemma 3.4.5.

3.4.1 **Definition:** A representation of B as union of two nonempty disjoint segments is called a *cut*.

3.4.2 **Definition:***) A subset $B \subset A$ is called *simple*, iff for each cut $B = B_1 \cup B_2$, $(B_1 < B_2)$, the following condition is fulfilled:

α) If $\sup B_1$ exists and belongs to B_1, then $\inf B_2$ exists and we have either $\sup B_1 = \inf B_2$ or $\inf B_2 \in B_2$.

β) If $\inf B_2$ exists and belongs to B_2, then $\sup B_1$ exists and we have either $\sup B_1 = \inf B_2$ or $\sup B_1 \in B_1$.

3.4.3 **Example:** The sets $(\leftarrow, 0] \cup (1, \rightarrow)$ and $(\leftarrow, 0) \cup [1, \rightarrow)$, considered as subsets of $\mathbb{R}$, are not simple. The sets $(\leftarrow, 0) \cup (1, \rightarrow)$ and $(\leftarrow, 0] \cup [1, \rightarrow)$, considered as subsets of $\mathbb{R}$, are simple.

3.4.4 **Lemma:** Each segment is simple.

Proof: Assume that $B \subset A$ is a segment and $B = B_1 \cup B_2$ a cut. Assume that $b_1 := \sup B_1$ exists and belongs to B_1; unless $b_1 = \inf B_2$, there exists $a \in A$ such that $b_1 < a \leqq B_2$. Because B_2 is not empty and B is a segment, a belongs to B and therefore to B_2. Thus, $B_2 \ni a = \inf B_2$. The other case is dealt with similarly.

3.4.5 **Lemma:** For a subset $B \subset A$ relative topology and interval topology coincide if and only if B is simple.

Proof: (i) First, we assume that B is simple. As $\mathscr{I}_B \subset \mathscr{I}_A \cap B$, we have to show that $B_1 := B \cap (\leftarrow, a) \in \mathscr{I}_B$ for all $a \in A$. Let $B_2 := B \cap [a, \rightarrow)$. If B_1 has no maximal element it is open in $\mathscr{I}_B$. If $b_1 := \sup B_1 \in B_1$, we have $b_1 < a \leqq B_2$. Because B is simple, this implies that $b_2 = \inf B_2$ exists and belongs to B_2. Therefore, $B_1 = \{b \in B : b < b_2\}$ is open in $\mathscr{I}_B$.

*) See Definition 3.5.1.

(ii) Second we show that B is simple if relative topology and interval topology coincide. Assume that $B = B_1 \cup B_2$ is a cut such that $b_1 := \sup B_1 \in B_1$. If b_1 is not the infimum of B_2, there exists $a \in A$, $a > b_1$, which is lower bound of B_2. Then $B_1 = B \cap (\leftarrow, a)$ is open in the relative topology and therefore open in the interval topology $\mathscr{I}_B$. As $b_1 \in B_1$, there exists $b_2 \in B$ such that $b_1 \in (\leftarrow, b_2) \subset B_1$. From the definition of b_1, the interval (b_1, b_2) contains no element of B_1 and as $(\leftarrow, b_2) \subset B_1$ no element of B. Thus, $\inf B_2 = b_2 \in B_2$.

3.4.6 **Corollary:** If B is a segment, interval topology and relative topology coincide.

Proof: Follows immediately from 3.4.4 and 3.4.5.

3.5 Order-Completeness and Connectedness

3.5.1 **Definition:** If B_1, B_2 are subsets of an ordered set A such that $b_1 < b_2$ for all $b_1 \in B_1$, $b_2 \in B_2$, we write $B_1 < B_2$. Similarly $a < B_2$ means: $a < b_2$ for all $b_2 \in B_2$ etc.

An element $a_0 \in A$ is an *upper (lower) bound* of a subset $B \subset A$ iff $a_0 \geqq B$ ($a_0 \leqq B$).

Let C be the set of all upper (lower) bounds of a subset $B \subset A$. An element $a_0 \in A$ is *supremum (infimum)* of B iff $a_0 \in C$ and $a_0 \leqq C$ ($a_0 \geqq C$). In this case we write $a_0 = \sup B$ ($a_0 = \inf B$).

An ordered set A is *order-complete* iff each nonempty subset which has an upper bound has a supremum.

3.5.2 **Lemma:** An ordered set is order-complete iff each nonempty subset which has a lower bound has an infimum.

Proof: Let B be a nonempty subset which has an upper bound. Thus, the set C of all upper bounds is not empty and has a lower bound, because B is not empty. By assumption, it has an infimum c, which is necessarily an upper bound of B and therefore a supremum of B. The reverse is proved similarly.

3.5.3 **Example:** The set of all positive and all negative real numbers is not order-complete, because the set of all positive real numbers has lower bounds but no infimum.

3.5.4 **Lemma:** In an order-complete set any monotone and bounded sequence has a limit point.

Proof: Let $(a_n)_{n=1,2,\ldots}$ be nondecreasing: $a_n \leqq a_{n+1}$ for all $n = 1, 2, \ldots$ If there exists an upper bound, say b, the set $\{a_1, a_2, \ldots\}$ has a supremum by order-completeness. As the sequence is nondecreasing, this supremum is a limit point.

3.5.5 Definition: A subset $B \subset A$ is *connected* iff it is not the union of two disjoint nonempty sets which are open in the relative topology of B.

3.5.6 Lemma: If an ordered set A is not connected, it is the union of two nonempty disjoint open segments.

Proof: Assume that $A = B \cup C$ where B, C are two nonempty disjoint open sets. Let $b_0 \in B$, $c_0 \in C$. Without loss of generality $b_0 < c_0$. We define: $B_0 := (\leftarrow, b_0) \cup \{x \in B : [b_0, x] \subset B\}$. B_0 is a nonempty segment. The following argument shows that B_0 is open: Let $b \in B_0$. If $b < b_0$, $b \in (\leftarrow, b_0)$. If $b \geqq b_0$ we have $b \in B$. Because B is open, there exist b', b'' such that $b \in (b', b'') \subset B$. We show that $(b', b'') \subset B_0$. Let $x \in (b', b'')$. If $x \leqq b$, $x \in B_0$ because B_0 is a segment. If $x > b$, we have $[b_0, x] = [b_0, b] \cup (b, x] \subset B$, because $[b_0, b] \subset B$ and $(b, x] \subset (b', b'') \subset B$. Thus, $x \in B_0$.

Let $C_0 = A - B_0$. As $C_0 \ni c_0$, it is a nonempty segment. We now show that C_0 is open: If $x \in C_0$, there exists $c \in C$ such that $b_0 < c \leqq x$. If $c < x$, $x \in (c, \rightarrow) \subset C_0$ and the proof is completed. If $c = x$, there exist $a', a'' \in A$ such that $c \in (a', a'') \subset C$. We show that $(a', a'') \subset C_0$. Let $y \in (a', a'')$. Because $y \in C$, $[b_0, y] \subset B$ does not hold, whence $y \notin B_0$.

3.5.7 Definition: A closed interval $[a, b]$ is a *gap*, iff $a < b$ and the open interval (a, b) is empty.

3.5.8 Example: The set $\{r \in \mathbb{R} : r \leqq 0\} \cup \{r \in \mathbb{R} : r \geqq 1\}$ has the gap $[0, 1]$.

3.5.9 Lemma: An ordered set is connected iff it is order-complete and has no gaps.

Proof: (i) A connected set has no gaps: If A has a gap at $a < b$, we have $A = (\leftarrow, b) \cup (a, \rightarrow)$ which contradicts connectedness.

(ii) A connected set is order-complete: Let B be a nonempty set which has an upper bound. Let C be the set of all upper bounds and $D := A - C$. By definition of D to each $d \in D$ there exists $b \in B$ such that $d < b$. If B has no supremum, b is no upper bound for B and therefore belongs to D. Therefore, $d \in \{x \in A : x < b\} \subset D$. Thus, D is open. If B has no supremum, C has no infimum and is therefore open.

(iii) An order-complete set without gaps is connected. Assume that A is not connected. According to lemma 3.5.6 there exist nonempty disjoint open segments $B < C$ such that $A = B \cup C$. As A is order-complete, B has a supremum, say b_0. If $b_0 \in B$, openness of B implies the existence of an element $b' \in A$ such that $b_0 \in (\leftarrow, b') \subset B$. As $b_0 = \sup B$, the set (b_0, b') is empty, which contradicts the assumption that A is without gaps. If $b_0 \notin B$, we have $b_0 \in C$. Openness of C implies the existence of an element c' such that $b_0 \in (c', \rightarrow) \subset C$. As any element of C is an upper bound of B and b_0 is the least upper bound of B, the set (c', b_0) is empty, which also contradicts the assumption that A has no gaps.

3.5.10 Lemma: A connected subset of an ordered set is a segment.

Proof: Let B be a connected subset of A. If there exist $a, b \in B$, any c with $a < c < b$ belongs to B: Otherwise, $B = \{x \in B : x < c\} \cup \{x \in B : x > c\}$ is a representation of B as union of two disjoint nonempty relatively open sets.

In general, a segment is not necessarily connected. However:

3.5.11 Lemma: In a connected ordered set any segment is connected.

Proof: Assume that a segment I is not connected. According to Lemma 3.5.6 there exist nonémpty disjoint open segments B, C such that $I = B \cup C$. Without loss of generality we may assume that the elements of B are smaller than the elements of C. Let B_0 be the union of B and all elements below I, C_0 the union of C and all elements above I. Then, B_0 and C_0 are nonempty, disjoint open segments and $A = B_0 \cup C_0$, which contradicts the connectedness of A.

3.6 Continuous and Monotone Maps

This section deals with maps of an ordered set A into an ordered set B. The main purpose is to study the relationship between continuity and monotony of such maps.

3.6.1 Definition: A map f of a topological space $(A,\mathcal{T})$ into a topological space $(B,\mathcal{S})$ is *continuous* iff $f^{-1}(\mathcal{S}) \subset \mathcal{T}$ (i.e. iff the inverse of each open set in B is open in A).

3.6.2 Criterion: A map f is continuous iff the inverse of each member of a subbase of $\mathcal{S}$ is open.

Proof: See Kelley (1955, p. 86).

3.6.3 Lemma: If a map $f: A \to B$ is continuous, then for each convergent sequence $(a_n)_{n=1,2,\ldots}$

$$\lim_{n\to\infty} f(a_n) = f(\lim_{n\to\infty} a_n)$$

Proof: Let V be an open subset of B containing $f(\lim_{n\to\infty} a_n)$. Then, $\lim_{n\to\infty} a_n \in f^{-1}(V)$ which is open by continuity of f. Hence there exists n_0 such that $a_n \in f^{-1}(V)$ for all $n \geqq n_0$ which implies $f(a_n) \in V$ for all $n \geqq n_0$.

3.6.4 Lemma: For a topological space A which satisfies the first axiom of countability, the converse is true: If

$$\lim_{n\to\infty} f(a_n) = f(\lim_{n\to\infty} a_n)$$

for each convergent sequence $(a_n)_{n=1,2,\dots}$, then f is continuous.

Proof: Assume that f is not continuous. Then there exists an open set V in B and $a_0 \in f^{-1}(V)$ such that a_0 is not contained in an open set contained in $f^{-1}(V)$. Let $U_1, U_2, \dots$ be the sets of the countable base for the neighborhood system of a_0. Since $\bigcap_{k=1}^{n} U_k$ is open and contains a_0, there exists $a_n \in \bigcap_{k=1}^{n} U_k - f^{-1}(V)$ for $n = 1, 2, \dots$; $a_0 = \lim_{n\to\infty} a_n$, because for each open set $U \ni a_0$ there exists n_0 such that $U_{n_0} \subset U$ and thus $a_n \in U$ for all $n \geqq n_0$. On the other hand, $f(a_n) \notin V$ as $a_n \notin f^{-1}(V)$ for all n. This implies that $(f(a_n))_{n=1,2,\dots}$ does not converge to $f(a_0)$.

3.6.5 **Lemma:** If $f: A \to B$ and $g: B \to C$ are continuous, then the composition $g \circ f: A \to C$ is continuous.

Proof: See Kelley (1955, p. 85).

3.6.6 **Lemma:** If f is a continuous map of A into B, the picture $f(A_0)$ of any connected set $A_0 \subset A$ is connected.

Proof: If $f(A_0)$ were not connected, it would be the union of two nonempty disjoint open sets. As the inverses of nonempty disjoint open sets contained in $f(A_0)$ are nonempty disjoint open sets, A_0 would not be connected.

3.6.7 **Definition:** A map f of a topological space $(A, \mathscr{T})$ into a topological space $(B, \mathscr{S})$ is *open* iff $f(\mathscr{T}) \subset \mathscr{S}$ (i.e. iff the picture of each open set of A is open in B).

In the following we consider maps of ordered sets into ordered sets.

3.6.8 **Criterion:** A map into an ordered set is continuous iff the inverse of each open ray is open.

Proof: As the system of open rays is a subbase for the interval topology, the assertion follows immediately from 3.6.2.

3.6.9 **Lemma:** If f and g are two continuous maps of an ordered set A into an ordered set B, the set $K := \{a \in A : f(a) < g(a)\}$ is open.

Proof: Let $a_0 \in K$. There are two disjoint open intervals I_1 and I_2 such that $f(a_0) \in I_1$, $g(a_0) \in I_2$.

Because f and g are continuous, the inverses $f^{-1}(I_1)$ and $g^{-1}(I_2)$ and therefore the intersection $f^{-1}(I_1) \cap g^{-1}(I_2)$ are open. Furthermore $a_0 \in f^{-1}(I_1) \cap g^{-1}(I_2) \subset K$; since for any $a \in f^{-1}(I_1) \cap g^{-1}(I_2)$: $f(a) \in I_1$ and $g(a) \in I_2$, whence $f(a) < g(a)$. Thus K is open by criterion 3.1.4.

3.6.10 **Definition:** A map f of an ordered set A into an ordered set B

is *monotone increasing* (*decreasing*) iff $a'<a''$ implies $f(a')<f(a'')$, $(f(a')>f(a''))$ for all $a', a'' \in A$. A map is called *monotone* iff it is either monotone increasing or monotone decreasing.

We remark that each monotone map is $1-1$. Therefore f^{-1} is a map from $f(A)$ onto A.

3.6.11 **Lemma:** A monotone map of A *onto* B is continuous.

Proof: Without loss of generality we may assume that f is monotone increasing. Then, $f^{-1}(\leftarrow, b)=(\leftarrow, f^{-1}(b))$. Hence $f^{-1}(\leftarrow, b)$ is open. By criterion 3.6.8 this implies continuity.

3.6.12 **Corollary:** If f is a monotone map of A into B and $f(A)$ is simple, then f is continuous.

Proof: As $f(A)$ is simple, Lemma 3.4.5 implies that the relative topology in $f(A)$ is the interval topology. Therefore, f is a continuous map of A onto $f(A)$ by Lemma 3.6.11.

3.6.13 **Lemma:** (Intermediate Value Theorem): Let f be a continuous map of a connected ordered set A into an ordered set B. If to an element $b \in B$ there exist elements $a', a'' \in A$ such that $f(a')<b<f(a'')$, then there exists a between a', a'' such that $f(a)=b$.

Proof: Without loss of generality let $a' < a''$. As A is connected, $[a', a'']$ is connected and — because f is continuous — $f([a', a''])$ is connected too by 3.6.6. As $f(a')$, $f(a'') \in f([a', a''])$, also $b \in f([a', a''])$ by 3.5.10.

3.6.14 **Lemma:** (Intersection Theorem): Let f and g be two continuous maps of a connected ordered set A into an ordered set B. If there exist two elements $a', a'' \in A$ such that $f(a')<g(a')$ and $f(a'')>g(a'')$, then there exists a between a', a'' such that $f(a)=g(a)$.

Proof: If there is no element a such that $f(a) = g(a)$, then $A = \{a \in A : f(a) < g(a)\} \cup \{a \in A : f(a) > g(a)\}$ is a representation of A as union of two disjoint nonempty sets which are open by lemma 3.6.9. This contradicts the connectedness assumed for A.

3.6.15 **Lemma:** A $1-1$ continuous map from a connected ordered set into an ordered set is monotone.

Proof: Assume, for example, that for $a' < a'' < a'''$ we have $f(a') < f(a''') < f(a'')$. According to the intermediate value theorem, there exists $a \in (a', a'')$ such that $f(a) = f(a''')$, which contradicts the assumption that f is $1-1$. The other cases are dealt with similarly.

3.7 Product Spaces

3.7.1 **Definition:** Let $(A_1, \mathscr{T}_1)$, $(A_2, \mathscr{T}_2)$ be two topological spaces. We define as *product topology* $\mathscr{T}_1 \times \mathscr{T}_2$ the smallest topology containing all sets $\mathscr{T}_1 \times A_2 := \{U_1 \times A_2 : U_1 \in \mathscr{T}_1\}$ and $A_1 \times \mathscr{T}_2 := \{A_1 \times U_2 : U_2 \in \mathscr{T}_2\}$.

The family of all cartesian products $U \times V$ with $U \in \mathscr{T}_1$, $V \in \mathscr{T}_2$ is a base for this topology which therefore consists of arbitrary unions of members of this family. By the *product space* $(A_1, \mathscr{T}_1) \times (A_2, \mathscr{T}_2)$ we mean the topological space $(A_1 \times A_2, \mathscr{T}_1 \times \mathscr{T}_2)$.

3.7.2 **Lemma:** If $g: A \to B$, $h: A \to C$ are continuous, then the map $(g, h): A \to B \times C$ defined by $(g, h)(x) = (g(x), h(x))$ is continuous with respect to the product topology.

Proof: The inverses of $U \times C$ and $B \times V$ for arbitrary open sets $U \subset B$, $V \subset C$ are open for $(g, h)^{-1}(U \times C) = g^{-1}(U)$ and $(g, h)^{-1}(B \times V) = h^{-1}(V)$.

3.7.3 **Corollary:** If $g: A \to B$, $h: A \to C$, $f: B \times C \to D$ are continuous, then $f \circ (g, h): A \to D$ defined by $f \circ (g, h)(x) = f(g(x), h(x))$ is continuous.

Proof: As f and (g, h) are continuous, the composition $f \circ (g, h)$ is continuous too.

3.7.4 **Definition:** A map $f: A \times B \to C$ is *continuous in the first variable* iff for all $b \in B$ the map $f_b: A \to C$ defined by $f_b(x) = f(x, b)$ is continuous. Similarly: f is *continuous in the second variable*, iff for all $a \in A$ the map $f_a: B \to C$ defined by $f_a(y) = f(a, y)$ is continuous.

3.7.5 **Lemma:** If $f: A \times B \to C$ is continuous, then f is continuous in both variables.

Proof: The maps $g: A \to A$ with $g(x) = x$ and $h: A \to B$ with $h(x) = b$ are continuous. As f is a continuous map, the map $f(g(x), h(x)) = f(x, b)$ is continuous according to 3.7.3. The continuity of $f(a, y)$ is proved similarly.

The converse of this lemma is not true in general. Consider the real valued function f on the Euclidean plane defined by

$$f(x, y) = \frac{x \cdot y}{x^2 + y^2} \text{ for } x \neq 0, y \neq 0 \text{ and } f(0, 0) = 0.$$

This function is continuous in both variables, but f itself is not continuous. The converse of lemma 3.7.5 will be proved, however, under more restrictive conditions (3.7.11).

3.7.6 **Definition:** A map $f\colon A\times B\to C$ is *cancellable* iff the maps f_b and f_a are $1-1$ for all $a\in A$, $b\in B$.

In the following we consider maps on the product space of two ordered sets A and B into an ordered set C.

3.7.7 **Definition:** A map $f\colon A\times B\to C$ is *monotone in the first (second) variable* iff the map f_b (f_a) is monotone for each $b\in B$ ($a\in A$). The map is called *monotone*, iff it is monotone in both variables.

3.7.8 **Proposition:** If A and B are connected ordered sets and $f\colon A\times B\to C$ is cancellable and continuous in both variables, then f is monotone.

Proof: This is an immediate consequence of Lemma 3.6.15.

3.7.9 **Definition:** A map $f\colon A\times B\to C$ is *consistently monotone in the first (second) variable* iff it is monotone in this variable and if the direction of increase is independent of the value of the other variable. The map is called *consistently monotone* iff it is consistently monotone in both variables.

3.7.10 **Proposition:** If A and B are connected ordered sets, $f\colon A\times B\to C$ is monotone and continuous in both variables, then f is consistently monotone.

Proof: Assume there exist $a', a''\in A$ such that $f_{a'}$ is increasing and $f_{a''}$ is decreasing. Then for $b'<b''$ we have $f_{a'}(b')<f_{a'}(b'')$ and $f_{a''}(b')>f_{a''}(b'')$ As the functions $f_{b'}, f_{b''}$ are continuous by 3.6.14 there exists $a\in A$ such that $f_{b'}(a)=f_{b''}(a)$ or $f_a(b')=f_a(b'')$. This, however, contradicts the monotony assumed for f_a.

3.7.11 **Lemma:** If a map $f\colon A\times B\to C$ is consistently monotone in one variable and continuous in both variables, it is continuous.

Proof: Assume that f is monotone increasing in the first variable. We have to show that $f^{-1}(\leftarrow, c)$ is open for all $c\in C$. Let $(a,b)\in f^{-1}(\leftarrow, c)$. As f_b is continuous, $f_b^{-1}(\leftarrow, c)$ is open. Furthermore, $a\in f_b^{-1}(\leftarrow, c)$ or $A\subset f_b^{-1}(\leftarrow, c)$. By monotony of f_b there exists $a'>a$ such that $(\leftarrow, a')\subset f_b^{-1}(\leftarrow, c)$.

Assume first that there exists a'' such that $a<a''<a'$. As $f_{a''}$ is continuous, $f_{a''}^{-1}(\leftarrow, c)$ is open. Furthermore, $b\in f_{a''}^{-1}(\leftarrow, c)$. Therefore $(a,b)\in(\leftarrow, a'')\times f_{a''}^{-1}(\leftarrow, c)$. We have $(\leftarrow, a'')\times f_{a''}^{-1}(\leftarrow, c)\subset f^{-1}(\leftarrow, c)$, because $x\in(\leftarrow, a'')$ and $y\in f_{a''}^{-1}(\leftarrow, c)$ together imply $f(x,y)<f(a'',y)<c$.

If, on the other hand, no element a'': $a<a''<a'$ exists, then $(a,b)\in(\leftarrow, a')\times f_a^{-1}(\leftarrow, c)\subset f^{-1}(\leftarrow, c)$.

If f is monotone decreasing in the first variable or monotone in the second variable, the proof runs similarly.

3.7.12 **Definition:** A map $f: A\times B\to C$ is $\begin{cases} \textit{iso-} \\ \textit{anti-} \end{cases}$ *monotone* if it is consistently monotone and if the direction of increase is $\begin{cases} \text{the same} \\ \text{different} \end{cases}$ for both variables.

3.8 Separability and Countable Base

The purpose of this section is to discuss the concept of separability which will be needed in Section 4.2.

3.8.1 **Definition:** A subset $A_0 \subset A$ is called *dense* in the topological space $(A, \mathscr{T})$, iff each nonempty open set contains at least one element of A_0.

3.8.2 **Criterion:** A subset $A_0 \subset A$ is dense in the ordered set A if each nonempty open interval contains at least one element of A_0.

Proof: Each nonempty open set contains a nonempty open interval.

3.8.3 **Definition:** A topological space $(A, \mathscr{T})$ is *separable*, iff there exists a countable set which is dense in $(A, \mathscr{T})$.

A simple example of a separable ordered set is the set of real numbers. The following is an example (HOFMANN 1963) of an ordered set which is not separable: Let $A=\{(r_1, r_2): 0<r_i<1,\ i=1, 2\}$ with the lexicographical order. If A were separable, each of the sets

$$\{(r_1, r_2)\in A: (r, \tfrac{1}{2}) < (r_1, r_2) < (r, \tfrac{3}{4})\},\quad 0<r<1,$$

would contain an element of the countable subset. This, however, would imply that the set of real numbers between 0 and 1 is countable.

3.8.4 **Lemma:** If a set is separable with respect to the interval topology, $(B, \mathscr{I}_B)$ is separable for any subset B.

Proof: Let A be an ordered set, A_0 a countable subset dense in A and $B \subset A$ an arbitrary subset. We define

$B_1:=\{\inf\{b\in B: b\geqq a\}$, if it exists and belongs to $B: a\in A_0\}$,
$B_2:=\{\sup\{b\in B: b\leqq a\}$, if it exists and belongs to $B: a\in A_0\}$,
$B_3:=\{$an arbitrary element of $(a_1, a_2)\cap B$, if this set is not empty: $a_1, a_2\in A_0\}$.

$B_0:=B_1\cup B_2\cup B_3$ is a countable subset of B. We will show that B_0 is dense in B:

(i) For all $b \in B$ and $a \in A_0$: $(b, a] \cap B \neq \emptyset$ implies $(b, a] \cap B_0 \neq \emptyset$, and $[a, b) \cap B \neq \emptyset$ implies $[a, b) \cap B_0 \neq \emptyset$:

If $B' := (b, a] \cap B$ is not empty and finite, then $\sup\{b \in B: b \leqq a\}$ exists and belongs to B_2; for B' infinite, there exists an element $b' \in B$ such that $b < b' < a$ and $(b, b') \neq \emptyset$ and $(b', a) \neq \emptyset$; hence there exist $a_1, a_2 \in A_0$ with $b < a_1 < b' < a_2 < a$ and therefore $b_0 \in B_3$ with $a_1 < b_0 < a_2$ which implies $b < b_0 < a$. The second part of (i) follows from the first one by considering the inverse order relation.

(ii) For all $b_1, b_2 \in B$: $(b_1, b_2) \cap B \neq \emptyset$ implies $(b_1, b_2) \cap B_0 \neq \emptyset$: $(b_1, b_2) \cap B \neq \emptyset$ implies that there exists an element $a \in A_0$ such that $b_1 < a < b_2$ and at least one of the sets $B' := (b_1, a] \cap B$, $B'' := [a, b_2) \cap B$ is not empty. Thus it follows by (i) that $(B' \cup B'') \cap B_0 \neq \emptyset$.

(iii) For all $b \in B$: $(b, \rightarrow) \cap B \neq \emptyset$ implies $(b, \rightarrow) \cap B_0 \neq \emptyset$, and $(\leftarrow, b) \cap B \neq \emptyset$ implies $(\leftarrow, b) \cap B_0 \neq \emptyset$: Let $(b, \rightarrow) \cap B$ be not empty. If there is $a \in A_0$ with $(b, a] \cap B \neq \emptyset$, then $(b, \rightarrow) \cap B_0 \neq \emptyset$ by (i). If $(b, a] \cap B = \emptyset$ for all $a \in A_0$, $(b, \rightarrow) \cap B$ consists of exactly one element b'. We have $[b', \rightarrow) \cap A_0 = \emptyset$. Separability implies that $(b, \rightarrow) \cap A_0 \neq \emptyset$. Hence there exists $a \in (b, b') \cap A_0$, whence $b' = \inf\{b \in B: b \geqq a\} \in B_1$. The second part of (iii) follows by considering the inverse order relation.

(ii) and (iii) together imply that B_0 is dense in B.

3.8.5 **Lemma:** The interval topology of a separable ordered set satisfies the first axiom of countability.

Proof: Let A be an ordered set, A_0 a countable subset dense in A and $a \in A$ an arbitrary element. Then the intersections of pairs of sets of the following system of sets constitute a countable neighborhood base of a:

(i) if a belongs to no gap:
$\{(a_1, \rightarrow), (\leftarrow, a_2): a_1, a_2 \in A_0, a_1 < a < a_2\}$,

(ii) if $[a, a'']$ is the only gap which contains a:
$\{(a_1, \rightarrow), (\leftarrow, a''): a_1 \in A_0, a_1 < a\}$,

(iii) if $[a', a]$ is the only gap which contains a:
$\{(a', \rightarrow), (\leftarrow, a_2): a_2 \in A_0, a < a_2\}$,

(iv) if $[a', a]$ and $[a, a'']$ are gaps:
$\{(a', \rightarrow), (\leftarrow, a'')\}$.

3.8.6 **Theorem:** Let A, B be ordered sets, B being separable. Then for a monotone map f of A into B, the following properties are equivalent:

(i) f is continuous,

(ii) for all sequences $(a_n)_{n=1,2,\ldots} \subset A$ and all $a \in A$:
$a = \lim_{n\to\infty} a_n$ iff $f(a) = \lim_{n\to\infty} f(a_n)$.

Proof: Since B is separable, the subset $f(A)$ of B is separable (3.8.4). As f is monotone, this implies separability of A. Hence $\mathscr{I}_A$ satisfies the first axiom of countability (3.8.5) (ii) implies (i) by 3.6.4. (i) implies (ii) by 3.6.3 and 3.6.11.

3.8.7 **Lemma:** The following three properties of an interval topology are equivalent:

(i) the interval topology has a countable base,

(ii) the set is separable in its interval topology and has not more than a countable number of gaps,

(iii) there exists a countable subset which has a nonempty intersection with each closed interval $[a, b]$ with $a < b$.

Proof: (i) implies (ii): Assume that there exists a countable base $\mathscr{I}_0 \subset \mathscr{I}$. To show that the set A is separable, we choose from each nonempty member of $\mathscr{I}_0$ an element a, thereby obtaining a countable set A_0 which is dense in A. To show that A has not more than a countable number of gaps, let G be the set of elements of all gaps. Let $g_0 \in G$. Without loss of generality we may assume that there exists $g_1 \in G$ such that (g_0, g_1) is empty. Because $g_0 \in (\leftarrow, g_1)$ which is an open set, there exists $U \in \mathscr{I}_0$ such that $g_0 \in U \subset (\leftarrow, g_1)$. Hence g_0 is supremum of U. This establishes that G is countable.

(ii) implies (iii): Let $A_0 \subset A$ be countable and dense in A. As A has not more than a countable number of gaps, the set $A_1 := A_0 \cup G$ is countable. The intersection of A_1 with each closed interval is not empty. For, if (a, b) is not empty there exists $x \in (a, b)$ with $x \in A_0$. If (a, b) is empty, then $[a, b]$ is a gap and $a, b \in G$.

(iii) implies (i): Assume that there exists a countable subset A_0 of A, which has a nonempty intersection with each closed interval. A contains not more than a countable number of gaps, for each gap contains an element of A_0. Let G be the set of elements of gaps. Then the set of open intervals $\mathscr{I}_0 = \{(c_1, c_2), (c_1, \rightarrow), (\leftarrow, c_2) : c_1, c_2 \in A_0 \cup G\}$ is countable. That $\mathscr{I}_0$ is a base for the interval topology can be seen as follows: Let (a, b) be a nonempty open interval containing the element x. (The cases $(a, \rightarrow)$ and $(\leftarrow, b)$ are dealt with similarly.) We distinguish the following three cases:

1.) x belongs to no gap: Then there exist $a', a'', b', b'' \in A$ such that $a < a' < a'' < x < b'' < b' < b$. Furthermore, there exist $u \in [a', a''] \cap A_0$, $v \in [b'', b'] \cap A_0$. Then $(u, v) \in \mathscr{I}_0$ and $x \in (u, v) \subset (a, b)$.

2.) x belongs to exactly one gap: Then without loss of generality we may assume that there exist $a', a'' \in A$ such that $a < a' < a'' < x$ and $v > x$ such that (x, v) is empty and $u \in [a', a''] \cap A_0$. Then $(u, v) \in \mathscr{I}_0$ and $x \in (u, v) \subset (a, b)$.

3.) x belongs to two gaps: Then there are $u, v \in G$ such that $[u, x]$ and $[x, v]$ are gaps. Therefore $(u, v) \in \mathscr{I}_0$ and $x \in (u, v) \subset (a, b)$.

3.8.8 **Corollary:** A connected ordered set has a countable base iff it is separable.

The following example (HOFMANN (1963)) shows that in general an ordered set might be separable without having a countable base:

3.8.9 **Example:** Let $E=[0, 1]$, let E_0 (E_1) be the subset of rational (irrational) numbers in E. Let $A=(E\times\{0\})\cup(E_1\times\{1\})$ with the lexicographical order. The countable set $B=E_0\times\{0\}$ is dense in A: Let $(r_1, \delta_1)<(r_2, \delta_2)$. If $r_1<r_2$, there exists $r_0\in E_0$ such that $r_1<r_0<r_2$. Then, $(r_1, \delta_1)<(r_0, 0)<(r_2, \delta_2)$. If $r_1=r_2$, we have $\delta_1=0$, $\delta_2=1$ and $\{(r, \delta):(r_1, 0)<(r, \delta)<(r_1, 1)\}$ is empty. Thus, A is separable. It has no countable base, however, because there exists an uncountable number of gaps, namely $[(r, 0), (r, 1)]$ with $r\in E_1$.

4. Nominal and Ordinal Scales

4.1 Nominal Scales

In section 1.8.1 a *nominal scale* was defined as a $1-1$ map of $\langle \tilde{\tilde{\mathbf{A}}}; =\rangle$ into $\langle \mathbb{R}; =\rangle$ where $\langle \tilde{\tilde{\mathbf{A}}};=\rangle$ is the irreducible r. s. corresponding to a r. s. $\langle \mathbf{A}; \approx\rangle$ with an equivalence relation $\approx$. Thus a nominale scale is a $1-1$ correspondence between equivalence classes (classes of empirical objects showing the same manifestation of the property in question) and real numbers.

The term nominal scale indicates the fact that scale values of such a scale are just names for the equivalence classes. They do not tell anything more: any other relationship between the scale values except equality is irrelevant, as no corresponding empirical relationship exists.

Nominal scales are unique up to $1-1$ transformations. Any transformation changing the names in such a way that objects with different names get different names and objects with identical names get identical names leads to a nominal scale again. It serves the same purpose as the original scale: to distinguish between equivalence classes.

The question of the existence of such a scale is trivial, if the number of equivalence classes is finite or countable. Then, a subset of the set of natural numbers can be used to name the indifference classes. Other cases are of purely theoretical interest only. A nominal scale exists, using $\langle \mathbb{R}; =\rangle$ as numerical relational system, iff the cardinal number of the set $\tilde{\tilde{A}}$ is at most the cardinal number of $\mathbb{R}$.

4.2 Ordinal Scales

By an *ordinal scale* we mean a monotone increasing and continuous map of an empirical order system $\langle A; =, <\rangle$ into the numerical system $\langle \mathbb{R}; =, <\rangle$. This section will give conditions which guarantee the existence of an ordinal scale.

4.2.1 Lemma: If an order system is countable, an ordinal scale exists.

Proof: Let $A = \{a_1, a_2, \ldots\}$. We construct a map $f: A \to \mathbb{R}$ as follows: We choose an arbitrary real number r_1 and put $f(a_1) = r_1$. If $f(a_1), \ldots, f(a_n)$ are already defined, we define $f(a_{n+1})$ in the following way: Let $(i_1, \ldots, i_n)$ be a permutation of $(1, \ldots, n)$ such that $a_{i_1} < a_{i_2} < \ldots < a_{i_n}$. If $a_{i_k} < a_{n+1} < a_{i_k+1}$ for some $i_k \in \{i_1, \ldots i_n\}$ [resp. $a_{n+1} < a_{i_1}$ resp. $a_{n+1} > a_{i_n}$] we choose an arbitrary real number r_{n+1} with $f(a_{i_k}) < r_{n+1} < f(a_{i_k+1})$ [resp. $r_{n+1} < f(a_{i_1})$ resp. $r_{n+1} > f(a_{i_n})$] and put $f(a_{n+1}) = r_{n+1}$.

Obviously the map thus constructed is monotone. It can be made continuous by the following adjustment: We choose an arbitrary element $r_0 \in f(A)$. To each cut $\{r \in f(A): r \geqq r_0\} = \mathbb{R}' \cup \mathbb{R}''$ which does not correspond to a gap, we subtract from all elements of $\mathbb{R}''$ the amount $\inf \mathbb{R}'' - \sup \mathbb{R}'$. To each cut $\{r \in f(A): r \leqq r_0\} = \mathbb{R}' \cup \mathbb{R}''$ which does not correspond to a gap, we add to each element of $\mathbb{R}'$ the amount $\inf \mathbb{R}'' - \sup \mathbb{R}'$. This procedure is justified as there exists an at most countable number of cuts with $\sup \mathbb{R}' < \inf \mathbb{R}''$. By this adjustment $f(A)$ becomes simple. According to Corollary 3.6.12 the adjusted map is continuous.

4.2.2 Remark: The map thus obtained has the property that for each cut $f(A) = \mathbb{R}' \cup \mathbb{R}''$ which does not correspond to a gap, we have $\sup \mathbb{R}' = \inf \mathbb{R}''$.

4.2.3 Theorem: An order system can be represented by an ordinal scale iff it has a countable base.

Proof: Proofs of this theorem were given by Debreu (1954) and Hofmann (1963). The following proof is an adjustment of Debreu's. The first proof for the case of a connected order system is due to Cantor (1895).

Let C be a countable subset dense in A containing all gap elements (see Lemma 3.8.7) and the elements $\inf A$ and $\sup A$ if they exist. By Lemma 4.2.1, a monotone and continuous map f from C into $\mathbb{R}$ exists. This map can be extended to A as follows: assume that $a \notin C$. Then $C = C_1 \cup C_2$ with $C_1 := \{c \in C: c < a\}$, $C_2 := \{c \in C: c > a\}$ is a cut. As C is dense in A, we have $\sup C_1 = \inf C_2 = a$: Assume that C_1 has a maximal element c_1. Because $a \notin C$, a is no gap element. Therefore, $c_1 < a$ implies the existence of an element $c \in C$ such that $c_1 < c < a$. This, however, contradicts the assumption that c_1 is the maximal element of C_1. Similarly there exists no upper bound a' of C_1 with $a' \in A$ and $a' < a$. Because of monotony $f(C) = f(C_1) \cup f(C_2)$ is a cut too. As f is monotone increacing on C, $f(C_1)$ has no maximal and $f(C_2)$ no minimal element. According to remark 4.2.2, in this case $\sup f(C_1) = \inf f(C_2)$. We define: $f(a) = \sup f(C_1) = \inf f(C_2)$. Obviously the extended map is monotone. It is continuous because $f(A)$ is simple.

On the other hand, if an order system can be represented by an ordinal scale, $f(A)$ has a countable base as a subset of the set of real numbers. As f is a continuous and open map of A onto $f(A)$, A itself has a countable base.

4.2.4 Corollary: A connected order system can be represented by an ordinal scale iff it is separable.

Proof: The assertion follows immediately from 4.2.3 and 3.8.8.

As the continuous image of a connected set is connected, the image is an interval in this case.

4.3 Ordinal Scales in Practice

MOH's scale for the hardness of minerals and BEAUFORT's scale for the strength of winds are usually cited as examples of typical ordinal scales. Though they are good illustrations for the ordinal assignment of numbers, they are not ordinal scales in the strict sense used here, because they are not $1-1$: a great number of different degrees of hardness, for example, are grouped together under one number.

As a typical example for an ordinal scale we will consider the blood sedimentation rate taken as an indicator for the intensity of pathological processes. In order to determine the blood sedimentation rate, a tube is filled with blood, then sodium citrate is added; the extent of sedimentation is measured on a mm-scale after an interval of one hour. Thus we obtain scale values in mm, which might give the illusion of an interval scale. In fact, these values are at best an ordinal scale for the intensity of the pathological process in question, an increase in which leads to an increase in the globulin content, which, in turn, increases the blood sedimentation rate and the height of the sediment within a given period of time. Hence, the height of the sediment is monotonely related to the intensity of the pathological process involved. The greater the intensity of this process, the greater is the height of the sediment. It is, however, not possible to conclude that a therapeutic agent A which decreases the sediment from 75 to 60 is more effective than an agent B decreasing the sediment from 65 to 55: The measurement procedure gives no justification for such a conclusion. That the blood sedimentation rate cannot be more than an ordinal scale is also illustrated by the fact that changes in the procedure of its determination (such as changes in the amount of sodium citrate or the time interval after which the height of sediment is determined) will not at all lead to a linear transformation of the scale (the transformation will at best be monotone).

Other illustrative examples for the concept of an ordinal scale can be obtained by considering the interaction between stimulus and response in the case of pitch. Experience shows that pitch is a monotone function of frequency. Though frequency is measured in an interval scale (cycles per unit of time) the frequency scale considered as a scale for pitch is only an ordinal scale: Any other scale, derived from frequencies by a monotone increasing transformation gives the same information about pitch: the order. To obtain an interval scale for pitch requires the consideration of additional relations between the manifestations of this property, such as obtained by the operation of bisection.

As another example, let us consider an intelligence test where the time needed for the solution of a task is measured. Though physical time is measured by an interval scale, time used as a measure of intelligence is an ordinal scale. To get more than an ordinal scale requires the discovery of a richer structure of the property intelligence.

These examples are typical for a widespread phenomenon: That properties measured in an interval scale are taken as indicants for other monotone related properties. Used as scales for the related property, the original interval scales become ordinal scales only. Ignorance of this fact occasionally leads to mistakes.

4.4 Continuity of Ordinal Scales

At first sight it might seem reasonable to use the term "ordinal scale" for a homomorphic (i e. monotone and therefore 1—1) map of an order system $\mathbf{A}=\langle A; =, <\rangle$ into $\langle\mathbb{R}; =, <\rangle$, because the order of A is then reflected by the order of $\mathbb{R}$. But this is achieved in an incomplete manner only: The order relation $<$ on A induces the interval topology $\mathscr{I}_A$ on A (see 3.3.4). Any scale m mapping A monotone onto $B := m(A) \subset \mathbb{R}$ is a continuous map onto the topological space $(B, \mathscr{I}_B)$, $\mathscr{I}_B$ being the interval topology defined by the order relation on B. This topology is coarser than the relative topology $B \cap \mathscr{I}_{\mathbb{R}}$ induced by the topology of the real numbers and not identical with it in general (see 3.4.5). Thus for a monotone map m the order of real numbers will reflect the order in A, but the topology on $m(A)$ induced by the topology of $\mathbb{R}$ will not describe the interval topology of A, except if m is continuous:

4.4.1 **Theorem:** A monotone increasing map m of A into $\mathbb{R}$ is a continuous and open map of $(A, \mathscr{I}_A)$ onto $(m(A), m(A) \cap \mathscr{I}_{\mathbb{R}})$ iff m is a continuous map of $(A, \mathscr{I}_A)$ into $(\mathbb{R}, \mathscr{I}_{\mathbb{R}})$.

Proof: As stated above, the topology $\mathscr{I}_{m(A)}$ is coarser than the relative topology $m(A) \cap \mathscr{I}_{\mathbb{R}}$ or, equivalently, $m^{-1}(\mathscr{I}_{\mathbb{R}}) \supset \mathscr{I}_A$ for each monotone map m. Continuity of m is equivalent to $m^{-1}(\mathscr{I}_{\mathbb{R}}) \subset \mathscr{I}_A$. Therefore $m^{-1}(\mathscr{I}_{\mathbb{R}}) = \mathscr{I}_A$ iff the monotone map m is continuous.

4.4.2 **Remark:** There are order systems which can be mapped into the real numbers by a monotone increasing map, but not by a monotone increasing and *continuous* map: In 3.8.9 an example of an ordered set A is given such that

i) A is separable and
ii) the interval topology of A has no countable base.

From i) it follows that there is a monotone map of A into $\mathbb{R}$ (the proof will not be given here), from ii) that $\langle A; < \rangle$ cannot be represented by an ordinal scale (see 4.2.3).

Beside a discussion of the "technical" character of continuity in 6.6 we remark:

1) From a finitistic point of view the claim of continuity is no restriction; each monotone map of a finite totally ordered r.s. into the real numbers is continuous.
2) Each at most countable totally ordered r.s. can be represented by an ordinal scale (see 4.2.1).
3) If an (infinite) totally ordered r.s. $\mathbf{A}$ can be mapped monotone increasing into $\mathbb{R}$ by the map m, m is an imbedding of $\mathbf{A}$ into an ordinal r.s., namely $\langle \mathbb{R}; < \rangle$, which can be represented by an ordinal scale; in other words, there always exists a suitable extension of $\mathbf{A}$ which can be represented by an ordinal scale.

The concept of an ordinal scale as a $1-1$ homomorphism and homomorphism of $\langle A; < \rangle$ into $\langle \mathbb{R}; < \rangle$ diverges from the general concept of a scale as defined in 1.6. It can, however, be subsumed under the general concept of a scale if we consider the formally enriched r.s. $\langle A; <, L \rangle$ instead of $\langle A; < \rangle$, where L is the limit-relation induced by the interval topology $\mathscr{I}_A$ on A. The *limit-relation* is uniquely determined by the interval topology and thus by the order relation. It may be formalized as follows:

4.4.3 **Definition:** Given any sequence $(a_n)_{n=0,1,2,\ldots}$ of elements of A, $L(a_0, a_1, a_2, \ldots)$ holds iff $a_0 = \lim_{n \to \infty} a_n$ (see 3.4.9 for the definition of lim).

Since all relevant e.r.s. involve finitary relations only – with the exception of the limit-relation – sections 1.3–1.5 are restricted to finitary r.s. We therefore remark that all definitions and propositions of 1.3 – 1.5 can be extended to r.s. with infinitary relations except propositions concerning the congruence relation (1.4.5 – 1.4.8, 1.5.9 ii). They break down since the remark 1.4.3 does not hold for infinitary relations; this exception is irrelevant, however, because $\langle A; < \rangle$ is irreducible. The term "1 – 1-homomorphism" of $\langle A; <, L \rangle$ into $\langle \mathbb{R}; <, L \rangle$, however, is meaningful. Thus we can characterize ordinal scales by the following version of 3.8.6.

4.4.4 **Theorem:** The map m of $\langle A; < \rangle$ into $\langle \mathbb{R}; < \rangle$ is an ordinal scale iff it is a scale of $\langle A; <, L \rangle$ into $\langle \mathbb{R}; <, L \rangle$.

Given any ordinal scale m_0, the transformation γ is admissible iff it maps $m_0(A)$ monotone increasing and continuous into $\mathbb{R}$. As shown in example 3 to 1.5.11, admissible transformations may not be induced by strictly monotone increasing and continuous maps of $\mathbb{R}$ onto $\mathbb{R}$, nor by 1 – 1-maps of $\mathbb{R}$ onto $\mathbb{R}$.

5. Operations

5.1 Monotony, Continuity and Separability

Let $\langle A; \approx, \prec \rangle$ be an order system and "$\circ$" a binary operation assigning to each pair $a, b \in A$ an element $a \circ b \in A$, such that "$\approx$" is also a congruence relation for the relation $R_\circ$ corresponding to the operation "$\circ$" (see 1.3), i.e. such that $a' \approx a''$ and $b' \approx b''$ together imply $a' \circ b' \approx a'' \circ b''$. As "$\approx$" is the coarsest congruence relation for $\mathbf{A} := \langle A; \approx, \prec, R_\circ \rangle$ (see 1.4.5) we may introduce the irreducible relational system $\mathbf{A}/\approx$ (see 1.4.6). As $(\tilde{a}, \tilde{\tilde{b}}, \tilde{\tilde{c}}) \in \tilde{\tilde{R}}_\circ$ iff $\tilde{\tilde{c}} = \widetilde{\widetilde{a \circ b}}$, to $\tilde{\tilde{R}}_\circ$ there corresponds an operation.

In the following we will restrict ourselves to irreducible systems of this kind which will be denoted by $\langle A; =, <, \circ \rangle$.

Thus an operation on A is a function of $A \times A$ into A. We remind the reader of the definitions of cancellability (3.7.6) and monotony (3.7.7, 3.7.9, 3.7.12). Especially we direct attention to the difference between continuity (with respect to the product topology) and continuity in both variables (3.7.4). Here and in the following the topology of A is always the order topology.

5.1.1 **Proposition:** Let $G(x)$, $H(x)$ be expressions formed by applying the operation "$\circ$" a finite number of times to fixed elements of A and to a variable element $x \in A$. If A is connected and "$\circ$" continuous, the following is true:

If there exist a', a'' such that $G(a') < H(a')$ and $G(a'') > H(a'')$, then there exists an element a between a' and a'' such that $G(a) = H(a)$.

Proof: $G(x)$, $H(x)$ are continuous functions of x according to 3.7.5 and 3.6.5. Hence the statement follows from the intersection theorem 3.6.14.

5.1.2 **Definition:** The operation "$\circ$" is *intern*, iff for all $a, b \in A$ the element $a \circ b$ lies between a and b, the values a and b themselves being excluded if $a \neq b$.

Starting from an operation "o" we define operations ${}_{n}\circ$ and $\circ_{n}$ by complete construction:

5.1.3 i) $a\ {}_{0}\circ\ b = b$

$a\ {}_{(n+1)}\circ\ b = a \circ (a\ {}_{n}\circ\ b),$

ii) $a\ \circ_{0}\ b = a$

$a\ \circ_{(n+1)}\ b = (a\ \circ_{n}\ b) \circ b.$

5.1.4 **Definition:** An intern operation is *archimedean* in the $\begin{cases}\text{first}\\ \text{second}\end{cases}$ variable, iff for all

$$a, b \in A \begin{cases} \lim\limits_{n\to\infty} a\ \circ_{n}\ b = b \\ \lim\limits_{n\to\infty} a\ {}_{n}\circ\ b = a\,. \end{cases}$$

5.1.5 **Lemma:** If an intern operation defined on an order-complete set is continuous in a variable, it is archimedean in this variable.

For a conversion of this Lemma under more restrictive conditions see section 5.2.

Proof: We will prove the theorem for continuity in the second variable. Without loss of generality we may assume $a < b$. As the operation is intern, this implies $a < a\ {}_{(n+1)}\circ\ b < a\ {}_{n}\circ\ b$. As A is order-complete and the sequence $(a\ {}_{n}\circ\ b)_{n=1,2,\ldots}$ monotone and bounded, $\lim\limits_{n\to\infty} a\ {}_{n}\circ\ b$ exists according to 3.5.4. From continuity we have

$$a \circ \lim_{n\to\infty} a\ {}_{n}\circ\ b = \lim_{n\to\infty} a \circ (a\ {}_{n}\circ\ b) = \lim_{n\to\infty} a\ {}_{(n+1)}\circ\ b = \lim_{n\to\infty} a\ {}_{n}\circ\ b.$$

As the operation is intern, this implies the archimedean property.

5.1.6 **Lemma:** If the domain of definition of a monotone increasing, continuous and intern operation is order-complete, then it is separable.

Proof: Let A be the domain of definition. Starting from two arbitrary elements $a, b \in A$ we define A_0 to be the smallest subset of A containing a and b such that

(i) $x, y \in A_0$ implies $x \circ y \in A_0$,

(ii) $a \circ z \in A_0$ implies $z \in A_0$,

$z \circ b \in A_0$ implies $z \in A_0$.

We remark that by (i) $x, y \in A_0$ implies $x\ {}_{n}\circ\ y \in A_0$ and $x\ \circ_{n}\ y \in A_0$ for any $n = 1, 2, \ldots$. From (ii) we obtain that for any $n = 1, 2, \ldots$: $a\ {}_{n}\circ\ z \in A_0$ implies $z \in A_0$, $z\ \circ_{n}\ b \in A_0$ implies $z \in A_0$.

1.) A_0 is countable: The set of elements obtained from a and b by applying (i) and (ii) a finite number of times is countable. It is furthermore contained in A_0 and closed under (i) and (ii) and therefore identical with A_0.

2.) A_0 is dense in A: Let x, y be two elements of A. We will show that an element $z \in A_0$ exists such that $x < z < y$. First, we assume $a \leqq x < b$. Then there exists m such that $x < x_{m\circ} b < y$. Now we construct a sequence $(z_n)_{n=1,2,\ldots}$ of elements of A_0 such that $x < z_n \leqq x_{n\circ} b$: Put $z_0 = b$. If z_n is constructed, we define $z_{n+1} = z_n$ if $z_n \leqq x_{(n+1)\circ} b$. If $x < x_{(n+1)\circ} b < z_n$, we consider the sequence $(a_{\circ k} z_n)_{k=1,2,\ldots}$. As $\lim_{k\to\infty} a_{\circ k} z_n = z_n$ according to 5.1.5, there exists k_0, such that $a_{\circ k_0} z_n \leqq x < a_{\circ(k_0+1)} z_n$. We define $z_{n+1} = a_{\circ(k_0+1)} z_n$. As $a, z_n \in A_0$, we have $z_{n+1} \in A_0$. Furthermore, we have $z_{n+1} \leqq x_{(n+1)\circ} b$: From $z_n \leqq x_{n\circ} b$ and $a_{\circ k_0} z_n \leqq x$ we obtain: $z_{n+1} = a_{\circ(k_0+1)} z_n = (a_{\circ k_0} z_n) \circ z_n \leqq x \circ (x_{n\circ} b) = x_{(n+1)\circ} b$.

To study the case $x \notin [a, b)$ we assume without loss of generality that $x \geqq b$. Then, there exists m such that $a < a_{m\circ} x < b$. From the result obtained above there exists $z \in A_0$ such that $a_{m\circ} x < z < a_{m\circ} y$. As "o" is intern, A has no gaps. Furthermore A is order-complete by assumption. This implies that A is connected (see 3.5.9). According to 5.1.1 the element z' defined by $a_{m\circ} z' = z$ exists. Furthermore z' belongs to A_0 and is between x and y.

5.2 Algebraic Properties of Binary Operations

We will consider the following algebraic properties:

2.5.1 **Reflexivity:**

(i) An element $a_0 \in A$ is *reflexive*, iff $a_0 \circ a_0 = a_0$.

(ii) The operation "o" is *reflexive* iff all elements of A are reflexive.

5.2.2 **Commutativity:** For all $a, b \in A$: $a \circ b = b \circ a$.

5.2.3 **Associativity:** For all $a, b, c \in A$: $(a \circ b) \circ c = a \circ (b \circ c)$.

5.2.4 **Bisymmetry:** For all $a, b, c, d \in A$:
$(a \circ b) \circ (c \circ d) = (a \circ c) \circ (b \circ d)$.

5.2.5 **Autodistributivity:** For all $a, b, c \in A$:
$(a \circ a) \circ (b \circ c) = (a \circ b) \circ (a \circ c)$
$(a \circ b) \circ (c \circ c) = (a \circ c) \circ (b \circ c)$.

We remark that commutativity and associativity together imply bisymmetry. Autodistributivity is obviously a special case of bisymmetry. The relation between bisymmetry and autodistributivity is further considered in section 5.4.

For cancellable operations reflexivity and autodistributivity can be combined into a single axiom:

5.2.6 $(a \circ b) \circ c = (a \circ c) \circ (b \circ c)$
$a \circ (b \circ c) = (a \circ b) \circ (a \circ c)$.

For $a = b$ we obtain reflexivity by cancellation. For reflexive operations, however, 5.2.6 and autodistributivity are equivalent.

For cancellable operations reflexivity, autodistributivity and commutativity can be combined into a single axiom:

5.2.7 $a \circ (b \circ c) = (a \circ b) \circ (c \circ a)$.

For $a = b = c$ we obtain reflexivity by cancellation. For $a = b$ we obtain commutativity from reflexivity and cancellation. For reflexive and commutative operations 5.2.7 is equivalent to autodistributivity.

5.2.8 **Proposition:** If a reflexive operation is isomonotone, it is increasing and therefore intern.

Proof: If the operations were decreasing in both variables, $a < b$ would imply $a = a \circ a > a \circ b > b \circ b = b$, which is a contradiction. Hence, the operation is increasing in both variables and we have $a = a \circ a < a \circ b < b \circ b = b$.

5.2.9 **Proposition:** If a consistently monotone operation is reflexive and commutative, it is increasing and intern.

Proof: Commutativity implies that the operation is isomonotone. Hence the proposition follows from 5.2.8.

For a relationship between associativity and monotony for continuous and cancellable operations see 5.5.2.

5.2.10 **Theorem*):** If a reflexive, autodistributive and monotone increasing operation is archimedean in a variable, it is continuous in this variable.

Proof: First we show

$$(a \circ b)\ {}_{n\circ}\ (a \circ c) = a \circ (b\ {}_{n\circ}\ c)$$

by mathematical induction.

For $n = 1$ the relation follows immediately from autodistributivity and reflexivity.

$$\begin{aligned}(a \circ b)\ {}_{(n+1)\circ}\ (a \circ c) &= (a \circ b) \circ \big((a \circ b)\ {}_{n\circ}\ (a \circ c)\big)\\ &= (a \circ b) \circ \big(a \circ (b\ {}_{n\circ}\ c)\big) = a \circ \big(b \circ (b\ {}_{n\circ}\ c)\big)\\ &= a \circ \big(b_{(n+1)\circ}\ c\big).\end{aligned}$$

We will proof the theorem for continuity in the second variable. As "$\circ$" is monotone, according to corollary 3.6.12 we have to show that $K :=$

---

*) See Fuchs (1950).

$\{a \circ x : x \in A\}$ is simple. Let $K = K_1 \cup K_2$ be a cut. If sup K_1 exists and belongs to K_1, then $\sup K_1 = \inf K_2$. For let be $\sup K_1 = a \circ x_1$. As K_2 is not empty, there exists $x_2 > x_1$. $a \circ x_1$ is the limit point of the sequence $(a \circ x_1) {}_{no} (a \circ x_2)$ with $x_2 > x_1$. The sequence $(a \circ x_1) {}_{no} (a \circ x_2)$, however, belongs to K_2 because $(a \circ x_1) {}_{no} (a \circ x_2) = a \circ (x_1 {}_{no}\, x_2)$. If, on the other hand, inf K_2 exists and belongs to K_2, the proof is dealt with similarly.

5.2.11 **Definition:** An operation is called *metrical* iff it is bisymmetric, continuous in both variables and cancellable.

5.2.12 **Proposition:** A metrical operation defined on a connected set A is consistently monotone and continuous.

Proof: The assertion follows from 3.7.8, 3.7.10 and 3.7.11.

5.2.13 **Definition:** A *middling* operation is a reflexive and commutative metrical operation. Middling operations will be denoted by "|".

5.2.14 **Theorem:** If A is connected, from any metrical operation "∘" a middling operation "ϕ"*) can be derived by the following implicit definition:

$$(u' \circ (a \phi b)) \circ ((a \phi b) \circ u'') = (u' \circ a) \circ (b \circ u'').$$

5.2.15 **Remark:** In the case of a commutative operation this definition reduces to

$$(a \phi b) \circ (a \phi b) = a \circ b.$$

In the case "∘" is a middling operation, the derived middling operation "ϕ" is identical with the original one.

Proof of the Theorem:

a) The operation "ϕ" as defined by 5.2.14 is uniquely determined and independent of u', u'':

1) To prove the existence of $a \phi b$, we assume $a < b$. If "∘" is isomonotone, we have

$$(u' \circ a) \circ (a \circ u'') < (u' \circ a) \circ (b \circ u'') < (u' \circ b) \circ (b \circ u'').$$

If "∘" is antimonotone, we have:

$$(u' \circ a) \circ (a \circ u'') > (u' \circ a) \circ (b \circ u'') > (u' \circ b) \circ (b \circ u'').$$

As A is connected, proposition 5.1.1 implies that in each of the two cases there exists an element $a \phi b$ satisfying 5.2.14.

2) Given u', u'', a and b, the element $a \phi b$ is uniquely determined by monotony of the operation "∘". In order to show that $a \phi b$ is independent of u', u'', we consider the following sequence of equations:

---

*) We use the symbol "ϕ" instead of "|" in this case in order to indicate the metrical operation "∘" from which the middling operation is derived.

$$
\begin{aligned}
&\{[(v' \circ v') \circ (v' \circ v')] \circ [(v' \circ v') \circ (v' \circ v')]\} \\
&\qquad \circ \{[(u' \circ x) \circ (y \circ u'')] \circ [(v'' \circ v'') \circ (v'' \circ v'')]\} \\
&= \{[(v' \circ v') \circ (v' \circ v')] \circ [(v' \circ v') \circ (v' \circ v')]\} \\
&\qquad \circ \{[(u' \circ x) \circ (v'' \circ v'')] \circ [(y \circ u'') \circ (v'' \circ v'')]\} \\
&= \{[(v' \circ v') \circ (v' \circ v')] \circ [(u' \circ x) \circ (v'' \circ v'')]\} \\
&\qquad \circ \{[(v' \circ v') \circ (v' \circ v')] \circ [(y \circ v'') \circ (u'' \circ v'')]\} \\
&= \{[(v' \circ v') \circ (u' \circ x)] \circ [(v' \circ v') \circ (v'' \circ v'')]\} \\
&\qquad \circ \{[(v' \circ v') \circ (v' \circ v')] \circ [(y \circ v'') \circ (u'' \circ v'')]\} \\
&= \{[(v' \circ u') \circ (v' \circ x)] \circ [(v' \circ v') \circ (v'' \circ v'')]\} \\
&\qquad \circ \{[(v' \circ v') \circ (v' \circ v')] \circ [(y \circ v'') \circ (u'' \circ v'')]\} \\
&= \{[(v' \circ u') \circ (v' \circ v')] \circ [(v' \circ x) \circ (v'' \circ v'')]\} \\
&\qquad \circ \{[(v' \circ v') \circ (v' \circ v')] \circ [(y \circ v'') \circ (u'' \circ v'')]\} \\
&= \{[(v' \circ u') \circ (v' \circ v')] \circ [(v' \circ v') \circ (v' \circ v')]\} \\
&\qquad \circ \{[(v' \circ x) \circ (v'' \circ v'')] \circ [(y \circ v'') \circ (u'' \circ v'')]\} \\
&= \{[(v' \circ u') \circ (v' \circ v')] \circ [(v' \circ v') \circ (v' \circ v')]\} \\
&\qquad \circ \{[(v' \circ x) \circ (y \circ v'')] \circ [(v'' \circ v'') \circ (u'' \circ v'')]\}
\end{aligned}
$$

Let $a \phi b$ be the solution of 5.2.14. The value of the first term obtained by the substitution $x = a$, $y = b$ is the same as that obtained by the subtitution $x = y = a \phi b$. Hence these subtitutions also lead to identical values of the last term. From this we see that $a \phi b$ fulfills the relation

$$(v' \circ (a \phi b)) \circ ((a \phi b) \circ v'') = (v' \circ a) \circ (b \circ v'').$$

b) The operation "ϕ" defined by 5.2.14 is a middling operation:

1) "ϕ" is cancellable, for $a \phi b' = a \phi b''$ implies $(u' \circ a) \circ (b' \circ u'') = (u' \circ a) \circ (b'' \circ u'')$, whence $b' = b''$ follows, as "$\circ$" is cancellable.

2) "ϕ" is continuous in both variables, as for isomonotone and continuous "$\circ$" the set $\{x \in A : a \phi x < c\} = \{x \in A : (u' \circ a) \circ (x \circ u'') < (u' \circ c) \circ (c \circ u'')\}$ is open. The corresponding argument holds for antimonotone "$\circ$".

3) "ϕ" is bisymmetric. This will be proved in corollary 5.3.23.

4) "ϕ" is commutative:

$$(u' \circ (a \phi b)) \circ ((a \phi b) \circ u'') = (u' \circ a) \circ (b \circ u'') = (u' \circ b) \circ (a \circ u'').$$

Uniqueness of $a \phi b$ implies $b \phi a = a \phi b$.

5) "ϕ" is reflexive: Putting $b = a$ in 5.2.14 we obtain $a \phi a = a$ from uniqueness.

5.2.16 **Theorem:** If the domain of definition of a metrical operation is connected, then it is separable.

Proof: According to theorem 5.2.14 there exists a middling operation with the same domain of definition. As each connected set is order-complete according to 3.5.9, the assertion follows from lemma 5.1.6, 5.2.12, 5.2.9.

We introduce another algebraic property of operations:

5.2.17 **Definition:** An operation is *singular* iff for all $a \in A$:

$$[a \circ (a \circ a)] \circ [(a \circ a) \circ a] = (a \circ a) \circ [((a \circ a) \circ (a \circ a)) \circ a]$$

Obviously each reflexive operation is singular.

Using theorem 5.2.14 we can express singularity of a metrical operation as follows:

5.2.18 **Proposition:** A metrical operation "o" is singular iff for all $a \in A$

$$a \circ a = a \,\phi\, [(a \circ a) \circ (a \circ a)].$$

Proof: 5.2.14 yields the assertion, as for $u' = u'' = a$ the operation "ϕ" is uniquely determined.

5.2.19 **Example:** As an example of a metrical operation we consider the operation (p, q, r) defined on some interval of the set of real numbers by:

$$x\,(p, q, r)\,y = px + qy + r$$

with real numbers $p \neq 0$, $q \neq 0$, r.

This operation is in fact a metrical operation: it is bisymmetric, continuous and cancellable.

Therefore, we can derive a middling operation according to theorem 5.2.14: $(u' \circ z) \circ (z \circ u'') = (u' \circ x) \circ (y \circ u'')$ yields $p\,(pu' + qz + r) + q\,(pz + qu'' + r) + r = p\,(pu' + qx + r) + q\,(py + qu'' + r) + r$ or

$$z = \frac{x+y}{2}.$$

In general the operation (p, q, r) has the following properties: It is monotone increasing in the first (resp. second) variable iff $p > 0$ (resp. $q > 0$). It is monotone decreasing in the first (resp. second) variable iff $p < 0$ (resp. $q < 0$).

Furthermore it is singular iff $p + q = 1$

reflexive iff $p + q = 1$ and $r = 0$

commutative iff $p = q$

middling iff $p = q = 1/2$ and $r = 0$

associative iff $p = q = 1$.

We will give the proof for singularity. The other statements are dealt with similarly: According to 5.2.18, singularity of (p, q, r) is equivalent to

$$px+qx+r=\frac{1}{2}x+\frac{1}{2}(p(px+qx+r)+q(px+qx+r)+r).$$

This relation is fulfilled for all x in some interval iff $p+q=1$.

5.3 Mappings and Algebraic Properties

From the definition of homomorphism of relational systems (1.5) we obtain for the special case of an operation: f: $\langle A;\circ\rangle \to \langle B;\bullet\rangle$ is a homomorphism iff "$(a, b, c)\in R_{\circ}$ iff $(f(a), f(b), f(c))\in R_{\bullet}$".

5.3.1 **Proposition:** Let "$\circ$" be a cancellable operation. Then f is a homomorphism of $\langle A;\circ\rangle$ into $\langle B;\bullet\rangle$ iff f is $1-1$ and for all $a, b\in A$:

5.3.2 $f(a\circ b)=f(a)\bullet f(b)$.

Proof: Assume that f is a homomorphism. As
$a\circ b = c$ iff $f(a)\bullet f(b) = f(c)$,

5.3.2 follows immediately. Furthermore $f(a') = f(a'')$ implies $f(a')\bullet f(b) = f(a'')\bullet f(b) = f(a''\circ b)$. But $f(a')\bullet f(b) = f(a''\circ b)$ implies $a'\circ b = a''\circ b$ and hence $a' = a''$ by cancellability. Hence f is $1-1$.

If, on the other hand, f is $1-1$ and fulfills 5.3.2, then it is a homomorphism.

A map f is an isomorphism of $\langle A;\circ\rangle$ to $\langle B;\bullet\rangle$ iff it is a $1-1$ homomorphism of $\langle A;\circ\rangle$ onto $\langle B;\bullet\rangle$. If such an isomorphism exists, the systems $\langle A;\circ\rangle$, $\langle B;\bullet\rangle$ as well as the operations "$\circ$", "$\bullet$" themselves are called isomorphic.

5.3.3 **Proposition:** If there exists a continuous and monotone homomorphism f: $\langle A;\circ\rangle\to\langle B;\bullet\rangle$, continuity and all algebraic properties as listed above of the operation "$\bullet$" imply the same property for the operation "$\circ$". If there exists an isomorphism, also the converse is true, i.e. isomorphic operations have the same properties.

Proof: We will give the proof only for cancellability and reflexivity, the other cases being dealt with similarly. If "$\bullet$" is cancellable, the following is true: $a\circ b' = a\circ b''$ implies $f(a\circ b') = f(a\circ b'')$, whence $f(a)\bullet f(b') = f(a)\bullet f(b'')$, whence $f(b') = f(b'')$, whence $b' = b''$. If "$\bullet$" is reflexive, we have: $f(a)\bullet f(a) = f(a)$, whence $f(a\circ a) = f(a)$, whence $a\circ a = a$.

A system $\langle A;\circ\rangle$ is not only a relational system, but also an algebra as defined in 1.3.3. According to 1.5.5, f is an algebraic homomorphism of $\langle A;\circ\rangle$ into $\langle B;\bullet\rangle$ iff 5.3.2 is fulfilled, i.e. iff

$f(a \circ b) = f(a) \bullet f(b)$.

5.3.4 **Proposition:** If f is an algebraic homomorphism of $\langle A; \circ \rangle$ into $\langle B; \bullet \rangle$, then f is also an algebraic homomorphism of $\langle A; \phi \rangle$ into $\langle B; \blacklozenge \rangle$.

Proof: The derived middling "ϕ" was defined in 5.2.14 by $(u' \circ (a \phi b)) \circ ((a \phi b) \circ u'') = (u' \circ a) \circ (b \circ u'')$. As f is an algebraic homomorphism, we have:

$$(f(u') \bullet f(a \phi b)) \bullet (f(a \phi b) \bullet f(u''))$$
$$= (f(u') \bullet f(a)) \bullet (f(b) \bullet f(u'')).$$

This implies: $f(a \phi b) = f(a) \blacklozenge f(b)$.

5.3.5 **Uniqueness Theorem for Algebraic Homomorphisms:** Let A be order-complete, "$\circ$" continuous, monotone increasing and intern, "$\bullet$" cancellable. If two continuous algebraic homomorphisms

$$f_i\colon \langle A; \circ \rangle \to \langle B; \bullet \rangle \ (i = 1, 2)$$

coincide for two different elements, they are identical*).

Proof: Let $A_1 = \{x \in A : f_1(x) = f_2(x)\}$. If $x, y \in A_1$, we have $x \circ y \in A_1$, because $f_1(x \circ y) = f_1(x) \bullet f_1(y) = f_2(x) \bullet f_2(y) = f_2(x \circ y)$. Furthermore, $x \in A_1$ and $x \circ z \in A_1$ together imply $z \in A_1$: $f_1(x) \bullet f_1(z) = f_1(x \circ z) = f_2(x \circ z) = f_2(x) \bullet f_2(z) = f_1(x) \bullet f_2(z)$. As "$\bullet$" is cancellable, we obtain $f_1(z) = f_2(z)$. Let a, b be two different elements for which f_1, f_2 coincide and let A_0 be the set defined in the proof of lemma 5.1.6. Then $A_0 \subset A_1$, because A_1 is closed under 5.1.6 (i) and (ii). As A_0 is dense in A according to 5.1.6, continuity of f_1, f_2 implies $A_1 = A$.

5.3.6 **Corollary:** Let A and B be two connected ordered sets, "$\circ$" and "$\bullet$" two metrical operations. If two continuous algebraic homomorphisms $f_i\colon \langle A; \circ \rangle \to \langle B; \bullet \rangle$ $(i = 1, 2)$ coincide for two different elements, they are identical.

Proof: The derived middling operations "ϕ", "$\blacklozenge$" are continuous, monotone increasing and intern. Furthermore f_i $(i = 1, 2)$ are algebraic homomorphisms of $\langle A; \phi \rangle$ into $\langle B; \blacklozenge \rangle$ according to 5.3.4. Now the statement follows from 5.3.5.

5.3.7 **Definition:** An element $a \in A$ is a *fixpoint* of a map $f\colon A \to A$ iff $f(a) = a$.

5.3.8 **Proposition:** Let "$\circ$" be a metrical operation defined on a connected set A. A continuous algebraic endomorphism of $\langle A; \circ \rangle$ which is not the identity map has at most one fixpoint.

---

*) This is a modified version of a theorem of ACZÉL (1964).

Proof: Let f_1 be the endomorphism in question. Let f_2 be the identity map. If f_1 has two different fixpoints, say a and b, we have $f_1(a) = a = f_2(a)$ and $f_1(b) = b = f_2(b)$. Hence f_1 is the identity map according to 5.3.6.

5.3.9 **Proposition:** A metrical operation defined on a connected set is either reflexive or has at most one reflexive element.

Proof: The map $f(a) = a \circ a$ is a continuous algebraic endomorphism: $f(a \circ b) = (a \circ b) \circ (a \circ b) = (a \circ a) \circ (b \circ b) = f(a) \circ f(b)$. The fixpoints of these endomorphisms are the reflexive elements. The assertion therefore follows from 5.3.8.

5.3.10 **Definition:** A map $f: A \to A$ is *singular* with respect to a metrical operation "o", iff for all $a \in A$:

$$f(a) = a \,\phi\, f(f(a)).$$

Each identity map is a singular algebraic automorphism. We remark that the algebraic endomorphism $f(a) = a \circ a$ is singular iff "o" is singular.

5.3.11 **Proposition:** Let "o" be a metrical operation defined on a connected set A. A singular continuous algebraic endomorphism has no fixpoints except it is the identity map.

Proof: If an algebraic endomorphism is singular and an element $b \neq f(b)$ exists, we have:

(*) $\quad x \,\phi\, f(b) = f(x) \,\phi\, b$ for all $x \in A$.

This can be seen as follows: $f_1(x) = x \,\phi\, f(b)$, $f_2(x) = f(x) \,\phi\, b$ are algebraic endomorphisms with respect to "ϕ". We have $f_1(b) = f_2(b)$ and $f_1(f(b)) = f_2(f(b))$. Hence, (*) holds for all $x \in A$. If there would exist a fixpoint, (*) would imply $f(b) = b$, which is a contradiction.

5.3.12 **Proposition:** If a singular metrical operation defined on a connected set is not reflexive, it has no reflexive elements.

Proof: If "o" is singular, the algebraic endomorphism $f(a) = a \circ a$ is singular too. The reflexive elements of "o" are the fixpoints of f. Thus the assertion follows from 5.3.11.

5.3.13 **Definition:** The operations "o" on A and "•" on B are *joined*, iff there exists a $1-1$ map f of A onto B such that for all $a, b, c, d \in A$:

5.3.14 $f^{-1}(f(a \circ b) \bullet f(c \circ d)) = f^{-1}(f(a) \bullet f(c)) \circ f^{-1}(f(b) \bullet f(d))$.
The map f itself will be called a *joining map*.

5.3.15 **Definition:** If 5.3.14 holds for $A = B$, $\circ = \bullet$, the map f is called *autojoining*.

5.3.16 **Definition:** The operations "$\circ$" on A and "$\bullet$" on B are *distributive*, iff there exists a $1-1$ map f of A onto B such that for all $a, b, c \in A$:

5.3.17
$$\begin{cases} f^{-1}(f(a \circ b) \bullet f(a \circ c)) = f^{-1}(f(a) \bullet f(a)) \circ f^{-1}(f(b) \bullet f(c)) \\ f^{-1}(f(a \circ c) \bullet f(b \circ c)) = f^{-1}(f(a) \bullet f(b)) \circ f^{-1}(f(c) \bullet f(c)) \\ f^{-1}(f(a) \bullet f(b)) \circ f^{-1}(f(a) \bullet f(c)) = f^{-1}(f(a \circ a) \bullet f(b \circ c)) \\ f^{-1}(f(a) \bullet f(c)) \circ f^{-1}(f(b) \bullet f(c)) = f^{-1}(f(a \circ b) \bullet f(c \circ c)) \end{cases}$$

Obviously, jointness implies distributivity. The converse relationship is studied in section 5.4.

If $A = B$, $\circ = \bullet$, and f is the identity map, jointness degenerates to bisymmetry, distributivity degenerates to autodistributivity.

If "$\circ$" on A and "$\bullet$" on B are distributive, then "$\bullet$" on B and "$\circ$" on A are distributive too.

5.3.18 **Proposition:** If the operations "$\circ$" on A and "$\bullet$" on B are bisymmetric and $\langle A; \circ\rangle$ and $\langle B; \bullet\rangle$ are isomorphic, then "$\circ$" and "$\bullet$" are joined.

Proof: Let "$\bullet$" be bisymmetric. As the operations are isomorphic, there exists a $1-1$ map f of A onto B such that: $f(a \circ b) = f(a) \bullet f(b)$. Hence

$$\begin{aligned} f^{-1}(f(a \circ b) \bullet f(c \circ d)) &= f^{-1}[(f(a) \bullet f(b)) \bullet (f(c) \bullet f(d))] \\ &= f^{-1}[(f(a) \bullet f(c)) \bullet (f(b) \bullet f(d))] \\ &= f^{-1}(f(a) \bullet f(c)) \circ f^{-1}(f(b) \bullet f(d)). \end{aligned}$$

5.3.19 **Proposition:** If the reflexive and commutative operations "$\circ$" on A and "$\bullet$" on B are joined, then the joining map is an isomorphism of $\langle A; \circ\rangle$ to $\langle B; \bullet\rangle$.

5.3.20 **Corollary:** For reflexive and commutative operations any autojoining map is an automorphism. For middling operations isomorphism is sufficient and necessary for jointness. If two middling operations on the same set A are joined by the identity map, they are identical.

If we restrict ourselves to bisymmetric operations, $\langle A; \circ\rangle$ and $\langle B; \bullet\rangle$ are joined for $A = B$ and $\circ = \bullet$ (f being the identity map). Thus the relation of jointness is reflexive. Furthermore it is symmetric, because an interchange of A and B, $\circ$ and $\bullet$, f and f^{-1}, a and $f(a)$ leaves 5.3.14 unchanged. The relation of jointness is, however, not transitive in general.

5.3.21 **Example:** $A = \mathbb{R}$, $a \circ b = a + b$, $a \bullet b = \frac{a+b}{2}$, $a * b = \frac{a+b}{2} + 1$. Then, "$\circ$" and "$\bullet$" as well as "$\bullet$" and "$*$" are joined, however, not "$\circ$" and "$*$".

5.3.22 **Theorem:** If the metrical operations "$\circ$" and "$\bullet$" are joined, the following pairs of operations are joined with the same map $f\colon A \to B$: "$\circ$" and "Φ", "ϕ" and "$\bullet$", "ϕ" and "Φ".

Proof:

$$(u' \circ (a \phi b)) \circ ((a \phi b) \circ u'') = (u' \circ a) \circ (b \circ u'') \text{ and}$$
$$(v' \circ (c \phi d)) \circ ((c \phi d) \circ v'') = (v' \circ c) \circ (d \circ v'')$$

together imply:

$$f^{-1}\{f[(u' \circ (a \phi b)) \circ ((a \phi b) \circ u'')] \bullet f[(v' \circ (c \phi d)) \circ ((c \phi d) \circ v'')]\}$$
$$= f^{-1}\{f[(u' \circ a) \circ (b \circ u'')] \bullet f[(v' \circ c) \circ (d \circ v'')]\}.$$

Using jointness of "$\circ$" and "$\bullet$", we obtain:

$$f^{-1}[f(u' \circ (a \phi b)) \bullet f(v' \circ (c \phi d))]$$
$$\circ f^{-1}[f((a \phi b) \circ u'') \bullet f((c \phi d) \circ v'')]$$
$$= f^{-1}[f(u' \circ a) \bullet f(v' \circ c)] \circ f^{-1}[f(b \circ u'') \bullet f(d \circ v'')]$$

$$\{f^{-1}[f(u') \bullet f(v')] \circ f^{-1}[f(a \phi b) \bullet f(c \phi d)]\}$$
$$\circ \{f^{-1}[f(a \phi b) \bullet f(c \phi d)] \circ f^{-1}[f(u'') \bullet f(v'')]\}$$
$$= \{f^{-1}[f(u') \bullet f(v')] \circ f^{-1}[f(a) \bullet f(c)]\}$$
$$\circ \{f^{-1}[f(b) \bullet f(d)] \circ f^{-1}[f(u'') \bullet f(v'')]\}.$$

Uniqueness of ϕ implies

$$f^{-1}[f(a \phi b) \bullet f(c \phi d)] = f^{-1}[f(a) \bullet f(c)] \phi f^{-1}[f(b) \bullet f(d)].$$

Hence "ϕ" and "$\bullet$" are joined. As jointness is a symmetric property, "$\circ$" and "Φ" are joined too. Because "$\circ$" and "Φ" are joined, another application of the theorem yields jointness of "ϕ" and "Φ".

5.3.23 **Corollary:** For any metrical operation "$\circ$" the derived operation "ϕ" (see 5.2.14) is bisymmetric.

Proof: This follows immediately from 5.3.22 for $A=B$, $\circ=\bullet$, and f the identity map.

5.4 Distributivity and Bisymmetry

In section 5.3 we have mentioned that jointness implies distributivity. In this section we will show the converse under additional assumptions.

5.4.1 **Theorem:** If two cancellable, continuous and autodistributive operations "$\circ$" and "$\bullet$" one of which is defined on a connected set A are distributive by a monotone map f, they are joined.

5.4.2 Corollary*): If A is connected, a cancellable, continuous and autodistributive operation is bisymmetric.

Proof: Let $a, b, c, d \in A$ be arbitrary. Without loss of generality we may assume that A is connected and that $a < b < c < d$; the other cases can be dealt with similarly. We define a function $\varepsilon : A \to A$ by:

5.4.3 $$f^{-1}[f(a \circ x) \bullet f(c \circ d)] = f^{-1}[f(a) \bullet f(c)] \circ f^{-1}[f(\varepsilon(x)) \bullet f(d)].$$

This function is defined for all x between a and d. We have

$$f^{-1}[f(a \circ a) \bullet f(c \circ d)] = f^{-1}[f(a) \bullet f(c)] \circ f^{-1}[f(a) \bullet f(d)]$$
$$f^{-1}[f(a \circ d) \bullet f(c \circ d)] = f^{-1}[f(a) \bullet f(c)] \circ f^{-1}[f(d) \bullet f(d)].$$

If x is between a and d, $f^{-1}[f(a \circ x) \bullet f(c \circ d)]$ is between $f^{-1}[f(a \circ a) \bullet f(c \circ d)]$ and $f^{-1}[f(a \circ d) \bullet f(c \circ d)]$ and therefore between $f^{-1}[f(a) \bullet f(c)] \circ f^{-1}[f(a) \bullet f(d)]$ and $f^{-1}[f(a) \bullet f(c)] \circ f^{-1}[f(d) \bullet f(d)]$. Thus according to 5.1.1 there exists $\varepsilon(x)$ between a and d such that 5.4.3 holds. As "$\circ$" and "$\bullet$" are monotone by 3.7.8, $\varepsilon(x)$ is uniquely determined. We have:

$$\varepsilon(a) = a, \ \varepsilon(d) = d.$$

We will show that $\varepsilon(x) = x$ for all x between a and d.

1.) First we show that $x' \circ y' = x'' \circ y''$ implies:

$$\varepsilon(x') \circ \varepsilon(y') = \varepsilon(x'') \circ \varepsilon(y'').$$

For this purpose consider the following sequence of equations:

$$\begin{aligned}
& f[(a \circ a) \circ (x \circ y)] \bullet f[(c \circ c) \circ (d \circ d)] \\
&= f[(a \circ x) \circ (a \circ y)] \bullet f[(c \circ d) \circ (c \circ d)] \\
&= f\{f^{-1}[f(a \circ x) \bullet f(c \circ d)] \circ f^{-1}[f(a \circ y) \bullet f(c \circ d)]\} \\
&= f\{[f^{-1}(f(a) \bullet f(c)) \circ f^{-1}(f(\varepsilon(x)) \bullet f(d))] \\
&\qquad \circ [f^{-1}(f(a) \bullet f(c)) \circ f^{-1}(f(\varepsilon(y)) \bullet f(d))]\} \\
&= f\{[f^{-1}(f(a) \bullet f(c)) \circ f^{-1}(f(a) \bullet f(c))] \\
&\qquad \circ [f^{-1}(f(\varepsilon(x)) \bullet f(d)) \circ f^{-1}(f(\varepsilon(y)) \bullet f(d))]\} \\
&= f\{f^{-1}[f(a \circ a) \bullet f(c \circ c)] \circ f^{-1}[f(\varepsilon(x) \circ \varepsilon(y)) \bullet f(d \circ d)]\}.
\end{aligned}$$

If $x' \circ y' = x'' \circ y''$, the value of the first term obtained by the substitution $x = x'$, $y = y'$ is the same as that obtained by the substitution $x = x''$, $y = y''$. Hence these substitutions also lead to identical values of the last term. From this we obtain by the cancellation properties:

$$\varepsilon(x') \circ \varepsilon(y') = \varepsilon(x'') \circ \varepsilon(y'').$$

---

*) This corollary generalizes a theorem by HOSSZU (1959, pp. 6–8) who proved 5.4.2 for the special case of A being a set of real numbers and "$\circ$" a reflexive operation.

2.) Second, we show that there exists an operation "$*$" which is continuous, intern, increasing in both variables, and which fulfills

$$\varepsilon(x * y) = \varepsilon(x) * \varepsilon(y).$$

For this purpose, we have to distinguish two cases:

(i) "$\circ$" is isomonotone. Without restriction of generality, we assume that "$\circ$" is increasing. We define an operation "$*$" by

$$(x * y) \circ (x * y) = x \circ y.$$

To see that this equation defines an operation, we assume without loss of generality: $x < y$. Then,

$$x \circ x < x \circ y < y \circ y.$$

Therefore, according to 5.1.1 $z \circ z = x \circ y$ has a solution. Because of monotony, this solution is unique. From 1.) we have

$$\varepsilon(x * y) \circ \varepsilon(x * y) = \varepsilon(x) \circ \varepsilon(y).$$

By definition of "$*$", we have

$$\varepsilon(x) \circ \varepsilon(y) = (\varepsilon(x) * \varepsilon(y)) \circ (\varepsilon(x) * \varepsilon(y)).$$

Therefore,

$$\varepsilon(x * y) = \varepsilon(x) * \varepsilon(y).$$

As can be easily seen, "$*$" is continuous, intern, and increasing in both variables.

(ii) "$\circ$" is antimonotone. Without loss of generality we assume that "$\circ$" is increasing in the first and decreasing in the second variable. We define an operation "$*$" by

$$x \circ (x * y) = (x * y) \circ y.$$

To see that this equation defines an operation, we may assume without loss of generality: $x < y$. Then,

$$x \circ x > x \circ y$$
$$x \circ y < y \circ y.$$

Therefore, according to 5.1.1 $x \circ z = z \circ y$ has a solution. This solution is unique: If $z' \leqq z''$ are both solutions, we have: $x \circ z' \geqq x \circ z'' = z'' \circ y \geqq z' \circ y = x \circ z'$. Therefore, $x \circ z' = x \circ z''$, whence by cancellation $z' = z''$ follows.

From 1.) we have

$$\varepsilon(x) \circ \varepsilon(x * y) = \varepsilon(x * y) \circ \varepsilon(y).$$

By definition of "$*$", we have

$$\varepsilon(x) \circ (\varepsilon(x) * \varepsilon(y)) = (\varepsilon(x) * \varepsilon(y)) \circ \varepsilon(y).$$

Therefore,

$$\varepsilon(x * y) = \varepsilon(x) * \varepsilon(y).$$

As can easily be seen, "$*$" is continuous. Furthermore, it is intern and increasing in both variables: If, for example, $y' < y''$ and $x * y' \geqq x * y''$, we obtain a contradiction from

$$x \circ (x * y') \leqq x \circ (x * y'') = (x * y'') \circ y'' < (x * y') \circ y'.$$

Similarly, we can show that "$*$" is intern.

3.) Finally we show that $\varepsilon(x) = x$ for all $x \in [a, d]$. As $\varepsilon(a) = a$ and $\varepsilon(d) = d$, this follows immediately from the uniqueness theorem for algebraic homomorphisms 5.3.5.

5.5 Additive Operations

5.5.1 **Definition:** An *additive operation* is an associative, commutative, and cancellable operation which is continuous in both variables.

For additive operations we will use the symbol "$+$" instead of "$\circ$".

Each additive operation is a metrical operation: Associativity together with commutativity imply bisymmetry. If $a, b \in A$ are reflexive elements for an additive operation "$+$", we have $a + (a + b) = (a+a)+b = a+b = a+(b+b) = (a+b)+b = b+(a+b)$, whence from cancellation $a=b$ follows. Therefore, A contains at most one reflexive element.

The axioms of additive operations given in literature usually differ somewhat from 5.5.1. Often, instead of a continuity axiom, a subtraction axiom is assumed: To elements $a, b, \in A$ with $a<b$ there exists $x \in A$ such that $a+x=b$. (HÖLDER (1901), p. 57, Axiom V; HEMPEL (1952), p. 66, Formula 12.4 g; BEHREND (1956), p. 347, Axiom $A_2^* r$.) This is natural, if one considers only the additive operation as such. In the connection with measurement, however, additive operations in an ordered, connected set are of interest. Under these circumstances, it seems feasible to use a continuity axiom instead of the subtraction axiom. If elements x', x'' exist such that $a+x'<b<a+x''$, then by continuity an element x exists such that $a+x=b$. On the other hand, continuity follows from the subtraction axiom.

Occasionally, it is also required that $a+b>a$ for all a, b (HÖLDER (1901), p. 7 (ck), axiom N; HEMPEL (1952), p. 66, Formula 12.4f; BEHREND (1956), p. 347, Axiom $A \circ_1 r$). This axiom is omitted here because it is not needed for our purposes and because operations of practical relevance exist, fulfilling 5.5.1 but not $a+b>a$. One example is connection in parallel of rheostats. More generally, if $f(x)$ is any decreasing nonnegative continuous function on $\mathbb{R}$, the operation "-$\blacklozenge$-" defined by a-$\blacklozenge$-$b = f^{-1}(f(a)+f(b))$ is an additive operation fulfilling a-$\blacklozenge$-$b<a$.

From 5.5.1 we conclude that $a+b$ is monotone increasing in both variables:

5.5.2 **Theorem:** A cancellable and associative operation which is continuous in both variables and defined on an ordered and connected set A is monotone increasing in both variables.

Proof: In 3.7.8 and 3.7.10 we have shown that a continuous cancellable operation is consistently monotone in both variables. We shall now show that in the case of associativity the operation is increasing in the second variable, the proof for the first one being similar.

Assume that the operation is decreasing in the second variable. If $c' < c''$, then $(a+b)+c' > (a+b)+c'' = a+(b+c'') > a+(b+c') = (a+b)+c'$ which is a contradiction.

One of the main points of the paper of Hölder (1901), p. 13, is to show that commutativity follows from his axioms. A modification of Hölder's proof was given by Behrend (1956), p. 349. Similarly, we can delete commutativity. In order to prove this, we need the following Lemma:

5.5.3 **Lemma:** Assume that "+" is an associative, continuous and cancellable operation defined on an ordered and connected set A. Let $a+a \gtrless a$ for all $a \in A$. Then, for each pair of elements $a, b \in A$ with $a \lessgtr b$, there exists a natural number n such that $(n+1)\,a \lessgtr nb$.

Proof: We restrict ourselves to the case $a+a>a$. We define a sequence $\{a_n : n = 1, 2, \ldots\}$ as follows: Let $\varphi_n(a) = n \cdot a$, and let φ_n^{-1} be the inverse function of φ_n. Then $a_n = \varphi_n^{-1}(\varphi_{n+1}(a))$. That this element always exists, can be seen as follows: We have $\varphi_n(a) < \varphi_{n+1}(a) \leqq \varphi_{2n}(a) = \varphi_n(a+a)$ By continuity, there exists an element a_n such that $\varphi_n(a_n) = \varphi_{n+1}(a)$. The sequence $\{a_n : n = 1, 2, \ldots\}$ is monotone decreasing: $\varphi_n^{-1}(\varphi_{n+1}(a)) = \varphi_{n(n+1)}^{-1}$ $(\varphi_{(n+1)(n+1)}(a)) > \varphi_{n(n+1)}^{-1}(\varphi_{n(n+2)}(a)) = \varphi_{n+1}^{-1}(\varphi_{n+2}(a))$. Furthermore $a_n > a$ for all $n = 1, 2, \ldots : \varphi_n^{-1}(\varphi_{n+1}(a)) > \varphi_n^{-1}(\varphi_n(a)) = a$. Therefore $\{a_n : n = 1, 2, \ldots\}$ is convergent the limit being $\geqq a$. We will show that $\lim a_n = a$. If this is true, for each pair a, b with $a<b$ there exists n such that $a_n < b$. Then, $\varphi_{n+1}(a) = \varphi_n(a_n) < \varphi_n(b)$, q.e.d.

In order to prove $\lim\limits_{n\to\infty} a_n = a$, we need the relation

$$\varphi_n(a+a_n) = \varphi_{2n}(a_{2n}).$$

We remark that $\varphi_n^{-1}(\varphi_p(x)) = \varphi_p(\varphi_n^{-1}(x))$ if $\varphi_n^{-1}(x)$ exists. For, $\varphi_p(\varphi_n(u)) = \varphi_n(\varphi_p(u))$ implies $\varphi_n^{-1}(\varphi_p(\varphi_n(u))) = \varphi_p(u)$ whence with $u = \varphi_n^{-1}(x)$ the assertion follows. Therefore we have: $\varphi_{2n+1}(a) + \varphi_n^{-1}(\varphi_{2n}(a_{2n})) = \varphi_n(\varphi_n^{-1}(\varphi_{2n+1}(a))) + \varphi_n^{-1}(\varphi_{2n+1}(a)) = \varphi_{n+1}(\varphi_n^{-1}(\varphi_{2n+1}(a))) = \varphi_n^{-1}(\varphi_{n+1}(\varphi_{2n+1}(a))) = \varphi_n^{-1}(\varphi_{2n+1}(\varphi_{n+1}(a))) = \varphi_{2n+1}(\varphi_n^{-1}(\varphi_{n+1}(a))) = \varphi_n(\varphi_n^{-1}(\varphi_{n+1}(a))) + \varphi_n(\varphi_n^{-1}(\varphi_{n+1}(a))) + \varphi_n^{-1}(\varphi_{n+1}(a))) = \varphi_{2n+1}(a) + a + a_n$. By cancellation this implies $\varphi_n^{-1}(\varphi_{2n}(a_{2n})) = a + a_n$ whence $\varphi_{2n}(a_{2n}) = \varphi_n(a + a_n)$.

Assume that $\lim a_n =: a_\infty > a$. From strict monotony we have

$$a + a_\infty < a_\infty + a_\infty .$$

Because of continuity there exists n, such that

$$a + a_n < a_\infty + a_\infty .$$

Hence $\varphi_{2n}(a_{2n}) = \varphi_n(a + a_n) < \varphi_n(a_\infty + a_\infty) = \varphi_{2n}(a_\infty)$. Therefore, $a_{2n} < a_\infty$, which contradicts $a_n \downarrow a_\infty$.

5.5.4 **Theorem:** An associative, continuous and cancellable operation defined on an ordered and connected set is commutative.

Proof: We have to distinguish three cases:

(i) $a + a > a$ for all $a \in A$. We remark that in this case also $a + b > a$ and $a + b > b$ for all $a, b : a + a > a$ implies $a + (a + b) = (a + a) + b > a + b$, whence $a + b > b$. The proof for $a + b > a$ runs similarly. Therefore, $\varphi_{n+1}(a + b) = a + \varphi_n(b + a) + b > \varphi_n(b + a)$ for all n. Together with lemma 5.5.3 this implies: $a + b \geqq b + a$. The same reasoning shows the opposite inequality whence commutativity follows.

(ii) $a + a < a$ for all $a \in A$: Proof analogous to (i).

(iii) If there exists a', a'' with $a' + a' < a'$, $a'' + a'' > a''$, continuity and connectedness imply the existence of an element o such that $o + o = o$. From $o + (o + a) = (o + o) + a = o + a$, we obtain: $o + a = a$ for all a. Similarly, $a + o = a$ for all a. This relation also implies the uniqueness of o. For $a \gtrless o$, we have $a + a \gtrless a + o = a$. By o, the set A is divided into two classes: The set of positive elements $a > o$ and the set of negative elements $a < o$. Within the positive and within the negative elements, the operation is commutative according to (i) and (ii). It remains to be shown that the operation is also commutative if a positive and a negative element are combined. Let $a < o < b$. Without loss of generality, we may assume that $a + b > o$. As $a + o < o < a + b$, an element a' exists such that $a + a' = o$, $o < a' < b$. From $(a' + a) + a' = a' + (a + a') = a' + o = a'$ we have $a' + a = o$ too. As $a' + o < b < a' + b$, there exists an element c such that $a' + c = b$, $o < c < b$. As both, a' and c, are positive elements, we also have $c + a' = b$. Therefore, $a + b = a + (a' + c) = (a + a') + c = c = c + (a' + a) = (c + a') + a = b + a$.

6. Theory of Interval Scales Based on Operations

6.1 Existence and Uniqueness of Interval Scales

In this section we will study the possibility of constructing interval scales based on metrical operations. Interval scales are scales which are unique up to positive linear transformations (see 1.8.3). We obtain such scales by a homomorphism of an irreducible empirical r.s. $\langle A; <, L, \circ\rangle$ into a numerical r.s. $\langle \mathbb{R}; <, L, (p, q, r)\rangle$ with the numerical operation (p, q, r) as defined in 5.2.19 and the limit-relation L as defined in 4.4.3.

6.1.1 **Theorem:** Let A be an ordered and connected set containing at least two elements. There exists a scale m of the irreducible r.s. $\langle A; <, L, \circ\rangle$ into a n.r.s. $\langle \mathbb{R}; <, L, (p, q, r)\rangle$ (i.e. a monotone increasing and continuous map m: $A \to \mathbb{R}$ such that: $m(a \circ b) = pm(a) + qm(b) + r$) iff "$\circ$" is a metrical operation. The scale m is unique up to positive linear transformations. The constants p, q are uniquely determined.

Proof: (i) If "$\circ$" is a metrical operation, then such a homomorphism m exists: According to theorem 5.2.16, A is separable as it is connected. By theorem 4.2.3 there exists a monotone increasing and continuous map g: $A \to \mathbb{R}$. As A is connected, the picture of A, $g(A)$, is an interval in $\mathbb{R}$.

On $g(A)$ we define an operation Φ by:

$$\Phi(x, y) = g\left(g^{-1}(x) \circ g^{-1}(y)\right).$$

It is easy to see that Φ is cancellable, continuous and bisymmetric. According to a theorem of Aczél (1966, p. 287) there exists a monotone and continuous function f: $\mathbb{R} \to \mathbb{R}$ which can always be choosen to be increasing and $p, q, r \in \mathbb{R}$ such that:

$$\Phi(x, y) = f^{-1}\left(pf(x) + qf(y) + r\right).$$

Therefore

$$g\left(g^{-1}(x) \circ g^{-1}(y)\right) = f^{-1}\left(pf(x) + qf(y) + r\right).$$

For $a = g^{-1}(x)$, $b = g^{-1}(y)$, $f(g(a)) = m(a)$, we obtain:

$$m(a \circ b) = pm(a) + qm(b) + r.$$

Thus m is a homomorphism of $\langle A; <, L, \circ\rangle$ into $\langle \mathbb{R}; <, L, (p, q, r)\rangle$. As g

and f are monotone increasing and continuous, m is monotone increasing and continuous too.

(ii) If there exists a homomorphism, then "o" is a metrical operation: As (p, q, r) is a metrical operation (5.2.19), this follows immediately from proposition 5.3.3.

(iii) Uniqueness: If there exist two continuous homomorphisms m_1: $\langle A; <, L, \circ\rangle \rightarrow \langle \mathbb{R}; <, L, (p_1, q_1, r_1)\rangle$ and m_2: $\langle A; <, L, \circ\rangle \rightarrow \langle \mathbb{R}; <, L, (p_2, q_2, r_2)\rangle$ we have

$$m_1 (a \circ b) = p_1 m_1 (a) + q_1 m_1 (b) + r_1$$
$$m_2 (a \circ b) = p_2 m_2 (a) + q_2 m_2 (b) + r_2 .$$

With $m_1 (a) = x$, $m_1 (b) = y$, $m_2 (m_1^{-1} (x)) = F(x)$ we obtain:

$$F(p_1 x + q_1 y + r_1) = p_2 F(x) + q_2 F(y) + r_2 .$$

According to Aczél (1966, p. 67) this implies

$p_1 = p_2$, $q_1 = q_2$, $F(x) = \alpha x + \beta$. As F is increasing, we have $\alpha > 0$.

6.1.2 **Theorem:** If there exists a homomorphism of $\langle A; <, \circ\rangle$ into $\langle \mathbb{R}; <, (p, q, r)\rangle$ and A contains at least two elements, the following is true:

$p>0$ (resp. $q>0$) iff "o" is monotone increasing in the first (resp. second) variable,

$p<0$ (resp. $q<0$)	iff "o" is monotone decreasing in the first (resp. second) variable,
$p+q=1$	iff "o" is singular,
$p+q=1$, $r=0$	iff "o" is reflexive,
$p=q$	iff "o" is commutative,
$p=q=1$	iff "o" is associative.

Proof: This follows immediately from example 5.2.19.

6.1.3 **Remark:** In principle also the numerical operation $[p, q, r]$ defined on the set of positive real numbers $\mathbb{R}^+$ by

$$x \, [p, q, r] \, y = x^p y^q e^r$$

can be used as corresponding to an empirical metrical operation "o".

If m is a homomorphism into the system $\langle \mathbb{R}; <, L, (p, q, r)\rangle$, then $n: n(a) = \exp [m(a)]$ is a homomorphism into the system

$$\langle \mathbb{R}^+; <, L, [p, q, r]\rangle .$$

Such scales are unique up to the transformation

$$\gamma (x) = \beta x^\alpha .$$

The statements about the constants p, q, r in theorem 6.1.2 remain true for this operation. In this case a middling operation has as corresponding numerical operation the geometric mean: $\sqrt{x \cdot y}$. Such a middling will be called a *geometric* middling. On the other hand, a middling which has as corresponding numerical operation the arithmetic mean will be called an *arithmetic* middling.

6.2 Inherent Zero Points

According to Theorem 6.1.1 the coefficients p and q are uniquely determined by the metrical operation, i.e. independent of the specific interval scale. This is not true, in general, for the additive constant r.

If we consider first the case of a nonsingular operation $(p+q \neq 1)$ the transformation $m(a) \to \alpha m(a) + \beta$ leads to $r \to \alpha r - \beta(p+q-1)$. Therefore, in this case we can always find a shift of the scale namely

$$m(a) \to m(a) + \frac{r}{p+q-1}$$

such that for the transformed scale the additive constant becomes 0. Using the transformed scale, we have therefore the representation

6.2.1 $\quad m(a \circ b) = p\,m(a) + q\,m(b).$

If we restrict ourselves to such distinguished representations, we restrict the class of admissible transformations to dilations (see 1.8.3) i.e. $m(a)$ is unique up to transformations $m(a) \to \alpha m(a)$ with $\alpha > 0$.

By the restriction to distinguished representations the zero point of the scale is fixed. It might happen, of course, that for the distinguished scales $m(A)$ does not contain 0 (i.e. there exists no element $\mathrm{o} \in A$ such that $m(\mathrm{o}) = 0$.) If, however, such an element o exists, then it is reflexive: $m(\mathrm{o} \circ \mathrm{o}) = p\,m(\mathrm{o}) + q\,n(\mathrm{o}) = 0$, whence $\mathrm{o} \circ \mathrm{o} = \mathrm{o}$. Thus, the restriction to distinguished representations 6.2.1 can also be interpreted as the restriction to scales which map the reflexive element (if one exists) into zero.

In the case of singular operations $(p+q=1)$, this requirement is not meaningful because they have no reflexive element unless they are reflexive operations (i.e. *all* elements are reflexive). In the case $p+q=1$, r also is invariant under shifts and is transformed into αr by the dilation $m(a) \to \alpha m(a)$. Therefore, r cannot be eliminated by linear transformations and no distinguished class of scales exists.

In the special case of a reflexive operation, we have $r=0$. Of course also in this case the whole class of scales (obtained from a given scale by positive linear transformations) is admissible.

As in the case of a singular operation no zero point inherent to the operation itself exists, extraneous criteria have to be applied in order to fix the zero point and to make the scale thereby unique up to dilations. If, for example, A has a smallest element, it seems natural to map this smallest element into 0. If A has no smallest element, but the set $m(A)$ has a infimum, it is natural to transform the scale such that the infimum becomes 0.

In order to distinguish a zero point determined by the properties of the scale from a zero point determined by extraneous considerations, we call the first one an inherent zero point. Thus, we have the result that an inherent zero point exists if and only if the scale is nonsingular.

6.3 Zero-Points from Endomorphisms

In this section we consider some special endomorphisms of an e. r. s. $\langle A; <, L, \circ\rangle$ where "$\circ$" is a metrical operation and A contains at least two elements.

6.3.1 **Example:** The subject is asked by the experimenter to determine a tone whose loudness is half that of a given tone.

6.3.2 **Proposition:** If f is an endomorphism of $\langle A; <, L, \circ\rangle$, and m an interval scale for $\langle A; <, L, \circ\rangle$, then $m \circ f$ is an interval scale for $\langle A; <, L, \circ\rangle$ too, i.e.

6.3.3 $m(f(a)) = \lambda m(a) + \mu.$

Proof: As f is a homomorphism of $\langle A; <, L, \circ\rangle$ into $\langle A; <, L, \circ\rangle$ and m a homomorphism of $\langle A; <, L, \circ\rangle$ into $\langle \mathbb{R}; <, L, (p, q, r)\rangle$, the composition $m \circ f$ is a homomorphism of $\langle A; <, L, \circ\rangle$ into $\langle \mathbb{R}; <, L, (p, q, r)\rangle$ according 1.5.5 and 4.4.3.

6.3.4 **Proposition:** The constant λ occurring in 6.3.3 is independent of the special scale m. Furthermore: $\lambda=1$ iff f is singular, i.e.

$$f(a) = a \,\phi\, f(f(a)).$$

Proof: If we transform in 6.3.3 $m(a) \to \alpha m(a) + \beta$, λ remains unchanged. Furthermore, if $\lambda = 1$, then, according to 5.3.4 and 5.2.19, $m[a \,\phi\, f(f(a))] = 1/2\,[m(a) + m(f(f(a)))] = 1/2\,[m(a) + m(a) + \mu +$

$\mu)] = m(f(a))$. Therefore, $a \diamond f(f(a)) = f(a)$. On the other hand, $f(a) = a \diamond f(f(a))$ implies $\lambda m(a) + \mu = 1/2\,[m(a) + \lambda(\lambda m(a) + \mu) + \mu]$ whence $\lambda = 1$.

If f is a nonsingular endomorphism, i.e. $\lambda \neq 1$, the shift

$$m(a) \rightarrow m(a) + \frac{\mu}{\lambda - 1}$$

transforms the constant μ in 6.3.3 into 0. Thus the endomorphism can be represented in the *distinguished* form:

6.3.5 $m(f(a)) = \lambda m(a)$.

If there exists an element o such that $m(\text{o}) = 0$, we have $m(f(\text{o})) = 0$ which implies $f(\text{o}) = \text{o}$, i.e. o is a fixpoint of the endomorphism f. If, moreover, A is connected, o is the only fixpoint as f is assumed to be nonsingular (see 5.3.8). Hence by restricting ourselves to scales with distinguished representation of the endomorphism, we fix the zero-point of the scale in such a way that the fixpoint of the endomorphism – if it exists – is mapped into zero. The scale is thereby uniquely determined up to dilations.

We summarize these remarks in the following theorem:

6.3.6 **Theorem:** If A is connected, for a nonsingular endomorphism f of $\langle A; <, L, \text{o} \rangle$, there exists a subclass of distinguished interval scales m^* such that:

(i) $m^*(f(a)) = \lambda m^*(a)$,

(ii) the fixpoint of f – if it exists – is the zero-point of m^*,

(iii) m^* is unique up to dilations.

The most important endomorphism in practical applications is halving:

6.3.7 **Definition:** An endomorphism f of $\langle A; <, L, \text{o} \rangle$ is a *halving* iff for all $a \in A$:

$$f(a) = (a \diamond f(a)) \diamond f(f(a))$$

and if f is not the identity map.

6.3.8 **Proposition:** If m is an interval scale, for a halving endomorphism we have $\lambda = 1/2$.

Proof: From 6.3.7 we obtain:

$$\lambda m(a) + \mu = \frac{1}{2}\left[\frac{1}{2} m(a) + \frac{1}{2}(\lambda m(a) + \mu)\right] + \frac{1}{2}[\lambda(\lambda m(a) + \mu) + \mu]$$

This implies

$$\lambda^2 - \frac{3}{2}\lambda + \frac{1}{2} = 0 \text{ and } \mu \cdot \left(\lambda - \frac{1}{2}\right) = 0$$

Hence we have either $\lambda = 1/2$ or $\mu = 0$ and $\lambda = 1$. In the last case f is the identity map and therefore not a halving.

6.3.9 **Remark:** A singular endomorphism f is represented by:

$$m(f(a)) = m(a) + \mu .$$

In the case of a singular endomorphism it might seem natural to map "ϕ" into the geometric instead of the arithmetic mean. If this is done, i.e. if the scale $n(a) = \exp m(a)$ is used, we have

$$n(f(a)) = \gamma n(a).$$

In some sense, this determines a zero-point. It does, however, not restrict the admissible transformations to a one-parameter family. Only if we have extraneous reasons to fix the value of γ (e.g. $\gamma = 1/2$), this determines the scale uniquely up to dilations, because γ remains unchanged under $n(a) \to \beta n(a)^\alpha$ only for $\alpha = 1$.

We remark that in the case of a geometric scale the result $\lambda = 1$ (i.e. $n(f(a)) = \gamma n(a)$) can also be obtained from the assumptions that (i) $f(a) < a$ for all $a \in A$, (ii) arbitrary large and arbitrary small positive scale values occur. In this case, $\gamma n(a)^\alpha < n(a)$ holds for all $a \in A$ only if $\alpha = 1$. If $\alpha < 1$, this relation would hold for

$$n(a) > \gamma^{\frac{1}{1-\alpha}}$$

only, if $\alpha > 1$ only for

$$n(a) < \gamma^{\frac{1}{1-\alpha}} .$$

6.4 Simultaneous Arithmetic and Geometric Middling

In section 6.3 we discussed the possibility of making a scale based on arithmetic or geometric middling unique up to dilations by using in addition the halving endomorphism. If for a property arithmetic and geometric middlings are available simultaneously, this is also sufficient to make the scale unique up to dilations. This idea goes ultimately back to STEVENS (1951, p. 24).

To make this intuitive idea more precise, we assume that two different middling operations "|" (to be interpreted as arithmetic middling) and "ϕ" (to be interpreted as geometric middling) are given, fulfilling the following condition:

6.4.1 $(a \phi c) \mid (b \phi c) = [(a \mid b) \mid (a \phi b)] \phi c$

for all $a, b, c \in A$.

Let m denote a scale obtained by mapping "|" into the arithmetic mean, n a scale obtained by mapping "ϕ" into the geometric mean, $\mathfrak{M}$ and $\mathfrak{N}$ the classes of equivalent scales. m is unique up to positive linear transformations, n is unique up to the transformation $\gamma(x) = \beta x^{\alpha}$.

6.4.2 **Theorem:** If for two middling operations defined on a connected set A containing at least two elements condition 6.4.1 is fulfilled, the following two cases are possible:

a) If the two operations are identical ($a \mid b = a \phi b$ for all $a, b \in A$), to each scale $m \in \mathfrak{M}$ there exists a scale $n \in \mathfrak{N}$ such that $m(a) = \log n(a)$ for all $a \in A$.

b) If the two operations are not identical ($a \mid b \neq a \phi b$ for at least one pair $a, b \in A$), $\mathfrak{M}$ and $\mathfrak{N}$ have a nonempty intersection. The scales in $\mathfrak{M} \cap \mathfrak{N}$ are identical up to dilations.

Proof: Let $m: \langle A; <, L, | \rangle \to \langle \mathbb{R}; <, L, (\frac{1}{2}, \frac{1}{2}, 0) \rangle$ and $n: \langle A; <, L, \phi \rangle \to \langle \mathbb{R}; <, L, [\frac{1}{2}, \frac{1}{2}, 0] \rangle$. Let

(*) $\quad g(x, y) = n(n^{-1}(x) \mid n^{-1}(y))$.

For $a = n^{-1}(x)$, $b = n^{-1}(y)$, $c = n^{-1}(z)$ we obtain from 6.4.1

$$g(\sqrt{xz}, \sqrt{yz}) = \sqrt{g(g(x, y), \sqrt{xy})}\sqrt{z}.$$

For $\sqrt{x} = u$, $\sqrt{y} = v$, $\sqrt{z} = w$ and $\sqrt{g(g(u^2, v^2), uv)} = k(u, v)$ we obtain

$$g(uw, vw) = k(u, v)\, w.$$

Hence for $w_0 \neq 0$: $g(uw, vw) = (w/w_0)\, g(uw_0, vw_0)$. Substituting u for uw_0, v for vw_0 and w for w/w_0 we obtain

(**) $\quad g(uw, vw) = g(u, v)\, w$.

On the other hand, $g(x, y)$ is a middling operation which implies (Aczél 1966, p. 287) that there exists a monotone and continuous function $h: \mathbb{R} \to \mathbb{R}$ such that

$$g(x, y) = h^{-1}\left(\frac{1}{2} h(x) + \frac{1}{2} h(y)\right).$$

Together with (**) this implies (Aczél 1966, p. 153) that h is one of the following two functions:

(i) $h(x) = \alpha \log x + \beta \qquad \alpha \neq 0,$

(ii) $h(x) = \gamma x^{\alpha} + \beta \qquad \alpha \neq 0, \ \gamma \neq 0.$

Hence, g is one of the following two functions:

(i) $g(x, y) = \sqrt{xy}$

(ii) $g(x, y) = \left(\frac{1}{2} x^{\alpha} + \frac{1}{2} y^{\alpha}\right)^{1/\alpha} \qquad \alpha \neq 0.$

Both functions are solutions of (**).
Ad (i): From (*) we obtain:

(***) $n(a \mid b) = \sqrt{n(a)\, n(b)}.$

As by assumption the same relation holds with "$|$" instead of "ϕ", we have

$$a \mid b = a \phi b \text{ for all } a, b \in A.$$

Let $x = \log n(a)$, $y = \log n(b)$ and $F(x) = m(n^{-1}(\exp x))$. Then, (***) yields

$$F\left(\frac{x+y}{2}\right) = \frac{1}{2} F(x) + \frac{1}{2} F(y).$$

The only monotone and continuous solution of this functional equation is (Aczél 1966, p. 43)

$$F(x) = \alpha x + \beta$$

which implies: $m(a) = \alpha \log n(a) + \beta$.
Ad (ii): From (*) we obtain:

$$n(a \mid b)^{\alpha} = \frac{1}{2} n(a)^{\alpha} + \frac{1}{2} n(b)^{\alpha}.$$

This implies $n(a)^{\alpha} \in \mathfrak{M}$ whence: $m(a) = \gamma n(a)^{\alpha} + \beta$.

Thus, among the scales n: $\langle A; <, L, | \rangle \to \langle \mathbb{R}; <, L, [\frac{1}{2}, \frac{1}{2}, 0] \rangle$ there exists a subclass of scales which are scales for

$$\langle A; <, L, | \rangle \to \langle \mathbb{R}; <, L, (\tfrac{1}{2}, \tfrac{1}{2}, 0) \rangle.$$

The scales in this subclass are unique up to dilations.

6.5 Joined Scaling

In this section we shall study the question how scales for two joined empirical systems are related.

6.5.1 **Theorem:** Let m be an interval scale for $\langle A; <, L, \circ \rangle$, n an interval scale for $\langle B; <, L, \bullet \rangle$ with metrical operations "$\circ$", "$\bullet$" and connected sets A, B. If there exists a continuous and monotone joining map $f\colon \langle A; \circ\rangle \rightarrow \langle B; \bullet\rangle$, we have:

(*) $n(f(a)) = \alpha m(a) + \beta.$

Proof: According to theorem 5.3.19 and 5.3.22 joined operations lead to isomorphic middling operations: $f(a \phi b) = f(a) \blacklozenge f(b)$. Hence,

$$n(f(a \phi b)) = \frac{1}{2} n(f(a)) + \frac{1}{2} n(f(b)),$$

which means that $n \circ f$ or $-n \circ f$ is an interval scale for $\langle A; <, L, \phi\rangle$. As m is an interval scale for the same r. s. (5.3.4), theorem 6.1.1 implies (*).

A practical application is the so-called Cross-modality (STEVENS, 1959).

6.5.2 **Example:** The subject is asked to adjust a tone of variable loudness such that it matches a given vibration in intensity. By this experiment, a map f is determined which assigns to each degree of loudness a specific intensity of vibration of subjectively equal intensity. If "ϕ" is bisection for loudness, "$\blacklozenge$" bisection for intensity of vibration, jointness becomes: $f(a \phi b) = f(a) \blacklozenge f(b)$; if $f(a)$ is a vibration of an intensity matching loudness of a tone a, $f(a) \blacklozenge f(b)$ has an intensity matching loudness of the tone $a \phi b$, obtained from a and b by bisection.

Now we study jointness for the special case, with $A = B$, f being the identity map. This case occurs if for a given property more than one operation is available.

6.5.3 **Example:** For subjective loudness, we have the following two different operations:

(i) To two given degrees of loudness a and b, a third degree of loudness, $a \mid b$, is determined which is midway between a and b (according to the judgement of an observer).

(ii) To the two given degrees of loudness, a and b, a third degree of loudness, $a \phi b$, is determined such that the loudness of $a \phi b$, presented through one ear is subjectively equal to the loudness obtained if loudness a is presented through one, loudness b through the other ear.

If more than one operation is available, the question arises, whether the two scales are essentially identical, i. e. whether they really measure the same property or not. In the following we will ask for the formal conditions sufficient to ascertain that scales obtained from different metrical operations are identical up to admissible transformations.

6.5.4 **Theorem:** Let A be an ordered and connected set.

(i) If two metrical, nonsingular operations are joined by the identity map then there exists an interval scale which leads to a distinguished representation of both operations simultaneously.

(ii) If a nonsingular and a singular operation are joined by the identity map, the singular one is reflexive.

(iii) If there exists an interval scale which leads to a distinguished representation of two metrical operations simultaneously then they are joined by the identity map.

Proof: (0) Let m be an interval scale $m: A \to \mathbb{R}$ such that

$$(*) \quad \begin{aligned} m(a \circ b) &= p_1 m(a) + q_1 m(b) + r_1 \\ m(a \bullet b) &= p_2 m(a) + q_2 m(b) + r_2 . \end{aligned}$$

The operations "$\circ$" and "$\bullet$" are joined iff

$$(**) \quad (p_1 + q_1 - 1)\, r_2 = (p_2 + q_2 - 1)\, r_1 .$$

As m maps $1-1$, the jointness condition is equivalent to

$$m((a \circ b) \bullet (c \circ d)) = m((a \bullet c) \circ (b \bullet d)).$$

By (*) this equality is equivalent to

$$\begin{aligned} p_2 [p_1 m(a) + q_1 m(b) + r_1] + q_2 [p_1 m(c) + q_1 m(d) + r_1] + r_2 \\ = p_1 [p_2 m(a) + q_2 m(c) + r_2] \\ + q_1 [p_2 m(b) + q_2 m(d) + r_2] + r_1 , \end{aligned}$$

whence equivalent to (**).

(i) According 6.5.1, there exists a scale m satisfying (*). As the two operations are nonsingular we have $p_i + q_i - 1 \neq 0$ for $i = 1, 2$. By (**) the shift $r_1 / (p_1 + q_1 - 1)$ leads to a simultaneously distinguished representation.

(ii) Let the operation "$\circ$" be nonsingular, the operation "$\bullet$" singular. Then $p_2 + q_2 - 1 = 0$ and $p_1 + q_1 - 1 \neq 0$ imply by (**) that $r_2 = 0$. Hence "$\bullet$" is reflexive.

(iii) By assumption there exists a scale m satisfying (*) with $r_1 = r_2 = 0$. Hence (**) holds which implies jointness by (0).

6.6 The Empirical Status of Axioms

Given an empirical relational system $\mathbf{A} = \langle A; <, L, \circ \rangle$ certain conditions ("axioms") must be satisfied to ensure the existence of an interval scale (see 6.1.1):

(i) $\circ$ is bisymmetric (5.2.4),
(ii) $\circ$ is cancellable (3.7.7),
(iii) $\circ$ is continuous,
(iv) A is connected.

In order to apply this theory we must decide whether for a given e.r.s. **A** the axioms (i)–(iv) are satisfied or not. It is a convenient principle to accept the "hypothesis" that the axioms are satisfied as long as there is no contradictory empirical evidence. Our empirical tools, however, are restricted: we can consider only a finite subset $A_0 \subset A$ and test whether the elements of A_0 satisfy the relations $<$ and $\circ$ or not. From this empirical point of view the axioms (i)–(iv) are of different nature:
If (i) does not hold there exists at least one subset $A_0 = \{a_1, \ldots, a_6\} \subset A$ such that $(a_1 \circ a_2) \circ (a_3 \circ a_4) = a_5$ and $(a_1 \circ a_3) \circ (a_2 \circ a_4) = a_6$ but $a_5 \neq a_6$.
If (ii) does not hold there exists at least one subset $A_0 = \{a_1, \ldots, a_4\} \subset A$ such that

$$a_1 \circ a_2 = a_4 \text{ and } a_1 \circ a_3 = a_4 \text{ but } a_2 \neq a_3 \text{ or}$$

$$a_2 \circ a_1 = a_4 \text{ and } a_3 \circ a_1 = a_4 \text{ but } a_2 \neq a_3 .$$

Thus it is possible, in principle, to falsify (i) and (ii) by empirical experience. But this is impossible for axiom (iii); to falsify this axiom we would need an infinite subset of A and this cannot be given empirically. Axioms of the first kind will be called *testable*, the latter *objectionable* (ADAMS, FAGOT, R. R. ROBINSON (1965b)). Axiom (iv) implies that A is infinite as each finite ordered set is not connected and we must know the whole system A for falsifying connectedness. In the same manner the subtraction axiom for additive operations (5.5.1) is objectionable: "For all $a, b \in A$ with $a < b$ there exists an element $x \in A$ such that $a + x = b$". If a given finite subset $A_0 \subset A$ does not contain a suitable element x we cannot conclude that it does not exist in the whole infinite set A.

Among the notions occurring in section 5 are
α) testable: the operation $\circ$ is intern (5.1.2), reflexive (5.2.1), commutative (5.2.2), associative (5.2.3), bisymmetric (5.2.4), autodistributive (5.2.5), cancellable (3.7.7), monotone in one or both variables, singular (5.2.17);
β) objectionable: the operation $\circ$ is continuous, archimedian (5.1.4) and the set A is connected in order topology.

At first sight we may accept an objectionable axiom as only "technical" as our empirical experience will not contradict it. But unfortunately there are systems of axioms implying testable consequences which do not follow from the testable axioms of the system only: If $\circ$ is cancellable, continuous and autodistributive, and A is connected, then $\circ$ is bisymmetric (5.4.2); but without A being connected bisymmetry does not follow. Similar examples are given by 5.5.2 and 5.5.4. Thus great care is in order if we consider objectionable axioms, added to a system of testable axioms, as purely technical. For a closer examination of this question we ought first to specify the concepts "testable axiom" and "consequence" of a system of axioms.

Let $\mathbf{A} = \langle A; (R_i)_{i \in I} \rangle$ be an e.r.s. with k_i-ary relations R_i and finite I. What we can do empirically is to consider a finite subset A_0 of A and to test whether the sentences X: "$R_i (a_1, ..., a_{k_i}) = 0$" or "$R_i (a_1, ..., a_{k_i}) = 1$" for $a_j \in A_0$, $i \in I$, are true. Moreover, denoting this finite set of sentences X by $\mathscr{X}$ we can test sentences constructed from the sentences of $\mathscr{X}$ by the rules of the calculus of sentences: If we can test X_1 and X_2 we can test the sentences $X_1 \cup X_2$ ($\cup$=or), $X_1 \cap X_2$ ($\cap$=and), $X_1 \supset X_2$ ($\supset$=implication) and $\overline{X}_1$ ($\overline{}$=negation); see 2.3.2b. The set of sentences is a BOOLEAN algebra (see 12.1.1) and $X_1 \supset X_2$ is equivalent to $\overline{X}_1 \cup X_2$. As $X \in \mathscr{X}$ implies $\overline{X} \in \mathscr{X}$ ("not $R_i (a_1, ..., a_{k_i}) = 1$" is the same as "$R_i (a_1, ..., a_{k_i}) = 0$"), the system of sentences which can be constructed by these rules from the sentences of $\mathscr{X}$ consists of the sentences

$$(*) \qquad Y := (X_{11} \cup X_{12} \cup \ldots \cup X_{1\,l_1}) \cap (X_{21} \cup \ldots \cup X_{2\,l_2}) \cap \ldots \cap (X_{m1} \ldots X_{m l_m})$$

where $m, l_i \in \mathbb{N}$ and $X_{ij} \in \mathscr{X}$. A sentence Y of this type will be denoted more explicitly by $Y(a_1, ..., a_r)$ where $a_1, ..., a_r$ are the elements of A occurring in the sentences X_{ij}; thus e.g. if $m=1$ and $l_1=2$ and X_{11} is given by "$R_1 (a_1, a_2) = 1$", X_{12} by "$R_2 (a_2, a_3) = 1$", $Y(a_1, a_2, a_3)$ is the sentence "$R_1 (a_1, a_2) = 1$ or $R_2 (a_2, a_3) = 1$". If we are able to show empirically the existence of not necessarily different elements $a_1, ..., a_r$ such that $Y(a_1, ..., a_r)$ does not hold, we have falsified the sentence "$Y(a_1, ..., a_r)$ holds for all $a_1, ..., a_r \in A$". This suggests the following

6.6.1 **Definition:** A *testable* sentence for the r.s. $\mathbf{A}$ is a sentence of the type "$Y(a_1, ..., a_r)$ holds for all $a_1, ..., a_r$" where Y is a sentence of type (*). (Testable axioms are called "universal" sentences in the general theory of relational systems (TARSKI (1954), A. ROBINSON (1965))).

Consider, for example, the axiom of bisymmetry in the relational system $\langle A; =, <, \circ \rangle$; Y is given by $Y(a_1, a_2, ..., a_{10})$:

$$(a_1 \circ a_2) \neq a_3 \cup (a_4 \circ a_5) \neq a_6 \cup (a_3 \circ a_6) \neq a_7 \cup (a_1 \circ a_4) \neq a_8 \cup (a_2 \circ a_5) \neq a_9 \cup (a_8 \circ a_9) \neq a_{10} \cup a_7 = a_{10}.$$

So far we have formulated sentences by the relations and objects of a fixed r.s. $\langle A; (R_i)_{i \in I} \rangle$. We will a sentence of this kind interpret, moreover, as a sentence on all r.s. $\mathbf{A}' = \langle A'; (R'_i)_{i \in I} \rangle$ of the same type substituting R_i by R'_i and a_j by a'_j.

6.6.2 **Definition:** The testable sentence "for all $a_1, \ldots, a_r$ holds $Y(a_1, \ldots, a_r)$" is a *consequence* of a system of axioms on a relational system $\langle A; (R_i)_{i \in I} \rangle$ iff the testable sentence is satisfied for each r.s. $\mathbf{A}' = \langle A'; (R'_i)_{i \in I} \rangle$ of the same type which satisfies the axioms.

In this definition we have not fixed the language in which the "axioms" are formulated. We remark that the axioms considered here can be formulated in higher predicate calculus. We omit this, because we think that it is intuitively clear how we have to interpret the "sentences" in our examples. For the reader acquainted with model theory we remark, moreover, that we have identified the symbols of language with the symbols of the model interpreting it.

6.6.3 **Definition:** Let S_1 and S_2 be systems of axioms. S_2 is *only technical* in $\{S_1, S_2\}$ iff each testable sentence which is a consequence of $\{S_1, S_2\}$ is a consequence of S_1.

Referring to the problem mentioned in the exposition of this section we must drop the infinitary relation L from $\langle A; <, L, \circ \rangle$ for our purposes as the concept of testability excludes r.s. with infinitary relations. This is no restriction, because it is not necessary to express continuity in the language of our relational system. We can reformulate the problem in the following way: given relational systems $\langle A; =, <, \circ \rangle$, are the axioms $S_2 = \{$(iii), (iv)$\}$ only technical in $\{$(i), (ii), (iii), (iv)$\}$?

This question was answered affirmatively for two special cases (ADAMS, FAGOT, R. ROBINSON (1965b)): additive operations and middling operations $\circ$.

6.6.4 **Definition:** Let $\mathbf{R}_+$ be $\langle \mathbb{R}; =, <, (1, 1, 0) \rangle$ and $\mathbf{R}_\phi$ be $\langle \mathbb{R}; =, <, (1/2, 1/2, 0) \rangle$. A r.s. $\mathbf{A} = \langle A; =, <, \circ \rangle$ is *representable* by $\mathbf{R}_+$ or $\mathbf{R}_\phi$ iff there exists a homomorphism of $\mathbf{A}$ into $\mathbf{R}_+$ or $\mathbf{R}_\phi$, respectively. For the definition of (1, 1, 0) and (1/2, 1/2, 0) see 5.2.19. $\mathbf{A}$ is *commensurable* iff it does not satisfy the testable sentence: $a_1 \circ a_1 > a_1$ and $a_2 \circ a_2 < a_2$ together imply $(a_1 \circ a_2) \circ (a_1 \circ a_2) \neq (a_1 \circ a_2)$ for all a_1, a_2.

If α is a positive irrational number the r.s. $\langle\{n-m\alpha : n, m \in \mathbb{N}\}; =, <, +\rangle$ is not commensurable.

6.6.5 **Theorem:** Let s be a testable sentence on r-systems $\langle A; =, <, \circ\rangle$ of type $k_1=k_2=2$, $k_3=3$.

a) If s is true in at least one nonvoid commensurable r.s. $\mathbf{A}_1$ for which the relation $\circ$ is an operation and which is representable by $\mathbf{R}_+$, then s is a consequence of the following axioms S_a:

(o) $<$ is an order relation and $\circ$ an operation,

(i) $\circ$ is commutative,

(ii) $\circ$ is increasing,

(iii) $\circ$ is associative,

together with those among the following axioms S_a' which are satisfied by $\mathbf{A}_1$:

(iv) $\circ$ is positive: $a \circ b > a$ for all $a, b \in A$

(iv′) $\circ$ is negative: $a \circ b < a$ for all $a, b \in A$

(v) $\circ$ is nonnegative: $a \circ b \geqq a$ for all $a, b \in A$

(v′) $\circ$ is nonpositive: $a \circ b \leqq a$ for all $a, b \in A$

(vi) $a = b$ for all $a, b \in A$.

b) If s is true in at least one r.s. $\mathbf{A}_1$ containing at least two elements for which $\circ$ is an operation and which is representable by $\mathbf{R}_\phi$ then s is a consequence of the axioms S_b:

(o), (i), (ii),

(vii) $\circ$ is reflexive

(viii) $\circ$ is bisymmetric.

Theorem 6.6.5 is stronger than the corresponding theorem given by Adams, Fagot, Robinson, even though we use the same method. They consider only testable sentences which are true in *each* r.s. $\langle A; =, <, \circ\rangle$ representable by $\mathbf{R}_+$, $\mathbf{R}_\phi$ and by the positive part of $\mathbf{R}_+$. An immediate consequence of 6.6.5 is

6.6.6 **Corollary:** Let S_a, S_b have the same meaning as in 6.6.5.

(a) If $\{S_a, S\}$ is a system of axioms which is satisfied by a commensurable subset of $\mathbb{R}$, containing at least one positive and one negative element, then S is only technical.

(a′) If the system $\{S_a, T, S\}$ of axioms —where T is one of the axioms (iv) or (iv′)— is satisfied by a nonvoid subset of $\mathbb{R}$, then S is only technical.

(b) If $\{S_b, S\}$ is a system of axioms which is satisfied by a subset of $\mathbb{R}$, containing at least two elements, then S is only technical.

Thus, if we add to S_a or S_b axioms such as continuity, connectedness or the archimedian axiom, these additional axioms will be only technical, because they are satisfied by the real numbers.

Remark: The axioms of additive operations (5.5.1) and middling operations (5.2.12) given in this book are not precisely the axioms S_a and S_b, respectively. In both cancellability and continuity is substituted for monotony. It is clear that continuity, cancellability and connectedness are here not only technical since together with the other axioms they imply the testable sentence of monotony. But we know by 6.6.6 that all testable sentences are consequences of S_a and S_b, respectively.

To prove theorem 6.6.5 we need a lemma known in the theory of convex polyedric cones and Linear Programming due to MOTZKIN (1936). We suppose that the reader is acquainted with linear algebra and elementary topology. For elements

$$x=\begin{pmatrix}x_1\\ \vdots \\ x_n\end{pmatrix}\in\mathbb{R}^n,\ y=\begin{pmatrix}y_1\\ \vdots \\ y_n\end{pmatrix}\in\mathbb{R}^n$$

we define

$$x^Ty:=\sum_{i=1}^{n} x_i y_i$$

as inner product, $|x|=(x^Tx)^{\frac{1}{2}}$ as Euclidean norm and $\overline{\mathbb{R}}^+=\{r\in\mathbb{R}, r\geqq 0\}$.

6.6.7 **Definition:** A subset M of $\mathbb{R}^n$ is a *convex cone* iff $0\in M$ and $x, x'\in M$, $\lambda, \lambda'\in\mathbb{R}^+$ implies $\lambda x+\lambda' x'\in M$. If M is a convex cone we define $M^*:=\{y\in\mathbb{R}^n : x^Ty\geqq 0 \text{ for all } x\in M\}$.

6.6.8 **Proposition:** If M is a convex cone then M^* is a convex cone, and for M closed, $M=(M^*)^*$.

Proof: It follows immediately from 6.6.7 that M^* is a closed convex cone and $M\subset(M^*)^*$. We have to show that for M closed $M\supset(M^*)^*$. For $M=\mathbb{R}^n$ this is obvious. Assume that $y\notin M$. Since M is closed there exists an element $x\in M$ such that the distance to y is minimal:

$$0<|x-y|\leqq|x'-y| \text{ for all } x'\in M.$$

For arbitrary $z \in M$ and $\beta \in \mathbb{R}^+$, we have $x + \beta z \in M$ and therefore

$$(x - y)^T (x - y) = |x - y|^2 \leqq |x + \beta z - y|^2$$
$$= (x - y)^T (x - y) + 2\beta (x - y)^T z + \beta^2 z^T z,$$

implying that for each $\beta > 0$, $(x - y)^T z \geqq -\beta 2^{-1} |z|^2$ and thus $(x - y)^T z \geqq 0$. Since $z \in M$ was arbitrary, $x - y \in M^*$. As $\alpha x \in M$ for $\alpha \in \mathbb{R}^+$ the function $\alpha \to |\alpha x - y|$ on $\mathbb{R}^+$ is minimal at $\alpha = 1$ and the derivation vanishes at $\alpha = 1$: $(x - y)^T x = 0$. Since $|x - y| > 0$ it follows that $(x - y)^T y = (x - y)^T (y - x) + (x - y)^T x = -|x - y|^2 < 0$. As $x - y \in M^*$, $y \notin (M^*)^*$.

6.6.9 **Proposition:** For $a_i \in \mathbb{R}^n$ $(i = 1, \dots, l)$, the convex cone M generated by $\{a_i : i = 1, \dots, l\}$, defined as

$$M = \left\{ \sum_{i=1}^{l} \lambda_i a_i : \quad \lambda_i \geqq 0 \right\},$$

is closed.

Proof: The proposition is obvious for $l = 1$. We assume by induction that it holds for a fixed $l - 1$ $(l \geqq 2)$. As $-a_i \in M$ for all i implies that M is a linear space and thus closed, we assume that $-a_1 \notin M$. Let M' be the convex cone generated by $\{a_i : i = 2, \dots, l\}$ which is closed by assumption, and let x be a boundary point of M. Then there exist sequences $\{\lambda_j\} \subset \overline{\mathbb{R}}^+$ and $\{b_j\} \subset M'$ such that

$\lim (\lambda_j a_1 + b_j) = x$ and

(i) $\lim \lambda_j = \lambda \in \mathbb{R}^+$ or

(ii) $\lim \lambda_j = +\infty$.

For (i), $\{b_j\}$ converges to an element $b \in M'$ and thus $x = \lambda a_1 + b \in M$. For (ii), $\{\lambda_j^{-1} b_j\}$ converges to $-a_1$ which implies that $-a_1 \in M' \subset M$ contradicting to the assumption that $-a_1 \notin M$.

6.6.10 **Proposition:** (FENCHEL-TUCKER) Let L be a linear subspace of $\mathbb{R}^n$, $L^\perp$ the linear space orthogonal to L. Then we get for each k, $0 \leqq k \leqq n$, that

(i) $\quad M := L \cap (\overline{\mathbb{R}}^+)^n \subset \{x \in \mathbb{R}^n : x_1 = x_2 = \dots = x_k = 0\} =: E_{k,n}$

iff there exists an $y \in L^\perp$ such that

(ii) $\quad -y \in (\overline{\mathbb{R}}^+)^n$ and $y_1 < 0, \dots, y_k < 0$.

Proof: a) If a^i $(i = 1, \dots, l)$ is a base for $L^\perp$, the convex cone $N := \{x + y : y \in L^\perp, x \in (\overline{\mathbb{R}}^+)^n\}$ is generated by $a^i, -a^i$ $(i = 1, \dots, l)$ and the unit vectors of $\mathbb{R}^n$ and hence closed (6.6.9). It is easy to verify that $N^* = M$ and by 6.6.8 $N = (N^*)^* = M^*$. If (i) is satisfied then $N = M^* \supset E^*_{k,n} = \{x \in \mathbb{R}^n : x_{k+1} = \dots = x_n = 0\}$. Hence N contains the element $z : z_1 = \dots = z_k = -1$, $z_{k+1} = \dots = z_n = 0$; by definition of N, $z = y + x$ where $y \in L^\perp$, $x \in (\overline{\mathbb{R}}^+)^n$. $-y = x - z \in (\overline{\mathbb{R}}^+)^n$ and $y_1 < 0, \dots, y_k < 0$.

b) We assume that $y \in L^\perp$ satisfies (ii) and $x \in M$. $x \in L$ implies $x^T y = 0$. As $x_i \geqq 0$ $(i = 1, \ldots, n)$, $y_i \leqq 0$ $(i = 1, \ldots, n)$ and $y_1 < 0, \ldots, y_k < 0$, we get $x_1 = \ldots = x_k = 0$.

For $x \in \mathbb{R}^n$ we define: $x \geqq 0$ iff $x \in (\overline{\mathbb{R}}^+)^n$, $x \geq 0$ iff $x \geqq 0$ and $x \neq 0$, $x > 0$ iff each component of x is positive.

6.6.11 **Lemma:** (MOTZKIN (1936)). Let G be a real (p, n)-matrix, $p \geqq 1$, H a real (q, n)-matrix and denote by G^T and H^T the transposed matrix of G and H, respectively. Then there exists an $x \in \mathbb{R}^n$ such that

(i) $Gx > 0$ and $Hx \geqq 0$

iff there exists no pair $y \in \mathbb{R}^p$, $z \in \mathbb{R}^q$ such that

(ii) $G^T y + H^T z = 0$ and $y \geq 0$, $z \geqq 0$.

Proof: The unsolvability of (ii) is equivalent to the inclusion

(*) $L \cap (\overline{\mathbb{R}}^+)^{p+q} \subseteq E_{p,p+q}$

where $E_{p,p+q}$ is defined in 6.6.10 and

$$L = \left\{ \begin{pmatrix} y \\ z \end{pmatrix} \in \mathbb{R}^{p+q} : G^T y + H^T z = 0 \right\}.$$

L consists of those vectors $\binom{y}{z}$ which are orthogonal to each row-vector of the $(n, p+q)$-matrix (G^T, H^T). Hence $L^\perp$ is the space generated by the row-vectors of this matrix:

$$L^\perp = \left\{ \begin{pmatrix} G \\ H \end{pmatrix} x : x \in \mathbb{R}^n \right\}.$$

By 6.6.10 the inclusion (*) is equivalent to the existence of an element $y \in L^\perp$ such that all components of y are nonpositive and the p first components are negative. This means that there is an element $x \in \mathbb{R}^n$ such that $Gx < 0$ and $Hx \leqq 0$. The element $-x$ is a solution of (i).

6.6.12 **Corollary:** Let G, H be matrices as in 6.6.11 and F a (r, n)-matrix. There exists an element $x \in \mathbb{R}^n$ such that

$$Gx > 0,\ Fx \geqq 0,\ Hx = 0$$

iff there is no triple $y \in \mathbb{R}^p$, $z \in \mathbb{R}^q$, $u \in \mathbb{R}^r$ such that

$$G^T y + F^T z + H^T u = 0 \text{ and } y \geq 0,\ z \geqq 0.$$

Proof: Apply 6.6.11 for the matrix $\begin{pmatrix} F \\ H \\ -H \end{pmatrix}$ instead of H.

6.6.13 **Corollary:** There exists an element $x \in \mathbb{R}^n$ such that

$$Gx>0,\ Hx=0,\ x>0$$

iff there are no $y \in \mathbb{R}^p$, $z \in \mathbb{R}^q$ such that

$$G^T y + H^T z \leq 0 \text{ and } y \geqq 0 \text{ or}$$

$$G^T y + H^T z \leqq 0 \text{ and } y \geq 0.$$

There exists an element $x \in \mathbb{R}^n$ such that

$$Gx>0,\ Hx=0 \text{ and } x \geqq 0$$

iff $G^T y + H^T z \leqq 0$, $y \geq 0$ is not solvable.

Proof: Apply 6.6.11 substituting $\binom{G}{I}$ for G and 6.6.12 substituting I for F where I is the unit (n, n)-matrix.

6.6.14 **Corollary:** If the coefficients of the matrices G, H, F are rational numbers, then $\mathbb{G}$ can be substituted for $\mathbb{R}$ in 6.6.11 – 13, where $\mathbb{G}$ denotes the set of integers.

Proof: It suffices to show that systems 6.6.11 (i) and (ii) which can be solved by real-valued vectors x, y, z, can also be solved by integer-valued vectors. Let x^0 be a real vector such that $Gx^0 > 0$, $Hx^0 \geqq 0$. Adding to G the l rows i of H for which

$$\sum_{j=1}^{n} h_{ij} x_j > 0$$

we get a $(p+l, n)$-matrix G' and a $(q-l, n)$-matrix H' with rational coefficients such that $G'x^0 > 0$, $H'x^0 = 0$. The linear space $L := \{x \in \mathbb{R}^n : Hx = 0\}$ can be generated by vectors the components of which are rational numbers. Thus the elements $x \in \mathbb{R}^n$ with rational components are dense in L. As the map $x \to G'x$ is continuous, $G'x > 0$ for all elements x of a neighborhood of x^0. But each neighborhood of x^0 contains, as stated above, elements $x \in L$ with rational components. Thus there exists $x \in \mathbb{R}^n$ such that $G'x > 0$, $H'x = 0$, and therefore $Gx > 0$, $Hx \geqq 0$, and that the components x_i $(i = 1, \ldots, n)$ of x are rational numbers. Multiplying the numbers x_i by their common denominator we obtain an integer-valued solution. By the same method it can be proved that (ii) can be solved by integer-valued elements y, z if there is a real-valued solution.

Proof of 6.6.5: Let $\mathbf{A}_1 = \langle A_1; =, <, \circ \rangle$ and $\mathbf{A}_2 = \langle A_2; =, <, \circ \rangle$ be r.s. with order $<$ and binary relation $\circ$, $A_1 \neq \emptyset$, $A_1 \cap A_2 = \emptyset$. (The last condition ensures that no ambiguity arises using the same symbols for the relations in both systems. If $A_1 \cap A_2 \neq \emptyset$ we substitute for $\mathbf{A}_1$ a suitable isomorphic r.s.). We assume that there is a testable sentence s which is true in $\mathbf{A}_1$ but not in $\mathbf{A}_2$, say "$Y(a_1, \ldots, a_r)$ holds for all $a_1, \ldots, a_r$" where Y is given by

$$(X_{11} \cup X_{12} \cup \ldots \cup X_{1l_1}) \cap (X_{12} \cup X_{22} \cup \ldots \cup X_{2l_2}) \cap \ldots$$
$$\cap (X_{m1} \cup X_{m2} \cup \ldots \cup X_{ml_m}), \quad X_{ij} \in \mathscr{X}.$$

There are elements $a_1, \ldots, a_r \in A_2$ satisfying $\overline{Y}(a_1, \ldots, a_r)$, but $\overline{Y}(a'_1, \ldots, a'_r)$ is false for arbitrary, not necessarily different, elements $a'_i \in A_1$. It follows that there exist different elements $a_1, \ldots, a_l \in A_2$, $l \leqq r$, satisfying $X(a_1, \ldots, a_l) := \overline{X}_{i1} \cap \overline{X}_{i2} \cap \ldots \cap \overline{X}_{il_i}$ but that $X(a'_1, \ldots, a'_l)$ is false for all $a'_1, \ldots, a'_l \in A_1$. The system $\mathscr{X}$ consists of sentences of the types $a \circ b = c$, $a \circ b \neq c$, $a > b$, $a \ngtr b$, $a = b$, $a \neq b$. Since $a \neq b$ is equivalent to $a > b$ or $b > a$, and $a \ngtr b$ is equivalent to $a = b$ or $b > a$, and $a \neq b \circ c$ is equivalent to $d = b \circ c$ and $a \neq d$, we obtain a system of sentences

6.6.15 $a_{k1} > a_{k2} \qquad (k = 1, \ldots, p), p \geqq 0$, and
$a_{k1} = a_{k2} \qquad (k = p+1, \ldots, p_1 + p), p_1 \geqq 0$, and
$a_{k1} = a_{k2} \circ a_{k3} \; (k = p + p_1 + 1, \ldots, p + q), p + q > 0$,

where each a_{ki} is a well determined element of the set $\{a_1, \ldots, a_l\} \in A_2$, and which is true but which will be false if we substitute arbitrary, not necessarily different elements $a'_i \in A_1$ for a_i, $i = 1, \ldots, l$.

Proof of part a): Assume that $\mathbf{A}_2$ satisfies the axioms S_a and that the commensurable r.s. $\mathbf{A}_1$ is represented by $\mathbf{R}_+$, m being the representing map.

We derive from 6.6.15 the incidence matrices G', G'', H', H'' with the following rational coefficients:

$k = 1, \ldots, p; \; j = 1, \ldots, l$:

$$g'_{kj} = \begin{cases} 1 \text{ for } a_{k1} = a_j \\ 0 \text{ elsewhere} \end{cases}, \quad g''_{kj} = \begin{cases} 1 \text{ for } a_{k2} = a_j \\ 0 \text{ elsewhere} \end{cases};$$

$k = 1, \ldots, q; \; j = 1, \ldots, l$:

$$h'_{kj} = \begin{cases} 1 \text{ for } a_{p+k,1} = a_j \\ 0 \text{ elsewhere} \end{cases}, \quad h''_{kj} = \begin{cases} 2 \text{ for } a_{p+k,2} = a_{p+k,3} = a_j \\ 1 \text{ for } a_{p+k,2} = a_j \text{ or } a_{p+k,3} = a_j; \\ 0 \text{ elsewhere} \end{cases}$$

in other words: g'_{kj} counts the occurrence of a_j on the left side, g''_{kj} on the right side of the kth inequality. Since 6.6.15 is false for arbitrary $a'_1, \ldots, a'_l \in A_1$, the system

$$\text{6.6.16} \quad \begin{cases} Gx > 0 \text{ and } Hx = 0 & \text{for } p > 0, \\ \phantom{Gx > 0 \text{ and }} Hx = 0 & \text{for } p = 0 \end{cases}$$

cannot be solved by an element $x \in (m(A_1))^l$ where $G = G' - G''$, $H = H' - H''$.

We define by induction: $1b := b$, $nb := b \circ (n-1)b$ for $n \in \mathbb{N}$, $b \in A_2$ and agree that $(0b) \circ a = a$; $\Omega\{b_1\} := b_1$ and

$$\Omega\{b_i : i = 1, \ldots, k\} = \Omega\{b_i : i = 1, \ldots, k-1\} \circ b_k.$$

Let $y \in \mathbb{R}^p$, $z \in \mathbb{R}^q$ be integervalued vectors such that $y \geqq 0$ and $|y| + |z| > 0$. As $\circ$ is monotone it follows from 6.6.15 that

6.6.17 $$\begin{cases} f_1(y,z) > f_2(y,z) & \text{for } y \geq 0, \\ f_1(y,z) = f_2(y,z) & \text{for } y = 0, \text{ where} \end{cases}$$

$$\begin{aligned} f_1(y,z) := \ & \Omega\{y_k a_{k1} : k = 1, \ldots, p_1\} \\ & \circ\, \Omega\{z_k a_{p+k,1} : k = 1, \ldots, q \text{ and } z_k > 0\} \\ & \circ\, \Omega\{-z_k a_{p+k,2} : k = 1, \ldots, p_1 \text{ and } z_k < 0\} \\ & \circ\, \Omega\{-z_k (a_{p+k,2} \circ a_{p+k,3}) : k = p_1 + 1, \ldots, q \text{ and } z_k < 0\}; \\ f_2(y,z) := \ & \Omega\{y_k a_{k2} : k = 1, \ldots, p\} \\ & \circ\, \Omega\{z_k a_{p+k,2} : k = 1, \ldots, p_1 \text{ and } z_k > 0\} \\ & \circ\, \Omega\{z_k (a_{p+k,2} \circ a_{p+k,3}) : k = p_1 + 1, \ldots, q \text{ and } z_k > 0\} \\ & \circ\, \Omega\{-z_k a_{p+k,1} : k = 1, \ldots, q \text{ and } z_k < 0\}. \end{aligned}$$

The formalism defining f_1 can be described intuitively in the following way: We change the sides of the kth equation in 6.6.15 for all k with $z_k < 0$. Then we "add" y_1 times the left side of the first inequality and y_2 times the left side of the second inequality and so on, and $|z_1|$ times the left side of the first equality and $|z_2|$ times the left side of the second equality and so on.

As $\circ$ is commutative and associative it follows from the definition of the matrices G', G'', H', H'' that

$$f_1(y,z) = \Omega\{u_i a_i : i = 1, \ldots, l\}, \quad f_2(y,z) = \Omega\{v_i a_i : i = 1, \ldots, l\}$$

where

6.6.18 $$\begin{cases} u_i(y,z) := \sum_{k=1}^{p} y_k g'_{ki} + \sum_{\substack{k=1 \\ z_k > 0}}^{q} z_k h'_{ki} - \sum_{\substack{k=1 \\ z_k < 0}}^{q} z_k h''_{ki} \quad \text{and} \\ v_i(y,z) := \sum_{k=1}^{p} y_k g''_{ki} + \sum_{\substack{k=1 \\ z_k > 0}}^{q} z_k h''_{ki} - \sum_{\substack{k=1 \\ z_k < 0}}^{q} z_k h'_{ki} \\ u(y,z) - v(y,z) = (G' - G'')^T y + (H' - H'')^T z = G^T y + H^T z. \end{cases}$$

As $|y| + |z| > 0$ we obtain $u \geq 0$ and $v \geq 0$. We have to consider the following cases:

I) $\mathbf{A}_1$ satisfies no axiom of the system S'_a. Then the set $m(A_1)$ contains at least one positive and at least one negative number. Moreover, as $\mathbf{A}_1$ is commensurable there exist a_0 and $b_0 \in A_1$ such that $m(a_0) = -m(b_0) > 0$. Using the map

$$m' : a \to \frac{1}{m(a_0)} m(a)$$

instead of m we may assume that $m(A_1) \supset \mathbb{G}$, the set of integers. Thus there is no integervalued vector $x \in \mathbb{R}^l$ solving the system 6.6.16. As $Hx = 0$ is solvable by $x = 0 \in m(A_1)^l$, we obtain $p > 0$. It follows from 6.6.14 and 6.6.12 that there exist $y \in \mathbb{G}^p$ and $z \in \mathbb{G}^q$ such that

$$(1)\ G^T y + H^T z = 0 \quad \text{and} \quad (2)\ y \geq 0.$$

The equations (1) and 6.6.18 imply that $u_i(y, z) = v_i(y, z)$ for $i = 1, \ldots, l$ and thus $f_1(y, z) = f_2(y, z)$. 6.6.17 and (2) together imply $f_1(y, z) > f_2(y, z)$. Thus the assumption that s is not true in $\mathbf{A}_2$ leads to a contradiction. As $\mathbf{A}_2$ was an arbitrary r.s. satisfying S_a, s is a consequence of S_a.

II) $\mathbf{A}_1$ satisfies at least one of the axioms of S'_a. We assume that $\mathbf{A}_2$ satisfies the same axioms of S'_a as $\mathbf{A}_1$. If $\mathbf{A}_1$ and $\mathbf{A}_2$ satisfy (vi) then $\mathbf{A}_1$ and $\mathbf{A}_2$ are isomorphic and nothing is to prove.

$\mathbf{A}_1$ and $\mathbf{A}_2$ satisfy (iv): Then there is $a_0 \in A_1$ with $m(a_0) > 0$. In the same reasoning as in I) we may assume that $\mathbb{N} \subset m(A_1)$. Thus there is no $x \in \mathbb{G}^l$, $x > 0$, solving 6.6.16. It follows from 6.6.14 and 6.6.13 that there exist $y \in \mathbb{G}^p$ and $z \in \mathbb{G}^q$ such that

(α) $G^T y + H^T z \leq 0$ and $y \geqq 0$ or

(β) $G^T y + H^T z \leqq 0$ and $y \geq 0$ for $p > 0$,

(γ) $H^T z \leq 0$ for $p = 0$.

Each of the first inequalities of (α), (β) and (γ) implies $u(y, z) \leqq v(y, z)$ because of 6.6.18; for (α) and (γ), moreover, $u(y, z) \leq v(y, z)$. We thus obtain by (iv) and the monotony

$$(*) \quad \begin{cases} f_1(y, z) < f_2(y, z) \text{ for } (\alpha) \text{ and } (\gamma) \text{ and} \\ f_1(y, z) \leqq f_2(y, z) \text{ for } (\beta). \end{cases}$$

As $y \geq 0$ for (β), 6.6.17 and (*) contradict each other. Hence s is a consequence of S_a and (iv).

$\mathbf{A}_1$ and $\mathbf{A}_2$ satisfy (v) but not (vi) and (iv): There exist $a_0, b_0 \in A_1$ such that $m(b_0) = 0 < m(a_0)$. As in case I) we can assume that $\mathbb{N} \cup \{0\} \subseteq m(A_1)$. Hence there is no $x \in \mathbb{G}^l$, $x \geqq 0$, solving 6.6.16. $p = 0$ is impossible in this case because $H0 = 0$ and $0 \in m(A_1)^l$. It follows from 6.6.14 and 6.6.13 that there exist $y \in \mathbb{G}^p$ and $z \in \mathbb{G}^q$ such that

$$(1)\ G^T y + H^T z \leq 0 \quad \text{and} \quad (2)\ y \geq 0.$$

(1), monotony, 6.6.18 and (v) imply together that $f_1(y, z) \leqq f_2(y, z)$, but (2) and 6.6.17 that $f_1(y, z) > f_2(y, z)$. By this contradiction s is a consequence of S_a and (v).

$\mathbf{A}_1$ and $\mathbf{A}_2$ satisfy (iv′) or (v′): If we consider $\mathbf{A}_1$, $\mathbf{A}_2$ and s in the inverse order these cases are reduced to the earlier ones.

Proof of part b): Assume that $\mathbf{A}_1$ and $\mathbf{A}_2$ satisfy the axioms S_b and that $\mathbf{A}_1$ is represented by $\mathbf{R}_\Phi$, m being the representing map. As $a \circ a = a$ for all a we can reduce 6.6.15 to the form

$$6.6.19 \quad \begin{cases} a_{k1} \circ a_{k2} > a_{k3} \circ a_{k4} \ (k = 1, \ldots, p), p > 0, \\ a_{k1} \circ a_{k2} = a_{k3} \circ a_{k4} \ (k = p + 1, \ldots, p + q) \end{cases}$$

where each a_{ki} is a determined element of $\{a_1, \ldots, a_l\}$. ($p = 0$ is impossible because the equations would be satisfied by $a_{k1} = a_{k2} = a_{k3} = a_{k4} = a$ ($k = p + 1, \ldots, q$) for an arbitrary $a \in A_1$). As in part a) we derive incidence matrices from 6.6.19 with the following rational coefficients:

$k = 1, \ldots, p; j = 1, \ldots, l$:

$$g'_{kj} = \begin{cases} 1 & \text{for } a_{k1} = a_{k2} = a_j, \\ 1/2 & \text{for } a_{k1} = a_j \text{ or } a_{k2} = a_j, \\ 0 & \text{elsewhere,} \end{cases}$$

$$g''_{kj} = \begin{cases} 1 & \text{for } a_{k3} = a_{k4} = a_j, \\ 1/2 & \text{for } a_{k3} = a_j \text{ or } a_{k4} = a_j, \\ 0 & \text{elsewhere,} \end{cases}$$

and for $k = 1, \ldots, q; j = 1, \ldots, l$:

$$h'_{kj} = \begin{cases} 1 & \text{for } a_{p+k,1} = a_{p+k,2} = a_j, \\ 1/2 & \text{for } a_{p+k,1} = a_j \text{ or } a_{p+k,2} = a_j, \\ 0 & \text{elsewhere,} \end{cases}$$

$$h''_{kj} = \begin{cases} 1 & \text{for } a_{p+k,3} = a_{p+k,4} = a_j, \\ 1/2 & \text{for } a_{p+k,3} = a_j \text{ or } a_{p+k,4} = a_j, \\ 0 & \text{elsewhere.} \end{cases}$$

$$G: = G' - G'', H: = H' - H''.$$

Since there are no elements $a'_1, \ldots, a'_l \in A_1$, not necessarily different, such that 6.6.19 is true if we substitute a'_i for a_i, there is no $x \in m(A_1)^l$ solving

6.6.20 $Gx > 0, Hx = 0$.

As A_1 contains at least two elements we can assume, applying a suitable positive linear transformation on m, that $\{1, -1\} \subset m(A_1)$ and thus $D: = \{n\, 2^{-m}: m, n \in \mathbb{G}, |n| \leqq 2^m\} \subset m(A_1)$. If there were an integervalued solution x^0 of 6.6.20 then $x = 2^{-m}x^0$ with $2^m \geqq \text{Max}\,\{|x_i^0| : i = 1, \ldots, l\}$ would solve 6.6.20 and $x \in m(A_1)^l$. It follows from 6.6.12 and 6.6.14 that there are $y \in \mathbb{G}^p$ and $z \in \mathbb{G}^q$ such that

6.6.21 1) $G^T y + H^T z = 0$ and 2) $y \geq 0$.

We define a "mean" operation Δ_n on the 2^n-tuples of elements of A_2 by induction: $\Delta_0(b) = b$, and

6.6.22 $\Delta_n(b_1, \ldots, b_{2^n}) = \Delta_{n-1}(b_1 \circ b_2, b_3 \circ b_4, \ldots, b_{2^n-1} \circ b_{2^n})$ for $n \in \mathbb{N}$.

It is easy to prove by induction, using commutativity and bisymmetry, that

6.6.23 Δ_n is invariant under all permutations of its arguments

and, using monotony, that

6.6.24 $\Delta_n(b_1, \ldots, b_{2^n}) > \Delta_n(b'_1, \ldots, b'_{2^n})$ if $b_i \geqq b'_i$ for all i and $b_i > b'_i$ for at least one i, $1 \leqq i \leqq 2^n$.

Let y and z be integervalued vectors solving 6.6.21, and let

$$Y_k: = \sum_{j=1}^{k} y_j,\ Z_k: = \sum_{j=1}^{k} |z_j|.$$

Let z_{q+1} and n be the smallest nonnegative integers such that $Y_p + Z_q + z_{q+1} = 2^n$. We consider the following 2^n-tuples $b, c, b', c' \in A_1^{2^n}$:

$$\left.\begin{array}{l} b_i = a_{k1},\ c_i = a_{k2} \\ b_i' = a_{k3},\ c_i' = a_{k4} \end{array}\right\} \text{ for } i \in (Y_{k-1}, Y_k],\ k = 1, \ldots, p,$$

$$\left.\begin{array}{l} b_i = a_{p+k,1},\ c_i = a_{p+k,2} \\ b_i' = a_{p+k,3},\ c_i' = a_{p+k,4} \end{array}\right\} \begin{array}{l} \text{for } i \in (Y_p + Z_{k-1}, Y_p + Z_k] \text{ and } z_k > 0, \\ \qquad k = 1, \ldots, q, \end{array}$$

$$\left.\begin{array}{l} b_i = a_{p+k,3},\ c_i = a_{p+k,4} \\ b_i' = a_{p+k,1},\ c_i' = a_{p+k,2} \end{array}\right\} \begin{array}{l} \text{for } i \in (Y_p + Z_{k-1}, Y_p + Z_k] \text{ and } z_k < 0, \\ \qquad k = 1, \ldots, q, \end{array}$$

$b_i = b_i' = c_i = c_i' = a_{l+1}$ for $i \in (Y_p + Z_q, 2^n]$ where a_{l+1} is an arbitrary element of A_2 different from $a_1, \ldots, a_l$. 6.6.19 implies that $b_i \circ c_i > b_i' \circ c_i'$ for $i = 1, \ldots, Y_p$ and $b_i \circ c_i = b_i' \circ c_i'$ for $i = Y_p + 1, \ldots, 2^n$. Thus we obtain from $y \geq 0$, 6.6.22 and 6.6.24

6.6.25 $$\Delta_{n+1}(b, c) = \Delta_n(\{b_i \circ c_i : i = 1, \ldots, 2^n\}) > \Delta_n(\{b_i' \circ c_i' : i = 1, \ldots, 2^n\}) = \Delta_{n+1}(b', c').$$

On the other hand, the element a_j occurs in the 2^{n+1}-tuple (b, c) exactly $2\, u_j(y, z)$ times, in (b', c') $2\, v_j(y, z)$ times $(j = 1, \ldots, l)$, and a_{l+1} occurs in both exactly z_{q+1} times. u_j and v_j are given by 6.6.18 where the values of g', h', g'', h'' on the right side are given by the incidence matrix derived from 6.6.19. Therefore 6.6.18 and 6.6.21 imply that (b', c') is a permutation of (b, c) and thus $\Delta_{n+1}(b, c) = \Delta_{n+1}(b', c')$, contradicting 6.6.25. As $\mathbf{A}_2$ was an arbitrary r.s. satisfying S_b, s is a consequence of S_b.

7. Psychophysical Applications of Interval Scales Based on Operations

7.1 Additive Operations

The theory of scaling originated in the field where measurement was first applied – in physics. Almost all physical properties admit an additive operation, the only outstanding exception being temperature. Obvious examples of additive properties are length and mass. In the case of mass, for example, the order relation is established by comparing two masses by a balance with equal arms. Addition is performed by putting the masses to be added in the same scale of the balance. A less obvious example of an additive physical property is intensity of lighting (CAMPBELL and DADDING, 1922).

Due to the overwhelming importance of additive properties in physics, the theory of measurement was restricted to this area in its earlier stages. It was started by v. HELMHOLTZ (1887) and continued at a more penetrating mathematical level by HÖLDER (1901). The further development of theory and practice was strongly influenced by CAMPBELL (1920, 1928), who insisted that genuine measurement is possible only for additive properties. How deeprooted this heresy was can be seen from the conclusions adopted by the "Committee Appointed to Consider and Report upon the Possibility of Quantitative Estimates of Sensory Events" (1938) which even denied the justification of the thermodynamic definition of temperature. CAMPBELL was one of the members of this committee.

7.2 Middling Operations

Contrary to physics, the properties dealt with in the behavioral sciences are hardly ever additive. The increasing use of quantitative methods in these sciences called for a methodological foundation of measurement on a more general basis than that of additivity. The theory developed in chapter 6 includes additive properties as well as properties with middling operations as special cases.

One of the first measurement procedures applied in psychophysics and psychology is the so-called *method of bisection*. The basic experiment is the following: The subject is asked to determine a manifestation $a|b$ which is midway between two given manifestations a and b. The somewhat diverging results of different experiments are averaged and this average is taken as an estimate of $a|b$.

As was already mentioned in section 2.5.1, the natural way of averaging would be to take the median. Nevertheless, in cases where an underlying physical scale is available, it is usual to take the arithmetic or geometric mean of the physical values and to take as $a|b$ the manifestation corresponding to the physical value thus obtained.

This procedure is unjustified except for special psychophysical laws, as for the subjective properties the physical scale values are only an ordinal scale. For this reason, STEVENS (1955) uses an iterative procedure.

The reader interested in further practical details is referred to TORGERSON (1958, p. 117–131). The earliest experiments with bisection were reported by PLATEAU (1872), LORENZ (1890), MÜNSTERBERG (1892), TITCHENER (1905), PRATT (1923), JUDD (1933) for saturation of yellow colors, STEVENS and VOLKMANN (1940) for pitch, GARNER (1954) for subjective loudness. In these experiments, instead of bisection also "equisection" is used. In equisection experiments, two fixed manifestations are given and the subject is asked to interpolate a given number n of manifestations ($n=1$ corresponding to bisection) such that all distances between neighboring manifestations are equal. In equisection experiments the subject can restrict himself to the comparison of adjacent intervals too. Occasionally, experiments are performed requiring the subject to compare distant intervals (MÜNSTERBERG).

The question as to whether the middling axioms are fulfilled will be discussed for two properties: pitch and subjective loudness. Regrettably, the information is not very accurate as the experiments were performed without being guided by any theory.

That $a|b$ is uniquely determined by a and b is true in the following sense: Though the estimates vary to some extent from subject to subject, the average over a great number of subjects is fairly stable in repeated experiments. There seems to be a lack of experiments to show whether $a|b$ is independent of other properties of the objects in question. If, for example, the experiments are concerned with pitch: is the pitch of $a|b$ influenced by qualities of the tones a and b other than pitch (e.g., loudness and timbre).

Cancellation: In the case of pitch, the cancellation axiom seems a reasonable idealization of reality as long as other properties of the tones are kept constant. If b' and b'' are tones of identical pitch but different loudness and/or timbre, it becomes simply a question of fact whether $a|b'$ and $a|b''$ are of equal pitch or not.

Continuity: Even if it is not testable, the continuity axiom seems a reasonable idealization of reality for subjective loudness: If one of the given degrees of loudness is changed by a small amount, the loudness of the medium tone will also change by a small amount only. This is not evident a priori for pitch: one could expect that by a small change of pitch of one of the original tones the interval ab might become such that it can be divided into two musical intervals (octave, quint). Then, the subject could tend to divide the interval into the two musical intervals instead of two equal intervals. For this reason, in the experiments performed by STEVENS and VOLKMANN (1940, p. 334), only intervals were used which cannot be divided into two musical intervals.

Before entering into the discussion of bisymmetry, we will deal with the last two axioms:

Reflexivity: Is obviously fulfilled.

Commutativity: If $a|b$ denotes the manifestation obtained by a bisection experiment where a is presented as the first and b as the second stimulus, then one cannot expect a priori that $a|b=b|a$. For subjective loudness, experiments of STEVENS (1957, p. 159ff.), have shown that $a|b$ is louder than $b|a$, if b is louder than a. As regards pitch, the situation is not so clear (STEVENS, 1957, p. 160ff.). For some persons, especially those possessing absolute power of audition, $a|b=b|a$, whereas for others the two pitches disagree. In principle, commutativity can be enforced if the tones a and b are presented several times in changing sequence. But even if commutativity would not hold, this is no obstacle against the construction of an interval scale. The linear operation, corresponding to the operation "$\circ$", is, in this case, $pm(a)+qm(b)$ with $p+q=1$, and $p \neq q$.

Bisymmetry: As bisection is reflexive, the following weaker relationship is necessary and sufficient for bisymmetry (corollary 5.4.2):

7.2.1 $(a|b) \mid c = (a|c) \mid (b|c)$.

Inserting $a|b$ for c we obtain as a necessary (but not sufficient) condition for bisymmetry:

7.2.2 $a|b = [a \mid (a|b)] \mid [b \mid (a|b)]$.

For pitch, 7.2.2 is probably fulfilled. In one of the experiments performed by STEVENS and VOLKMANN (1940), the subject had to divide a given interval into four intervals of given length. First, the interval from a to b was bisected and then, each of the intervals from a to $a|b$ and from $a|b$ to b were bisected once more. Finally, the subject checked whether the four intervals were of equal length. As the operation "|" is commutative for pitch, the intervals from $a \mid (a|b)$, to $a|b$ and from $a|b$ to $(a|b) \mid b$ would be of different length if 7.2.2 were not fulfilled. Thus the task of dividing a given interval into four intervals of equal length would be insoluble in this case. As no such contradiction occurred, this can be taken as an indirect confirmation of bisymmetry.

As far as subjective loudness is concerned, experiments performed by GAGE (1934) have shown that $[a \mid (a|b)] \mid [(a|b) \mid b]$ is louder than $a|b$. This is, however, no contradiction to bisymmetry. As $a|b$ is louder than $b|a$ if b is louder than a, we have $(a|b) \mid b$ louder than $b \mid (a|b)$. Hence this result is to be expected from 7.2.2. In later experiments, NEWMAN, VOLKMANN and STEVENS (1937) succeeded in diminishing the divergence between $[a \mid (a|b)] \mid [(a|b) \mid b]$ and $a|b$ by changing the sequence repeatedly. Finally, in experiments performed by GARNER (1954), the subject had to divide a given interval into four equal intervals. As this task could be solved without contradiction, this is an indirect confirmation of bisymmetry, as was discussed in detail for pitch.

In practice, other methods germane to bisection are used together with or instead of bisection itself. In the following we will give a brief survey of such methods which are substitute methods from a theoretical point of view. The reader interested in more detail is referred to TORGERSON (1958, p. 61–116). One argument in favor of other methods is that bisection is not applicable if only a few manifestations are available. Even if a connected set of manifestations is available, other methods are often applied. We have already mentioned a) equisection and b) comparison of distant intervals. Though it would be wholly sufficient for the determination of a scale if the subjects were able to give an order of intervals according to length fulfilling the distance axioms (section 9.1), in many experiments the subjects are faced with a more difficult task:

They are required to give direct numerical estimates of the scale values of a given manifestation, where the scale is fixed, for example, by specifying the scale values of the largest and the smallest of the given manifestations. The scales thus obtained are called category rating scales. Another method is to require direct numerical estimates of the ratios of the manifestations. All these "estimation" methods can also be inverted to so-called "production" methods: In these the subject is required to produce a stimulus with a manifestation corresponding to a given numerical value. These direct methods were first applied by STEVENS and GALANTER (1957) for scaling subjective length, duration, heaviness, loudness, etc. and have since been applied to a great variety of properties, including the taste value of fruits (BJÖRKMANN, 1959), the aesthetic value of drawings (EKMAN and KÜNNAPAS 1962a) and handwriting (EKMAN and KÜNNAPAS 1962b) and the moral judgement of actions (EKMAN 1962).

A comprehensive examination of scales obtained by such direct methods is still missing. J. C. STEVENS (1958) has shown that so-called category rating scales for loudness are heavily dependent on which manifestations are used in the experiments. In magnitude estimation such an influence is not present according to J. C. STEVENS.

7.3 Endomorphisms

The endomorphism (see section 6.3) most widely used is "halving". It is based on experiments in which the subject is asked to assign to a given manifestation a (say a pitch) the manifestation which is half the given one. To make the performance of this task easier, often a second manifestation near the lower bound of A (e.g. a very deep tone) is given for reference.

We remark that – contrary to common opinion – halving alone is not sufficient to establish a scale. In a number of experiments, S. S. STEVENS tried to apply the method of halving to obtain a scale of subjective magnitudes. Starting from a given manifestation a_1 one obtains a sequence $(a_n)_{n=1,2,\ldots}$ with $a_{n+1}=f(a_n)$. If this endomorphism is really a halving, we have

$$m(a_n)=\frac{m(a_1)}{2^{n-1}}$$

(see 6.3.8). We obtain, however, only scale values for manifestations occurring in the sequence $(a_n)_{n=1,2,\dots}$ Furthermore, in order to check whether the endomorphism is really a halving, one needs in addition a middling operation (see 6.3.7). Otherwise there is no possibility to check the internal consistency, and the assumption

$$m(f(a))=\frac{1}{2}m(a)$$

becomes completely arbitrary.

If, for example, A is a subjective property which corresponds to an objective property (such as pitch to frequency), a sequence obtained by halving might be enough to determine the scale with a sufficient degree of accuracy. In this case the assumption that there exists a simple (or "smooth") psychophysical law relating the subjective to the objective property (if both are measured in interval scales) together with the scale values of the sequence will determine the scale of the subjective property sufficiently accurately.

Simultaneous experiments on bisection and halving were per formed by S. S. STEVENS and VOLKMANN (1940, p. 336, 338) for pitch.

For loudness simultaneous experiments with bisection and halving were performed by CHURCHER (1935) and GARNER (1954). The value of these results is somewhat dubious, as in some experiments halving was performed by determining the loudness of a tone which – presented to both ears – is of the same loudness as the original tone presented to one ear. Later experiments (S. S. STEVENS, 1962) have shown that the loudness thus determined does not agree with the loudness which is half the original according to direct judgement.

In his method of corrected ratios, GARNER (1954) considered still another type of endomorphism applied to loudness. In addition to equisection, he performed the following "equal ratio"-experiment: Two tones of different loudness were given as reference. The subject had to determine from a given tone a the tone $f(a)$ such that the ratio of the loudness a and $f(a)$ is the same as the ratio of the loudnesses of the reference tones. Thus, he obtained a sequence $(a_n)_{n=1,2,\dots}$ of subjective loudnesses with $a_{n+1} = f(a_n)$. For the scale m_0 with natural origin, we have

$$m_0(a_n)=\lambda^n m_0(a).$$

Therefore, starting from any interval scale m, we can determine the scale $m_0(a)=m(a)+\beta$ by choosing β such that

$$m(a_n)+\beta=\lambda^n(m(a)+\beta).$$

Practically, this was done by plotting $\log (m(a_n)+\beta)$ as function of n for different values of β. For the shift β, leading to the natural origin, this curve should be a straight line:

$$\log (m(a_n)+\beta)=n\cdot\log \lambda+\log (m(a)+\beta).$$

From the slope of this straight line the value of λ can be determined. At the same time this procedure is a test of the hypothesis that the ratios $a_n : a_{n+1}$ are constant.

In the experiments performed by GARNER it turned out that 13 of 18 subjects were unable to distinguish between distance and ratio: in fact, the loudnesses a_n, a_{n+1} were of equal distance. Therefore, GARNER performed experiments with halving. Though the subjects were asked to perform a halving, GARNER determined the values of λ by the graphical method. He obtained results in good agreement with the equisection scales, i.e. for appropriate values of β he obtained straight lines.

7.4 Empirical Comparison of Arithmetic and Geometric Bisection Scales

If subjects were able to distinguish correctly between distance and ratio (and therefore between arithmetic and geometric bisection), the arithmetic bisection scale (obtained by mapping arithmetic bisection on the arithmetic mean) and the geometric bisection scale (obtained by mapping geometric bisection on the geometric mean) should lead to the same class of scales: Any geometric scale of a property should be in a linear relationship to any arithmetic scale. Such comparisons were made among others by STEVENS (1957) and STEVENS and GALANTER (1957). They arrived at the conclusion that the linear relationship to be expected is true only for some of the properties. These are called *metathetic*. Metathetic properties are usually of a qualitative nature, such as the subjective position of a point on a straight line, or the subjective slope of straight lines. Also pitch is considered by STEVENS as a metathetic property, though in this case the agreement of geometric and arithmetic is not satisfactory. The other properties are called *prothetic*. They are of a more quantitative nature, such as intensities. An additional explanation given by STEVENS is the following: In going from one stimulus to a higher one, for prothetic properties the stimuli are accumulated, whereas for metathetic properties the lower stimulus is substituted by a different one. For prothetic properties the values of the arithmetic scale are concave functions of the values of the geometric scale.

Other inquiries have shown that the values of the arithmetic scale are linearly related to the logarithms of the geometric scale (TORGERSON (1960), EKMAN (1962), EKMAN and KÜNNAPAS (1962)). The natural explanation of this phenomenon is that in these cases the subjects are unable to distinguish between arithmetic and geometric bisection: Regardless whether the subjects are asked to bisect a given interval from a to b such that the ratio $a : a \phi b$ equals the ratio $a \phi b : b$ or such that the interval from a to $a|b$ equals the interval from $a|b$ to b, they always perform the same operation. This is also suggested by experiments of GARNER (1954). If this were true, case a) of theorem 6.4.2 would apply and a logarithmic relationship would exist between arithmetic and geometric scales. Intuitively, this is obvious: If both operations are in fact identical and the operation is one time mapped into the arithmetic mean and the other time into the geometric mean, the values of the first scale are related to the logarithms of the values of the second scale.

EISLER (1962) used the concept of complementary properties to argue for a logarithmic relationship between geometric and arithmetic bisection scales from a theoretical point of view.

7.5 Cross-Modality and the Psychophysical Law

We start from a map $g: A_1 \to A_2$ to be interpreted as assigning to each manifestation $a_1 \in A_1$ an equivalent manifestation $g(a_1) \in A_2$, e.g.: assigning to each degree of loudness a_1 a vibration of subjectively equal intensity (see example 6.5.2).

Let the two psychophysical laws be given by:

$$m_1(a_1) = F_1(n_1(a_1))$$
$$m_2(a_2) = F_2(n_2(a_2)).$$

The map $a_1 \to g(a_1) \in A_2$ determines functional relationships between the scales m_1 and m_2 as well as between n_1 and n_2: If g is a joining map, according to 6.5.1 we have $m_2(g(a_1)) = m_1(a_1)$ for appropriately chosen scales m_1, m_2. Hence

$$n_2(g(a_1)) = F_2^{-1}(F_1(n_1(a_1))).$$

According to STEVENS (1959), experiments have shown that $F_2^{-1}(F_1(x))$ is a power function:

7.5.1 $F_2^{-1}(F_1(x)) = \gamma x^\delta$.

This fact was used by STEVENS as an additional argument for his claim that the psychophysical laws are power functions. In fact, if $F_1(x) = \mu_1 x^{\lambda_1}$, $F_2(x) = \mu_2 x^{\lambda_2}$, 7.5.1 holds with

$$\gamma = \left(\frac{\mu_1}{\mu_2}\right)^{1/\lambda_2} \text{ and } \delta = \frac{\lambda_1}{\lambda_2}.$$

Therefore 7.5.1 is a necessary condition for the psychophysical laws being power functions. There are, however, other psychophysical laws leading to 7.5.1, among them the WEBER-FECHNER law

$$F_i(x) = \lambda_i \log x + \mu_i$$

which implies 7.5.1 with

$$\gamma = \exp\left[\frac{\mu_1 - \mu_2}{\lambda_2}\right] \text{ and } \delta = \frac{\lambda_1}{\lambda_2}.$$

An essential difference between these two cases was pointed out by LUCE and GALANTER (1963, p. 280): In the case of power laws the exponents λ_1, λ_2 and hence $\delta = \lambda_1/\lambda_2$ are uniquely determined. Therefore, starting from the two psychophysical laws, δ can be predicted and then corroborated by matching data. In the case of the WEBER-FECHNER law the constants λ_1, λ_2 are arbitrary and the ratio $\delta = \lambda_1/\lambda_2$ is not uniquely determined until the two scales are adjusted such that matched sensations are assigned the same scale value. Hence in this case the matching data are necessary for the determination of δ.

8. Order Relations on Product Sets

Throughout this chapter we use some definitions and theorems about interval topologies from chapter 3. Contrary to chapter 3 we consider in this chapter interval topologies based on nonirreducible order systems. However, the results obtained in chapter 3 remain true also for this case if we substitute "unique up to equivalences" for "unique".

8.1 Order Relations in A Derived from Order Relations in $A \times A$

Starting from a given order relation in $A \times A$, an order relation in A is defined and the relationship between these two order relations is studied. Basic for the following considerations is the condition:

8.1.1 **Order in $A \times A$ (o):** An order relation "$\prec$, $\approx$" is defined between the elements of $A \times A$ which fulfills the order axioms 3.2.2.

This assumption will be made throughout the following chapter without special reference. Now we define relations "$\prec_1$" and "$\approx_1$" between the elements of A by:

8.1.2 **Definition:** $a \prec_1 b$ iff $ab \prec ba$ and $a \approx_1 b$ iff $ab \approx ba$. For the sake of brevity this will be denoted by

$$a \begin{Bmatrix} \prec_1 \\ \approx_1 \end{Bmatrix} b \text{ iff } ab \begin{Bmatrix} \prec \\ \approx \end{Bmatrix} ba$$

in the following.

To ensure that the relations "$\prec_1$" and "$\approx_1$" thus defined fulfill the order axioms, additional conditions concerning the order in $A \times A$ are needed. A patent necessary and sufficient condition is the following:

8.1.3 **Weak Transitivity (wt):**

$ab \{\lessapprox\}\ ba$ and $bc \{\lessapprox\}\ cb$ together imply $ac \{\lessapprox\}\ ca$.

The maps $A \to A \times A$ defined by $a \to ab$ with arbitrary $b \in A$ will not be monotone in general. To ensure monotony, a stronger condition than weak transitivity is needed, namely:

8.1.4 **Left Monotony (lm)*):**

$ab \{\lesssim\} ba$ implies $ac \{\lesssim\} bc$ for all $c \in A$.

This condition is obviously necessary and sufficient for $a \to ab$ being monotone increasing. To ensure that $a \to ba$ is monotone decreasing, we need the corresponding condition:

8.1.5 **Right Monotony (rm):**

$ab \{\lesssim\} ba$ implies $ca \{\gtrsim\} cb$ for all $c \in A$.

Left and right monotony are connected by the following symmetry condition:

8.1.6 **Symmetry (s):**

$ac \{\lesssim\} bc$ implies $ca \{\gtrsim\} cb$.

Obviously symmetry together with left (right) monotony implies right (left) monotony. On the other hand, left and right monotony together imply symmetry (because $ac \prec bc$ implies $ab \prec ba$ which implies $ca \succ cb$).

8.1.7 **Proposition:** Symmetry has the following trivial consequences:

$ab \{\lesssim\} ba$ implies $ab \{\lesssim\} aa$ and $bb \{\lesssim\} ba$ and therefore $ab \approx ba$ implies $aa \approx bb$.

Proof: If we had $aa \lesssim ab$, symmetry would imply $aa \gtrsim ba$ and hence $ba \lesssim ab$.

8.1.8 **Proposition:** Left or right monotony implies weak transitivity (*wt*).

Proof: We will treat the case of left monotony: $ab \prec ba$ and $bc \prec cb$ imply $ad \prec bd$ and $bd \prec cd$ for all d. Hence $ad \prec cd$, which implies $ac \prec ca$.

In general, weak transitivity is weaker than (left or right) monotony. In the presence of symmetry (*s*), however, monotony is equivalent to the following strong transitivity:

8.1.9 **Strong Transitivity (st):**

$ab \prec ba$ and $bc \prec cb$ imply $ac \prec \min(ab, bc)$

$ab \approx ba$ and $bc \lesssim cb$ imply $ac \approx \min(ab, bc)$

$ab \lesssim ba$ and $bc \approx cb$ imply $ac \approx \min(ab, bc)$.

---

*) Each of the conditions 8.1.4, 8.1.5, 8.1.6, 8.2.1 implies a corresponding condition which we obtain by substituting "$\succ$" for "$\prec$".

8.1.10 **Proposition:** In the presence of symmetry (s), strong transitivity (st) implies weak transitivity.

Proof: $ab \prec ba$ and $bc \prec cb$ imply $ac \prec \min(ab, bc)$. Therefore, $ac \prec ab$. Because of (s) we have $ca \succ ba \succ ab \succ ac$. Furthermore, $ab \approx ba$ and $bc \approx cb$ imply $ac \approx \min(ab, bc)$. If $ac \approx ab$, we have $ca \approx ba \approx ab \approx ac$. If $ac \approx bc$, we have $ca \approx cb \approx bc \approx ac$.

8.1.11 **Proposition:** In the presence of symmetry (s), left monotony (lm) and strong transitivity (st) are equivalent.

Proof: (i) (st) implies (lm)

α) Let $ab \prec ba$. Let c be arbitrary.

$\alpha\alpha$) $bc \prec cb$. Then, (st) implies $ac \prec bc$.

$\alpha\beta$) $ca \prec ac$. Then, (st) implies $cb \prec ca$ whence $ac \prec bc$ follows by (s).

$\alpha\gamma$) If $cb \lessapprox bc$ and $ac \lessapprox ca$, (s) implies because of 8.1.7 $cb \lessapprox cc \lessapprox ca$. As $ab \prec ba$, at most one of the equivalence signs holds. Hence $cb \prec ca$ which implies $ac \prec bc$ by (s).

β) Let $ab \approx ba$.

$\beta\alpha$) If $bc \lessapprox cb$, (st) implies $ac \approx \min(ab, bc) \approx bc$.

$\beta\beta$) If $cb \prec bc$, (st) implies $ca \approx \min(cb, ba) \approx cb$ which implies $ac \approx bc$ by (s).

(ii) (lm) implies (st)

$ab \prec ba$ implies $ac \prec bc$ by (lm).

$bc \prec cb$ implies $ba \prec ca$ by (lm) whence $ac \prec ab$ by (s).

Hence $ac \prec \min(ab, bc)$.

The other cases are dealt with similarly.

For each c, $A \times \{c\}$ is a subset of the ordered set $A \times A$ and thus ordered itself. The order in $A \times \{c\}$ in turn induces an order in A. This order will be independent of c if the following condition is fulfilled:

8.1.12 **Independence (i):** For all $a, b \in A$: If there exists $c_0 \in A$ such that $ac_0 \{\lessapprox\} bc_0$, then $ac \{\lessapprox\} bc$ for all $c \in A$.

In the case of independence (i), we define:

8.1.13 **Definition:**

$$a \begin{Bmatrix} \prec_2 \\ \approx_2 \end{Bmatrix} b \text{ iff } ac \begin{Bmatrix} \prec \\ \approx \end{Bmatrix} bc \text{ for all } c \in A.$$

It is clear that under the independence condition (i), the order "$\prec_2, \approx_2$" fulfills axioms 3.2.2. Furthermore, the map $a \rightarrow ab$ is monotone increasing for each fixed $b \in A$. In the case of symmetry (s), the map $a \rightarrow ba$ is monotone decreasing for any $b \in A$.

In the presence of left monotony (*lm*), the two order relations "$\prec_1, \approx_1$" and "$\prec_2, \approx_2$" are identical.

8.1.14 **Proposition:** Left monotony (*lm*) implies independence (*i*). In the presence of symmetry (*s*), independence (*i*) and monotony (*lm*) are equivalent.

Proof: α) (*lm*) implies (*i*): $ac_0 \prec bc_0$ implies $ab \prec ba$ which in turn implies $ac \prec bc$ for all $c \in A$.

β) (*i*) implies (*lm*) in the presence of (*s*): $ab \{\lesssim\} ba$ implies $ab\{\lesssim\}\, aa$ by 8.1.7. Because of (*s*) this implies $aa \{\lesssim\} ba$, whence $ac \{\lesssim\} bc$ for all c by (*i*).

Thus in the presence of (*o*) and (*s*) we have the following relationships:

$$\begin{array}{c} rm \\ \updownarrow \\ st \leftrightarrow lm \leftrightarrow i \\ \downarrow \\ wt \end{array}$$

8.2 n-Tuple Conditions

A condition much stronger than the conditions discussed hitherto is the following:

8.2.1 **Quadruple Condition (q):**

$ab \{\lesssim\} cd$ implies $ac \{\lesssim\} bd$.

8.2.2 **Proposition:** The quadruple condition (*q*) implies:

$ab \{\lesssim\} cd$ implies $ba \{\gtrsim\} dc$.

As a special case for $b=d$ we obtain symmetry (*s*).

Proof: $ab \prec cd$ implies $db \prec ca$, because $ca \{\lesssim\} db$ would lead to $cd \{\lesssim\} ab$ which is a contradiction. (*q*) applied to $db \prec ca$ yields $dc \prec ba$. The case of equivalence is dealt with similarly.

(*q*) has the consequence $aa \approx bb$. This can easily be seen by applying (*q*) to $ab \approx ab$.

8.2.3 **Diagonal Condition (d):**

$aa \approx bb$ for all $a, b \in A$.

8.2.4 **Proposition:** The quadruple condition (*q*) implies the diagonal condition (*d*) and the monotony conditions (*lm*) and (*rm*).

Proof: (q) applied to $ab \approx ab$ immediately yields (d). Assume, furthermore, that there exists c_0 such that $ac_0 \prec bc_0$. Then, by (q) $ab \prec c_0c_0 \approx aa$. Hence $ab \prec aa$ which yields by (q) $aa \prec ba$ and therefore $ab \prec ba$. The case of equivalence is dealt with similarly. By 8.2.2 (q) and (lm) imply (rm).

In the following we will discuss the relation between the quadruple condition (q) and two different sextuple conditions:

8.2.5 **Weak Sextuple Condition (ws):**

$ab \{\lesssim\} a'b'$ and $bc \{\lesssim\} b'c'$ together imply $ac \{\lesssim\} a'c'$.

8.2.6 **Strong Sextuple Condition (ss)**

$ab \prec b'a'$ and $bc \approx c'b'$ together imply $ac \prec c'a'$

$ab \approx b'a'$ and $bc \approx c'b'$ together imply $ac \approx c'a'$.

8.2.7 **Proposition:** The strong sextuple condition (ss) implies the quadruple condition (q). The quadruple condition (q) implies the weak sextuple condition (ws).

Proof: (i) (ss) implies (q): $ab \prec cd$ and $bc \approx bc$ together imply $ac \prec bd$. $ab \approx cd$ and $bc \approx bc$ together imply $ac \approx bd$.

(ii) (q) implies (ws): $ab \prec a'b'$ implies $aa' \prec bb'$; $bc \prec b'c'$ implies $bb' \prec cc'$, whence $aa' \prec cc'$ which in turn implies $ac \prec a'c'$.

The case of equivalence is dealt with similarly.

Many of the concepts are introduced in this section may be found in DAVIDSON and MARSCHAK.

8.3 Continuity Conditions:

In this section we will assume throughout that conditions (o) and (q) are fulfilled. The underlying topology is always the interval topology of $A \times A$.

8.3.1 **Continuity Condition (c):** For each $b \in A$ the set $A \times \{b\}$ is connected in $A \times A$.

8.3.2 **Proposition:** In the presence of (o) and (q) the continuity condition (c) implies: For each $b \in A$, the set $\{b\} \times A$ is connected in $A \times A$.

Proof: The map $A \times \{b_0\} \to \{b_0\} \times A$ defined by $ab_0 \to b_0a$ is continuous: on account of (q) (see 8.2.2): $b_0a \prec cd$ iff $ab_0 \succ dc$. Thus the inverse image of $\{b_0a : b_0a \prec cd\}$ is $\{ab_0 : ab_0 \succ dc\}$ which is open in $A \times \{b_0\}$. As the map is continuous, connectedness of $A \times \{b_0\}$ implies connectedness of $\{b_0\} \times A$.

8.3.3 **Proposition:** In the presence of (*o*), (*q*) and (*c*), the maps $A \to A \times A$ defined by

(i) $a \to ab$

(ii) $a \to ba$

are continuous for all $b \in A$.

Proof: Because of (*q*), the maps are monotone (8.2.4). As $A \times \{b\}$ and $\{b\} \times A$ are connected and therefore (3.5.10, 3.4.4) simple, the maps are continuous (3.6.12).

8.3.4 **Proposition:** If (*o*), (*q*) and (*c*) hold, *A* is connected.

Proof: The proposition is an immediate consequence (3.6.6) of the fact that *A* is the picture of the connected set $A \times \{b\}$ under the monotone and therefore (3.6.11) continuous map $ab \to a$.

8.3.5 **Proposition:** If (*o*), (*q*) and (*c*) hold, the following is true: If a', a'' exist such that $a'b \prec cd \prec a''b$, then there exists *a* such that $ab \approx cd$.

If b', b'' exist such that $ab' \prec cd \prec ab''$, then there exists *b* such that $ab \approx cd$.

Proof: As *A* is connected and the map $a \to ab$ ($a \to ba$) continuous, the proposition follows from the intermediate value theorem 3.6.13.

8.3.6 **Proposition:** If (*o*), (*q*) and (*c*) hold, the following is true: If b', b'' exist such that $ab' \prec b'c$ and $ab'' \succ b''c$, then there exists *b* such that $ab \approx bc$.

Proof: As *A* is connected and the maps $a \to ab$ and $a \to ba$ are both continuous, the proposition is an immediate consequence of the intersection theorem 3.6.14.

8.3.7 **Proposition:** (*o*), (*q*) and (*c*) together imply the strong sextuple condition (*ss*).

Proof: Assume, for example, $ab \approx b'a'$, $bc \approx c'b'$ and $a \prec b \prec c$. Then, $ac \prec bc \prec cc \approx aa$ (8.2.4 and 8.2.3). By 8.3.5 there exists *x* such that $ax \approx bc$. Therefore, $ax \approx c'b'$. Furthermore, from (*q*) we have $ab \approx xc$, whence $xc \approx b'a'$. By 8.2.7 we obtain (*ws*) and therefore $ac \approx c'a'$.

The case "$\prec$" is dealt with similarly.

8.4 Relations between Derived and Given Order

Up to now we have studied the orders induced in *A* by a given order in $A \times A$. Often, in addition to the order in $A \times A$ an order in *A*, say $(\prec_3, \approx_3)$, is given in advance:

8.4.1 **Order in A (g_1):** An order relation "$\prec_3$, $\approx_3$" is defined between the elements of A which fulfills axioms 3.2.2.

Given order and derived order coincide if the following condition is fulfilled:

8.4.2 **Coincidence Condition (g_2):**

$$a' \begin{Bmatrix} \prec_3 \\ \approx_3 \end{Bmatrix} a'' \text{ implies } a'c \begin{Bmatrix} \prec \\ \approx \end{Bmatrix} a''c \text{ for all } c \in A\,.$$

(g_2) implies that the map $\langle A; \prec_3, \approx_3 \rangle \to \langle A \times A; \prec, \approx \rangle$ defined by $a \to ac$ is monotone increasing. Together with (s) this implies that the map $\langle A; \prec_3, \approx_3 \rangle \to \langle A \times A; \prec, \approx \rangle$ defined by $a \to ca$ is monotone decreasing.

If an order is given in A, it seems natural to substitute continuity condition (c) by the following two conditions:

8.4.3 **Condition (g_3):** $\langle A; \prec_3, \approx_3 \rangle$ is connected.

8.4.4 **Condition (g_4):** The map $\langle A; \prec_3, \approx_3 \rangle \to \langle A \times A; \prec, \approx \rangle$ defined by $a \to ac$ is continuous for any $c \in A$.

(g_3) and (g_4) together immediately imply (c). On the other hand, (c) together with (g_2) and (q) imply (g_3) and (g_4) as can be seen from the proofs of 8.3.3 and 8.3.4.

If order relations are given in A and $A \times A$ which are connected by conditions (g_3) and (g_4), the following condition is sufficient to ensure monotony of the maps $a \to ac$ and $a \to ca$:

8.4.5 **Condition (g_5):** For all $a, b \in A$: $a \approx_3 b$ iff $ac \approx bc$ for all $c \in A$.

An equivalent condition, in closer correspondence to (g_4) would be: The map $\langle A; \prec_3, \approx_3 \rangle \to \langle A \times A; \prec, \approx \rangle$ defined by $a \to ac$ is $1-1$ for all $c \in A$.

8.4.6 **Proposition:** In the presence of (o), (i) and (g_1) the conditions (g_3), (g_4) and (g_5) imply that the order "$\prec_3$, $\approx_3$" is identical with "$\prec_2$, $\approx_2$" or its inverse. If furthermore (s) holds, then one of the following statements is true:

(i) $a \to ac$ is monotone increasing and $a \to ca$ monotone decreasing for all c,

(ii) $a \to ac$ is monotone decreasing and $a \to ca$ monotone increasing for all c.

Proof: As the map $a \to ac_0$ is $1-1$ and continuous and as A is connected, theorem 3.6.15 implies that it is monotone. Because of (i) the direction of monotony is the same for all $c_0 \in A$. Because of (s), $a \to ca$ is monotone decreasing if $a \to ac$ is monotone increasing and vice versa.

In the sections above, the derived order was always defined in such a way as to make the map $a \to ac$ monotone increasing (and thus $a \to ca$ monotone decreasing). We could have defined the derived orders as well such that $a \to ac$ is monotone decreasing (and $a \to ca$ monotone increasing), namely

$$a \begin{Bmatrix} \prec_1 \\ \approx_1 \end{Bmatrix} b \text{ iff } ba \begin{Bmatrix} \prec \\ \approx \end{Bmatrix} ab$$

and

$$a \begin{Bmatrix} \prec_2 \\ \approx_2 \end{Bmatrix} b \text{ iff } ca \begin{Bmatrix} \prec \\ \approx \end{Bmatrix} cb.$$

8.5 Order Relations in $A_1 \times A_2$

Let A_1 and A_2 be two possibly different sets. Part of the material presented in the foregoing sections for the case $A_1 = A_2$ will now be developed for the general case. Conditions which are generalizations of conditions introduced above will be denoted by the same number and distinguished from the original ones by *.

8.5.1 **Order in $A_1 \times A_2$ (o*):** An order relation "$\prec, \approx$" is defined between the elements of $A_1 \times A_2$ which fulfills axioms 3.2.2.

Similarly as in 8.1, we consider the order of the subset $A_1 \times \{c_2\}$ and the order thereby induced in A_1. This order will be independent of c_2, if the following condition is fulfilled:

8.5.2 **Independence (i*):** For all $a_1, b_1 \in A_1$, $a_2, b_2 \in A_2$:
(i_1^*) if there exists c_2^0 such that

$$a_1 c_2^0 \{\precsim\} b_1 c_2^0, \text{ then } a_1 d_2 \{\precsim\} b_1 d_2 \text{ for all } d_2 \in A_2,$$

(i_2^*) if there exists c_1^0 such that

$$c_1^0 a_2 \{\precsim\} c_1^0 b_2, \text{ then } d_1 a_2 \{\precsim\} d_1 b_2 \text{ for all } d_1 \in A_1.$$

If independence condition (i_1^*), $[(i_2^*)]$ is fulfilled, we can define an order in A_1 $[A_2]$:

8.5.3 **Definition:**

$$a_1 \{\gtrapprox\} b_1 \text{ iff } a_1 c_2 \{\lessapprox\} b_1 c_2 \text{ for all } c_2 \in A_2.$$

The definition of the order in A_2 is analoguous. In some instances it might seem natural to define the order in A_2 in the reversed sense.

The order relations thus defined fulfill axioms 3.2.2. Furthermore, the maps $A_1 \to A_1 \times \{c_2\}$ defined by $a_1 \to a_1 c_2$ and $A_2 \to \{c_1\} \times A_2$ defined by $a_2 \to c_1 a_2$ are monotone increasing (with respect to the order relations in A_i as defined above).

The following additional condition will enable us to define order relations in the spaces $A_1 \times A_1$ and $A_2 \times A_2$:

8.5.4 **Generalized Quadruple Condition (q*):** There exists a map $A_1 \to A_2$ assigning to each element $a_1 \in A_1$ an element $F(a_1) \in A_2$ and a map $A_2 \to A_1$ assigning to each element $a_2 \in A_2$ an element $G(a_2) \in A_1$ such that

$$a_1 a_2 \{\lessapprox\} b_1 b_2 \text{ iff } a_1 F(b_1) \{\lessapprox\} G(a_2) b_2.$$

This condition which is an immediate generalization of the quadruple condition (q), has the following consequences:

8.5.5 **Proposition:** If (q^*) holds, for any $a_1 \in A_1$ and $a_2 \in A_2$ we have $a_1 F(a_1) \approx G(a_2) a_2$.

This also implies: $a_1 F(a_1) \approx b_1 F(b_1)$ for all $a_1, b_1 \in A_1$ and $G(a_2) a_2 \approx G(b_2) b_2$ for all $a_2, b_2 \in A_2$.

Proof: This follows immediately by applying (q^*) to $a_1 a_2 \approx a_1 a_2$.

8.5.6 **Proposition:** (o^*) and (q^*) together imply (i^*).

Proof: $a_1 c_2 \prec b_1 c_2$ implies $a_1 F(b_1) \prec G(c_2) c_2$. Because $G(c_2) c_2 \approx G(d_2) d_2$ for all $d_2 \in A_2$, we have $a_1 F(b_1) \prec G(d_2) d_2$ and therefore $a_1 d_2 \prec b_1 d_2$ for all $d_2 \in A_2$.

8.5.7 **Proposition:** If (o^*) and (q^*) hold, F and G are both monotone decreasing (with respect to the order relations in A_i as defined above).

Proof: $a_1 \prec b_1$ implies $a_1 c_2 \prec b_1 c_2$ whence $a_1 F(b_1) \prec G(c_2) c_2 \approx a_1 F(a_1)$. Hence $F(b_1) \prec F(a_1)$. The corresponding proof for G runs similarly.

8.5.8 **Proposition:** If (o^*) and (q^*) hold, G is the inverse of F: $G(F(a_1)) \approx a_1$ for all $a_1 \in A_1$.

Proof: (q^*) applied to $a_1 F(a_1) \approx a_1 F(a_1)$ implies $a_1 F(a_1) \approx G(F(a_1))$ $F(a_1)$. Because of (i^*) this implies $a_1 \approx G(F(a_1))$.

In the following we will give conditions which are sufficient for (q^*).

8.5.9 **Solution Condition (so*):** There exists an element $c_1^0 c_2^0 \in A_1 \times A_2$ such that

(i) for each $a_1 \in A_1$ there exists $a_2 \in A_2$

(ii) for each $a_2 \in A_2$ there exists $a_1 \in A_1$

such that $a_1 a_2 \approx c_1^0 c_2^0$.

This condition is a weaker form of the solution condition as used by Luce and Tukey (1964).

8.5.10 **Sextuple Condition (ss*):** $a_1 b_2 \prec b_1 a_2$ and $b_1 c_2 \approx c_1 b_2$ together imply $a_1 c_2 \prec c_1 a_2$. $a_1 b_2 \approx b_1 a_2$ and $b_1 c_2 \approx c_1 b_2$ together imply $a_1 c_2 \approx c_1 a_2$.

This condition was used by Suppes and Winet (1955), Adams and Fagot (1959), Debreu (1960) and Luce and Tukey (1964) (cancellation axiom, p. 8). It is well known as the Thompsen condition in the theory of webs. See also Aczél, Pickert, and Radó (1960).

Starting from (so^*) we define F and G by $a_1 F(a_1) \approx c_1^0 c_2^0$ and $G(a_2)\, a_2 \approx c_1^0 c_2^0$, respectively.

8.5.11 **Proposition:** If (o^*), (ss^*) and (so^*) hold, then (q^*) holds with the functions F, G as defined above.

Proof: $a_1 a_2 \prec b_1 b_2$ and $b_1 F(b_1) \approx G(a_2)\, a_2$ together imply $a_1 F(b_1)$ $\prec G(a_2)\, b_2$.

Furthermore, we need a continuity condition corresponding to (c).

8.5.12 **Continuity Condition (c*):** For each $c_2 \in A_2$ the set $A_1 \times \{c_2\}$ is connected in $A_1 \times A_2$; for each $c_1 \in A_1$ the set $\{c_1\} \times A_2$ is connected in $A_1 \times A_2$.

8.5.13 **Definition:** Let F, G be functions satisfying (q^*). For all $a_1, b_1, c_1, d_1 \in A_1$, $a_2, b_2, c_2, d_2 \in A_2$:

$$a_1 b_1 \begin{Bmatrix} \prec_1 \\ \approx_1 \end{Bmatrix} c_1 d_1 \text{ iff } a_1 F(b_1) \begin{Bmatrix} \prec \\ \approx \end{Bmatrix} c_1 F(d_1)$$

$$a_2 b_2 \begin{Bmatrix} \prec_2 \\ \approx_2 \end{Bmatrix} c_2 d_2 \text{ iff } G(a_2)\, b_2 \begin{Bmatrix} \succ \\ \approx \end{Bmatrix} G(c_2)\, d_2.$$

8.5.14 **Proposition:** The relations $(\prec_i, \approx_i)$ thus defined by 8.5.13 are independent of the special map F, i.e. any map for which (q^*) holds leads to same the relations $(\prec_i, \approx_i)$.

Proof: Let F, F' be two maps for which (q^*) holds. We have to show that $a_1F(b_1) \prec c_1F(d_1)$ implies $a_1F'(b_1) \prec c_1F'(d_1)$. (q^*) for F applied to the trivial relations $c_1F'(c_1) \approx d_1F'(d_1)$ leads to $c_1F(d_1) \approx G(F'(c_1))\, F'(d_1)$. Hence $a_1F(b_1) \prec G(F'(c_1))\, F'(d_1)$. Applying (q^*) for F again, we obtain: $a_1F'(c_1) \prec b_1F'(d_1)$. Finally, we apply (q^*) for F' and obtain $a_1F'(b_1) \prec c_1F'(d_1)$.

8.5.15 **Theorem:** The relations $(\prec_i, \approx_i)$ on $A_i \times A_i$ defined by 8.5.13 fulfill the conditions (o) (order), (q) (quadruple) and (c) (continuity), if the order relation $(\prec, \approx)$ in $A_1 \times A_2$ fulfills (o^*), (q^*) and (c^*).

Proof: (o): Of the order axioms we prove transitivity only: $a_1b_1 \prec_1 c_1d_1$ and $c_1d_1 \prec_1 e_1f_1$ together imply $a_1b_1 \prec_1 e_1f_1$. This is true because $a_1F(b_1) \prec c_1F(d_1)$ and $c_1F(d_1) \prec e_1F(f_1)$ together imply $a_1F(b_1) \prec e_1F(f_1)$ on account of transitivity of "$\prec$".

(q): $a_1b_1 \prec_1 c_1d_1$ implies $a_1c_1 \prec_1 b_1d_1$, because $a_1F(b_1) \prec c_1F(d_1)$ implies $a_1F(c_1) \prec b_1F(d_1)$.

(c): $A_1 \times \{c_1\}$ is connected for all $c_1 \in A_1$; the map $A_1 \times \{F(c_1)\} \to A_1 \times \{c_1\}$ defined by $a_1F(c_1) \to a_1c_1$ is continuous with respect to the relative topologies because the inverse of the open set $\{a_1c_1 : a_1c_1 \prec_1 d_1e_1\}$ is $\{a_1F(c_1) : a_1F(c_1) \prec d_1F(e_1)\}$ which is open again. As $A_1 \times \{F(c_1)\}$ is connected by (c^*) the picture $A_1 \times \{c_1\}$ is connected too.

8.5.16 **Proposition:** (o^*) and (q^*) imply

$$a_1b_1 \begin{Bmatrix} \prec_1 \\ \approx_1 \end{Bmatrix} c_1d_1 \text{ iff } F(a_1)F(b_1) \begin{Bmatrix} \succ_2 \\ \approx_2 \end{Bmatrix} F(c_1)\,F(d_1).$$

Proof: If we put $F(a_1) = a_2$, $F(b_1) = b_2$, $F(c_1) = c_2$, $F(d_1) = d_2$, then: $a_1b_1 \approx_1 c_1d_1$ iff $a_1F(b_1) \approx c_1F(d_1)$ iff $G(a_2)\, b_2 \approx G(c_2)\, d_2$ iff $a_2b_2 \approx_2 c_2d_2$ iff $F(a_1)\,F(b_1) \approx_2 F(c_1)\,F(d_1)$. The same holds true for "$\prec$".

8.5.17 **Remark:** As in section 1, an order in $A_1 \times A_1$ can be used to define an order in A_1 by:

$$a_1 \begin{Bmatrix} \prec \\ \approx \end{Bmatrix} b_1 \text{ iff } a_1c_1 \begin{Bmatrix} \prec_1 \\ \approx_1 \end{Bmatrix} b_1c_1 \text{ for all } c_1 \in A_1 .$$

By going back to the definition of order in $A_1 \times A_1$ by order in $A_1 \times A_2$ (8.5.13) we obtain

$$a_1 \{\lesssim\}\, b_1 \text{ iff } a_1c_2 \{\lesssim\}\, b_1c_2 \text{ for all } c_2 \in A_2.$$

Thus the order in A_1 derived from the order in $A_1 \times A_1$ coincides with the order naturally induced in A_1 by the order in $A_1 \times A_2$ as defined by 8.5.3. The same holds true for the order in A_2.

8.6 Order Relations in $A_1 \times \ldots \times A_k$

Let $A_1, \ldots, A_k$ be k possibly different sets. In this section it will be shown that the case $k \geqq 3$ is of a nature essentially different from the case $k=2$. The difference consists in the fact that nothing like the generalized quadruple condition (q^*) or the sextuple condition (ss^*) is needed: conditions of this type follow in the case $k \geqq 3$ from independence except the trivial case where all elements of $A_1 \times \ldots \times A_k$ are equivalent.

8.6.1 **Order in $A_1 \times \ldots \times A_k$ (o**):** An order relation "$\prec, \approx$" is given on $A_1 \times \ldots \times A_k$ which fulfills the axioms 3.2.2.

8.6.2 **Independence (i**):** For all a_i, a_j, b_i, b_j: $i, j=1, \ldots, k$, $i \leqq j$, the following condition holds:
If there exist

$$c_1^0, \ldots, c_{i-1}^0, c_{i+1}^0, \ldots, c_{j-1}^0, c_{j+1}^0, \ldots, c_k^0$$

such that

$$c_1^0 \ldots c_{i-1}^0 a_i c_{i+1}^0 \ldots c_{j-1}^0 a_j c_{j+1}^0 \ldots c_k^0 \; \{\precsim\}$$
$$c_1^0 \ldots c_{i-1}^0 b_i c_{i+1}^0 \ldots c_{j-1}^0 b_j c_{j+1}^0 \ldots c_k^0$$

$$\text{then } c_1 \ldots c_{i-1} a_i c_{i+1} \ldots c_{j-1} a_j c_{j+1} \ldots c_k \; \{\precsim\}$$
$$c_1 \ldots c_{i-1} b_i c_{i+1} \ldots c_{j-1} b_j c_{j+1} \ldots c_k$$

for all $c_l \in A_l$, $l=1, \ldots, i-1, i+1, \ldots, j-1, j+1, \ldots, k$.

We remark that (i^{**}) also implies the corresponding independence condition for one component only.

8.6.3 **Continuity Condition (c**):** For all $i=1, \ldots, k$ and all $c_j \in A_j$, $j=1, \ldots, i-1, i+1, \ldots, k$, the set $\{c_1\} \times \ldots \times \{c_{i-1}\} \times A_i \times \{c_{i+1}\} \times \ldots \times \{c_k\}$ is connected.

8.6.4 **Solution Condition (so**):** There exists an element $c_1^0 \ldots c_k^0 \in A_1 \times \ldots \times A_k$ such that for each pair $i, j=1, \ldots, k$, $i \neq j$, and each $a_i \in A_i$ there exists an element $F_{ij}(a_i) \in A_j$ such that

$$c_1^0 \ldots, c_{i-1}^0 a_i c_{i+1}^0 \ldots c_{j-1}^0 F_{ij}(a_i)\, c_{j+1}^0 \ldots c_k^0 \approx c_1^0 \ldots c_k^0 .$$

The general case for $k \geqq 3$ will be handled by reducing it to the case $k=2$. As the case $k=3$ shows all the properties of the general case with arbitrary $k \geqq 3$, the proofs will be written out for $k=3$ only.

Because of (i^{**}), we can define an order in $A_1 \times A_2$ as follows:

8.6.5 **Definition:** $a_1a_2 \{\lesssim\} b_1b_2$ iff $a_1a_2c_3 \{\lesssim\} b_1b_2c_3$ for all $c_3 \in A_3$.

It is straightforward to show that the order axioms 3.2.2 are fulfilled.

8.6.6 **Proposition:** If (o^{**}), (i^{**}) and (so^{**}) hold, the order in $A_1 \times A_2$ fulfills the generalized quadruple condition (q^*): $a_1a_2 \{\lesssim\} b_1b_2$ iff $a_1F_{12}(b_1) \{\lesssim\} F_{21}(a_2)\, b_2$.

Proof: By definition of order in $A_1 \times A_2$ we have $a_1a_2F_{23}(a_2) \{\lesssim\} b_1b_2F_{23}(a_2)$. Furthermore, by definition of F_{ij} and (i^{**}): $a_1a_2F_{23}(a_2) \approx a_1b_2F_{23}(b_2)$ and $F_{21}(a_2)\, a_2F_{23}(a_2) \approx F_{21}(a_2)\, b_2F_{23}(b_2)$. Combining the first and second relation, we obtain $a_1b_2F_{23}(b_2) \{\lesssim\} b_1b_2F_{23}(a_2)$ whence by (i^{**}) $a_1F_{12}(b_1)\, F_{23}(b_2) \{\lesssim\} b_1F_{12}(b_1)\, F_{23}(a_2)$. As $F_{21}(a_2)\, a_2c_3^0 \approx c_1^0c_2^0c_3^0 \approx b_1F_{12}(b_1)\, c_3^0$, we have $a_1F_{12}(b_1)\, F_{23}(b_2) \{\lesssim\} F_{21}(a_2)\, b_2F_{23}(b_2)$.

8.6.7 **Proposition:** If (o^{**}) and (i^{**}) are satisfied, then (c^{**}) implies (c^*) for the order in $A_1 \times A_2$ defined by 8.6.5.

Proof: For any c_3, the map from $A_1 \times A_2 \times \{c_3\}$ into $A_1 \times A_2$ defined by $a_1a_2c_3 \rightarrow a_1a_2$ is continuous, as the inverse image of the open set $\{a_1a_2 : a_1a_2 \prec b_1b_2\}$ is $\{a_1a_2c_3 : a_1a_2c_3 \prec b_1b_2c_3\}$ which is open again. As $A_1 \times \{c_2\} \times \{c_3\}$ is connected, its image $A_1 \times \{c_2\}$ is connected too.

Finally, we define an order in $A_1 \times A_1$ in the same way as in 8.5.13.

8.6.8 **Definition:** $a_1b_1 \{\lesssim\} c_1d_1$ iff $a_1F_{12}(b_1) \{\lesssim\} c_1F_{12}(d_1)$.

We have to show that the order thus induced in $A_1 \times A_1$ is independent of which one of the spaces $A_1 \times A_j$ $(j = 2, \ldots, k)$ is used in the definition.

8.6.9 **Proposition:** Assume (o^{**}), (i^{**}) and (so^{**}). Then $a_1F_{12}(b_1) \{\lesssim\}$ $c_1F_{12}(d_1)$ iff $a_1F_{13}(b_1) \{\lesssim\} c_1F_{13}(d_1)$ for all $a_1, b_1, c_1, d_1 \in A_1$.

Proof: First, we remark that $b_1F_{12}(b_1)\, c_3^0 \approx c_1^0c_2^0c_3^0 \approx b_1c_2^0F_{13}(b_1)$ and therefore from (i^{**}): $a_1F_{12}(b_1)\, c_3^0 \approx a_1c_2^0F_{13}(b_1)$. The relation $a_1F_{12}(b_1)$ $\{\lesssim\}$ $c_1F_{12}(d_1)$ implies $a_1F_{12}(b_1)\, c_3^0 \{\lesssim\} c_1F_{12}(d_1)\, c_3^0$, whence $a_1c_2^0F_{13}(b_1)$ $\{\lesssim\}$ $c_1c_2^0F_{13}(d_1)$ which implies $a_1F_{13}(b_1) \{\lesssim\} c_1F_{13}(d_1)$.

The order in A_1 derived from the order in $A_1 \times A_1$ by 8.1.13 is identical with: $a_1 \{\lesssim\} b_1$ iff $a_1c_2 \ldots c_k \{\lesssim\} b_1c_2 \ldots c_k$.

We remark that except for the trivial case that all elements of $A_1 \times \ldots \times A_k$ are equivalent, each component space A_i contains at least two nonequivalent elements. If not all elements of $A_1 \times \ldots \times A_k$ are equivalent, there exist i and $c_i^1 \in A_i$ such that, e. g., $c_1^0 \ldots c_i^0 \ldots c_k^0 \prec c_1^0 \ldots c_i^1 \ldots c_k^0$.

Let $j \neq i$ be arbitrary. There exists $F_{ij}(c_i^1) \in A_j$ such that

$$c_1^0 \ldots c_i^1 \ldots F_{ij}(c_i^1) \ldots c_k^0 \approx c_1^0 \ldots c_i^0 \ldots c_j^0 \ldots c_k^0.$$

Hence $c_1^0 \ldots c_i^1 \ldots F_{ij}(c_i^1) \ldots c_k^0 \prec c_1^0 \ldots c_i^1 \ldots c_j^0 \ldots c_k^0$ which implies $F_{ij}(c_i^1) \prec c_j^0$.

9. The Theory of Interval Scales Based on Distances

9.1 Distance Systems

In this section we shall summarize the results of chapter 8 which will be needed in the following two sections.

9.1.1 **Definition:** A *distance system* is a r.s. $\langle A; \approx, \prec\rangle$ with "$\approx$", "$\prec$" being quarternary relations on A as well as binary relations on $A^2 = A \times A$ such that:

(i) $\langle A^2; \approx, \prec\rangle$ is an order system,

(ii) the quadruple condition (q) holds: For all $a, b, c, d \in A$
$ab \{\precapprox\} cd$ implies $ac \{\precapprox\} bd$,

(iii) for each $b \in A$, $A \times \{b\}$ is connected in $A \times A$.

9.1.2 **Definition:** An *ordered distance system* is a r.s. $\langle A; \approx_1, \prec_1, \approx, \prec\rangle$ such that

(i) $\langle A; \approx_1, \prec_1\rangle$ is an order system,

(ii) $\langle A; \approx, \prec\rangle$ is a distance system,

(iii) the map $a \to ab$ is either monotone increasing for all $b \in A$ or monotone decreasing for all $b \in A$.

9.1.3 **Remark:** As we have seen in 8.1.2, from each distance system an ordered distance system can be derived by $a \approx_1 b$ iff $ab \approx ba$ and $a \prec_1 b$ iff $ab \prec ba$. If, on the other hand, an order in A is given in advance, it is more natural to substitute 9.1.1 (iii) by topological properties of A and of the map $a \to ab$ as carried through in the following lemma. The proof of this lemma shows that the derived order of A is the same as the given one or its inverse.

9.1.4 **Lemma:** The r.s. $\langle A; \approx_1, \prec_1, \approx, \prec\rangle$ is an ordered distance system iff the following is true:

(i) $\langle A; \approx_1, \prec_1\rangle$ is an order system,

(ii) A is connected,

(iii) $\langle A^2; \approx, \prec \rangle$ is an order system,

(iv) for each $b \in A$ the map $a \to ab$ is $1-1$, i.e. $a \approx_1 c$ iff $ab \approx cb$,

(v) for each $b \in A$ the map $a \to ab$ is continuous,

(vi) the quadruple condition holds.

Proof: The conditions of 9.1.4 together imply 9.1.2 (iii) according to 8.4.6, as 9.1.4 (vi) implies symmetry (8.2.2) and independence (8.2.4 and 8.1.14). Furthermore, 9.1.4 (ii) and 9.1.4 (v) together imply 9.1.1 (iii) by 3.6.6. On the other hand, 9.1.1 (iii) and 9.1.2 (iii) together imply 9.1.4 ((ii), (iv), (v)).

9.1.5 **Remark:** The proof of 9.1.4 shows that 9.1.2 (iii) can be substituted by: $a \to ab$ is monotone for all $b \in A$. Without loss of generality we will consider throughout this chapter only distance systems with $a \to ab$ being monotone increasing.

9.1.6 **Remark:** If the r.s. $\mathbf{A} = \langle A; \approx_1, \prec_1, \approx, \prec \rangle$ is an ordered distance system, the equivalence relation "$\approx_1$" is a congruence relation for $\mathbf{A}$. Therefore we can consider the quotient r.s. of $\mathbf{A}$ modulo "$\approx_1$": $\mathbf{A}/\approx_1$. Obviously $\mathbf{A}/\approx_1$ is an ordered distance system too. For the sake of simplicity we will write: $\mathbf{A}/\approx_1 = \langle A; <, \approx, \prec \rangle$.

9.1.7 **Example:** As an example of a numerical ordered distance system we consider $\langle \mathbb{R}; <, \approx, \prec \rangle$ where "$<$" is the usual order relation and "$\approx$", "$\prec$" are defined by:

$$xy \left\{ \precsim \right\} uv \text{ iff } x-y \left\{ \leqq \right\} u-v.$$

Another numerical ordered distance system is $\langle \mathbb{R}^+; <, \approx_1, \prec_1 \rangle$, with the quaternary relations $\approx_1$, $\prec_1$ defined by:

$$xy \begin{Bmatrix} \prec_1 \\ \approx_1 \end{Bmatrix} uv \text{ iff } \frac{x}{y} \begin{Bmatrix} < \\ = \end{Bmatrix} \frac{u}{v}.$$

9.2 Distance Systems and Operations

9.2.1 **Theorem:** From a r.s. $\langle A; <, \circ \rangle$ with the metrical operation "$\circ$" on a connected set A an ordered distance system $\langle A; <, \approx, \prec \rangle$ can be derived by:

9.2.2 $ab \left\{ \precsim \right\} cd$ iff $(u' \circ a) \circ (d \circ u'') \left\{ \geqq \right\} (u' \circ b) \circ (c \circ u'')$.
The right relations are independent of u', u''.

9.2.3 **Remark:** In the case of a commutative and monotone increasing operation this definition reduces to

$$ab \{\lesseqgtr\} cd \text{ iff } a \circ d \{\geqq\} b \circ c.$$

Proof: (a) The distance defined by 9.2.2 is independent of u', u''. By repeated application of bisymmetry we obtain:

$$(*) \qquad [(x \circ y) \circ z] \circ [(x' \circ y') \circ z'] = [(x \circ x') \circ z] \circ [(y \circ y') \circ z'].$$

Let us consider, for example, the case

$$(u' \circ a) \circ (d \circ u'') < (u' \circ b) \circ (c \circ u'').$$

We remark that "o" is consistently monotone by 5.2.12. Without loss of generality we assume that "o" is increasing in the second variable. We obtain:

$$[(w \circ v') \circ z] \circ [(u' \circ a) \circ (d \circ u'')] < [(w \circ v') \circ z] \circ [(u' \circ b) \circ (c \circ u'')].$$

By (*) we obtain:

$$[(w \circ u') \circ z] \circ [(v' \circ a) \circ (d \circ u'')] < [(w \circ u') \circ z] \circ [(v' \circ b) \circ (c \circ u'')],$$

whence by the cancellation property:

$$(v' \circ a) \circ (d \circ u'') < (v' \circ b) \circ (c \circ u'').$$

This shows that relation 9.2.2 is independent of u'. Independence of u'' is proved similarly.

(b) The distance defined by 9.2.2 fulfills the conditions (iii)—(vi) of lemma 9.1.4.

(iii): A proof will be given only for transitivity, the proofs of the other axioms being similar. By repeated application of bisymmetry we obtain

$$(**) \qquad \begin{aligned}&[(x' \circ y') \circ (r' \circ s')] \circ [(r'' \circ s'') \circ (x'' \circ y'')] = \\ &[(x' \circ y') \circ (r' \circ s'')] \circ [(r'' \circ s') \circ (x'' \circ y'')].\end{aligned}$$

By 9.2.2

$$ab \prec cd \text{ implies } (u' \circ a) \circ (d \circ u'') > (u' \circ b) \circ (c \circ u'')$$

$$cd \prec ef \text{ implies } (v' \circ c) \circ (f \circ v'') > (v' \circ d) \circ (e \circ v'').$$

If we assume that "o" is isomonotone (the case of antimonotony being similar), we obtain:

$$\begin{aligned}&\{(x' \circ y') \circ [(u' \circ a) \circ (d \circ u'')]\} \circ \{[(v' \circ c) \circ (f \circ v'')] \circ (x'' \circ y'')\} > \\ &\{(x' \circ y') \circ [(u' \circ b) \circ (c \circ u'')]\} \circ \{[(v' \circ d) \circ (e \circ v'')] \circ (x'' \circ y'')\}.\end{aligned}$$

By (**) we obtain:

$$\begin{aligned}&\{(x' \circ y') \circ [(u' \circ a) \circ (f \circ v'')]\} \circ \{[(v' \circ c) \circ (d \circ u'')] \circ [x'' \circ y'']\} > \\ &\{(x' \circ y') \circ [(u' \circ b) \circ (e \circ v'')]\} \circ \{[(v' \circ d) \circ (c \circ u'')] \circ [x'' \circ y'']\}.\end{aligned}$$

As $(v' \circ c) \circ (d \circ u'') = (v' \circ d) \circ (c \circ u'')$, we obtain:

$$(u' \circ a) \circ (f \circ v'') > (u' \circ b) \circ (e \circ v''),$$

which means $ab \prec ef$.

(iv): $ab' \approx ab''$ implies $(u' \circ a) \circ (b'' \circ u'') = (u' \circ b') \circ (a \circ u'')$. Bisymmetry together with the cancellation property implies $b' = b''$.

(v): $\{x : xb \prec cd\} = \{x : (u' \circ x) \circ (d \circ u'') > (u' \circ b) \circ (c \circ u'')\}$ is open, as "$\circ$" is continuous.

(vi): From $ab \{\precsim\} cd$ and bisymmetry we obtain

$$(u' \circ a) \circ (d \circ u'') \{\geqq\} (u' \circ b) \circ (c \circ u'') = (u' \circ c) \circ (b \circ u'')$$

which implies $ac \{\precsim\} bd$.

9.2.4 **Theorem:** For each irreducible ordered distance system a middling operation "|" can be defined by:

9.2.5 $a\,(a|b) \approx (a|b)\,b$.

Before entering into the proof of the theorem, we state two elementary properties of the operation defined by 9.2.5.

9.2.6 **Proposition:** $ab \{\precsim\} cd$ is equivalent to $a|d \{\leqq\} b|c$.

Proof: $ab \{\precsim\} cd$ and $b\,(b \mid c) \approx (b \mid c)\,c$ imply $a\,(b \mid c) \{\precsim\} (b \mid c)\,d$ by the strong sextuple condition (8.3.7) whence $a \mid d \leqq b \mid c$ follows. The reverse is proved similarly.

9.2.7 **Remark:** If distance, in turn, was defined by a metrical operation, $a|b$ is defined in terms of this metrical operation by

$$(u' \circ (a|b)) \circ ((a|b) \circ u'') = (u' \circ a) \circ (b \circ u'').$$

Hence "|" is in this case identical to the middling operation "ϕ" derived from "$\circ$" as defined by 5.2.14.

9.2.8 **Proposition:** $(a|c)\,(b|c)$ is independent of c.

Proof: If this were not the case, there would exist c_0 such that $a\,(a \mid b) \prec (a \mid c_0)\,(b \mid c_0)$. Then by quadruple condition $a\,(a \mid c_0) \prec (a \mid b)\,(b \mid c_0)$ and therefore $(a \mid c_0)\,c_0 \prec (a \mid b)\,(b \mid c_0)$. As $b\,(b \mid c_0) \approx (b \mid c_0)\,c_0$, we obtain from the weak sextuple condition and the quadruple condition: $(a \mid c_0)\,(b \mid c_0) \prec (a \mid b)\,b$ which is a contradiction.

Proof of Theorem 9.2.4: a) The operation "|" defined by 9.2.5 is uniquely determined: If $a < b$, we have $ab \prec bb$ and by 8.2.4: $aa \succ ab$. Therefore, 8.3.6 implies the existence of an element $a \mid b$ such that $a\,(a \mid b) \approx (a \mid b)\,b$. On account of monotony, $a \mid b$ is unique.

b) The operation "|" defined by 9.2.5 is a middling operation

Cancellability: $a \mid b' = a \mid b''$ implies by 9.2.6 and commutativity: $ab'' \approx ab'$ which implies $b'' = b'$ by 9.1.4 (iv).

Continuity: $\{x : x \mid b < c\} = \{x : xc \prec cb\}$. This set is open by 9.1.4 (v).

Bisymmetry: From 9.2.8 we have $(a \mid c)(b \mid c) \approx (a \mid d)(b \mid d)$. Together with 9.2.6 and commutativity this yields: $(a \mid b) \mid (c \mid d) = (a \mid c) \mid (b \mid d)$.
Commutativity: $ab \approx ab$ implies $a \mid b = b \mid a$ by 9.2.6.
Reflexivity: $aa \approx aa$ implies $a \mid a = a$.

9.3 Existence and Uniqueness of Interval Scales Based on Distances

9.3.1 **Theorem:** For any ordered distance system $\langle A; <, L, \approx, \prec \rangle$ there exists a homomorphism m into the numerical distance system $\langle \mathbb{R}; <, L, \approx, \prec \rangle$, i. e. a monotone increasing and continuous map m: $A \to \mathbb{R}$ such that:

9.3.2 $ab \{\lesssim\} cd$ iff $m(a) - m(b) \{\leqq\} m(c) - m(d)$.

Such a homomorphism is uniquely determined up to positive linear transformations, i.e. it is an interval scale.

Proof: (i) *Existence:* According to theorem 9.2.4 there exists a middling operation "|" on A. Therefore according to theorems 6.1.1 and 6.1.2 there exists a monotone increasing and continuous map $m: A \to \mathbb{R}$ such that $m(a \mid b) = 1/2\,(m(a) + m(b))$. By 9.2.6: $ab \{\lesssim\} cd$ iff $a|d \{\leqq\} b|c$ iff $1/2\,(m(a) + m(d)) \{\leqq\} 1/2\,(m(b) + m(c))$ iff $m(a) - m(b) \{\leqq\} m(c) - m(d)$.

(ii) *Uniqueness:* Let m_1, m_2 be two homomorphisms of $\langle A; <, L, \approx, \prec \rangle$ into $\langle \mathbb{R}; <, L, \approx, \prec \rangle$. For $F = m_2 \circ m_1^{-1}$ we obtain: $F(x) - F(y) = F(u) - F(v)$ iff $x - y = u - v$, i.e. $F(x) - F(y) = \Phi(x - y)$. According to Aczél (1966, p. 142) the only monotone solution of this functional equation is

$$F(x) = \alpha x + \beta, \qquad \Phi(x) = \alpha x.$$

9.3.3 **Remark:** Instead of the numerical system $\langle \mathbb{R}; <, L, \approx, \prec \rangle$ also the system $\langle \mathbb{R}^+; <, L, \approx_1, \prec_1 \rangle$ (see example 9.1.7) can be used as corresponding to an empirical distance system.

If m is a homomorphism into $\langle \mathbb{R}; <, L, \approx, \prec \rangle$, then the map n defined by $n(a) = \exp[m(a)]$ is a homomorphism into $\langle \mathbb{R}^+; <, L, \approx_1, \prec_1 \rangle$, i.e.

$$ab \{\lesssim\} cd \text{ iff } \frac{n(a)}{n(b)} \{\leqq\} \frac{n(c)}{n(d)}.$$

Such scales are unique up to the transformation

$$\gamma(x) = \beta x^{\alpha}.$$

By this scale the empirical distances are represented by ratios of scale values instead of differences.

9.3.4 **Theorem:** Let m_i be a scale of $\mathbf{A}_i = \langle A_i;\ <_i,\ L,\ \approx_i,\ \prec_i\rangle$ into $\langle \mathbb{R};\ <, L,\ \approx,\ \prec\rangle$, $i=1,2$. If f is a homomorphism of $\mathbf{A}_1$ into $\mathbf{A}_2$, then

$$m_2\,(f\,(a_1)) = \alpha m_1\,(a_1) + \beta, \quad \alpha > 0.$$

Proof: As f is a homomorphism of $\mathbf{A}_1$ into $\mathbf{A}_2$ and m_2 is a homomorphism of $\mathbf{A}_2$ into $\langle \mathbb{R};\ <, L,\ \approx,\ \prec\rangle$, the composition $m_2 \circ f$ is a homomorphism of $\mathbf{A}_1$ into $\langle \mathbb{R};\ <, L,\ \approx,\ \prec\rangle$, i.e. an interval scale for $\mathbf{A}_1$.

9.4 Conjoint Measurement

In this section we consider a special model for the simultaneous measurement of k properties. The problem of measuring several properties simultaneously occurs in a number of cases. Here are a few examples:

(i) Intelligence tests are performed in order to determine a) the intelligence of subjects, b) the difficulty of tasks.

(ii) k-tuples of commodities are ranked according to (subjective) utility in order to determine the utility function for each of the k commodities.

(iii) Experiments on the evaluation of wagers based on uncertain events are used to measure a) subjective probability of uncertain events, b) utility.

The model to be considered in this section is suitable to deal with cases (i) and (ii) (case (iii) will be dealt with in chapter 12). Basic for these considerations is the general theory of order relations on product sets as developed in sections 8.5 and 8.6. As mentioned in 8.6 there is an essential difference between the case of two and the case of more than two component spaces.

First we will consider the case of two component spaces.

9.4.1 **Definition:** A *two-dimensional conjoint measurement system* is a r. s. $\langle A_1 \times A_2;\ \approx,\ \prec\rangle$ such that

(i) $\langle A_1 \times A_2;\ \approx,\ \prec\rangle$ is an order system,

(ii) the generalized quadruple condition (q^*) holds (see 8.5.4),

(iii) the continuity condition (c^*) holds (see 8.5.12).

As we have seen in 8.5.13, 8.5.14, 8.5.15, from each two-dimensional conjoint measurement system two distance systems $\langle A_1;\ \approx_1, \prec_1\rangle$, $\langle A_2;\ \approx_2, \prec_2\rangle$ can be derived. Furthermore, from these distance systems two ordered distance systems $\langle A_1; <_1, \approx_1, \prec_1\rangle$, $\langle A_2; <_2, \approx_2, \prec_2\rangle$ can be derived (see 9.1.3 and 9.1.6).

9.4.2 **Theorem:** To each two-dimensional conjoint measurement system $\langle A_1 \times A_2; \approx, \prec\rangle$ there exist maps $m_1: A_1 \to \mathbb{R}$, $m_2: A_2 \to \mathbb{R}$ such that

(i) m_1, m_2 are interval scales of the derived ordered distance systems $\langle A_1; <_1, L, \approx_1, \prec_1\rangle$, $\langle A_2; <_2, L, \approx_2, \prec_2\rangle$ into $\langle \mathbb{R}; <, L, \approx, \prec\rangle$,

(ii) $m_1 + m_2$ is a homomorphism of $\langle A_1 \times A_2; \approx, \prec\rangle$ into $\langle \mathbb{R}; =, <\rangle$,

(iii) for maps m_1', m_2' satisfying (ii) there exist $\alpha \in \mathbb{R}^+$ and $\beta_i \in \mathbb{R}$ with $m_i' = \alpha m_i + \beta_i$ $(i = 1, 2)$.

Proof: (i) The assertion follows immediately from theorem 9.3.1.

(ii) According to 8.5.7, 8.5.8, 8.5.13 and 8.5.16 there exists an isomorphism F of $\langle A_1; <_1, \approx_1, \prec_1\rangle$ to $\langle A_2; >_2, \approx_2, \succ_2\rangle$. By 3.6.11 F is continuous, as it is a monotone map onto. As m_1 is an interval scale of $\langle A_1; <_1, \approx_1, \prec_1\rangle$, $-m_2$ an interval scale of $\langle A_2; >_2, \approx_2, \succ_2\rangle$, we have by 9.3.4: $-m_2(F(a_1)) = \alpha m_1(a_1) + \beta$, $\alpha > 0$. Thus we can adjust the scales such that $m_2(F(a_1)) = -m_1(a_1)$ or $m_1(F^{-1}(a_2)) = -m_2(a_2)$. Furthermore, we have by 8.5.13: $a_1 a_2 \{\precsim\} b_1 b_2$ iff $a_1 F^{-1}(a_2) \{\precsim_1\} b_1 F^{-1}(b_2)$ iff $m_1(a_1) - m_1(F^{-1}(a_2)) \{\leqq\} m_1(b_1) - m_1(F^{-1}(b_2))$ iff $m_1(a_1) + m_2(a_2) \{\leqq\} m_1(b_1) + m_2(b_2)$.

(iii) As $m_1 + m_2$ and $m_1' + m_2'$ are monotone increasing there exists a real monotone function G such that

$$G(m_1(a_1) + m_2(a_2)) = m_1'(a_1) + m_2'(a_2) \text{ for all } a_i \in A_i.$$

With $g_i(x_i) := m_i' \circ m_i^{-1}(x_i)$ for $x_i \in B_i := m_i(A_i)$
we obtain

$$G(x_1 + x_2) = g_1(x_1) + g_2(x_2) \text{ for all } x_i \in B_i \ (i = 1, 2).$$

As the sets B_i are real intervals there exist $\alpha \in \mathbb{R}^+$ and $\beta_i \in \mathbb{R}$ such that $g_i(x) = \alpha x + \beta_i$. (See ACZÉL (1966), p. 142.) The assertion follows immediately.

Now we will consider the case of more than two component sets:

9.4.3 **Definition:** A *k-dimensional conjoint measurement system* (with $k > 2$) is a r.s. $\langle A_1 \times \ldots \times A_k; \approx, \prec\rangle$ such that

(i) $\langle A_1 \times \ldots \times A_k; \approx, \prec\rangle$ is an order system,

(ii) the independence condition (i^{**}) holds (see 8.6.2),

(iii) the continuity condition (c^{**}) holds (see 8.6.3),

(iv) the solution condition (so^{**}) holds (see 8.6.4).

From each k-dimensional conjoint measurement system k ordered distance systems $\langle A_i; <_i, L, \approx_i, \prec_i\rangle$ $(i = 1, \ldots, k)$ can be derived (see 8.6.8).

9.4.4 **Theorem:** For each k-dimensional conjoint measurement system there exist k maps m_i: $A_i \to \mathbb{R}$ such that

(i) m_i is an interval scale of the derived ordered distance system $\langle A_i; <_i, L, \approx_i, \prec_i\rangle$ into $\langle \mathbb{R}; <, L, \prec\rangle$ $(i=1, \ldots, k)$,

(ii) $\sum_{i=1}^{k} m_i$ is a homomorphism of $\langle A_1 \times A_2 \times \ldots \times A_k; \approx, \prec\rangle$ into $\langle \mathbb{R}; =, <\rangle$,

(iii) for maps m'_i $(i = 1, \ldots, k)$ satisfying (ii) there exist $\alpha \in \mathbb{R}^+$ and $\beta_i \in \mathbb{R}$ such that $m'_i = \alpha m_i + \beta_i$.

Proof: (i) and (ii): $A_1 \times A_2$ ordered by 8.6.5 is a two-dimensional conjoint measurement system $\mathbf{A}'$ (see 8.6.6 and 8.6.7). By 9.4.2 there exist scales m'_1, m'_2 satisfying (i) and (ii) for $\mathbf{A}'$. Similarly as in 8. 6. 5, the order $\prec$ on $A_1 \times A_2 \times \ldots \times A_k$ induces an order on $A_2 \times \ldots \times A_k$ such that we obtain a $(k-1)$-dimensional conjoint measurement system $\mathbf{A}''$. Let $m_2, \ldots, m_k$ be maps satisfying (i) and (ii) for $\mathbf{A}''$. The existence of these maps follows from 9.4.2 for $k = 3$; for $k > 3$ we assume it by induction. The order relations of $\mathbf{A}'$ and $\mathbf{A}''$ induce the same distance system on A_2 (see 8.6.9). Thus there exist $\alpha \in \mathbb{R}^+$ and $\beta \in \mathbb{R}$ such that $m_2 = \alpha m'_2 + \beta$ (see 9.3.1). $m_1 := \alpha m'_1$ and m_2 satisfy (i) and (ii) for $\mathbf{A}'$.

For each k-tuple $x_1 \ldots x_k \in B_1 \times \ldots \times B_k$, $B_i := m_i(A_i)$, let $\psi(x_1, \ldots, x_k)$ be the equivalence class of $\langle A_1 \times \ldots \times A_k; \approx\rangle$ which contains $m_1^{-1}(x_1) \ldots m_k^{-1}(x_k)$. Then

$$\psi(x_1, x_2, \ldots x_k) = \psi(x_1, y_2, \ldots, y_k) \text{ iff } \sum_{i=2}^{k} x_i = \sum_{i=2}^{k} y_i$$

by definition of $\mathbf{A}''$. This implies the existence of a map H such that

$$\psi(x_1, \ldots, x_k) = H\left(x_1, \sum_{i=2}^{k} x_i\right) \text{ for all } (x_1, \ldots, x_k) \in B_1 \times \ldots \times B_k.$$

By the same argument, applied for $\mathbf{A}'$, there exists a map G such that

$$\psi(x_1, \ldots, x_k) = G(x_1 + x_2, x_3, \ldots, x_k)$$

and therefore

$$H\left(x_1, \sum_{i=1}^{k} x_i\right) = G(x_1 + x_2, x_3, \ldots, x_k) \text{ for all } (x_1, \ldots, x_k) \in B_1 \times \ldots \times B_k.$$

Let $(y_1, \ldots, y_k) \in B_1 \times \ldots \times B_k$ be arbitrary.

With $\gamma := \sum_{i=3}^{k} y_i$ we obtain

$$\psi(x_1, \ldots, x_k) = H\left(x_1, \sum_{i=2}^{k} x_i\right) = H\left(x_1, \left(\sum_{i=2}^{k} x_i - \gamma\right) + \sum_{i=3}^{k} y_i\right)$$

$$= G\left(\sum_{i=1}^{k} x_i - \gamma, y_3, \ldots, y_k\right)$$

for all $(x_1, ,.., x_k)$ satisfying

$$(*) \qquad \sum_{i=2}^{k} x_i - \sum_{i=3}^{k} y_i \in B_2 .$$

Hence for $(x_1, \ldots, x_k)$ and $(x'_1, \ldots, x'_k)$ satisfying $(*)$, $\sum_{i=1}^{k} x_i = \sum_{i=1}^{k} x'_i$ implies the equivalence of the corresponding k-tuples of $A_1 \times \ldots \times A_k$. Especially, $\sum_{i=1}^{k} x_i = \sum_{i=1}^{k} y_i$ and

$$(**) \qquad y_2 + (y_1 - x_1) \in B_2 \text{ or } x_2 - (y_1 - x_1) \in B_2$$

imply the equivalence of $m_1^{-1}(x_1) \ldots m_k^{-1}(x_k)$ and $m_1^{-1}(y_1) \ldots m_k^{-1}(y_k)$. W.l.o.g. (see 8.6) we may assume that B_2 is an interval consisting of more than one point. For an arbitrary pair $x: = (x_1, \ldots, x_k)$, $y: = (y_1, \ldots, y_k)$ of k-tuples of $B_1 \times \ldots \times B_k$ with $\sum_{i=1}^{k} x_i = \sum_{i=1}^{k} y_i$ we choose an integer $n \geqq 2$ such that

$$n > \frac{4|y_1 - x_1|}{|y_2 - x_2|} \quad \text{for } x_2 \neq y_2,$$

$$x_2 + \frac{1}{n}(y_1 - x_1) \in B_2 \text{ or } x_2 - \frac{1}{n}(y_1 - x_1) \in B_2 \text{ for } x_2 = y_2,$$

and define for $m = 0, 1, \ldots, n$

$$x_i^m = \left(1 - \frac{m}{n}\right) x_i + \frac{m}{n} y_i \quad (i = 1, \ldots, k).$$

As $B_1 \times \ldots \times B_k$ is convex, $x^m \in B_1 \times \ldots \times B_k$. Moreover,

$$\sum_{i=1}^{k} x_i^m = \sum_{i=1}^{k} x_i^l \quad \text{for all } m, l$$

and for $m = 0, 1, \ldots, n-1$

$$x_2^{m+1} + (x_1^{m+1} - x_1^m) = x_2^{m+1} + \frac{1}{n}(y_1 - x_1) \in B_2 \quad \text{or}$$

$$x_2^m - (x_1^{m+1} - x_1^m) = x_2^m - \frac{1}{n}(y_1 - x_1) \in B_2,$$

i.e. each pair x^m, x^{m+1} satisfies $(**)$. Since $x^0 = x$ and $x^n = y$, the k-tuples of $A_1 \times \ldots \times A_k$ corresponding to x and y are equivalent. Thus we have proved that

$$\sum_{i=1}^{k} m_i(a_i) = \sum_{i=1}^{k} m_i(a'_i) \text{ implies } a_1 \ldots a_k \approx a'_1 \ldots a'_k .$$

For $\sum_{i=1}^{k} x_i > \sum_{i=1}^{k} y_i$ there exists $(z_1, \ldots, z_k) \in B_1 \times \ldots, \times B_k$ such that

$$z_i \leqq x_i \text{ for } i = 1, \ldots, k \text{ and } \sum_{i=1}^{k} z_i = \sum_{i=1}^{k} y_i .$$

As m_i is monotone increasing we obtain

$$m_1^{-1}(x_1)\dots m_k^{-1}(x_k) \succ m_1^{-1}(z_1)\dots m_k^{-1}(z_k) \approx m_1^{-1}(y_1)\dots m_k^{-1}(y_k).$$

(iii) The assertion follows immediately from 9.4.2 (iii) by induction.

9.4.5 **Remark:** The model of conjoint measurement goes back to ideas of ADAMS and FAGOT (1959) and DEBREU (1960) developed in connection with utility measurement. An elaborate axiomatization for the two-dimensional case was given by LUCE and TUKEY (1964) and KRANTZ (1964). The most general results available until now are those of LUCE (1966) and TVERSKY (1967). The approach to conjoint measurement outlined above differs from those of LUCE and TVERSKY by the use of topological instead of algebraic concepts. We are of the opinion that the indirect way over distances makes the whole approach more intuitive.

9.5 Empirical Status of Axioms for Product Structures

As in 6.6 we will treat the problem whether the objectionable axioms ensuring the existence of a scale for distance systems and conjoint measurement are only technical.

The axioms of irreducible ordered distance systems $\langle A; =, \approx, \prec\rangle$ (9.1.2) are all testable with the exception of the topological axiom 9.1.1 (iii). But this system of axioms has testable consequences which do not follow without the topological axiom, for example, according to 8.3.7 the

(i) strong sextuple condition (*ss*) (8.2.6).

Moreover there are objectionable algebraic consequences such as the

(ii) bisection: For all $a, b \in A$ there exists $c \in A$ such that $ac \approx cb$ (9.2.4).

Thus the axioms (9.1.2) are stronger than the system of axioms which we obtain by substituting (i) and (ii) for the topological axiom 9.1.1 (iii). But as (9.1.2) is satisfied by the r. s. $\mathbf{R} = \langle \mathbb{R}; =, <, \approx, \prec\rangle$ (defined in 9.1.7) the following theorem shows that (9.1.2) implies no testable sentence which is not implied by the weakened system of axioms.

9.5.1 **Definition:** A *closed subsystem* of $\mathbf{R}$ is a subsystem $\mathbf{R}' = \langle R; =, <, \approx, \prec\rangle$ of $\mathbf{R}$, $R \subset \mathbb{R}$, satisfying (ii).

9.5.2 **Theorem:** Let s be a testable sentence on a r. s. $\mathbf{A} = \langle A; =, <, \approx, \prec\rangle$ of type $k_1 = k_2 = 2$, $k_3 = k_4 = 4$. If s holds in at least one closed subsystem $\mathbf{R}'$ of $\mathbf{R}$ containing at least two elements, s is a consequence of the following axioms S:

(o) $<, \prec$ are order relations and $\approx$ the equivalence relation for $\prec$,

(i) strong sextuple condition,

(ii) bisection,

(iii) "left increasing monotony": $a<b$ implies $ac \prec bc$ for all c.

Proof: As $\mathbf{R}'$ is closed, it satisfies the axioms S. Let $\mathbf{A}$ be a r.s. satisfying S and assume that s is a testable sentence which holds in $\mathbf{R}'$. In both r.s. a unique binary operation $|$ is defined by 9.2.5: For the definition we use (ii), for uniqueness (iii) and (i): they imply the right decreasing monotony ($a<b$ implies $cb \prec ca$). As (i) implies the weak sextuple condition and the quadruple condition (8.2.7), the propositions 9.2.6—9.2.8 hold even without topological conditions. Thus the operation $|$ is bisymmetric, commutative and reflexive (see Proof of 9.2.4). It is, moreover, monotone by 9.5.2 (iii).

$ab \approx cd$ is equivalent to $a \mid d = b \mid c$ by (9.2.6). $ab \prec cd$ is equivalent to $a \mid d < b \mid c$ (by (i) and the monotony). Thus we can formulate s by the relations $=, <$ and $|$. As $|$ in $\mathbf{R}'$ is the operation ϕ, it follows from 6.6.5b) that s holds in $\mathbf{A}$.

9.5.3 **Corollary:** A testable sentence which holds in at least one irreducible ordered distance system containing more than one element is a consequence of the axioms S.

Proof: By 9.3.1 the distance system can be represented by a subsystem $\mathbf{R}'$ of $\mathbf{R}$. $\mathbf{R}'$ is closed because the bisection property (ii) holds in the distance system (see 9.2.4).

Even though the testable sentences which hold in distance systems are consequences of S, they may be consequences of an objectionable axiom, namely (ii), the bisection.

9.5.4 **Definition:** $\mathbf{R}_2 = \langle \mathbb{R}^2; \approx, \prec \rangle$ where $(x_1, x_2) \prec (y_1, y_2)$ iff $x_1 + x_2 < y_1 + y_2$.

9.5.5 **Theorem:** Let $\mathbf{A} = \langle A_1 \times A_2; \approx, \prec \rangle$ be a r.s. of type $k_1 = k_2 = 2$ and s a testable sentence on $\mathbf{A}$. If s holds in $\mathbf{R}_2$, it is a consequence of the axioms S':

(o) $\prec$ is an order relation with equivalence $\approx$,

(i) strong solvability: (so^*) (8.5.9) and for all $a_1 a_2 \in A_1 \times A_2$ there is an $x_2 \in A_2$ such that $a_1 x_2 \approx c_1^0 a_2$,

(ii) strong sextuple condition (ss^*) (8.5.10).

Proof: Without loss of generality we may assume that $\mathbf{A}$ is reduced such that the solution x_2 of (i) is unique. Let F and G be the functions of 8.5.11 and denote by $<$ the order in A_1 induced by $\approx, \prec$. (As (ss^*) and (i) imply (q^*) (8.5.11), (ss^*) implies (i^*) (8.5.6).) We define a binary operation $\circ$ on A_1:

For $a, b \in A_1$ let $a \circ b$ be the unique element of A_1 determined by

$$aF(a \circ b) \approx c_1^0 F(b).$$

$\circ$ is commutative: By (q^*) and (8.5.8) $c_1^0 F(b) \approx aF(a \circ b)$ implies $c_1^0 F(a) \approx G(F(b)) F(a \circ b) \approx bF(a \circ b)$. Thus $F(a \circ b) = F(b \circ a)$.
$\circ$ is increasing: $a > c$ and $aF(a \circ b) \approx cF(c \circ b)$ imply $cF(c \circ b) \approx aF(a \circ b) \succ cF(a \circ b)$, and thus $F(c \circ b) > F(a \circ b)$. As F is decreasing, $a \circ b > c \circ b$.
$\circ$ is associative: For all $a, b, c \in A_1$ we have $aF(a \circ (b \circ c)) \approx c_1^0 F(b \circ c)$, $bF(b \circ (a \circ c)) \approx c_1^0 F(a \circ c)$ and $aF(a \circ c) \approx bF(b \circ c)$. Applying ($ss^*$) for the first and third relation we get: $bF(a \circ (b \circ c)) \approx c_1^0 F(a \circ c)$. This and the second relation imply $F(a \circ (b \circ c)) = F(b \circ (a \circ c))$. We have shown:

(*) $\langle A_1; =, <, \circ \rangle$ satisfies the axioms S_a of 6.6.5.

Moreover,

(**) $$\begin{cases} a_1 a_2 \succ b_1 b_2 \text{ iff } a_1 \circ G(b_2) > b_1 \circ G(a_2) \text{ and} \\ a_1 a_2 \approx b_1 b_2 \text{ iff } a_1 \circ G(b_2) = b_1 \circ G(a_2). \end{cases}$$

If $a_1 \circ G(b_2) > b_1 \circ G(a_2)$, then $c_1^0 F(a_1 \circ G(b_2)) \prec c_1^0 F(b_1 \circ G(a_2))$. This implies together with $c_1^0 a_2 = c_1^0 F(G(a_2)) \approx b_1 F(b_1 \circ G(a_2))$ by (ss) $b_1 F(a_1 \circ G(b_2)) \prec c_1^0 a_2$. As $a_1 F(a_1 \circ G(b_2)) \approx c_1^0 F(G(b_2)) = c_1^0 b_2$ we obtain by (ss) $b_1 b_2 \prec a_1 a_2$.

By (**) s can be formulated in $\langle A_1; =, <, \circ \rangle$ and $\langle \mathbb{R}; =, <, + \rangle$. Therefore s is a consequence of S' by 6.6.5a).

9.5.6 **Corollary:** A testable sentence s which is a consequence of the axioms 9.4.1 for two-dimensional conjoint measurement systems is a consequence of the axioms S'.

Proof: As $\mathbf{R}_2$ satisfies 9.4.1 the sentence s holds in $\mathbf{R}_2$. Thus it is a consequence of S' according to 9.5.5.

We have seen in this section that the continuity conditions and (q^*) are only technical if we enrich the systems of axioms by algebraic axioms ((ss) and bisection for distance systems, (ss^*) and strong solvability for conjoint measurement systems). For conjoint measurement this result is unsatisfactory as the enriched system of axioms is stronger than the original system 9.4.1: The strong solution condition does not follow from 9.4.1. Thus it may be possible to improve Corollary 9.5.6 by substituting a weaker system of axioms for S'.

All axioms of S' are testable with the exception of strong solvability. Thus we must accept one objectionable axiom in each of the two theories considered in this section. Implicitly we have to accept a non-universal sentence in the systems S_a and S_b too by the axiom that the relation is an operation.

The Theorems 9.5.2 and 9.5.5 are due to Adams, Fagot, Robinson (1965b).

10. Canonical Representations

10.1 The Principle of Canonical Representations

Let $F(a_1, \ldots, a_k, b)$ be a function mapping $A^k \times B$ into a set C. Our assumptions about the sets A, B, C vary from case to case and will be specified separately in each particular instance.

In a number of instances it turns out that an empirically given function F can be transformed into a very simple function H by maps $m: A \to \mathbb{R}$ and $n: B \to \mathbb{R}$: $F(a_1, \ldots, a_k, b) = H(m(a_1), \ldots, m(a_k), n(b))$ for all $a_i \in A$, $i = 1, \ldots, k$ and $b \in B$. If these maps are unique up to linear transformations, we will speak of a *canonical representation*. This definition depends, of course, wholly on the undefined concept of simplicity used in connection with the function H.

In the following we will give a few examples of such canonical representations and prove that in these examples the scales are in fact unique up to linear transformations. The question of sufficient conditions which F has to fulfill in order for a canonical representation to exist will be treated only occasionally.

The approach outlined above is a natural generalization of ideas presented by L. L. THURSTONE (1925, 1927). In the author's opinion these papers relating to applications to mental testing are the only ones in this field successfully striving for a methodological foundation of the whole testing business. Essentially the same ideas connected with completely different applications are contained in SHEPARD (1965) and in an abstract framework in LEVINE (1967).

The question naturally arises as to whether this kind of measurement is fundamental or derived measurement. Obviously, the scale is determined by the structure of the property as exhibited by the empirically given function F. In general the structure does not lend itself to a description by a relational system in a natural way. Although in some cases (see e.g. 10.3) a distance structure can be defined in a natural way, it seems hardly justifiable to consider such scales as fundamental and other scales as derived.

10.2 Uniqueness of Translation Invariant Representations

10.2.1 **Definition:** Let $D \subset \mathbb{R}^k$ be a set for which $(a_1, \ldots, a_k) \in D$ implies $(a_1 + a, \ldots, a_k + a) \in D$ for all $a \in \mathbb{R}$. Then a function $G: D \to C$ is translation invariant iff

$$G(x_1 + u, \ldots, x_k + u) = G(x_1, \ldots, x_k) \text{ for all } (x_1, \ldots, x_k) \in D \text{ and } u \in \mathbb{R}.$$

For $U, V \subset \mathbb{R}^k$ and $v \in \mathbb{R}^k$ we define $U \dot{-} V := \{u - v : u \in U, v \in V\}$, $U \dot{-} v = \{u - v : u \in U\}$. The symbol $\dot{+}$ is defined correspondingly.

10.2.2 **Definition:** Let $D \subset A^k \times B$. Then a function $G: D \to C$ is *cancellable* iff for all $i = 1, \ldots, k+1$ and all $x_1, \ldots, x_{i-1}, x_{i+1}, \ldots, x_{k+1}, x_i', x_i'' \in A$, respectively B, with

$$(x_1, \ldots, x_{i-1}, x_i', x_{i+1}, \ldots, x_{k+1}), (x_1, \ldots, x_{i-1}, x_i'', x_{i+1}, \ldots, x_{k+1}) \in D$$

$$G(x_1, \ldots, x_{i-1}, x_i', x_{i+1}, \ldots, x_{k+1}) = G(x_1, \ldots, x_{i-1}, x_i'', x_{i+1}, \ldots, x_{k+1})$$

implies $x_i' = x_i''$.

10.2.3 **Theorem:** Assume that for $F: A^k \times B \to C$ there exists a representation

$$F(a_1, \ldots, a_k, b) = H(m(a_1), \ldots, m(a_k), n(b))$$

by a translation invariant function $H: D_{m,n} \to C$, where

$$D_{m,n} := \{(m(a_1) + x, \ldots, m(a_k) + x, n(b) + x) : a_i \in A, b \in B, x \in \mathbb{R}\}$$

and functions m, n, such that $m(A)$ and $n(B)$ are connected. Let A and B contain at least two elements. Assume furthermore that either

(a) F is cancellable, C is ordered, and H is either monotone (1) or continuous (2) in the last variable on $\{(m(a), \ldots, m(a), n(b)) : b \in B\}$ for all $a \in A$, or

(b) H is cancellable, A, B are ordered and m, n are monotone.

Then the functions m, n H are unique up to the simultaneous transformation

$$m^*(a) = \alpha m(a) + \beta$$

$$n^*(b) = \alpha n(b) + \gamma$$

$$H^*(x_1, \ldots, x_k, y) = H\left(\frac{x_1 - \beta}{\alpha}, \ldots, \frac{x_k - \beta}{\alpha}, \frac{y - \gamma}{\alpha}\right)$$

for $x_i \in m^*(A)$, $y \in n^*(B)$.

Proof: Assume that there exist two different representations:

10.2.4 $H(m(a_1), \ldots, m(a_k), n(b)) = H^*(m^*(a_1), \ldots, m^*(a_k), n^*(b))$.

Let $a_1 = \ldots = a_k = a$. Then from translation invariance we obtain:

10.2.5 $H(0, \ldots, 0, n(b) - m(a)) = H^*(0, \ldots, 0, n^*(b) - m^*(a))$.

Let $n(b) = u$, $m(a) = -v$. Furthermore, let H' be such that

$$H'(H^*(0, \ldots, 0, x)) = x \text{ for } x \in n^*(B) \dot{-} m^*(A).$$

Let $f(x) := H'(H(0, \ldots, 0, x))$ for $x \in n(B) \dot{-} m(A)$

$g(u) := n^* n^{-1}(u)$ for $u \in n(B)$

$h(v) := -m^* m^{-1}(-v)$ for $-v \in m(A)$.

That H' exists is clear in case $(a, 1)$ and follows from cancellability of H^* in case (b). That H' exists in case $(a, 2)$ can be seen as follows: $H^*(0, \ldots, x)$ is a continuous and 1—1 map on the connected set $n^*(B) \dot{-} m^*(a)$, $H^*(0, \ldots, x)$ is monotone on $n^*(B) \dot{-} m^*(a)$ by 3.6.15. That m^{-1} and n^{-1} exist is clear in case (b) and follows from cancellability of F in case (a).

Hence we obtain from 10.2.5:

10.2.6 $f(u + v) = g(u) + h(v)$.

In case (a) we obtain that f is monotone, in case (b) that g, h are monotone. According to Aczél (1966, p. 142), 10.2.6 implies

$$g(x) = \alpha x + \gamma$$
$$h(x) = \alpha x - \beta$$
$$f(x) = \alpha x + \gamma - \beta,$$

whence

$$m^*(a) = \alpha m(a) + \beta,$$
$$n^*(b) = \alpha n(b) + \gamma.$$

Substituting this result into 10.2.4 we obtain:

$H^*(\alpha m(a_1) + \beta, \ldots, \alpha m(a_k) + \beta, \alpha n(b) + \gamma) = H(m(a_1), \ldots, m(a_k), n(b))$.

As $a_1, \ldots, a_k, b$ are arbitrary, we have

$$H^*(x_1, \ldots, x_k, y) = H\left(\frac{x_1 - \beta}{\alpha}, \ldots, \frac{x_k - \beta}{\alpha}, \frac{y - \gamma}{\alpha}\right)$$

for $x_i \in m^*(A)$, $y \in n^*(B)$.

10.2.7 **Corollary:** If $B = A$ the theorem also holds true for the particular case $n = m$.

10.2.8 **Corollary:** If we put $H(x_1, \ldots, x_k, 0) = H_0(x_1, \ldots, x_k)$, we obtain the representation $F(a_1, \ldots, a_k, b) = H_0(m(a_1) - n(b), \ldots, m(a_k) - n(b))$.

Applications of Theorem 10.2.3 and its corollaries are given in 10.3.8, 11.3.1, 11.4.1.

10.2.9 **Remark:** Under the assumptions of Theorem 10.2.3 (a) we can define an order in A and B by

$$a' \{\lesssim\} a'' \text{ iff } m(a') \{\leqq\} m(a''),$$

and

$$b' \{\lesssim\} b'' \text{ iff } n(b') \{\leqq\} n(b'').$$

With respect to this order, F is monotone in each variable.

Up to now we were exclusively concerned with the question of uniqueness of the scale as determined by a canonical representation. Much more important and much more difficult is the question as to which properties a function must have in order that it can be transformed into a canonical function. The conditions depend, of course, on the type of the function H used for the canonical representation.

10.3 Existence of Translation Invariant Representations

For translation invariant representations the question of existence was answered in a paper by M. LEVINE (1967). In this section we will present a somewhat weaker version of LEVINE's Theorem with a proof taking advantage of the results obtained in section 9.3.

Let $\langle A; <_1\rangle$ be an ordered and connected set containing at least two elements. Let $F_\lambda : A \to \mathbb{R}$, $\lambda \in \Lambda$ be a family of functions such that:

10.3.1 F_λ is monotone increasing for all $\lambda \in \Lambda$.

10.3.2 $F_\lambda(A) = I$ is independent of $\lambda \in \Lambda$.

10.3.3 F_λ, F_μ do not intersect for $\lambda \neq \mu$, i. e. $F_\lambda(a) \neq F_\mu(a)$ for $\lambda \neq \mu$.

10.3.4 To each pair $(a, x) \in A \times I$ there exists $\lambda \in \Lambda$ such that $x = F_\lambda(a)$.

10.3.5 For all $\lambda, \mu, \nu \in \Lambda$: $F_\lambda^{-1} \circ F_\nu \circ F_\mu^{-1} = F_\mu^{-1} \circ F_\nu \circ F_\lambda^{-1}$.

10.3.6 **Proposition:**

F_λ is continuous and open for all $\lambda \in \Lambda$.

Proof: The continuity of F follows from 10.3.1 and 10.3.2 by 3.6.12, 3.5.10 and 3.4.4. As F_λ^{-1} is monotone, F_λ^{-1} is continuous according to 3.6.11. F_λ is therefore an open map.

10.3.7 Theorem: If a family F_λ, $\lambda \in \Lambda$ fulfills conditions 10.3.1–10.3.5, it admits a translation invariant representation, i.e. there exist monotone and continuous maps

$$m\colon A \to \mathbb{R}$$
$$H\colon \mathbb{R} \to \mathbb{R}$$

and a map $k\colon \Lambda \to \mathbb{R}$ such that

(*) $\quad F_\lambda(a) = H(m(a) - k(\lambda))$.

The maps H, m and k are unique up to the simultaneous transformation

$$m^*(a) = \alpha m(a) + \beta$$
$$H^*(v) = H((v - \beta + \gamma)/\alpha)$$
$$k^*(\lambda) = \alpha k(\lambda) + \gamma.$$

Furthermore $m(A) = k(\Lambda) = \mathbb{R}$.

Proof: Let $\lambda_0 \in \Lambda$ be arbitrary. We define an order in $A \times A$ as follows: According to 10.3.4 to each pair $(a, b) \in A \times A$ there exists an unique $\lambda = \lambda(a, b)$ such that $F_\lambda(a) = F_{\lambda_0}(b)$. We define

$ab \{\precsim\} cd$ iff $F_\lambda(c) \{\leqq\} F_{\lambda_0}(d)$ with $\lambda = \lambda(a, b)$.

(i) It is easy to see that $\langle A; <_1, \approx, \prec\rangle$ thus defined is a reduced ordered distance system. Proofs will be given for transitivity, cancellation, continuity and the quadruple condition.

Transitivity: $ab \prec cd$ implies: $F_\lambda(a) = F_{\lambda_0}(b)$ and $F_\lambda(c) < F_{\lambda_0}(d)$. $cd \prec ef$ implies: $F_\mu(c) = F_{\lambda_0}(d)$ and $F_\mu(e) < F_{\lambda_0}(f)$. Therefore, $F_\lambda(c) < F_\mu(c)$. As F_λ is continuous for all $\lambda \in \Lambda$, 10.3.3 implies, on account of the Intersection Theorem 3.6.14, that $F_\lambda(v) < F_\mu(v)$ for all $v \in A$. Hence $F_\lambda(e) < F_\mu(e)$, whence $F_\lambda(e) < F_{\lambda_0}(f)$. This, however, implies $ab \prec ef$ by definition.

Cancellation: $a'b \approx a''b$ implies $F_\lambda(a') = F_{\lambda_0}(b)$ and $F_\lambda(a'') = F_{\lambda_0}(b)$. Hence $F_{\lambda_0}(a') = F_{\lambda_0}(a'')$ whence $a' = a''$.

Continuity: We show that $\{x \in A\colon ab \prec xc\}$ is open. Let $F_\lambda(a) = F_{\lambda_0}(b)$. As $ab \prec xc$ iff $F_\lambda(x) < F_{\lambda_0}(c)$, we have $\{x \in A\colon ab \prec xc\} = \{x \in A\colon x <_1 F_\lambda^{-1} F_{\lambda_0}(c)\}$ which is open.

Quadruple Condition: $ab \prec cd$ implies $F_\lambda(a) = F_{\lambda_0}(b)$ and $F_\lambda(c) < F_{\lambda_0}(d)$. Let $F_\mu(a) = F_{\lambda_0}(c)$. Using 10.3.5, we obtain $F_\mu^{-1} F_{\lambda_0}(d) > F_\mu^{-1} F_\lambda(c) = F_\mu^{-1} F_\lambda F_{\lambda_0}^{-1} F_{\lambda_0}(c) = F_{\lambda_0}^{-1} F_\lambda F_\mu^{-1} F_{\lambda_0}(c) = F_{\lambda_0}^{-1} F_\lambda(a) = b$. Hence $F_\mu(b) < F_{\lambda_0}(d)$.

(ii) As all ordered distance axioms are fulfilled, 9.3.1 implies the existence of a monotone and continuous map $m\colon A \to \mathbb{R}$ such that $ab \gtreqless cd$ iff $m(a) - m(b) \gtreqless m(c) - m(d)$. By definition of distance we have $a(F_{\lambda_0}^{-1} F_\lambda(a)) \approx b(F_{\lambda_0}^{-1} F_\lambda(b))$ for all $a, b \in A$. Hence, $m(a) - m(F_{\lambda_0}^{-1} F_\lambda(a)) = m(b) - m(F_{\lambda_0}^{-1} F_\lambda(b))$, i.e. $k(\lambda) := m(a) - m(F_{\lambda_0}^{-1} F_\lambda(a))$ is independent of a. Hence $F_\lambda(a) = F_{\lambda_0}(m^{-1}(m(a) - k(\lambda)))$. Let now $H := F_{\lambda_0} \circ m^{-1}$. We have $k(\Lambda) = \{m(a) - m(F_{\lambda_0}^{-1} F_\lambda(a))\colon \lambda \in \Lambda\} = m(a) \dot{-} \{m(F_{\lambda_0}^{-1} F_\lambda(a))\colon \lambda \in \Lambda\} = m(a) \dot{-} m(A)$

for all $a \in A$, according to 10.3.4. This implies $k(\Lambda) = \mathbb{R}$ and $m(A) = \mathbb{R}$. Therefore H is defined on $\mathbb{R}$. Since H is monotone and continuous, the existence assertion of the theorem holds.

If we have a representation of the type (*), then $I = \{F_\lambda(a): \lambda \in \Lambda\} = H(m(a) \dot{-} k(\Lambda))$. Therefore $m(a) \dot{-} k(\Lambda) = H^{-1} I$ for all $a \in A$, i. e. $k(\Lambda) = \mathbb{R}$, and analogously $m(A) = \mathbb{R}$. The uniqueness assertion follows now from 10.2.3(a).

In the following we give a sufficient condition for the case of arbitrary k.

10.3.8 **Theorem:** Let $F: A^k \times B \to C$. Assume that C is ordered and that there exists a function $F_0: A \times B \to C$ such that:

(i) $F(a_1', \ldots, a_k', b') = F(a_1'', \ldots, a_k'', b'')$ iff
$F_0(a_i', b') = F_0(a_i'', b'')$ for all $i = 1, \ldots, k$,

(ii) F_0 is cancellable,

(iii) $\{F_0(a, b): a \in A\}$, $\{F_0(a, b): b \in B\}$ are connected in the interval topology of C for all $b \in B$, $a \in A$ respectively,

(iv) there exists a one-to-one map φ from A onto B such that
$F_0(a', b') \{\leqq\} F_0(a'', b'')$ iff
$F_0(a', \varphi(a'')) \{\leqq\} F_0(\varphi^{-1}(b'), b'')$.

Under these assumptions we may define an order in A by

10.3.9 $a' \{\leqq\} a''$ iff $F_0(a', b) \{\leqq\} F_0(a'', b)$, and correspondingly in B. Furthermore there exists a map $m: A \to \mathbb{R}$, monotone and continuous with respect to this order, and a translation invariant function H: $D_{m,n} \to C$ such that

$$F(a_1, \ldots, a_k, b) = H(m(a_1), \ldots, m(a_k), n(b)), \quad \text{with } n = m \circ \varphi^{-1}$$

and $D_{m,n} := \{(m(a_1)+x, \ldots, m(a_k)+x, n(b)+x): a_i \in A, b \in B, x \in \mathbb{R}\}$.

The maps m and H are unique up to the transformation

$$m^*(a) = \alpha m(a) + \beta$$

$$H^*(x_1, \ldots, x_k, y) = H\left(\frac{x_1-\beta}{\alpha}, \ldots, \frac{x_k-\beta}{\alpha}, \frac{y-\beta}{\alpha}\right), \text{ for } x_i, y \in m^*(A).$$

Proof: We define an order on $A \times B$ by

10.3.10 $a'b' \{\lesssim\} a''b''$ iff $F_0(a', b') \{\leqq\} F_0(a'', b'')$.

Now we shall show that with the order in $A \times B$ thus defined the assumptions of Theorem 9.4.2 are fulfilled: The generalized quadruple condition (q^*) immediately follows from (iv) with $F = \varphi$, $G = \varphi^{-1}$, for $a'\,b' \{\lesssim\} a''\,b''$

iff $F_0(a', \varphi(a''))\{\leqq\} F_0(\varphi^{-1}(b'), b'')$. This is equivalent to $a' \varphi(a'')\{\precsim\}$ $\varphi^{-1}(b')\, b''$. We remark that 10.3.9 defines an order relation in A, as can be seen from 8.5.6.

(ii) and (iii) imply the continuity condition. We will prove that $A_0 := \{(a, b) : a \in A\}$ is a connected subset of $A \times B$, endowed with the interval topology. As the map $F_0(a, b) \rightarrow ab$ is a monotone map from the connected set $\{F_0(a, b) : a \in A\}$ onto A_0, A_0 is connected with respect to the interval topology of A_0 (3.6.11, 3.6.6). As A_0 is simple, which can be easily seen from (ii) and (iii), the interval topology and relative topology coincide (3.4.5).

Hence by Theorem 9.4.2 there exists an interval scale m such that

$m(a_1) - m(a_2)\{\leqq\} m(a_3) - m(a_4)$ iff $a_1 a_2 \{\precsim\} a_3 a_4$ iff $a_1 \varphi(a_2)\{\precsim\}$ $a_3 \varphi(a_4)$.

This implies the existence of a monotone function H_0 such that

10.3.11 $F_0(a, b) = H_0(m(a) - n(b))$ with $n = m \circ \varphi^{-1}$.

Hence $F(a'_1, \ldots, a'_k, b') = F(a''_1, \ldots, a''_k, b'')$ iff $m(a'_i) - n(b') = m(a''_i) - n(b'')$ for all $i = 1, \ldots, k$ by (i) and therefore $F(a_1, \ldots, a_k, b) = H_1(m(a_1) - n(b),$ $\ldots, m(a_k) - n(b))$ for some function H_1. The assertion now follows with $H(x_1, \ldots, x_k, y) := H_1(x_1 - y, \ldots, x_k - y)$.

Using the representation 10.3.11, uniqueness of m and n follows by 10.2.3 (a). Therefore also H is unique up to linear transformations.

10.4 Linear Representations

10.4.1 **Definition:** By a *linear* representation we mean a representation of the type

$$F(a, b) = H\left(\frac{m(a) - n(b)}{s(b)}\right), \quad a \in A, b \in B.$$

A translation invariant representation $F(a, b) = H_0(m(a) - n(b))$ is always a special linear representation. We will use the term *genuine linear* representation for a representation with $s(b)$ not identical to a constant.

If $F(a, b) = H_0(m(a) - n(b))$, the transformation

$m'(a) = \exp(m(a))$

$n'(b) = \exp(n(b))$

$H'_0(u) = H_0(\log(1 + u))$

leads to

$$F(a, b) = H'_0\left(\frac{m'(a) - n'(b)}{n'(b)}\right),$$

a genuine linear representation. From this example it becomes clear that there might exist several linear representations which are not connected by a linear transformation. Hence the existence of a linear representation does not determine the scale uniquely up to linear transformations. Theorem 10.4.5 shows, however, that uniqueness up to linear transformations can be achieved by the following

10.4.2 **Convention:** If among the linear representations of $F(a, b)$ there are translation invariant representations, we will not use genuine linear representations.

Furthermore, any genuine linear representation has an intrinsic indeterminatness:

If

$$F(a,b)=H\left(\frac{m(a)-n(b)}{s(b)}\right),$$

we also have

$$F(a,b)=H'\left(\frac{m(a)-n'(b)}{s(b)}\right)$$

with $n'(b)=n(b)+\beta s(b)$,

$H'(u)=H(u+\beta)$.

This indetermination can be eliminated by the

10.4.3 **Standardization** $H(0)=\frac{1}{2}$.

We remark that in particular cases H may be interpreted as distribution function. Then standardization 10.4.3 makes the median of the pertaining random variable equal to zero. It suggests itself in these cases to standardize H further such that the pertaining variance equals one.

In the following let A and B be ordered and connected sets.

The following Lemma is due to ACZÉL, DJOKOVIĆ and PFANZAGL (1968).

10.4.4 **Lemma:** Let m and n be monotone increasing functions defined on A and B, respectively, having the same real interval as range. Let m^* and n^* be another such pair of functions. Let s and s^* be positive functions defined on B. Assume that the functions $s \circ m^{-1}$ and $s^* \circ m^{-1}$ are differentiable.

Finally assume that

$$F(a,b)=H\left(\frac{m(a)-n(b)}{s(b)}\right)=H^*\left(\frac{m^*(a)-n^*(b)}{s^*(b)}\right),$$

$$H(0)=H^*(0)=\frac{1}{2}$$

with monotone increasing functions H and H^*. Then one of the following four relations between m, n, s, H and m^*, n^*, s^*, H^* obtains:

$$\text{(i)}\quad \begin{cases} m^*(a)=\alpha m(a)+\beta \\ n^*(b)=\alpha n(b)+\beta \\ s^*(b)=\gamma s(b) \\ H^*(t)=H\left(\dfrac{t\gamma}{\alpha}\right) \text{ for } t\in\left\{\dfrac{m^*(a)-n^*(b)}{s^*(b)}: a\in A, b\in B\right\} \end{cases}$$

$$\text{(ii)}_1\quad \begin{cases} m^*(a)=\alpha\exp(\beta m(a))+\gamma \\ n^*(b)=\alpha\exp(\beta n(b))+\gamma \\ s^*(b)=\delta\exp(\beta n(b)) \\ s(b)=\varepsilon \\ H^*(t)=H\left(\dfrac{1}{\beta\varepsilon}\log\left(1+\dfrac{\delta t}{\alpha}\right)\right) \text{ for } t\in\left\{\dfrac{m^*(a)-n^*(b)}{s^*(b)}: a\in A, b\in B\right\} \end{cases}$$

$$\text{(ii)}_2\quad \begin{cases} m(a)=\alpha\exp(\beta m^*(a))+\gamma \\ n(b)=\alpha\exp(\beta n^*(b))+\gamma \\ s(b)=\delta\exp(\beta n^*(b)) \\ s^*(b)=\varepsilon \\ H(t)=H^*\left(\dfrac{1}{\beta\varepsilon}\log\left(1+\dfrac{\delta t}{\alpha}\right)\right) \text{ for } t\in\left\{\dfrac{m(a)-n(b)}{s(b)}: a\in A, b\in B\right\} \end{cases}$$

$$\text{(iii)}\quad \begin{cases} m^*(a)=\lambda\,|m(a)+\beta|^{\gamma}+\varepsilon \\ n^*(b)=\lambda\,|n(b)+\beta|^{\gamma}+\varepsilon \\ s^*(b)=\delta\,|n(b)+\beta|^{\gamma} \\ s(b)=\alpha(n(b)+\beta) \\ H(t)=H^*\left(\dfrac{\lambda}{\delta}(|1+\alpha t|\gamma-1)\right) \text{ for } t\in\left\{\dfrac{m(a)-n(b)}{s(b)}: a\in A, b\in B\right\} \end{cases}$$

with appropiate constants α, β, γ, δ, ε, λ.

10.4.5 **Theorem:** If there exist linear representations

$$(*)\qquad F(a,b)=H\left(\frac{m(a)-n(b)}{s(b)}\right),\quad H(0)=\frac{1}{2}$$

with a positive function s and monotone increasing functions m, n, H, such that $s\circ n^{-1}$ is differentiable and m, n have the same interval as range, then the application of convention 10.4.2 leads to scales m, n which are unique up to linear representations. More precisely, the maps m, n, s and H are unique up to the simultaneous transformation:

$$\text{(i)}\qquad \begin{cases} m^*(a)=\alpha m(a)+\beta \\ n^*(b)=\alpha n(b)+\beta \\ s^*(b)=\gamma s(b) \\ H^*(t)=H\left(\dfrac{t\gamma}{\alpha}\right)\text{ for } t\in\left\{\dfrac{m^*(a)-n^*(b)}{s^*(b)}: a\in A, b\in B\right\} \end{cases}$$

Proof: According to 10.4.4 the solutions of the functional equation (*) are given by (i), (ii) or (iii). We shall show that according to convention 10.4.2 the scales m^*, n^* in case $(ii)_1$ and m, n in case $(ii)_2$ or (iii) are not admitted.

In case $(ii)_1$ or $[(ii)_2]$ a difference representation

$$F(a,b)=H\left(\frac{m(a)-n(b)}{\varepsilon}\right)\qquad \left[H^*\left(\frac{m^*(a)-n^*(b)}{\varepsilon}\right)\right]$$

is possible.

According to convention 10.4.2 m^*, n^* $[m, n]$ are not admitted. In case (iii), a difference representation is possible too. As $s(b)>0$ for all $b\in B$, $n(b)+\beta>0$ $(n(b)+\beta<0)$ for all $b\in B$ and therefore $m(a)+\beta>0$ $(m(a)+\beta<0)$ for all $a\in A$.

Hence with

$$\begin{aligned} m_0(a)&=\log(m(a)+\beta) && [-\log(-(m(a)+\beta))] \\ n_0(b)&=\log(n(b)+\beta) && [-\log(-(n(b)+\beta))] \\ H_0(t)&=H\left(\frac{1}{\alpha}(\exp(t)-1)\right) && \left[H\left(\frac{1}{\alpha}\exp(-t)-1\right)\right] \end{aligned}$$

we obtain:

$$F(a,b)=H_0(m_0(a)-n_0(b)).$$

Therefore the scales m, n are not admitted by convention 10.4.2.

11. Scales Derived from Response

11.1 Response, Judgment and Valuation

Let A be a set of stimuli, B a set of subjects and C the set of possible responses. An experiment consists in subjecting subject $b \in B$ to stimulus $a \in A$ and registering the response $c \in C$. Thus, $(a, b, c) \in A \times B \times C$ is a complete description of the experiment (a, b) together with its outcome c. It is assumed that independent repetitions of the experiment (a, b) are possible. This entails that the outcomes $c_1, c_2, \ldots$ in a sequence of independent repetitions $(a_1, b_1), (a_2, b_2), \ldots$ with $a_i = a$ and $b_i = b$ for $i = 1, 2, \ldots$ behave like a sequence of realizations of independent random variables (i.e. there is no perseverance, no learning, etc.). Then it is adequate to base the analysis of the experiment on the assumption that to each experiment (a, b) there corresponds a probability measure $R(a, b, D)$, defined on a σ-algebra $\mathscr{D}$ of subsets $D \subset C$ and which governs the distribution of the outcomes of the individual performances of the experiment.

To illustrate the generality of this description we shall consider an experiment in which the subject is asked to rank a set of k stimuli according to some criterion. Then we can choose: $A = A_0^k$, i.e. the set of all k-tuples $(a_1, \ldots, a_k)$ with $a_i \in A_0$, and for C the set of all permutations of the numbers $1, \ldots, k$. If $a_1, \ldots, a_k$ are ranked in order $(a_{i_1}, \ldots, a_{i_k})$, this outcome can be described by $c = (i_1, \ldots, i_k)$. As C consists of a finite number of points (namely $k!$), the probability measure $R(a, b, D)$ is given by a finite number of probabilities. Written explicitly, $P(a_1, \ldots, a_k, b, i_1, \ldots, i_k)$ is the probability that stimuli $a_1, \ldots, a_k$ are ranked in the order $a_{i_1}, \ldots, a_{i_k}$ by subject b.

Another possible interpretation of the stochastic element is that for each subject the response is uniquely determined by the stimulus, the stochastic element entering from sampling the subject from a homogeneous population. In this case, b characterizes the population (rather than the individual subject). With this interpretation the following results hold if the word "population" is substituted for "subject". Instead of different subjects we have to think of different homogeneous populations (e.g. distinct only by age or sex).

As we are interested in the foundational aspects only, we may neglect the fact that in practice our knowledge is always restricted to a finite number of experiments. Hence we will assume that $R(a, b, D)$ is known. If we consider an infinite number of independent performances of the same experiment (a, b) as a single experiment with the response being the probability measure $R(a, b, D)$, we are back to the original model: We have only to change the concept of experiment and the set of possible responses which is now the set of all possible probability measures on a σ-algebra over C instead of C itself. Thus, considering the foundational aspects only, the distinction between stochastic and uniquely determined response becomes irrelevant.

The variable c, characterizing the outcome of the experiment (a, b), is also called the *response* of subject b to stimulus a. Accordingly, $R(a, b, D)$ will be called *response probability measure* (or shortly: *response distribution*) of the experiment (a, b) (or of subject b to stimulus a). We will speak of *judgment*, if $R(a, b, D)$ is independent of $b \in B$. If the response distribution function is not independent of b (i.e. if there exist $a \in A$ and $b', b'' \in B$ such that not $R(a, b', D) = R(a, b'', D)$ for all D of the σ-algebra), we will speak of *valuation*.

The intuitive idea behind this terminology is the following: If $R(a, b, D)$ is independent of the subject, it reflects the judgment of the subjects about a property of the stimuli which is intersubjective. Judgments of pitch or subjective loudness are typical examples. If the response distribution $R(a, b, D)$ is not uniquely determined by the stimulus, it depends on a property of the subject, which will be called *disposition*. The stimulus is valuated from the viewpoint of a specific disposition. Opinions on ethical or esthetical statements are typical examples of valuation. But also the responses of the subjects to tasks in a performance test are valuations in this terminology.

In short: A comparison of ice creams according to sweetness is judgment, a comparison according to taste is valuation. To rank statements on the racial issue according to the degree in which they favor integration is judgment. To rank them according to the subject's personal consent is valuation.

The distinction between judgment and valuation is decisive in the theory of measurement: In the case of judgment we obtain an intersubjective scale for some property of the stimulus. In the case of valuation we primarily obtain a different scale for each subject. It might, however, turn out that there is a common scale for stimuli and dispositions of subjects such that the response of the subject to the stimulus depends on the relative position of the pertaining scale values on this common scale. (In performance testing, for example, we might obtain a common scale measuring the difficulty of the task (stimulus) and the disposition of the subject, with the outcome of the experiment depending on the position of the subject relative to the task on this scale.)

While judgment can only lead to measurement of an intersubjective property of the stimuli, valuation may lead to simultaneous measurement of stimuli *and* subjects. In sections 3 and 4 we will develop a general foundation of measurement for these cases based on canonical representation. In sections 5 to 12 we will consider a few applications. Section 2 gives a discriminal dispersion model for the response behavior.

11.2 A Discriminal Dispersion Model*)

The fact that the response of a subject to a stimulus is stochastic rather than uniquely determined was explained by THURSTONE (1927) using a model of the discriminal process. The following is an adaptation of THURSTONE's model to the more general case treated here. The basic assumption is that the response is uniquely determined by the psychophyical process (called *sensation* in the following) which is initiated by the stimulus: the process itself, however, is a random variable. This model is made more specific by the assumption that to each stimulus a there corresponds an *ideal sensation* with a scale value $m(a)$. The sensation actually perceived in a specific performance of the experiment (a, b) has the scale value α. According to THURSTONE's assumption α is a random variable distributed somehow about the ideal sensation $m(a)$. In case A is a Cartesian product, to the k-tuple of stimuli $(a_1, \ldots, a_k)$ there corresponds a k-tuple of sensations $(\alpha_1, \ldots, \alpha_k)$ distributed in $\mathbb{R}^k$ about $(m(a_1), \ldots, m(a_k))$. Observable is the response $R(\alpha_1, \ldots, \alpha_k)$. We assume that we are given the distribution $P(a_1, \ldots, a_k, D)$ (i.e. the probability that the response belongs to the set $D \in \mathscr{B}^k$ if the stimuli are $(a_1, \ldots, a_k)$, where $\mathscr{B}^k$ denotes the BOREL algebra of $\mathbb{R}^k$).

*) The knowledge of this section is not essential for the understanding of the following sections.

Let the probability for $(\alpha_1, \ldots, \alpha_k) \in D \in \mathscr{B}^k$ be of the form

11.2.1 $Q(D \dot{-} (m(a_1), \ldots, m(a_k)))$, where

$$D \dot{-} (r_1, \ldots, r_k) := \{(x_1 - r_1, \ldots, x_k - r_k) : (x_1, \ldots, x_k) \in D\}.$$

(The symbol $\dot{+}$ is defined correspondingly.) Furthermore, we assume that any set in $\mathscr{B}^k$ is of positive Q-measure iff it is of positive LEBESGUE measure.

11.2.2 **Proposition:** For all $i = 1, 2, \ldots, k$:

$$Q(D \dot{-} (x_1, \ldots, x_i', \ldots, x_k)) = Q(D \dot{-} (x_1, \ldots, x_i'', \ldots, x_k)) \text{ for all } D \in \mathscr{B}^k$$

implies $x_i' = x_i''$.

Proof: If 11.2.2 holds for all $D \in \mathscr{B}^k$, it also holds for $D = \{(\xi_1, \ldots, \xi_i, \ldots, \xi_k) : \xi_i \leqq 0\}$. Then, $D' = D \dot{-} (x_1, \ldots, x_i', \ldots, x_k) = \{(\xi_1, \ldots, \xi_i, \ldots, \xi_k) : \xi_i \leqq -x_i'\}$, $D'' = D \dot{-} (x_1, \ldots, x_i'', \ldots, x_k) = \{(\xi_1, \ldots, \xi_i, \ldots, \xi_k) : \xi_i \leqq -x_i''\}$. If $x_i' > x_i''$, then $D'' - D' = \{\xi_1, \ldots, \xi_i, \ldots, \xi_k) : -x_i' < \xi_i \leqq -x_i''\}$ is of positive LEBESGUE measure whence $Q(D'' - D') > 0$. Because $D' \subset D''$, this contradicts $Q(D') = Q(D'')$.

Finally, we assume that the response depends on the relative position of the stimuli only, i.e.

11.2.3 $R(\alpha_1 + u, \ldots, \alpha_k + u) = R(\alpha_1, \ldots, \alpha_k)$.

Let $R^{-1}(D) = \{(\alpha_1, \ldots, \alpha_k) : R(\alpha_1, \ldots, \alpha_k) \in D\}$. Then $P(a_1, \ldots, a_k, D) = Q(R^{-1}(D) \dot{-} (m(a_1), \ldots, m(a_k)))$. From 11.2.3 we obtain that $R^{-1}(D) \dot{+} (u, \ldots, u) = R^{-1}(D)$. If we define $Q^*(x_1, \ldots, x_k, D) := Q(R^{-1}(D) \dot{-} (x_1, \ldots, x_k))$ we therefore have $Q^*(x_1 + u, \ldots, x_k + u, D) = Q^*(x_1, \ldots, x_k, D)$. Furthermore by 11.2.2 $Q^*(x_1, \ldots, x_i', \ldots, x_k, D) = Q^*(x_1, \ldots, x_i'', \ldots, x_k, D)$ for all $D \in \mathscr{B}^k$ implies $x_i' = x_i''$, if $R^{-1}\mathscr{B}^k = \mathscr{B}^k$. Therefore $P(a_1, \ldots, a_k, D)$ admits a canonical representation $P(a_1, \ldots, a_k, D) = Q^*(m(a_1), \ldots, m(a_k), D)$. If A is an ordered set, m is a monotone function, and $m(A)$ is a connected set, then the last equation determines the scale m uniquely up to linear transformations (10.2.3(b)).

The semantical meaning of condition 11.2.1 becomes more clear if we respresent Q by its density with respect to the LEBESGUE measure. Then 11.2 1 is equivalent to the requirement that the density be of the type

11.2.4 $\varphi(\alpha_1 - m(a_1), \ldots, \alpha_k - m(a_k))$,

where φ is independent of the $m(a_i)$. It is not required that $\alpha_1, \ldots, \alpha_k$

are stochastically independent. Nevertheless, condition 11.2.4 is rather restrictive because it is assumed that the density depends on the $m(a_i)$ in a very simple manner. In the case of a normal distribution, e.g., 11.2.4 implies that neither the variances nor the covariances depend on $m(a_i)$. This means that the stochastic dependence between (α_1, α_2) is the same regardless of whether the stimuli a_1, a_2 generating (α_1, α_2) are identical or markedly different.

Formula 11.2.4 suggests to consider other modes in which the density depends on $m(a_1), \ldots, m(a_k)$, e.g.

11.2.5 $$\varphi\left(\frac{\alpha_1 - m(a_1)}{f(m(a_1))}, \ldots, \frac{\alpha_k - m(a_k)}{f(m(a_k))}\right) \cdot \prod_1^k \frac{1}{f(m(a_i))}.$$

This allows for discriminal dispersions depending on the "ideal" stimuli. Inherently this model requires the scale values $m(a)$ to be unique up to dilations.

We remark that there is a special case of 11.2.5 which is essentially equivalent to 11.2.4, namely the case that the random variables are essentially positive, that $m(a) > 0$ for all $a \in A$ and $f(m(a)) = \varkappa m(a)$. Then we may put

$$\psi(x_1, \ldots, x_k) := \varphi\left(\frac{1}{\varkappa}(e^{x_1} - 1), \ldots, \frac{1}{\varkappa}(e^{x_k} - 1)\right) \prod_1^k \frac{e^{x_i}}{\varkappa};$$

$\beta_i = \log \alpha_i$ and $n(a_i) = \log m(a_i)$ and obtain that the density is

$$\psi(\beta_1 - n(a_1), \ldots, \beta_k - n(a_k)), \text{ i.e. of type 11.2.4.}$$

Of course, there is no way to distinguish between these two assumptions on empirical grounds: If one of the two models fits the data, so does the other one. The decision between these two models (which is equivalent to a choice between the scales m and $\log m$) has to be made on prior grounds. The situation becomes different, if an additional scale is available. Then, the question whether the discriminal dispersion is constant or not if the sensations α are measured in the given scale becomes meaningful. Such a situation occurred e.g. with experiments performed by EKMAN and KÜNNAPAS (1962a, b, 1963). In these experiments it turned out that scales of aesthetic values obtained by ratio estimation were identical with paired comparison scales obtained on the assumption of discriminal dispersions being proportional to the means.

11.3 Measurement of Stimuli

In this section we consider the case that the response $R(a, b)$ is independent of $b \in B$. Then, we can simply write $R(a)$. If a canonical representation is possible, this might determine an interval scale for A. We will give an example for the case that $R(a)$ is a probability measure, say $P(a, D)$.

11.3.1 **Theorem:** Assume that both A and C are ordered and connected sets containing at least two elements and that $\mathscr{D}$ is the σ-algebra generated by the sets $(\leftarrow, d)$ with $d \in C$. Assume, furthermore, that
* $P(a', D) = P(a'', D)$ for a set $D = (\leftarrow, d)$ implies $a' = a''$, and

(*) $P(a, I) > 0$ for any nondegenerate interval $I \in \mathscr{D}$. If there exist monotone and continuous functions

$m: A \to \mathbb{R}$

$k: C \to \mathbb{R}$ such that $\mathscr{D} = k^{-1} \mathscr{B}$

and a function $Q(x, B): \mathbb{R} \times \mathscr{B} \to \mathbb{R}$ with $Q(x+u, B \dotplus u) = Q(x, B)$ for all $x, u \in \mathbb{R}$, $B \in \mathscr{B}$ such that $P(a, D) = Q(m(a), k(D))$ for all $D \in \mathscr{D}$, then the functions m, k and Q are unique up to the simultaneous transformation

$$m^*(a) = \alpha m(a) + \beta$$

$$k^*(c) = \alpha k(c) + \gamma$$

$$Q^*(x, B) = Q\left(\frac{x-\beta}{\alpha}, \frac{B \dotminus \gamma}{\alpha}\right) \quad \text{for } x \in m^*(A)$$

if the direction of increase is the same for m^* and m, and for k^* and k.
Furthermore $k(C) = \mathbb{R}$.
We remark that $\nu B \dotplus \mu := \{\nu x + \mu : x \in B\}$.

Proof: Assume that $k(C) \subsetneqq \mathbb{R}$. Since C is connected and k continuous, we may assume without loss of generality that $\alpha := \sup k(C) < \infty$. This implies $1 = P(a, C) = Q(m(a), k(C)) \leqq Q(m(a), (-\infty, \alpha])$, i.e. $Q(m(a), (-\infty, \alpha]) = 1$ for all $a \in A$. Let $a_i \in A$ for $i = 1, 2, 3$ be chosen such that $m(a_1) < m(a_2) < m(a_3)$. Then $Q(m(a_3) + m(a_i) - m(a_3), (-\infty, \alpha + m(a_i) - m(a_3)]) = Q(m(a_3), (-\infty, \alpha])$ for $i = 1, 2$.

If $\varepsilon < m(a_3) - m(a_i)$ for $i = 1, 2$, we have $Q(m(a_i), (-\infty, \alpha - \varepsilon)) = 1$ for $i = 1, 2$, and therefore $Q(m(a_i), k(C) \cap (-\infty, \alpha - \varepsilon)) = 1$ for $i = 1, 2$. There exists $d \in C$ with $k(C) \cap (-\infty, \alpha - \varepsilon) = k((\leftarrow, d))$ if k is monotone increasing and $k(C) \cap (-\infty, \alpha - \varepsilon] = k([d, \to))$ if k is monotone decreasing. Therefore we have $P(a_i, (\leftarrow, d)) = Q(m(a_i), k(\leftarrow, d)) = 1$ or $P(a_i, [d, \to)) = Q(m(a_i), k([d, \to))) = 1$ respectively; according to $*$ this implies $a_1 = a_2$ which contradicts $m(a_1) < m(a_2)$.

Assume that two such representations exist: $Q(m(a), k(D)) = Q^*(m^*(a), k^*(D))$. Let $\varphi = m \circ m^{*-1}$, $\psi = k \circ k^{*-1}$, $m^*(a) = x$, $k^*(D) = B$. Then, for all $x \in m^*(A)$ and $B \in k^*(\mathscr{D})$: $Q(\varphi(x), \psi(B)) = Q^*(x, B)$. Let $B = (\leftarrow, y)$. Then, $\psi(B) = (\leftarrow, \psi(y))$, and $B \dotplus u = (\leftarrow, y + u)$.

Let $Q(v, (\leftarrow, w)) =: H(v, w)$, and $Q^*(x, (\leftarrow, y)) =: H^*(x, y)$. Then

(**) $H(\varphi(x), \psi(y)) = H^*(x, y)$, and

$$H(v + u, w + u) = H(v, w), \quad H^*(x + u, y + u) = H^*(x, y).$$

From (*) we obtain that H is increasing in y for $x \in m(A)$; the same holds true for H^*.

Now (**) yields $H_0(\varphi(x) - \psi(y)) = H_0^*(x - y)$, where $H_0(x - y) := H(x, y)$ and H_0, H are monotone functions. This is equivalent to $f(x - y) = \varphi(x) - \psi(y)$ with a monotone function $f(u) := H_0^{-1} H_0^*(u)$. Similarly as in the proof of 10.2.3 we obtain

$$m^*(a) = \alpha m(a) + \beta$$

$$k^*(c) = \alpha k(c) + \gamma$$

$$H^*(x, y) = H\left(\frac{x - \beta}{\alpha}, \frac{y - \gamma}{\alpha}\right) \text{ for } x \in m^*(A)$$

whence the assertion follows for all $B = (\leftarrow, d)$, $d \in \mathbb{R}$, and therefore for all $B \in \mathscr{B}$.

11.3.2 **Remark:** If m, k are monotone increasing functions with $k(C) = \mathbb{R}$, then a representation as described in Theorem 11.3.1 exists iff there exists a distribution function H_0 such that $P(a, (\leftarrow, c)) = H_0(k(c) - m(a))$.

11.4 Simultaneous Measurement of Stimuli and Subjects

In this section we consider the case that the response $R(a, b)$ actually depends on b. We define an equivalence relation on B by $b' \approx b''$ iff $R(a, b') = R(a, b'')$ for all $a \in A$. Let A and B contain at least two elements.

11.4.1 **Theorem:** Let C be an ordered set and $A = A_0^k$ with $k \geqq 1$. Assume that $R: A_0^k \times B \to C$ is cancellable and that there exist functions $m: A_0 \to \mathbb{R}$, $n: B \to \mathbb{R}$, with $m(A_0)$, $n(B)$ being connected sets, and a continuous function $H: \mathbb{R}^k \to C$, such that

$$R(a_1, \ldots, a_k, b) = H(m(a_1) - n(b), \ldots, m(a_k) - n(b)).$$

Then these functions are unique up to the simultaneous transformation

$$m^*(a)=\alpha m(a)+\beta$$

$$n^*(b)=\alpha n(b)+\gamma$$

$$H^*(x_1,\ldots,x_k)=H\left(\frac{x_1-\beta+\gamma}{\alpha},\ldots,\frac{x_k-\beta+\gamma}{\alpha}\right) \quad \text{for}$$

$$x_i\in m^*(A_0)\dot{-}n^*(B).$$

Proof: Let $H'(x_1,\ldots,x_k,y)=H(x_1-y,\ldots,x_k-y)$. Then, H' fulfills the assumptions of Theorem 10.2.3(a), and the assertion follows.

11.5 Matching of Stimuli

The first application of the general theory developed in sections 11.3 and 11.4 is to the following experiment:

Subject b is asked to adjust a variable stimulus a_2 such that it matches a given standard a_1. Thus, the outcome of the experiment (a_1, b) is a stimulus a_2. Therefore, $C=A$ in this case. A is assumed to be an ordered set. Let $P(a_1, b, D)$ be the probability measure governing the distribution on A. In many applications it turns out that $P(a_1, b, D)$ is independent of b. As both a_1, a_2 belong to the same set A we naturally assume the two scales to be identical.

Then, Theorem 11.3.1 applied for a_1 instead of a and a_2 instead of d yields: If there exists a monotone increasing function $m\colon A\to\mathbb{R}$ with $m(A)=\mathbb{R}$ and a monotone increasing probability distribution function $H_0(u)$ such that $P(a_1,(\leftarrow,a_2))=H_0(m(a_2)-m(a_1))$, they are uniquely determined up to the simultaneous transformation

$$m^*(a)=\alpha m(a)+\beta$$

$$H_0^*(u)=H_0\left(\frac{u}{\alpha}\right).$$

This method is essentially FECHNER's method of average error. The experiments performed by FECHNER (1860) yielded frequency distributions (which were estimates of the probability distribution $P(a, D)$) for several values of the standard stimulus a_1. The scale was constructed such that the interquartile range became constant for all frequency distributions. This was at that time an excellent nonparametric procedure.

11.6 Paired Comparisons

Paired comparisons render another application of the general theory developed in sections 11.3 and 11.4. Let us consider the following experiment:

Subject b is asked to rank two given stimuli a_1, a_2 according to some criterion, i.e. to make either

statement 1: "$a_1 > a_2$" or statement 2: "$a_2 > a_1$".

Therefore, we may choose $C = \{1, 2\}$ in this case.

We remark that it suggests itself not to admit the statement $a_1 \sim a_2$, because indifference might depend on other characteristics of the subject than inability to discriminate between a_1 and a_2. Hence the subject is forced to decide for one of the two admitted statements, even in case of inability to discriminate. This implies $P(a_1, a_2, b, \{1\}) + P(a_1, a_2, b, \{2\}) = 1$. Hence one of these probabilities suffices to characterize the whole probability distribution. We will choose $P(a_1, a_2, b, \{1\})$ and denote it for short by $P(a_1, a_2, b)$.

In many applications it turns out that this probability measure is independent of b. (The case where it depends on b will be dealt with in section 11.12). If A contains at least two elements, then an interval scale $m: A \to \mathbb{R}$ can be obtained according to the following

11.6.1 **Theorem:** If there exists a 1—1 map $m: A \to \mathbb{R}$ and a monotone increasing function H defined on $m(A) \dot{-} m(A)$, such that $m(A)$ is connected and

11.6.2 $P(a_1, a_2) = H(m(a_1) - m(a_2))$,
then m and H are uniquely determined up to the simultaneous transformation

$$m^*(a) = \alpha m(a) + \beta$$

$$H^*(u) = H\left(\frac{u}{\alpha}\right) \quad \text{for } u \in m^*(A) \dot{-} m^*(A).$$

Proof: This Theorem is an immediate consequence of Theorem 10.2.3 (a).

11.6.3 **Theorem:** If P is cancellable, the following conditions on $P(a_1, a_2)$ are sufficient for the existence of a representation 11.6.2 with monotone increasing and continuous functions m, H, where the order on A is derived from 11.6.7:

11.6.4 *Continuity condition:*

For all $a_2 \in A : \{P(a_1, a_2) : a_1 \in A\}$ is an interval.

For all $a_1 \in A : \{P(a_1, a_2) : a_2 \in A\}$ is an interval.

11.6.5 *Quadruple condition:*

$P(a_1, a_2) \{\leqq\} P(a_3, a_4)$ implies $P(a_1, a_3) \{\leqq\} P(a_2, a_4)$.

Proof: We define an order in $A \times A$ by

11.6.6 $a_1 a_2 \{\lesssim\} a_3 a_4$ iff $P(a_1, a_2) \{\leqq\} P(a_3, a_4)$,
and an order in A by

11.6.7 $a_1' \{\leqq\} a_1''$ iff $P(a_1', a_2) \{\leqq\} P(a_1'', a_2)$.

Definition 11.6.7 is independent of a_2 in consequence of 8.2.4 and 8.1.14. Similarly as in the proof of Theorem 10.3.8 we obtain that for each $a \in A$ the set $A \times \{a\}$ is connected in $A \times A$. Therefore all the assumptions of Theorem 9.3.1 are fulfilled and the assertion follows easily.

If the experiment is performed in such a way that there is no asymmetry between the experiment (a_1, a_2) and the experiment (a_2, a_1), then

11.6.8 $P(a_1, a_2) + P(a_2, a_1) = 1$

is fulfilled, and H has the property

$$H(-x) = 1 - H(x) \text{ for } x \in m(A) \dot{-} m(A).$$

We remark that for functions P fulfilling 11.6.8 one of the two conditions 11.6.4 is sufficient.

Basically, the method of paired comparisons is nothing else than FECHNER's method of the right and wrong cases (FECHNER, 1860, Vol. 1, p. 74). To choose $P(a_1, a_2)$ as an indicator of distance is essentially FECHNER's principle "equally often noticed differences are equal".

In this connection it might be illustrative to mention THORNDIKE (1910) containing an early and straightforward application of this principle to the measurement of excellence of handwriting. His description of the scale was given by a sequence, say $a_1, a_2, \ldots, a_n, \ldots$ of equidistant specimens of handwritings, the elements of the sequence being chosen such that $P(a_{i+1}, a_i) = .8$.

11.7 Logit Models

In a number of papers (BRADLEY and TERRY (1952), BRADLEY (1954a, b, 1955), LUCE (1959)) the problem of paired comparisons is treated under the additional assumption that

11.7.1 $$\frac{P(a,b)}{P(b,a)}\cdot\frac{P(b,c)}{P(c,b)}=\frac{P(a,c)}{P(c,a)}.$$

This assumption presumes that $P(a,b)>0$ for all $a,b\in A$. Furthermore, we shall assume that 11.6.8 holds.

A general choice model leading to this assumptions is discussed in section 11.10. Condition 11.7.1 is very restrictive, indeed. First of all, it implies the quadruple condition, as $P(a,b)\{\leqq\}P(c,d)$ implies:

$$\frac{P(a,c)}{P(c,a)}\{\leqq\}\frac{P(c,d)}{P(d,c)}\cdot\frac{P(b,c)}{P(c,b)}=\frac{P(b,d)}{P(d,b)},$$

whence $P(a,c)\{\leqq\}P(b,d)$.

Therefore, under suitable conditions on A and P (see Theorem 11.6.3) $P(a,b)$ can be represented as

11.7.2 $P(a,b)=H(m(a)-m(b))$.

Whereas the question of how to determine the functions H and m is very complicated in the general case, it is easy if 11.7.1 holds: It can be checked immediately that

$$H(u)=\frac{1}{1+\exp(-u)},\quad m(a)=\log\frac{P(a,e)}{P(e,a)},$$

with arbitrary $e\in A$, are solutions of 11.7.2.

If the arbitrarily fixed element e is changed into an element e', the scale m is subjected to a shift:

$$m'(a)=\log\frac{P(a,e')}{P(e',a)}=\log\left[\frac{P(a,e)}{P(e,a)}\cdot\frac{P(e,e')}{P(e',e)}\right]=m(a)+\beta$$

with

$$\beta=\log\frac{P(e,e')}{P(e',e)}.$$

Let

$$u(a):=\frac{P(a,e)}{P(e,a)}.$$

Then 11.7.1 implies

11.7.3 $P(a,b)=\dfrac{u(a)}{u(a)+u(b)}$.

It is interesting to note that this model usually ascribed to BRADLEY and TERRY (1952) was used by ZERMELO as early as 1929 in order to measure the playing power $u(a)$ of player a (applied to chess). ZERMELO also discussed the question of how the playing power can be estimated from relative frequencies corresponding to $P(a, b)$ (i.e. fraction of times player a has beaten playeı b), using an estimate of maximum likelihood type.

11.8 The Method of just Noticeable Differences

The purpose of this section is to discuss the relationship between the method of just noticeable differences (jnd) and the method of paired comparisons. It will be shown that for ordered sets A, the method of jnd can be considered as a special application of the method of paired comparisons. This section follows closely the papers by LUCE and EDWARDS (1958) and PFANZAGL (1962).

The basic idea of the method of jnd's is to assign to each manifestation a a manifestation a', which exceeds a by a just noticeable amount. Experiments of this kind were first performed by WEBER (1834). The idea of considering all jnd's as subjectively equal and to use them as a basis for the construction of a subjective scale is due to FECHNER (1860).

In order to make this idea more precise, we have to remark that:

1. The concept of a jnd is not precisely defined. The definition: „jnd's are differences which are noticed *almost* anytime" is not satisfactory because of the phrase "almost anytime". We can make this concept precise by specifying the probability p that a jnd is noticed and assigning to each manifestation a a manifestation a' which is classified higher than a with prescribed probability p. A common value is $p=.75$.

2. Even if the concept of jnd is clearly defined in this way, and if the principle is accepted that all jnd's are equal, this is not sufficient for the construction of a scale: We only obtain scale values for manifestations occurring in the sequence $a, a', a'', \dots$ and there is no possibility whatsoever of determining the scale value of a manifestation between say a and a'. It can hardly be denied that in the presence of a physical scale

"interpolation" will be sufficient for any practical purposes. It must, however, not be overlooked that this interpolation yields scale values which are not defined — more precisely: which are only defined by the interpolation procedure itself and which are therefore without operational meaning.

In order to obtain a complete scale, we have to consider the jnd's for all probabilities, not for one probability only. To be more precise, we define a map $w(a, p)$ from a subset of $A \times \mathbb{R}$ into A by:

11.8.1 $P(w(a, p), a) = p$.

If P is strictly monotone and continuous, $w(a, p)$ is uniquely defined. It is the manifestation which will be classified higher than a with probability p.

In agreement with the terminology introduced by LUCE and EDWARDS, $w(a, p)$ will be called stochastic WEBER*ian function.*

Now we will study relations between properties of P and the following properties of the corresponding WEBERian functions:

11.8.2

a) To each a there exists an nondegenerate interval $I_a \subset [0, 1]$ such that $w(a, p)$ is defined for all $p \in I_a$,

b) for all $a \in A$: $\{w(a, p) : p \in I_a\} = A$,

c) $w(a_0, p') = w(a_0, p'')$ for some $a_0 \in A$ implies $p' = p''$,

d) A is an ordered and connected set and the map $a \to w(a, p)$ is monotone increasing, i. e. $a_1 < a_2$, and $p \in I_{a_1} \cap I_{a_2}$ imply $w(a_1, p) < w(a_2, p)$,

the map $p \to w(a, p)$ is monotone increasing, i. e. $p_1 < p_2$, and $p_1, p_2 \in I_a$ imply $w(a, p_1) < w(a, p_2)$,

11.8.3 $w(w(a, p), q) = w(w(a, q), p)$ for $p, q \in I_a$, $p \in I_{w(a, q)}$, $q \in I_{w(a, p)}$

(i.e. the maps $a \to w(a, p)$ and $a \to w(a, q)$ are commutable),
if $p \in I_a$ then $1 - p \in I_{w(a, p)}$, and

11.8.4 $w(w(a, p), 1 - p) = a$.

Conditions 11.8.2b) and c) together imply that, for all $a \in A$, each element of A occurs among $w(a, p)$; $p \in I_a$ exactly once.

Definition 11.8.1 immediately implies:

11.8.5 $w(b, P(a, b)) = a.$

On the other hand, 11.8.5 may be used to define P in terms of w. Because of 11.8.2b), $P(a, b)$ is defined for any pair $a, b \in A$. $P(a, b)$ is uniquely determined because of 11.8.2c).

11.8.6 **Theorem:**

(i) If P is cancellable and fulfills 11.6.4, 11.6.5 and 11.6.8, then w defined by 11.8.1 fulfills 11.8.2–11.8.5, where the order on A is the order induced by P (see 11.6.7).

(ii) If w fulfills 11.8.2, 11.8.3 and 11.8.4 and $I_a = I$ is independent of a, then P defined by 11.8.5 is cancellable and fulfills 11.6.4, 11.6.5, 11.6.8 and 11.8.1. The order induced by P (see 11.6.7) is the order given in advance by 11.8.2.

Proof: (i) We define an order in A and $A \times A$ according to 11.6.7 and 11.6.6, respectively. Then A is connected, P is continuous and monotone increasing in the first variable and decreasing in the second variable.

α) $\{P(b, a) : b \in A\} = I_a$ implies 11.8.2a), b); c) holds because $w(a_0, p') = w(a_0, p'')$ implies $p' = P(w(a_0, p'), a_0) = P(w(a_0, p''), a_0) = p''$.

d) Let $a < b$ and $p \in I_a \cap I_b$, then
$P(w(a, p), a) = p = P(w(b, p), b) < P(w(b, p), a)$; therefore
$w(a, p) < w(b, p)$.

If $p_1 < p_2$ and $p_1, p_2 \in I_a$, then
$P(w(a, p_1), a) = p_1 < p_2 = P(w(a, p_2), a)$; therefore
$w(a, p_1) < w(a, p_2)$.

β) By definition, we obtain
$P(w(a, p), a) = p$ for $p \in I_a$, and $P(w(w(a, q), p), w(a, q)) = p$ for $q \in I_a$, $p \in I_{w(a, q)}$. As $P(w(w(a, q), p), w(a, q)) = P(w(a, p), a)$, 11.6.5 implies
$P(w(w(a, q), p), w(a, p)) = P(w(a, q), a)$.

On the other hand

$P(w(w(a, p), q), w(a, p)) = P(w(a, q), a)$ for $p, q \in I_a$, $q \in I_{w(a, p)}$.

Hence 11.8.3 follows.

γ) If $p \in I_a$, then $P(w(a, p), a) = p$. Therefore $1 - p = P(a, w(a, p))$, according to 11.6.8. This implies $1 - p \in I_{w(a, p)}$, and $a = w(w(a, p), 1 - p)$.

δ) By definition, $P(w(b, P(a, b)), b) = P(a, b)$.
Hence cancellability implies $w(b, P(a, b)) = a$.
(ii) We have $w(a, P(b, a)) = b$. Therefore, $w(b, 1—P(b, a)) = w(w(a, P(b, a)), 1—P(b, a)) = a$. Now 11.8.5 and 11.8.2c together imply 11.6.8.

α) By definition of P and 11.8.2d, P is monotone increasing in the first variable and therefore (see 11.6.8) monotone decreasing in the second variable. This implies that P is cancellable and that, furthermore, the order induced by P and the order given in advance coincide.

β) We have $\{P(b, a) : b \in A\} = I_a$, according to 11.8.5. Therefore, 11.6.4 holds, since I_a is connected.

γ) $w(a, P(b, a)) = b$ implies $P(w(a, P(b, a)), a) = P(b, a)$.
Therefore $P(w(a, p), a) = p$ for all $p \in I_a$.

δ) We first show that
$P(a, b) = P(w(a, p), w(b, p))$ for all $p \in I$.
For this purpose we substitute in 11.8.1
$a = w(b, p)$ and $p = P(a, b)$.
Using 11.8.5 we obtain
$$P(a, b) = P[w(w(b, p), P(a, b)), w(b, p)]$$
$$= P[w(w(b, P(a, b)), p), w(b, p)] = P[w(a, p), w(b, p)].$$
Now let $P(a', b') = P(a'', b'')$. Then
$P(b', b'') = P(w(b', P(a', b')), w(b'', P(a'', b''))) = P(a', a'')$.
For $P(a', b') < P(a'', b'')$, the proof runs similarly.

11.8.7 **Theorem:** If a WEBERian function fulfills 11.8.2, 11.8.3, and 11.8.4, and I_a is independent of a, there exist continuous and monotone increasing maps $m: A \to \mathbb{R}$ and $h: I \to \mathbb{R}$ such that

11.8.8 $w(a, p) = m^{-1}(m(a) + h(p))$.

Moreover the maps m and h are unique up to the simultaneous transformation

$$m^*(a) = \alpha m(a) + \beta,$$
$$h^*(p) = \alpha h(p),\ p \in I.$$

Proof: Follows immediately by applying definition 11.8.1 to the representation 11.6.2. Then 11.8.8 holds with $h = H^{-1}$. Uniqueness follows from 11.6.1.

This theorem is closely related to a theorem of HOSSZÚ (1962); see also ACZÉL (1966), p. 272/273.

We shall remark that the map $a \to w\big(w(a, p), q\big)$ is a WEBERian function again i.e. that $P\big(w\big(w(a,p)\,q\big), a\big)$ is independent of a. This follows immediately from 11.8.7, because

$$\begin{aligned} w(w(a,p),q) &= m^{-1}(m(w(a,p)) + h(q)) \\ &= m^{-1}(m(a) + h(p) + h(q)) \\ &= w(a, h^{-1}(h(p) + h(q))). \end{aligned}$$

For more details on stochastic WEBERian functions see PFANZAGL (1962) and LUCE and GALANTER (1963), p. 191–244.

11.9 Choices

A natural generalization of paired comparisons are choices from $k > 1$ stimuli $a_1, \ldots, a_k$: The subject b is asked to choose according to some criterion one from k stimuli $\{a_1, \ldots, a_k\}$. The choice can be described by stating one of the numbers $1, \ldots, k$. Thus, we may take $C = \{1, \ldots, k\}$.

For $k = 2$ we are back to the case of paired comparison, because the statement "$a_1 > a_2$" can be considered as the choice of a_1 from the set $\{a_1, a_2\}$.

Let $P(a_1, \ldots, a_k, b, t)$ be the probability that subject b chooses stimulus a_t from the set $\{a_1, \ldots, a_k\}$. This presumes that the experiment is performed in such a way that there is no asymmetry between e.g. the experiment (a_3, a_1, a_2) and the experiment (a_1, a_2, a_3). In many applications it turns out that this probability is independent of b.

11.9.1 **Theorem:** If $P: A^k \times C \to \mathbb{R}$ is cancellable and if there exists a representation

11.9.2 $P(a_1, \ldots, a_k, t) = H(m(a_1), \ldots, m(a_k), m(a_t))$

by a translation invariant function $H: D_{m,m} \to \mathbb{R}$ which is continuous in the last variable and a map $m: A \to \mathbb{R}$ such that $m(A)$ is a connected set, then m and H are unique up to the simultaneous transformation

$$\begin{aligned} m^*(a) &= \alpha\, m(a) + \beta, \\ H^*(x_1, \ldots, x_k, y) &= H\left(\frac{x_1 - \beta}{\alpha}, \ldots, \frac{x_k - \beta}{\alpha}, \frac{y - \beta}{\alpha}\right). \end{aligned}$$

Proof: Follows immediately from Theorem 10.2.3 (a).

11.9.3 **Remark:** From 11.9.2 we obtain the following properties of H:

(i) $\sum_{t=1}^{k} H(x_1, \ldots, x_k, x_t) = 1$ for $x_i \in m(A)$

(ii) $H(x_1, \ldots, x_k, x_t) = H(x_{i_1}, \ldots, x_{i_k}, x_t)$ for $x_i \in m(A)$ and all permutations $(x_{i_1}, \ldots, x_{i_k})$ of $(x_1, \ldots, x_k)$ and for all $t = 1, \ldots, k$.

11.9.4 **Axiom:** If $a'_1, \ldots, a'_k$ and $a''_1, \ldots, a''_k$ are indexed in increasing order, then $P(a'_1, \ldots, a'_k, t) = P(a''_1, \ldots, a''_k, t)$ for all $t = 1, \ldots, k$ is equivalent to $P(a'_i, a'_t) = P(a''_i, a''_t)$ for all $i, t = 1, \ldots, k$.

11.9.5 **Theorem:** If $P(a_1, a_2)$ is cancellable and if conditions 11.6.4, 11.6.5, and 11.9.4 are fulfilled, then a representation of $P(a_1, \ldots, a_k, t)$ of the type 11.9.2 exists.

Proof: Follows immediately from Theorem 10.3.8.

Starting from choice probabilities, GUILFORD (1937) uses

11.9.6 $$\frac{P(a_1, \ldots, a_k, i)}{P(a_1, \ldots, a_k, i) + P(a_1, \ldots, a_k, j)}$$

as substitute for $P(a_i, a_j)$. His argument is that the choice probabilities contain information about the ranking of a_i and a_j if either a_i is preferred to all other a's (and therefore also to a_j), or a_j is preferred to all other a's (and therefore also to a_i). Then, 11.9.6 is the probability with which a_i is preferred among the cases in which we have information about the ranking of a_i and a_j. Assuming tacitly that the preference between a_i, a_j is not influenced by the presence of other stimuli, GUILFORD concludes that 11.9.6 is equal to $P(a_i, a_j)$. Formally, this argument is valid iff

$$\frac{P(a_i, a_j)}{P(a_j, a_i)} = \frac{P(a_1, \ldots, a_k, i)}{P(a_1, \ldots, a_k, j)}.$$

This assumption was formalized by LUCE (1959) as follows: Let $P(S, R)$ be the probability that the stimulus, chosen from a given set S, belongs to the set $R \subset S$. He postulates*):

11.9.7 **Independence:** For $R \subset S \subset T$:

$$P(S, R) = \frac{P(T, R)}{P(T, S)}.$$

---

*) We avoid the term "choice axiom" suggested by LUCE because it has already a definite meaning in mathematics. The term "independence postulate" is suggested by the terminology of ARROW and means "independence of irrelevant alternatives".

If the choice is restricted to S, then the probability of choosing a stimulus belonging to R is equal to the probability of R among those choices from T, for which the chosen stimulus belongs to S. Intuitively, this axiom expresses that the conditional choice probabilities within the set S are not influenced by stimuli not belonging to S: If R', R'' are two subsets of S, 11.9.7 implies:

$$11.9.8 \quad \frac{P(S, R')}{P(S, R'')} = \frac{P(T, R')}{P(T, R'')}.$$

At first sight, this axiom looks plausible. A closer examination however reveals that this is not the case: Consider, for example, the situation where a subject has to choose among three different dishes: $a_1 =$ pork, $a_2 =$beef, $a_3 =$fish. Assume that the subject prefers meat to fish with probability p (e.g. $p = 6/7$ for Roman Catholics), and that he is indifferent to either pork or beef (i.e. he prefers pork to beef with probability 1/2). If we take $R' = \{\text{beef}\}$, $R'' = \{\text{fish}\}$, $S = \{\text{beef, fish}\}$, 11.9.7 implies:

$$\frac{P(\{\text{beef, fish}\}, \{\text{beef}\})}{P(\{\text{beef, fish}\}, \{\text{fish}\})} = \frac{P(\{\text{pork, beef, fish}\}, \{\text{beef}\})}{P(\{\text{pork, beef, fish}\}, \{\text{fish}\})}.$$

Assuming that the subject decides first between meat and fish and then – if it has decided in favor of meat – between beef and pork, we have

$$P(\{\text{beef, fish}\}, \{\text{beef}\}) = p,$$

$$P(\{\text{beef, fish}\}, \{\text{fish}\}) = 1 - p,$$

$$P(\{\text{pork, beef, fish}\}, \{\text{beef}\}) = p \cdot 1/2,$$

$$P(\{\text{pork, beef, fish}\}, \{\text{fish}\}) = 1 - p.$$

Therefore, 11.9.7 is not fulfilled in this case. Of course, GUILFORD's method is inadmissible then. His estimate of $P(\{\text{beef, fish}\}, \{\text{beef}\}) = p$ would be

$$\frac{P(\{\text{pork, beef, fish}\}, \{\text{beef}\})}{P(\{\text{pork, beef, fish}\}, \{\text{beef}\}) + P(\{\text{pork, beef, fish}\}, \{\text{fish}\})} =$$

$$\frac{p/2}{p/2 + (1-p)} = \frac{p}{2-p}.$$

A similar objection against 11.9.7 was already raised in DEBREU (1960). That these objections are valid in practice has been shown by empirical tests performed by BECKER, DE GROOT and MARSCHAK (1963).

There might be other cases, however, in which axiom 11.9.7 is more realistic. One such case is described by CLARKE (1957).

Another objection against 11.9.7 can be raised from a formal point of view: If 11.9.7 is postulated for choosing the best stimulus from S – why not also for choosing the worst? If 11.9.7 is valid for the best as well as for the worst stimulus, together with the so called ranking postulate 11.10.6 this implies $P(a_1, \ldots, a_k, t) = 1/k$ for all $t = 1, \ldots, k$ (see theorem 11.10.9).

The independence postulate 11.9.7 has a number of nice consequences:

As it implies

$$P(a_1, a_2) = \frac{P(a_1, a_2, a_3, 1)}{P(a_1, a_2, a_3, 1) + P(a_1, a_2, a_3, 2)},$$

we immediately obtain 11.7.1 (see LUCE, 1959, p. 16, Theorem 2).

11.9.9 **Theorem:** If 11.9.7 holds, then there exist positive functions $v(a)$, unique up to dilations, such that

11.9.10 $$P(a_1, \ldots, a_k, t) = \frac{v(a_t)}{\sum_1^k v(a_j)}.$$

We remark that this is an immediate generalization of 11.7.3.

Proof: Let $e \in A$ be an arbitrary but fixed element and define:

$$v(a) = \frac{P(a, e)}{P(e, a)}.$$

$$\frac{v(a_i)}{\sum_1^k v(a_j)} = \frac{v(a_i)/v(a_1)}{\sum_1^k v(a_j)/v(a_1)} = \frac{P(a_i, a_1)/P(a_1, a_i)}{\sum_1^k P(a_j, a_1)/P(a_1, a_j)}$$

$$= \frac{P(a_1, \ldots, a_k, i)/P(a_1, \ldots, a_k, 1)}{\sum_{j=1}^k P(a_1, \ldots, a_k, j)/P(a_1, \ldots, a_k, 1)} = P(a_1, \ldots, a_k, i).$$

To show uniqueness, suppose that v' is another such function. For any $a_t \in \{a_1, \ldots, a_k\}$, we have

$$v'(a_t) = \sum_1^k v'(a_j) P(a_1, \ldots, a_k, t)$$

$$= \frac{\sum_1^k v'(a_j)}{\sum_1^k v(a_j)} v(a_t).$$

The representation 11.9.10 of choice probabilities was suggested by THURSTONE (1930), BRADLEY and TERRY (1952), GULLIKSEN (1953), PENDERGRASS and BRADLEY (1960). It was derived from (11.9.7) by LUCE (1959), p. 23, Theorem 3.

If the choice probabilities are explained by a discriminal process, the independence postulate 11.9.7 is not valid in general. Conditions on the discriminal process assuring 11.9.7 seem to be unknown.

11.10 Rankings

Another generalization of paired comparisons are rankings of k stimuli: Subject b is asked to rank k given stimuli, say $a_1, \ldots, a_k$, according to some criterion. The ranking $a_{i_1} > \ldots > a_{i_k}$ may be described by the sequence $(i_1, \ldots, i_k)$. Thus we can take C to consist of all $k!$ permutations of the numbers $1, \ldots, k$.

For $k=2$ we are back to the case of paired comparisons. (There is just a formal difference between the spaces of outcomes: Formerly, we had $C=\{1, 2\}$, now we have $C=\{(1, 2), (2, 1)\}$. There is, however, a $1-1$ correspondence $1 \to (1, 2), 2 \to (2, 1)$.)

Let $P(a_1, \ldots, a_k, b, i_1, \ldots, i_k)$ be the probability that subject b ranks the stimuli $a_1, \ldots, a_k$ in the order $a_{i_1} > \ldots > a_{i_k}$. In many applications, $P(a_1, \ldots, a_k, b, i_1, \ldots, i_k)$ is independent of b. We will write $P(a_1, \ldots, a_k, i_1, \ldots, i_k)$ in these cases.

11.10.1 **Axiom:** If $a'_1, \ldots, a'_k$ and $a''_1, \ldots, a''_k$ are indexed in increasing order, then $P(a'_1, \ldots, a'_k, i_1, \ldots, i_k) = P(a''_1, \ldots, a''_k, i_1, \ldots, i_k)$ for all permutations $(i_1, \ldots, i_k)$ of $(1, \ldots, k)$ is equivalent to $P(a'_i, a'_{i_j}) = P(a''_j, a''_{i_j})$ for all $i, j = 1, \ldots, k$.

11.10.2 **Theorem:** If $P(a', a'')$ is cancellable, and if conditions 11.6.4, 11.6.5, and 11.10.1 are fulfilled, then there exist functions $m: A \to \mathbb{R}$ and $H: (m(A) \dot{-} m(A))^k \to \mathbb{R}$, such that

$$*P(a_1, \ldots, a_k, i_1, \ldots, i_k) = H(m(a_1) - m(a_{i_1}), \ldots, m(a_k) - m(a_{i_k})).$$

Proof: Theorem 10.3.8 yields the existence of monotone functions m and H_0, such that $P(a', a'') = H_0(m(a') - m(a''))$. By 11.10.1 this implies the representation*.

Rankings have the practical advantage that much more information can be collected per unit time than in the case of paired comparisons: For k stimuli there is one ranking experiment, but $k(k-1)/2$ pairwise comparisons. For $k = 10$, this means: 1 ranking versus 45 pairwise comparisons. Therefore, a great number of experiments is concerned with rankings. The analysis of the data is, however, not always correct. Usually it is taken for granted in advance, that the pairwise probabilities $P(a_\nu, a_\mu)$ can be inferred from $P(a_1, \ldots, a_k, i_1, \ldots, i_k)$ by summing over all $(i_1, \ldots, i_k)$ for which ν precedes μ, i. e.

$$i_m = \nu, \quad i_n = \mu \quad \text{imply} \quad m < n.$$

11.10.3 **Consistency of Rankings:**

$$P(a_\nu, a_\mu) = \sum_{\nu \text{ precedes } \mu} P(a_1, \ldots, a_k, i_1, \ldots, i_k)$$

The justification for this condition lies in the fact that for these (and only these) rankings, a_μ is ranked higher than a_ν and would be chosen from the set $\{a_\mu, a_\nu\}$ if the other stimuli were not available. An assumption like this is made by HEVNER (1930) and THURSTONE (1931).

In LUCE (1959, p. 71) an example is given to illustrate that consistency of rankings does not necessarily hold. This example starts from the assumption that a ranking is built up from paired comparisons in the following way: The subject selects a pair out of $\{a_1, a_2, a_3\}$ at random and ranks the elements of this pair. Then he picks one of these at random and compares it with the remaining third. If this does not produce a ranking, he compares the remaining two. For this procedure, we have

$$P(a_1, a_2, a_3, i_1, i_2, i_3) = \frac{1}{3} P(a_{i_1}, a_{i_2}) P(a_{i_2}, a_{i_3}) [2P(a_{i_1}, a_{i_3}) + 1].$$

It is easily seen that the consistency condition is not fulfilled in this case.

For this reason, LUCE tries to give intuitive conditions, sufficient to ensure consistency of rankings. Following LUCE (1959, p. 73) we obtain

11.10.4 **Theorem:** For ranking processes based on discriminal processes with independent sensations (see 11.2.4), rankings are consistent (11.10.3).

Proof: If $P(a_1, a_2, a_3, i_1, i_2, i_3)$ can be described by a model of the discriminal process (section 11.2) there exists a density $\varphi(\alpha_1 - m(a_1), \alpha_2 - m(a_2), \alpha_3 - m(a_3))$ such that

11.10.5 $P(a_1, a_2, a_3, i_1, i_2, i_3)$

$$= \int_{\alpha_{i1}=-\infty}^{+\infty} \int_{\alpha_{i2}=-\infty}^{\alpha_{i1}} \int_{\alpha_{i3}=-\infty}^{\alpha_{i2}} \varphi(\alpha_1 - m(a_1), \alpha_2 - m(a_2), \alpha_3 - m(a_3)) \, d\alpha_1 \, d\alpha_2 \, d\alpha_3 .$$

Representation 11.10.5 immediately implies

$$P(a_1, a_2, a_3, 1, 2, 3) + P(a_1, a_2, a_3, 1, 3, 2) + P(a_1, a_2, a_3, 3, 1, 2)$$
$$= \int_{\alpha_1=-\infty}^{+\infty} \int_{\alpha_2=-\infty}^{\alpha_1} \varphi_0(\alpha_1 - m(a_1), \alpha_2 - m(a_2)) \, d\alpha_1 \, d\alpha_2 ,$$

with

$$\varphi_0(\xi_1, \xi_2) = \int_{-\infty}^{+\infty} \varphi(\xi_1, \xi_2, \xi_3) \, d\xi_3 .$$

In general, the discriminal process $\varphi(\alpha_1 - m(a_1), \alpha_2 - m(a_2))$ governing the ranking of a_1, a_2 may be different from $\varphi_0(\alpha_1 - m(a_1), \alpha_2 - m(a_2))$ for the presence of a_3 might influence the sensations α_1 and α_2. As independence is assumed, we have

$$\varphi(\alpha_1 - m(a_1), \alpha_2 - m(a_2), \alpha_3 - m(a_3)) = \varphi(\alpha_1 - m(a_1)) \cdot$$
$$\varphi(\alpha_2 - m(a_2)) \cdot \varphi(\alpha_3 - m(a_3))$$

and therefore

$$\int_{\alpha_1=-\infty}^{+\infty} \int_{\alpha_2=-\infty}^{\alpha_1} \varphi_0(\alpha_1 - m(a_1), \alpha_2 - m(\alpha_2)) \, d\alpha_1 \, d\alpha_2$$
$$= P(a_1, a_2, 1, 2) = P(a_1, a_2) .$$

Another theoretical model assuring consistency of rankings, also due to LUCE (1959, p. 72), is based on the so called

11.10.6 **Ranking Postulate:**

$$P(a_1, \ldots, a_k, i_1, \ldots, i_k) = P(a_1, \ldots, a_k, i_1)$$
$$\cdot P(a_1, \ldots, a_{i_1-1}, a_{i_1+1}, \ldots, a_k, i_2, \ldots, i_k) .$$

A plausible situation where the ranking postulate is not fulfilled may be obtained from the example outlined in section 11.9, p. 182. If the subject first decides between fish and meat and then between pork and beef, the ranking "pork> beef> fish" will have probability $p/2$. However,

$$P(\{\text{pork, beef, fish}\}, \text{pork})=p/2,$$

$$P(\{\text{beef, fish}\}, \text{beef, fish})=p.$$

Hence 11.10.6 does not hold in this case.

We remark that even in the case of a discriminal process with independent sensations, the ranking postulate does not necessarily hold. Conditions sufficient to assure the ranking postulate in this case seem to be unknown.

The following theorem, due to BLOCK and MARSCHAK (1960, p. 110, Theorem 3.7), generalizes LUCE (1959, p. 72, Theorem 9).

11.10.7 **Theorem:** If independence postulate (11.9.7) and the ranking postulate (11.10.6) are both fulfilled, then rankings are consistent (11.10.3).

Proof: The theorem is trivially true for $k = 2$. To prove it for arbitrary k, we have to show that it holds for k if it holds for $k - 1$. 11.10.6 together with 11.9.7 and 11.9.10 implies

$$\sum_{i_1=\gamma} P(a_1, \dots, a_k, i_1, \dots, i_k) = P(a_1, \dots, a_k, \gamma) = \frac{v(a_\gamma)}{\sum\limits_{i=1}^{k} v(a_i)}.$$

Furthermore, 11.9.7 and 11.9.10 imply

$$P(a_\nu, a_\mu) = \frac{v(a_\nu)}{v(a_\nu)+v(a_\mu)}, \quad \sum_{\nu \text{ precedes } \mu} P(a_1, \dots, a_k, i_1, \dots, i_k)$$

$$= \sum_{i_1=\nu} P(a_1, \dots, a_k, i_1, \dots, i_k)$$

$$+ \sum_{\substack{\gamma \neq \nu, \mu \\ \gamma=1, \dots, k}} \; \sum_{\substack{i_1=\gamma \\ \nu \text{ precedes } \mu}} P(a_1, \dots, a_k, i_1, \dots, i_k).$$

Using 11.10.6 again and then the inductive assumption, we obtain

$$\sum_{\substack{i_1=\gamma \\ \nu \text{ precedes } \mu}} P(a_1, \dots, a_k, i_1, i_2, \dots, i_k)$$

$$= \sum_{\nu \text{ precedes } \mu} P(a_1, \dots, a_k, \gamma) P(a_1, \dots, a_{\gamma-1}, a_{\gamma+1}, \dots, a_k, i_2, \dots, i_k)$$

$$= P(a_1, \dots, a_k, \gamma) \frac{v(a_\nu)}{v(a_\nu)+v(a_\mu)}.$$

As

$$\sum_{\gamma=1}^{k} P(a_1, \ldots, a_k, \gamma) = 1,$$

we obtain

$$\sum_{\nu \text{ precedes } \mu} P(a_1, \ldots, a_k, i_1, \ldots, i_k)$$

$$= \frac{v(a_\nu)}{\Sigma v(a_i)} + \left(1 - \frac{v(a_\nu)}{\Sigma v(a_i)} - \frac{v(a_\mu)}{\Sigma v(a_i)}\right) \frac{v(a_\nu)}{v(a_\nu) + v(a_\mu)}$$

$$= \frac{v(a_\nu)}{v(a_\nu) + v(a_\mu)} = P(a_\nu, a_\mu).$$

That independence postulate and ranking postulate are far from being necessary for consistency of rankings may be seen from the example in 11.9, where neither the independence postulate nor the ranking postulate holds. Nevertheless, the rankings are consistent. Essentially the same situation holds for any discriminal process with independent sensations.

Besides the objections raised on p. 182 against the independence postulate on empirical grounds, together with the ranking postulate it leads to a very restrictive result, if 11.9.7 is assumed for choice of the best as well as choice of the worst. The following theorem generalizes

The following theorem, due to BLOCK and MARSCHAK (1960, p. 111, Theorem 3.8), generalizes LUCE (1959, p. 69, Theorem 8).

11.10.8 **Theorem:** If the independence postulate 11.9.7 is assumed for choice of the best as well as choice of the worst, together with the ranking postulate 11.10.6 this implies

$$P(a_1, \ldots, a_k, t) = 1/k \text{ for } t = 1, \ldots, k.$$

Proof: Let $P(a_1, \ldots, a_k, t)$ be the probability that a_t is chosen as the best from $a_1, \ldots, a_k$, and $P^*(a_1, \ldots, a_k, t)$ be the probability that a_t is chosen as the worst from $a_1, \ldots, a_k$. Then, if 11.9.7 holds for both types of choices, we have the two representations:

11.10.9 $$P(a_1, \ldots, a_k, t) = \frac{v(a_t)}{\Sigma v(a_j)},$$

$$P^*(a_1, \ldots, a_k, t) = \frac{v^*(a_t)}{\Sigma v^*(a_j)}.$$

For $k = 2$: $P(a_1, a_2, 1) = P^*(a_1, a_2, 2)$. Together with 11.10.9 this implies: $v(a_1) \cdot v^*(a_1) = v(a_2) \cdot v^*(a_2)$. Therefore

(*) $P(a_1, \ldots, a_k, t) \cdot P^*(a_1, \ldots, a_k, t)$ is independent of t.

We will take $k=3$ in the following:

$$P(a_1, a_2, a_3, i_1, i_2, i_3) = P(a_1, a_2, a_3, i_1)\cdot\frac{v(a_{i_2})}{v(a_{i_2})+v(a_{i_3})}$$

$$= P(a_1, a_2, a_3, i_1)\cdot\frac{P(a_1, a_2, a_3, i_2)}{P(a_1, a_2, a_3, i_2)+P(a_1, a_2, a_3, i_3)}.$$

Similarly,

$$P(a_1, a_2, a_3, i_1, i_2, i_3)=P^*(a_1, a_2, a_3, i_3)\cdot\frac{v^*(a_{i_2})}{v^*(a_{i_1})+v^*(a_{i_2})}$$

$$=P^*(a_1, a_2, a_3, i_3)\cdot\frac{P^*(a_1, a_2, a_3, i_2)}{P^*(a_1, a_2, a_3, i_1)+P^*(a_1, a_2, a_3, i_2)}.$$

Together with (*), these two equations imply:

$$P(a_1, a_2, a_3, i_1) + P(a_1, a_2, a_3, i_2) = P^*(a_1, a_2, a_3, i_2) + P^*(a_1, a_2, a_3, i_3).$$

Similarly,

$$P(a_1, a_2, a_3, i_2) + P(a_1, a_2, a_3, i_1) = P^*(a_1, a_2, a_3, i_1) + P^*(a_1, a_2, a_3, i_3).$$

Thus: $P^*(a_1, a_2, a_3, i_1) = P^*(a_1, a_2, a_3, i_2)$ for all i_1, i_2 and therefore

$$P^*(a_1, a_2, a_3, t)=\frac{1}{3} \text{ for } t=1,2,3.$$

Then, also $P(a_1, a_2, a_3, t) = 1/3$ for $t = 1, 2, 3$.

11.11 Similarity Response

Another application of the general theory developed in sections 9.3 and 9.4 is the following:

(i) The subject has to choose from a given set of stimuli $\{a_1, \ldots, a_k\}$ the one which is most similar (according to some criterion) to a standard stimulus a_0 (which might be identical to one of the stimuli $a_1, \ldots, a_k$ or not, depending on the specific case).

(ii) The subject is trained to respond to each stimulus $a \in A$ in a specific way. Let $c(a)$ be the response specifical for a. Then the subject is subjected to a stimulus a_0 and the response c is registered.

The reader will realize, that this is a generalization of stimulus matching, if we identify the response $c(a)$ with the stimulus matched to a. If the assignment $A \leftrightarrow C$ is such that similar responses correspond to similar stimuli and vice versa, we can take the probability with which $c(a)$ occurs as response to a_0 as indicator of similarity between a_0 and a. More precisely: If the specific experiment is restricted to responses corresponding to the stimuli $a_1, \ldots, a_k$, then the response $c(a_i)$ to stimulus a_0 can be considered as equivalent to the judgment that a_i is the one stimulus from among $a_1, \ldots, a_k$ which is most similar to a_0. In this specific case the experiment becomes from an abstract point of view equivalent to the experiment described in (i).

We remark that the task (i) may also be considered as a generalization of pairwise comparison. This is the case if we consider the task to identify a_0 with one of the stimuli $a_1, a_2, \ldots, a_k$ as equivalent to assign a_0 to one of the intervals $(\leftarrow, a_1|a_2), (a_1|a_2, a_2|a_3), \ldots, (a_{k-1}|a_k, \rightarrow)$ where $a'|a''$ denotes the middle of a' and a''. Pairwise comparison, i.e. the task to rank a_0 and a_1, is equivalent to assign a_0 to one of the intervals $(\leftarrow, a_1)$ and $(a_1, \rightarrow)$ and can therefore be considered as a case to which the assignment task degenerates for $k=1$.

(iii) The subject has to rank the stimuli $a_1, \ldots, a_k$ according to their similarity to a standard stimulus a_0.

In cases (i) and (ii) the experiment renders the probability that a_i is judged most similar to a_0 among $a_1, \ldots, a_k$: $P(a_1, \ldots, a_k, a_0, i)$. We have

$$\sum_1^k P(a_1, \ldots, a_k, a_0, i) = 1\,.$$

In case (iii) the experiment renders the probability that $a_{i_1}, \ldots, a_{i_k}$ is the order of $a_1, \ldots, a_k$ according to similarity to a_0 : $P(a_1, \ldots, a_k, a_0, i_1, \ldots, i_k)$. We have

$$\sum_{(i_1, \ldots, i_k)} P(a_1, \ldots, a_k, a_0, i_1, \ldots, i_k) = 1\,.$$

Scales might be obtained similarly as in section 10.3.

11.12 Dichotomous Valuation

The response functions so far considered were all of the judgment type, i.e. the response probability measures were independent of the subject. Now we consider the simplest case of valuation, (i.e. of a response function depending on the subject), the case of dichotomous response.

We will show that a canonical respresentation leads simultaneously to a scale for stimuli and a scale for disposition of subjects, which are unique up to linear transformation.

The subject b is subjected to a stimulus a under a condition which allows for two different modes of response, called positive and negative. If we assign to a positive response the symbol "1", to a negative response the symbol "0", we have $C=\{0, 1\}$. As outlined in connection with paired comparisons, (see p. 174) in the case of a dichotomous response one function suffices to characterize the whole response probability distribution. For this, we choose $P(a, b, \{1\})$, the probability of a positive response which will be denoted by $P(a, b)$.

We remark that $P(a, b)$ considered for fixed a (stimulus or item) as a function of b (disposition) is called *trace line* in latent structure analysis and *item characteristic curve* in mental test theory.

The following list gives a few typical examples for experiments of this type:

Field	Subjects	Stimuli	Disposition	Property of Stimulus	negative Response	positive Response
Dosis-mortality	animals	dosage	resistance	strength*) of dosis	death	survival
Performance	subjects	tasks	ability	difficulty	failure	solution
Attitude	subjects	statements	attitude	attitude expressed in statement	disagreement	agreement

*) Here strength is of course to be interpreted as a measure of efficiency of the stimuli in the experiment, not as strength in a physical sense.

In the case of dichotomous response, it is convenient to distinguish between two cases:

(i) For all b, $P(a, b)$ is a monotone function of a,

(ii) this is not the case.

The first case naturally occurs with stimuli for which a positive response to stimulus a' essentially implies a positive response to any stimulus $a'' < a'$ except for random deviations. This is e.g. the case with dosage-mortality curves. If a subject survives a dosage a', then it ought to survive also a dosage $a'' < a'$. The same holds true for achievement tests: If a task a' is solved by a subject, it ought to solve also an easier task a''. Following MOESTLLER (1949) we will call stimuli of this kind *cumulative stimuli*.

The second case occurs with attitude measurement. If, for example, the stimuli consist of statements concerning the racial issue, we will expect that some individuals might have a somewhat moderate position. They will disagree with extreme statements of either kind. Though the response function might be monotone for some subjects also in this case, this is not necessarily true for all subjects. Stimuli of this kind will be called *point stimuli* (MOSTELLER, 1949)*).

If P is cancellable and if there exists a representation

$$P(a, b) = H(m(a) - n(b))$$

with a continuous function $H: \mathbb{R} \to \mathbb{R}$, and if $m(A)$ and $n(B)$ are connected sets, it is unique up to the simultaneous transformation

$$m^*(a) = \alpha m(a) + \beta$$

$$n^*(b) = \alpha n(b) + \gamma$$

$$H^*(x) \to H\left(\frac{x - \beta + \gamma}{\alpha}\right) \quad \text{for } x \in m^*(A) \dot{-} n^*(B)$$

according to Theorem 11.4.1.

If such a representation exists this suggests to consider $m(a)$ as a measure of the intensity of the stimulus, $n(b)$ as a measure of the disposition of the subject.

It seems natural to consider also other canonical representations such as

$$P(a, b) = H\left(\frac{m(a) - n(b)}{s(b)}\right).$$

In this case, the maps are unique up to linear transformations too if a natural convention for the exclusion of inexpedient scales (see section 10.4) is adopted.

---

*) Other terms than "*cumulative*" and "*point*" stimuli are used too in literature; TORGERSON for example speaks of "*monotone*" and "*point*", LOEVINGER of "*cumulative*" and "*differential*", COOMBS of "*monotone*" and "*nonmonotone*", THURSTONE and CHAVE of "*increasing probability*" and "*maximum probability*".

One of the first practical applications of this model, assuming that H is a normal distribution function, is due to THURSTONE (1925) in the field of intelligence and achievement measurement. In this application the different b corresponded to different age groups. Here the assumption that the standard deviation depends on b seems quite natural.

This procedure yields simultaneous estimates of scale values of the stimuli $a_1, \ldots, a_k$ and of the scale values of the subjects $b_1, \ldots, b_m$. It is *not* necessary, as usual in intelligence testing, to obtain "scores" (scale values) for the different "items" (tasks) by the assumption that the scores attained by the subjects in a homogeneous population are normally distributed.

We remark that case (i) of monotone P is closely related to paired comparisons, case (ii) of not necessarily monotone P to stimulus generalization. If we identify A with B (and pose accordingly the additional requirement that $m=n$) we obtain a problem where instead of subject b stimulus a_0 occurs. The formal problem of finding *two* scales m, n such that a representation exists reduces to the simpler problem of finding *one* scale m such that a canonical representation exists.

We remark that in the determination of $P(a, b)$ as a function of a for fixed b, the responses of one and the same subject to different stimuli are assumed to be independent. Only under this assumption the response function gives a complete description of the reactions of the subject to the stimuli. In principle, also the case of dependent response could be dealt with by the method of canonical representations. Consider an experiment in which the subject is subjected to k stimuli $a_1, \ldots, a_k$. Let z_i be a random variable assuming the value 1 in case of a positive response to stimulus i and 0 in case of a negative response. Then the complex response to the set of stimuli $a_1, \ldots, a_k$ can be described by a vector $(z_1, \ldots, z_k)$ with components equal to 0 or 1. This vector has 2^k possible values, called response patterns in latent structure analysis. Let $P(a_1, \ldots, a_k, b, z_1, \ldots, z_k)$ be the probability of response pattern $(z_1, \ldots, z_k)$ if subject b is subjected to the stimuli $a_1, \ldots, a_k$. If these 2^k probabilities can be represented in the form

$$P(a_1, \ldots, a_k, b, z_1, \ldots, z_k) = H_{z_1, \ldots, z_k}(m(a_1) - n(b), \ldots, m(a_k) - n(b))$$

the scales m and n are also unique up to linear transformations (see Theorem 11.4.1).

The practical determination of the scale values $m(a_1), \ldots, m(a_k)$ and $n(b)$ for different subjects b is greatly simplified if these estimates depend on $(z_1, \ldots, z_k)$ only through the sufficient statistic $\sum_{i=1}^{k} z_i$ (i. e. if the estimate depends on the *number* of positive responses to the stimuli $a_1, \ldots, a_k$ only and not on the distribution of the positive responses over the stimuli. Conditions under which this particularly simple model holds are discussed by RASCH (1960) and BIRNBAUM (1965).

12. Events, Utility and Subjective Probability

In this chapter we present a special approach for the simultaneous measurement of utility and subjective probability. The connection with some related theories is discussed in section 12.6. The original plan to include a comprehensive survey on the measurement of utility was abandoned because of the survey paper by P. FISHBURN (1968) and a monography (1970) by the same author.

12.1 The Algebra of Events

Let $\mathscr{E}$ be a system of events. These events will be denoted by capital letters like $P, Q, R, \ldots$. We will assume that for events in $\mathscr{E}$ the following three operations are defined: the *join* ($\cup$), the *meet* ($\cap$) and the *complementation* (*negation*) ($^-$). $P \cup Q$ is to be interpreted as the event which obtains if at least one of the events P, Q obtains. $P \cap Q$ is to be interpreted as the event which obtains if both, P and Q, obtain. $\bar{P}$ is to be interpreted as the event which obtains if P does not obtain. We shall assume that $\mathscr{E}$ is closed under these three operations.

Furthermore, we shall assume that the following axioms are fulfilled:

12.1.1 **Definition:** A system $\mathscr{E}$ is a *Boolean algebra* if operations $\cup$, $\cap$, $^-$ with the following properties are defined:

12.1.2 commutativity $\quad P \cap Q = Q \cap P, \quad P \cup Q = Q \cup P$

12.1.3 associativity $\quad P \cup (Q \cup R) = (P \cup Q) \cup R,$
$\quad P \cap (Q \cap R) = (P \cap Q) \cap R$

12.1.4 distributivity $\quad P \cap (Q \cup R) = (P \cap Q) \cup (P \cap R),$
$\quad P \cup (Q \cap R) = (P \cup Q) \cap (P \cup R)$

12.1.5 absorption law $\quad (P \cup Q) \cap Q = Q, \quad (P \cap Q) \cup Q = Q$

12.1.6 $(P \cap \bar{P}) \cup Q = Q, \quad (P \cup \bar{P}) \cap Q = Q$

This system of axioms remains unchanged if we interchange $\cap$ and $\cup$. Therefore from the proof of any consequence of this system of axioms we obtain a proof of the "dual" consequence by interchanging $\cap$ and $\cup$. In the following we will prove only one of the two "dual" consequences.

In the sections following 12.2 we will use the shorter expression PQ instead of $P \cap Q$.

12.1.7 **Proposition:** The elements of a Boolean algebra are *idempotent:* $Q \cup Q = Q$ and $Q \cap Q = Q$ for all $Q \in \mathscr{E}$.

Proof: For all $P, Q \in \mathscr{E}$ we have from 12.1.2, 12.1.4 and 12.1.5

$$\begin{aligned} Q &= (P \cap Q) \cup Q = Q \cup (P \cap Q) = (Q \cup P) \cap (Q \cup Q) \\ &= ((Q \cup P) \cap Q) \cup ((Q \cup P) \cap Q) \\ &= ((P \cup Q) \cap Q) \cup ((P \cup Q) \cap Q) = Q \cup Q. \end{aligned}$$

The proof for $Q \cap Q = Q$ runs similarly.

Now we can define a binary relation between events by

12.1.8 **Definition:** $P \subset Q$ iff $P \cap Q = P$.

By the absorption law (12.1.5), "$P \subset Q$ iff $P \cup Q = Q$" is an equivalent definition.

The intuitive interpretation of this relation is that P implies Q, i.e. Q obtains if P obtains.

12.1.9 **Theorem:** The inclusion $\subset$ defined by 12.1.8 induces a *partial order* between the elements of the Boolean algebra, i.e.

(i) $P \subset P$ for all $P \in \mathscr{E}$,

(ii) for all $P, Q \in \mathscr{E}$: $P \subset Q$ and $Q \subset P$ together imply $P = Q$,

(iii) for all $P, Q, R \in \mathscr{E}$: $P \subset Q$ and $Q \subset R$ together imply $P \subset R$.

Proof: (i) follows immediately from 12.1.7.

(ii) If $P \subset Q$ and $Q \subset P$ then $P = P \cap Q = (P \cup Q) \cap Q = Q$ by 12.1.5.

(iii) If $P \subset Q$ and $Q \subset R$ then $P = P \cap Q = P \cap (Q \cap R)$ $= (P \cap Q) \cap R = P \cap R$ by 12.1.3 and therefore $P \subset R$.

12.1.10 **Proposition:** For all $P, R \in \mathscr{E}$:

(i) $P \cap \bar{P} = R \cap \bar{R}$,

(ii) $P \cup \bar{P} = R \cup \bar{R}$.

Proof: (i) Replacing Q by $R \cap \bar{R}$ in 12.1.6 we obtain $(P \cap \bar{P}) \cup (R \cap \bar{R}) = (R \cap \bar{R})$, and therefore $P \cap \bar{P} \subset R \cap \bar{R}$. As this relation holds for all $P, R \in \mathscr{E}$, equality follows.

As a consequence of 12.1.10 the events $P \cap \bar{P}$ and $P \cup \bar{P}$ are independent of $P \in \mathscr{E}$. We will denote them by O and E, respectively. From 12.1.6 we obtain $O \cup Q = Q$ and $E \cap Q = Q$, and therefore $O \subset Q$ and $Q \subset E$ for all $Q \in \mathscr{E}$. The event O is called the *impossible event*, the event E is called the *sure event* of the Boolean algebra $\mathscr{E}$.

12.1.11 **Proposition:** If $P \cap R = O$ and $P \cup R = E$, then $R = \bar{P}$.

Proof: From 12.1.2 and 12.1.4 we obtain $R \subset \bar{P}$: $R = R \cap E = R \cap (P \cup \bar{P}) = (R \cap P) \cup (R \cap \bar{P}) = (P \cap R) \cup (R \cap \bar{P}) = O \cup (R \cap \bar{P}) = R \cap \bar{P}$. The dual argumentation yields $R \supset \bar{P}$, whence the assertion follows.

12.1.12 **Theorem:** The map $P \rightarrow \bar{P}$ induces a *dual automorphism*:

(i) $\bar{\bar{P}} = P$ for all $P \in \mathscr{E}$,

(ii) $\overline{P \cap Q} = \bar{P} \cup \bar{Q}$ for all $P, Q \in \mathscr{E}$,

(iii) $\overline{P \cup Q} = \bar{P} \cap \bar{Q}$ for all $P, Q \in \mathscr{E}$.

Proof: (i) From the definition of O and E we obtain $\bar{P} \cap P = O$ and $\bar{P} \cup P = E$ by 12.1.2. The assertion follows by application of 12.1.11 to $\bar{P}$ instead of P.

(ii) By 12.1.4 we obtain

$$(P \cap Q) \cap (\bar{P} \cup \bar{Q}) = (P \cap Q \cap \bar{P}) \cup (P \cap Q \cap \bar{Q}) = O \cup O = O$$

$$(P \cap Q) \cup (\bar{P} \cup \bar{Q}) = (P \cup \bar{P} \cup \bar{Q}) \cap (Q \cup \bar{P} \cup \bar{Q}) = E \cap E = E$$

On account of 12.1.11 this implies (ii).

(iii) follows by the dual argumentation.

12.1.13 **Definition:** A nonempty subset $\mathscr{J} \subset \mathscr{E}$ is an *ideal* iff

(i) $P, Q \in \mathscr{J}$ implies $P \cup Q \in \mathscr{J}$,

(ii) $Q \in \mathscr{J}$ and $P \subset Q$ together imply $P \in \mathscr{J}$.

To the ideal $\mathscr{J}$ there corresponds an equivalence relation $\approx_{\mathscr{J}}$ defined as follows: For all $P, Q \in \mathscr{J}$:

$$P \approx_{\mathscr{J}} Q \text{ iff } P \cap \bar{Q} \in \mathscr{J} \text{ and } \bar{P} \cap Q \in \mathscr{J}.$$

The system of all subelements of a fixed element, say $R \in \mathscr{E}$ is an ideal. Ideals of this type are called *principal ideals*. For reasons stemming from the interpretation of $\mathscr{E}$ as an algebra of events and which will become more clear later on, it is the principal ideal generated by $\bar{R}$ rather than the principal ideal generated by R which is of interest. For this reason we will denote by $\mathscr{J}_R$ the principal ideal generated by $\bar{R}$; i.e.:

$$\mathscr{J}_R := \{Q \in \mathscr{E} : Q \cap R = O\}.$$

Instead of $\approx_{\mathscr{J}_R}$ we will simply write $\approx_R$.

12.1.14 **Proposition:** The equivalence relation $\approx_{\mathscr{J}}$ is an algebraic congruence relation with respect to join, meet and complementation, explicitely: For all $P, Q, R \in \mathscr{E}$, $P \approx_{\mathscr{J}} Q$ implies

(i) $P \cup R \approx_{\mathscr{J}} Q \cup R$,

(ii) $P \cap R \approx_{\mathscr{J}} Q \cap R$,

(iii) $\bar{P} \approx_{\mathscr{J}} \bar{Q}$.

Proof: (i) From 12.1.4 and 12.1.12 we obtain

$$(P \cup R) \cap \overline{(Q \cup R)} = (P \cup R) \cap (\bar{Q} \cap \bar{R}) = (P \cap \bar{Q} \cap \bar{R}) \subset P \cap \bar{Q} \in \mathscr{J}$$

$$\overline{(P \cup R)} \cap (Q \cup R) = (\bar{P} \cap \bar{R}) \cap (Q \cup R) = (\bar{P} \cap \bar{R} \cap Q) \subset \bar{P} \cap Q \in \mathscr{J}$$

By 12.1.13 this implies the equivalence.

(ii) This assertion follows by the dual argumentation.

(iii) Is an immediate consequence of the definition.

12.1.15 **Proposition:** For all $P, Q, R \in \mathscr{E}$:

$$P \approx_R Q \text{ iff } P \cap R = Q \cap R.$$

Proof: 12.1.13 and the definition of $\mathscr{J}_R$ imply $P \approx_R Q$ iff $P \cap \bar{Q} \in \mathscr{J}_R$ and $\bar{P} \cap Q \in \mathscr{J}_R$ iff $P \cap \bar{Q} \cap R = O$ and $\bar{P} \cap Q \cap R = O$. Now we obtain

(i) $P \cap R = Q \cap R$ implies $P \approx_R Q$: $P \cap R = Q \cap R$ implies $P \cap R \cap \bar{Q} = Q \cap R \cap \bar{Q} = O$ and $Q \cap R \cap \bar{P} = P \cap R \cap \bar{P} = O$ whence the assertion follows.

(ii) $P \approx_R Q$ implies $P \cap R = Q \cap R$: $((P \cap R) \cap \overline{(Q \cap R)}) \cup (\overline{(P \cap R)} \cap (Q \cap R)) = ((P \cap R) \cap (\bar{Q} \cup \bar{R})) \cup ((\bar{P} \cup \bar{R}) \cap (Q \cap R)) = (P \cap R \cap \bar{Q}) \cup (\bar{P} \cap Q \cap R) = O$. Hence $P \cap R = Q \cap R$.

Any congruence relation divides $\mathscr{E}$ into disjoint classes (equivalence classes). The equivalence class containing P will be denoted by $\tilde{\tilde{P}}^{\mathscr{J}}$ or $\tilde{\tilde{P}}$ if there is no doubt concerning the ideal defining the equivalence relation.

12.1.16 **Definition:** The *quotient algebra* $\mathscr{E} \mid \mathscr{J}$ of $\mathscr{E}$ modulo $\mathscr{J}$ consists of the elements $\tilde{\tilde{P}}$ $(P \in \mathscr{E})$ together with the operations $\cup$, $\cap$, $^-$ defined by $\tilde{\tilde{P}} \cap \tilde{\tilde{Q}} = \widetilde{\widetilde{P \cap Q}}$, $\tilde{\tilde{P}} \cup \tilde{\tilde{Q}} = \widetilde{\widetilde{P \cup Q}}$, $\overline{\tilde{\tilde{P}}} = \tilde{\tilde{\bar{P}}}$.

These definitions are unique according to 12.1.14.

If $\mathscr{J}$ is the principal ideal $\mathscr{J}_R$, we denote the quotient algebra by $\mathscr{E} \mid R$ and the equivalence classes by $\tilde{\tilde{Q}}^R$ (or $\tilde{\tilde{Q}}$). The map $m: \mathscr{E} \to \mathscr{E} \mid \mathscr{J}$ defined by $m(P) = \tilde{\tilde{P}}$ is the (natural) homomorphism of $\mathscr{E}$ onto $\mathscr{E} \mid \mathscr{J}$. Under this homomorphism the events of $\mathscr{J}$ are mapped into the impossible event of $\mathscr{E}|\mathscr{J}$. Especially the ideal $\mathscr{J}_E = \{O\}$ induces an isomorphism of $\mathscr{E}$ onto $\mathscr{E}|E$.

12.1.17 **Proposition:** For all $P, Q \in \mathscr{E}$:

(i) $m(P) \cup m(Q) = m(P \cup Q)$,

(ii) $m(P) \cap m(Q) = m(P \cap Q)$,

(iii) $\overline{m(P)} = m(\bar{P})$.

Obviously, $\mathscr{E} \mid \mathscr{J}$ is a Boolean algebra again and we have a partial order between the equivalence classes, defined by

$$m(P) \subset m(Q) \text{ iff } m(P) \cap m(Q) = m(P).$$

12.1.18 **Lemma:** For all $P, Q \in \mathscr{E}$:

$$m(P) \subset m(Q) \quad \text{iff} \quad P \cap \bar{Q} \in \mathscr{J}.$$

Proof: Using 12.1.17 and 12.1.13 we obtain $m(P) \cap m(Q) = m(P)$ iff $m(P \cap Q) = m(P)$ iff $P \cap Q \approx P$ iff $(P \cap Q) \cap \bar{P} \in \mathscr{J}$ and $\overline{(P \cap Q)} \cap P \in \mathscr{J}$ iff $P \cap \bar{Q} \in \mathscr{J}$.

12.1.19 **Proposition:** $P \subset Q$ implies $m(P) \subset m(Q)$.

Proof: $P \subset Q$ implies $P \cap Q = P$. Therefore $P \cap \bar{Q} = (P \cap Q) \cap \bar{Q} = O \in \mathscr{J}$. The assertion now follows from 12.1.18.

We remark that the converse of 12.1.19 is not true. This may be seen by taking $Q = \bar{P}$. Then we have $P \cap \bar{Q} = P \in \mathscr{J}_Q$, and therefore $m(P) \subset m(Q)$; however, $P \subset Q$ is equivalent to $P = O$.

The quotient algebra $\mathscr{E}|R$ has an obvious interpretation. If event R obtains, an equivalence relation in $\mathscr{E}$ is induced: Two events P and Q are equivalent if they belong to the same equivalence class modulo $\mathscr{J}_R$, i.e. if—given R obtains—the occurrence of P leads to the same event as the occurrence of Q. As we may interpret $\tilde{\tilde{Q}}^R$ as the conditional event $Q|R$, the quotient algebra introduced here is essentially the same as COPELAND's implicative algebra.

A fundamental difference between this and COPELAND's approach consists in the fact that COPELAND regards conditional events as elements of $\mathscr{E}$ rather than classes of elements of $\mathscr{E}$. We hesitate to follow him on his way, as an expression like $P \cap (Q \mid R)$ admits no semantic interpretation.

Now we consider conditioning in $\mathscr{E} \mid R$. Let

$$\mathscr{J}_{Q \mid R} := \{P \mid R \in \mathscr{E} \mid R : (P \mid R) \cap (Q \mid R) = O \mid R\}$$

be the principal ideal generated by $\overline{Q \mid P}$ (i.e. $\mathscr{J}_{Q \mid R} = \mathscr{J}_{m\,(Q)}$, m being the natural homomorphism of $\mathscr{E}$ onto $\mathscr{E} \mid R$). The equivalence relation in $\mathscr{E} \mid R$ pertaining to $Q \mid R$ reduces the algebra $\mathscr{E} \mid R$ further to the algebra $(\mathscr{E} \mid R) \mid (Q \mid R)$.

In the following let $\mathscr{J}_1$ be an ideal in $\mathscr{E}$, $\mathscr{J}_2$ an ideal in $\mathscr{E} \mid \mathscr{J}_1$, m_1 the natural homomorphism of $\mathscr{E}$ onto $\mathscr{E} \mid \mathscr{J}_1$ and m_2 the natural homomorphism of $\mathscr{E} \mid \mathscr{J}_1$ onto $(\mathscr{E} \mid \mathscr{J}_1) \mid \mathscr{J}_2$.

12.1.20 **Definition:**

$$\mathscr{J}_1 \mathscr{J}_2 = m_1^{-1} \mathscr{J}_2 = \{P \in \mathscr{E} : m_1 (P) \in \mathscr{J}_2\}.$$

12.1.21 **Proposition:** $\mathscr{J}_1 \mathscr{J}_2$ is an ideal in $\mathscr{E}$.

Proof: According to 12.1.17 we obtain

$m_1 (P \cup Q) = m_1 (P) \cup m_1 (Q) \in \mathscr{J}_2$ for all $P, Q \in \mathscr{J}_1 \mathscr{J}_2$

and

$m_1 (P) = m_1 (P \cap Q) = m_1 (P) \cap m_1 (Q) \in \mathscr{J}_2$ for all $Q \in \mathscr{J}_1 \mathscr{J}_2$

and all $P \subset Q$.

12.1.22 **Theorem:** $(\mathscr{E} \mid \mathscr{J}_1) \mid \mathscr{J}_2$ is isomorphic to $\mathscr{E} \mid \mathscr{J}_1 \mathscr{J}_2$.

Proof: Let $\mathscr{J}$ be the ideal $\mathscr{J}_1 \mathscr{J}_2$ and m be the natural homomorphism of $\mathscr{E}$ onto $\mathscr{E} \mid \mathscr{J}$. By 12.1.13, $P \approx_{\mathscr{J}} Q$ iff $P \cap \bar{Q} \in \mathscr{J}$ and $\bar{P} \cap Q \in \mathscr{J}$. The latter is equivalent to $m_2 \circ m_1 (P \cap \bar{Q}) = O = m_2 \circ m_1 (\bar{P} \cap Q)$ where O denotes the impossible event of $\mathscr{E} \mid \mathscr{J}$ (see 12.1.20). As the maps m_i are algebraic homomorphisms we obtain (see 12.1.11) that

$$P \approx_{\mathscr{J}} Q \text{ iff } m_2 \circ m_1 (P) = m_2 \circ m_1 (Q).$$

Thus $m_2 \circ m_1 \circ m^{-1}$ is a $1-1$ map of $\mathscr{E} \mid \mathscr{J}$ onto $(\mathscr{E} \mid \mathscr{J}_1) \mid \mathscr{J}_2$. This map is, moreover, an isomorphism.

12.1.23 **Corollary:** $(\mathscr{E} \mid R) \mid (Q \mid R)$ is isomorphic to $\mathscr{E} \mid (Q \cap R)$ for all $P, Q, R \in \mathscr{E}$.

Proof: For all $P, Q, R \in \mathscr{E}$ we have:

$P \mid R \in \mathscr{J}_{Q \mid R}$ iff $P \mid R \cap Q \mid R = O \mid R$ iff $(P \cap Q) \mid R = O \mid R$ iff
$P \cap Q \in \mathscr{J}_R$ iff $P \cap Q \cap R = O$ iff $P \in \mathscr{J}_{Q \cap R}$.

Therefore $\mathscr{J}_R \mathscr{J}_{Q \mid R} = \mathscr{J}_{Q \cap R}$ and the assertion follows from 12.1.22.

The content of 12.1.23 corresponds to COPELAND's axiom $(P|R) \mid (Q|R) = P \mid (Q \cap R)$.

12.2 The Space of Wagers

The approach developed here may be considered as a generalization of the MORGENSTERN-VON NEUMANN approach to the measurement of subjective utility (12.6). It is based on the evaluation of wagers (gambles options, bets, lotteries). By a wager we mean a situation with a finite number of possible outcomes, exactly one of which is to occur. Which one of the possible outcomes occurs depends on some uncertain event.

The interpretation of the word "outcome" requires some care. Let the uncertain event be the tossing of a coin. If you are offered a 1:1 bet that tail will obtain, the decision upon acceptance of this bet has to be based on the comparison between the utility of your status quo and the utility of the wager with the two possible outcomes "status quo + 1 $" and "status quo − 1 $" strictly speaking, the two possible outcomes are "status quo +1 $ and the coin shows tail" and "status quo −1 $ and the coin shows head". Besides of its consequence (gain versus loss of 1 $) the question whether the coin shows head or tail is irrelevant for the evaluation of the outcomes. Therefore, they are described exhaustively by "status quo + 1 $" and "status quo − 1 $". If, on the other hand, the uncertain event is the outcome of the next presidential elections, the decision about a 1:1 bet that the next president will be republican has to be based on the utility of the following two wagers, each of them having two possible outcomes

Wager 1	"The next president is republican"
(bet not accepted)	"The next president is democrate"
Wager 2	"The next president is republican and you get 1 $"
(bet accepted)	"The next president is democrate and you loose 1 $"

In this case, the consequences of the uncertain event itself influence your utility and have, therefore, to be considered as part of the outcome.

We shall assume that the evaluation of wagers is governed by the following two general principles:

a) **"Lack of Illusion" Principle:**

Virtually identical wagers presented in different ways have the same utility;

b) **"Sure-thing" Principle:**

(i) The utility of a wager remains unchanged if an outcome is substituted by an outcome of the same utility.

(ii) If one of the outcomes is substituted by an outcome with higher utility, then the utility of the wager either increases or remains unchanged for all possible substitutions of this outcome.

The reader will realize that the above formulation is essentially that of SAVAGE ((1954), pp. 21/22). It is somewhat stronger than SAMUELSON's "strong independence axiom" ((1952), p. 672), as it is not confined to even–change wagers.

The set of events will be denoted by $\mathscr{E}$, the set of possible outcomes by A. By a *simple wager* aPb with $a, b \in A$ and $P \in \mathscr{E}$, we mean the wager leading to outcome a if P obtains and to outcome b if P does not obtain.

For sake of brevity let

$APA := \{aPb : a, b \in A\}$ and $A\mathscr{E}A := \{aPb : a, b \in A, P \in \mathscr{E}\}$.

About $\mathscr{E}$ and A we will make the following basic assumptions

12.2.1 $\mathscr{E}$ is a Boolean algebra.

12.2.2 A is an ordered and connected set containing at least two elements.

In the simplest case $\mathscr{E}$ might consist of the events O, E, P, $\bar{P}$ and A of different quantities of a simple commodity (e.g. money), filling an interval.

Of basic importance for the following is

12.2.3 **Order Axiom:** $A\mathscr{E}A$ is an order system (3.2.1).

According to the order axiom, between any two elements of $A\mathscr{E}A$ exactly one of the relations $\succ$, $\approx$ or $\prec$ holds. The intuitive meaning of this order is an order according to utility. The relation $\approx$ is to be interpreted as an equivalence (in the sense of equal utility) not as an equality. Such an order relation may, for instance, be defined by means of the (objective) probability with which one element of $A\mathscr{E}A$ is preferred to another, equivalence (preference) being the case in which this probability equals (is greater than) 1/2.

The order in $A\mathscr{E}A$ induces an order in $\mathscr{E}$, if the following axiom is fulfilled (see SAVAGE (1954), p. 31, p. 4).

12.2.4 Uniqueness Axiom: If for a special pair $a_0, b_0 \in A$ with $a_0 > b_0$: $a_0Pb_0 \gtreqless a_0Qb_0$, then $aPb \gtreqless aQb$ for all $a, b \in A$ with $a > b$.

If 12.2.4 is fulfilled, we may define an order in $\mathscr{E}$ by

12.2.5 Definition: $P \gtreqless Q$ iff $aPb \gtreqless aQb$ for all $a, b \in A$ with $a > b$.
We remark that under suitable assumptions the order defined by 12.2.5 refines the order defined by 12.1.8 (see 12.3.4).

A special role is played by the events equivalent to O, called "*almost impossible*", and the events equivalent to E, called "*almost sure*".

Interpreting $\prec$ on $A\mathscr{E}A$ as an order of wagers according to utility and $<$ on A as an order of outcomes according to utility we obtain as a formalized consequence of the principles a) and b) the following

12.2.6 Postulate:

a) $aPb \approx b\bar{P}a$ for all $P \in \mathscr{E}$ and $a, b \in A$,

b) $P \approx O$ implies $aPb \approx a'Pb$ for all $a, a', b \in A$ and
$P \not\approx O$ implies $aPb \prec a'Pb$ for all $a, a', b \in A$ with $a < a'$.

We remark that part (i) of the sure-thing principle is contained in 12.2.2: By assuming $<$ to be an order relation for which the equivalence relation is the identity, we identify outcomes of equal utility.

As a consequence of 12.2.6 we obtain that

12.2.6.c) $P \approx O$ iff $\bar{P} \approx E$.

Proof: 12.2.5 and 12.2.6a) imply that $\bar{P} \approx E$ iff $bPa \approx bOa$ for all $b < a$. By 12.2.6b) this is equivalent to $P \approx O$.

12.2.7 Continuity Axiom:

$a \to aPb$ is continuous for all $b \in A$.

Together with 12.2.6a) this implies that

$b \to aPb$ is continuous for all $a \in A$.

12.2.8 Proposition: The map of $A \times A$ into APA defined by $(a, b) \to aPb$ is continuous.

Proof: If P is almost impossible or almost sure, the assertion is trivial. If $P \not\approx O, E$ we argue as follows. As each one of the maps $a \to aPb$ and $b \to aPb$ is monotone increasing and continuous, $(a, b) \to aPb$ is continuous by 3.7.11.

A special role is played by the wagers aPa leading to outcome a regardless whether P obtains or not. Though it seems most natural to require such wagers to be equivalent to a (for all $P \in \mathscr{E}$), it turns out to be unnecessary to formalize such an assumption in this section.

12.2.9 **Proposition:** The map $a \to aPa$ of A into APA is monotone increasing and continuous.

Proof: If P is almost impossible or almost sure the assertion is trivial. If $P \not\approx O, E$ we argue as follows: From 12.2.6 we obtain for $a < b: aPa \prec aPb \prec bPb$. Continuity follows immediately from the fact that $a \to (a, a)$ is continuous by (3.7.2) and $(a, a) \to aPa$ is continuous by 12.2.8.

12.2.10 **Theorem:** For all $a, b \in A$ with $a \neq b$ there exists exactly one c between a and b such that $cPc \approx aPb$.

Proof: Follows immediately from (12.2.9) and the intermediate value theorem (3.6.13).

12.2.11 **Definition:** "$\circ_P$" is the operation which assigns to each pair $a, b \in A$ an element $a \circ_P b \in A$ defined by $aPb \approx (a \circ_P b)\, P\, (a \circ_P b)$.

We remark that the existence of such an element is guaranteed by 12.2.10. $a \circ_P b$ will be called *safety equivalent* of the wager aPb, for the subject is indifferent between the wager aPb and the amount $a \circ_P b$.

12.2.12 **Theorem:** The operation $\circ_P$ and the relation $\approx$ have the following properties

(i) $\circ_P$ is intern except $P \approx O$ or $P \approx E$.

(ii) $a \circ_E b = a$.

(iii) $\circ_P$ is increasing in both variables except $P \approx O$ or $P \approx E$.

(iv) $(a, b) \to a \circ_P b$ is continuous.

(v) $a \circ_P b = b \circ_P a$ for all $a, b \in A$, $P \in \mathscr{E}$.

(vi) The following three sentences are equivalent:

a) $a \circ_P b = a \circ_Q b$ for at least one pair $a, b \in A$, $a \neq b$,

b) $a \circ_P b = a \circ_Q b$ for all $a, b \in A$, and

c) $P \approx Q$.

Proof:

(i) See 12.2.10.

(ii) Follows immediately from $aEb \approx aEa$ (12.2.6).

(iii) We shall prove monotony in the first variable only: If $a' < a''$, 12.2.6 implies $a'Pb \prec a''Pb$. Let $c' = a' \circ_P b$, $c'' = a'' \circ_P b$. We have $c'Pc' \approx a'Pb \prec a''Pb \approx c''Pc''$. Hence 12.2.9 implies $c' < c''$.

(iv) We have to show that: $\{(a, b) \in A \times A : a \circ_P b < c\}$ is open for all $c \in A$. We have $a \circ_P b < c$ iff $aPb \approx (a \circ_P b)\, P\, (a \circ_P b) \prec cPc$. Hence $\{(a, b) \in A \times A : a \circ_P b < c\} = \{(a, b) \in A \times A : aPb \prec cPc\}$. As $(a, b) \to aPb$ is continuous (12.2.8), this is an open set for all $c \in A$. The other cases are dealt with similarly.

(v) Follows immediately from 12.2.6a).

(vi) Follows immediately from the uniqueness axiom (12.2.4) and (v).

12.3 Compound Wagers

In section 12.2 we considered simple wagers, the outcomes being elements of a given set A. In this section we shall consider wagers with outcomes being simple wagers. $(aQ|Pb)\, P\, (cQ|\bar{P}d)$ will denote the compound wager leading to wager $a\,(Q|P)\,b$ if P obtains, to wager $c\,(Q|\bar{P})\,d$ if $\bar{P}$ obtains. We may also regard this compound wager as a wager with four possible outcomes: $PQ \to a$, $P\bar{Q} \to b$, $\bar{P}Q \to c$, $\bar{P}\bar{Q} \to d$.

So far we have assumed that the wagers depending on events of $\mathscr{E}$ satisfy the order axiom 12.2.3, the uniqueness axiom 12.2.4 and the continuity axiom 12.2.7. Now we shall make the same assumptions for wagers depending on events of $\mathscr{E} \mid P$ instead of $\mathscr{E}$ (where P is an arbitrary fixed element of $\mathscr{E}$ which is not almost impossible). Furthermore, we presume the sure-thing principle and the lack of illusion principle. From these assumptions we obtain an operation $\circ_{Q|P}$ on $A \times A$ for each $P, Q \in \mathscr{E}$ (with not almost impossible P) which satisfies 12.2.12 and, in addition, 12.3.2 and 12.3.3 below.

The sure-thing principle and the lack of illusion principle are to be considered as normative principles defining "rational behavior" rather than a description of actual behavior. This point is stressed by the following example (ELLSBERG, (1961), 653/4), showing that the application of the sure-thing principle to combined wagers occasionally leads to results contradictory to intuition.

12.3.1 **Example:** An urn contains 30 red balls and 60 black and yellow balls, the latter in unknown proportion. If one of these balls is drawn at random, we have an uncertain event with three possible outcomes:

"red", "black", "yellow". The following table shows four different wagers (with numbers representing the gain in terms of money):

wager \ result	red	black	yellow
I	100	0	0
II	0	100	0
III	100	0	100
IV	0	100	100

Ellsberg asked subjects to choose first between I and II and then between III and IV. He found that most of them preferred I to II and IV to III. This, however, contradicts the sure-thing principle:

Let P be the event "red or black" and Q the event "red" ($\bar{P} \cap Q = O$). Then these four wagers may be written as

I: $(100\,(Q\,|\,P)\;\;0\;)\,P\;\;0$

II: $(\;0\;\;(Q\,|\,P)\;100)\,P\;\;0$

III: $(100\,(Q\,|\,P)\;\;0\;)\,P\;100$

IV: $(\;0\;\;(Q\,|\,P)\;100)\,P\;100$

A subject preferring I to II (i.e. $100\,(Q\,|\,P)\,0 \succ 0\,(Q\,|\,P)\,100$) ought to prefer III to IV according to the sure-thing principle.

Another example of this kind was given by Allais (1953) and discussed by Savage (1954). The reader is furthermore referred to Markowicz (1965).

Though examples of this kind are rather plausible, we are of the opinion that the sure-thing principle must necessarily be accepted by any "rational" person. Everybody having preferences in contradiction to the sure-thing principle is bound to a revision of his preferences, as well as everybody being intuitively convinced of the truth of a specific mathematical theorem is bound to a revision of this conviction, if a careful logical analysis shows this theorem to be wrong.

The two wagers $(a\,(Q\,|\,P)\,b)\,P\,(c\,(Q\,|\,\bar{P})\,d)$ and $(a\,(P\,|\,Q)\,c)\,Q\,(b\,(P\,|\,\bar{Q})\,d)$ are identical, as for both wagers $PQ \to a$, $P\bar{Q} \to b$, $\bar{P}Q \to c$, $\bar{P}\bar{Q} \to d$. Hence they are judged equivalent due to our lack of illusion principle. Furthermore $uRv \approx (u \circ_R v)\,R\,(u \circ_R v)$. Hence it follows from the sure-thing principle that the following wagers are identical:

$$(a\,(Q\,|\,P)\,b)\,P\,(c\,(Q\,|\,\bar{P})\,d),\;(a \circ_{Q\,|\,P} b)\,P\,(c \circ_{Q\,|\,P} d),$$
$$(a \circ_{Q\,|\,P} b) \circ_P (c \circ_{Q\,|\,P} d),$$

$$(a\,(P|Q)\,c)\,Q\,(b\,(P|\bar{Q})\,d),$$
$$(a \circ_{P|Q} c)\,Q\,(b \circ_{P|\bar{Q}} d),$$
$$(a \circ_{P|Q} c) \circ_Q (b \circ_{P|\bar{Q}} d).$$

This leads to the following

12.3.2 **Postulate:** For all $a, b, c, d \in A$ and all $P, Q \in \mathscr{E}$, $(\not\approx O, E)$:

$$(a \circ_{Q|P} b) \circ_P (c \circ_{Q|P} d) = (a \circ_{P|Q} c) \circ_Q (b \circ_{P|\bar{Q}} d).$$

Furthermore the wagers $(a\,(Q|P)\,b)\,Pb$ and $aPQb$ are identical, as for both wagers $PQ \to a$, $P\bar{Q} \to b$, $\bar{P}Q \to b$, $\bar{P}\bar{Q} \to b$. Hence they are judged equivalent due to our lack of illusion principle. Furthermore we obtain from the sure-thing principle $(a\,(Q|P)\,b)\,Pb \approx (a \circ_{Q|P} b)\,Pb \approx (a \circ_{Q|P} b) \circ_P b$ and $aPQb \approx a \circ_{PQ} b$. This suggests the following

12.3.3 **Postulate:** For all $a, b \in A$ and all $P, Q \in \mathscr{E}$ $(P \not\approx O)$:

$$(a \circ_{Q|P} b) \circ_P b = a \circ_{PQ} b.$$

12.3.4 **Theorem:** The order in $\mathscr{E}$ defined by 12.2.5 refines the order defined by 12.1.8: $P \supset Q$ implies $aPb \gtrsim aQb$ for all $a, b \in A$ with $a > b$.

Proof: By definition 12.1.8, $P \supset Q$ is equivalent to $P \cap Q = Q$. Hence 12.3.3 implies $(a \circ_{Q|P} b) \circ_P b = a \circ_Q b$.

By 12.2.12 (ii) and (iii) $a > b$ implies $a \geqq a \circ_{Q|P} b$. Hence $a \circ_P b \geqq a \circ_Q b$ which proves the assertion.

In the following sections we shall only use properties of the operation $\circ_P$ which are stated in 12.2.12, 12.3.2 and 12.3.3. Instead of deriving these postulates from more general axioms (order, uniqueness and continuity) and principles (sure-thing and lack of illusion), another possible approach would be to forget about these general axioms and principles and to state 12.2.12, 12.3.2 and 12.3.3 together with the continuity axiom as fundamental axioms.

12.3.5 **Proposition:** Let $P \in \mathscr{E}$ be not almost impossible. Then $Q \mid P$ is almost impossible (sure) iff PQ ($P\bar{Q}$) is almost impossible.

Proof: i) If $Q \mid P$ is almost impossible, $a \circ_{P|Q} b$ does not depend on a (12.2.12.ii). Hence $a \circ_{PQ} b$ does not depend on a (12.3.3) implying $PQ \approx O$ (12.2.12.ii). $PQ \approx O$ implies that $(a \circ_{Q|P} b) \circ_P b$ does not depend on a (12.3.3 and 12.2.12.ii). As $P \not\approx O$, $a \circ_{Q|P} b$ does not depend on a and thus $Q \mid P$ is almost impossible. By 12.2.6.c), $Q \mid P$ is almost sure iff $\bar{Q} \mid P$ is almost impossible.

12.3.6 **Proposition:** $P \approx E$ implies $\overline{PQ} \approx P\bar{Q} \approx \bar{Q}$ for all $Q \in \mathscr{E}$.

Proof: $P \approx E$ implies by 12.2.12.ii) and 12.3.3 that $a \circ_{Q|P} b = (a \circ_{Q|P} b) \circ_P b = a \circ_{PQ} b$. Thus $a \circ_{P\bar{Q}} b = a \circ_{\bar{Q}|P} b = b \circ_{Q|P} a = b \circ_{PQ} a$

$= a \circ_{\bar{P}Q} b$. From this we obtain $P\bar{Q} \approx \bar{P}Q$ by 12.2.12 vi). As $\bar{P}Q \supset \bar{Q} \supset P\bar{Q}$, the assertion follows from 12.3.4.

For $P \approx O$, $Q \approx O$ we obtain from 12.3.6 that $\bar{P}\bar{Q} \approx E$ and thus $P \cup Q \approx O$. Together with 12.3.4 this implies the

12.3.7 **Corollary:** The system $\{P \in \mathscr{E} : P \approx O\}$ of almost impossible events is an ideal.

12.4 Preliminary Lemmas

For the sake of brevity, we will use the following notation:

12.4.1 **Definition:** Let U_0, U_1 be two functions mapping A into $\mathbb{R}$. We will write $U_0 \approxeq U_1$, if $U_0(a) - U_1(a)$ is independent of $a \in A$.

12.4.2 **Lemma:** The representation of a function in the form

$$U_0^{-1}(V_0(a) + W_0(b) + k_0)$$

with monotone and continuous real-valued functions U_0, V_0, W_0 defined on an ordered and connected set, and a constant k_0, is essentially unique: If there exists another representation of the same type with functions U_1, V_1, W_1 and a constant k_1, then:

$$U_1 \approxeq \alpha U_0$$
$$V_1 \approxeq \alpha V_0$$
$$W_1 \approxeq \alpha W_0.$$

Proof: From $U_0^{-1}(V_0(a) + W_0(b) + k_0) = U_1^{-1}(V_1(a) + W_1(b) + k_1)$ we obtain $U_1 U_0^{-1}(\xi + \eta) = V_1 V_0^{-1}(\xi) + W_1^* W_0^{*-1}(\eta)$ with $W_i^*(b) = W_i(b) + k_i$, $\xi = V_0(a)$, $\eta = W_0^*(b)$. This equation is a generalization of CAUCHY's functional equation. As the functions involved in this functional equation are monotone and continuous, the general solution is (see ACZÉL (1966), p. 142):

$$U_1 U_0^{-1}(t) = \alpha t + \beta + \gamma$$
$$V_1 V_0^{-1}(t) = \alpha t + \beta$$
$$W_1^* W_0^{*-1}(t) = \alpha t + \gamma$$

whence the assertion follows immediately.

12.4.3 **Lemma:** Let A be connected and assume that

i) $\mathscr{E}' = \{P \in \mathscr{E} : P \not\approx O \text{ and } P \not\approx E\}$ is not empty,

ii) for each $P \in \mathscr{E}'$ there exists $Q \in \mathscr{E}$ such that

(*) $PQ \not\approx O$, $P\bar{Q} \not\approx O$, $\bar{P}Q \not\approx O$ and $\bar{P}\bar{Q} \not\approx O$, and for each $a, b \in A$ there exist $x, y \in A$ with $x \circ_P a \geqq b$, $y \circ_P a \leqq b$.

Then there exist increasing and continuous functions U and U_R ($R \in \mathscr{E}'$) such that

(a) $U(a \circ_P b) \approxeq U_P(a) + U_{\bar{P}}(b)$

and

(b) $U_P(a \circ_{Q|P} b) \approxeq U_{PQ}(a) + U_{P\bar{Q}}(b)$.

The functions U and U_R are unique up to linear transformations. If one of the functions, e.g. U, is fixed, all other functions are uniquely dertermined up to an additive constant. Moreover, $P \approx P'$ implies $U_P \approxeq U_{P'}$. Defining U_P by U for $P \approx E$ and U_P by zero for $P \approx O$, the relation (*a*) holds for all $P \in \mathscr{E}$ and the relation (*b*) holds for all $P, Q \in \mathscr{E}$ with $P \not\approx O$.

Proof: As A is connected, it is order complete and has no gaps (3.5.9). Hence it is separable by (5.1.6). According to (4.2.4) this implies the existence of a monotone and continuous auxiliary map of the order system $\langle A; =, <\rangle$ into the numerical system $\langle \mathbb{R}; =, <\rangle$. Let P, Q be a pair of events satisfying (*). Then the events $P, Q, Q \mid P, Q \mid \bar{P}, P \mid Q$ are neither almost impossible nor almost sure (12.3.5) and thus the corresponding operations increasing in both variables (12.2.12.iii). Therefore we obtain from (12.3.2) according to Aczél (1966, p. 314), the existence of strictly monotone and continuous functions $U, U_P, \bar{U}_P, U_Q, \bar{U}_Q, U_{Q|P}, \bar{U}_{Q|P}, U_{Q|\bar{P}}$ and $\bar{U}_{Q|\bar{P}}$ such that:

12.4.4 $U(a \circ_P b) = U_P(a) + \bar{U}_P(b)$.

12.4.5 $U(a \circ_Q b) = U_Q(a) + \bar{U}_Q(b)$.

12.4.6 $U_P(a \circ_{Q|P} b) = U_{Q|P}(a) + \bar{U}_{Q|P}(b)$

$\bar{U}_P(a \circ_{Q|\bar{P}} b) = U_{Q|\bar{P}}(a) + \bar{U}_{Q|\bar{P}}(b)$

$U_Q(a \circ_{P|Q} b) = U_{Q|P}(a) + U_{Q|\bar{P}}(b)$

$\bar{U}_Q(a \circ_{P|\bar{Q}} b) = \bar{U}_{Q|P}(a) + \bar{U}_{Q|\bar{P}}(b)$

We have to face the problem that, in principle, all functions $U, U_P, \bar{U}_P, U_Q, \bar{U}_Q$, depend on both, P and Q. We shall show, however, that the functions $U_P, \bar{U}_P$ can be chosen independent of Q, and U can be chosen independent of both, P and Q. This follows from the fact that representations of the form 12.4.4—12.4.6 are essentially unique according to 12.4.2.

If we take an event Q^* instead of Q we obtain instead of 12.4.4:

$U^*(a \circ_P b) = U_P^*(a) + \bar{U}_P^*(b)$.

Because of 12.4.2, this implies together with 12.4.4 $U^*(a) \approxeq \alpha U(a)$, $U_P^*(a) \approxeq \alpha U_P(a)$, $\bar{U}_P^*(a) \approxeq \alpha \bar{U}_P(a)$. Hence, for given P the functions U, U_P and $\bar{U}_P$

are unique up to linear transformations. Therefore, we can choose U, U_P and $\bar{U}_P$ independent of Q, that is, a representation 12.4.4 based on a specific event Q^* is valid for any event Q.

By applying the same argument to equation 12.4.5 we see that for given Q, the functions U, U_Q and $\bar{U}_Q$ are unique up to linear transformations. Hence we can choose U independent of P and Q.

12.4.2 implies that all the functions occurring in 12.4.4—12.4.6 are uniquely determined up to an additive constant, if one of them, say U, is fixed.

Moreover, $P \approx P'$ implies by 12.2.12.vi) and 12.4.2 that $U_P \approxeq U_{P'}$.

Starting from 12.4.4 and 12.4.6:

$$U(a \circ_P b) = U_P(a) + \bar{U}_P(b),$$

$$U_P(a \circ_{Q \mid P} b) = U_{Q \mid P}(a) + \bar{U}_{Q \mid P}(b),$$

we obtain from $a \circ_P b = b \circ_{\bar{P}} a$ and $a \circ_{\bar{Q} \mid P} b = b \circ_{Q \mid P} a$ (12.2.12.v) that $\bar{U}_P \approxeq U_{\bar{P}}$ and $\bar{U}_{Q \mid P} \approxeq U_{\bar{Q} \mid P}$. Furthermore, from 12.4.4, 12.3.3 and 12.4.6 we obtain for $PQ \in \mathscr{E}'$: $U_{PQ}(a) + \bar{U}_{PQ}(b) = U(a \circ_{PQ} b) = U\big((a \circ_{Q \mid P} b) \circ_P b\big) = U_P\ (a \circ_{Q \mid P} b) + \bar{U}_P(b) = U_{Q \mid P}(a) + \bar{U}_{Q \mid P}(b)$ and thus, by 12.4.2, $U_{Q \mid P} \approxeq U_{PQ}$, whence the assertion follows.

For $P \approx E$ or $P \approx O$ the relation (a) is satisfied because of 12.2.12(ii). For $P \approx E$, 12.3.3 and 12.2.12 imply $a \circ_{Q \mid P} b = a \circ_{PQ} b$; thus (b) follows for $P \approx E$ immediately from (a) and 12.3.6.

12.5 Theorems on Utility and Subjective Probability

12.5.1 **Definition:** The event $Q \in \mathscr{E}$ is *independent* of the event $P \in \mathscr{E}'$ iff $\circ_{Q|P} = \circ_{Q|\bar{P}}$.

This definition is justified by the fact that $\circ_{Q|P} = \circ_{Q|\bar{P}}$ means that the knowledge of whether P or $\bar{P}$ obtains is irrelevant for the evaluation of wagers based on Q. It will be shown in 12.5.14 that independence is a symmetric property, i. e. if Q is independent of P, then also P is independent of Q.

12.5.2 **Axiom:** For each event $P \in \mathscr{E}'$ there exists an element $Q \in \mathscr{E}'$ which is independent of P, and $x \to x \circ_P a$ maps onto A for each $a \in A$.

The first part of this axiom is not very strong, of course, because any rational person will be willing to consider the tossing of a coin as an event which is independent of all other uncertain events. If there is only a subsystem $\mathscr{E}_0$ of $\mathscr{E}'$ satisfying this axiom, the following proportions concerning the subjective probability s will be true for $P \in \mathscr{E}_0$.

12.5.3 **Proposition:** If P, $Q \in \mathscr{E}'$ and if Q is independent of P then $PQ \not\approx O$, $P\bar{Q} \not\approx O$, $\bar{P}Q \not\approx O$ and $\bar{P}\bar{Q} \not\approx O$.

Proof: As both, Q and $\bar{Q}$, are independent of P and $\bar{P}$, it suffices to show that $PQ \not\approx O$. Supposing $PQ \approx O$ we obtain by 12.3.5 that $Q \mid P$ and thus $Q \mid \bar{P}$ is almost impossible (12.5.1 and 12.2.12) implying $\bar{P}Q \approx O$. As the union of two almost impossible events is almost impossible (12.3.7), $Q = \bar{P}Q \cup PQ \approx O$ in contradiction to $Q \not\approx O$.

Excluding the trivial case $P \approx O$ or E for all $P \in \mathscr{E}$, the axiom 12.5.2 implies the assumptions of 12.4.3. Thus there is a sys tem of functions U, U_R $(R \in \mathscr{E})$ satisfying the assertions of 12.4.3.

12.5.4 **Decomposition-Theorem:** For each $P \in \mathscr{E}$ there exist a real number $s(P)$ such that for all $a \in A$:

(*) $\quad U_P(a) \approxeq s(P)\, U(a).$

Proof: By definition, $s(P) = 0$ for $P \approx O$, and $s(P) = 1$ for $P \approx E$. For $P \in \mathscr{E}'$ we choose an event $Q \in \mathscr{E}'$ which is independent of P (12.5.2). By use of 12.5.1 we obtain from 12.4.3:

$$U_P^{-1}\left(U_{PQ}(a) + U_{P\bar{Q}}(b) + k_P\right) = U_{\bar{P}}^{-1}\left(U_{\bar{P}Q}(a) + U_{\bar{P}\bar{Q}}(b) + k_{\bar{P}}\right)$$

and therefore from 12.4.2: $U_{\bar{P}}(a) \approxeq t\, U_P(a)$ with a constant t depending on P. Using 12.4.3 a), the assertion follows from:

$$U(a) = U(a \circ_P a) \approxeq U_P(a) + U_{\bar{P}}(a) \approxeq U_P(a) + t(P)\, U_P(a)$$
$$= (1 + t(P))\, U_P(a).$$

12.5.5 **Corollary:** $s(E) = 1$ and $s(O) = 0$.

12.5.6 **Representation-Theorem:** If $P, Q \in \mathscr{E}$ and $P \not\approx O$ then for all $a, b \in A$:

$$U(a \circ_{Q\mid P} b) = \frac{s(PQ)}{s(P)}\, U(a) + \left(1 - \frac{s(PQ)}{s(P)}\right) U(b).$$

Proof: 12.5.4 (*) together with 12.4.3 b) implies

(**) $\quad s(P)\, U(a \circ_{Q\mid P} b) \approxeq s(PQ)\, U(a) + s(P\bar{Q})\, U(b).$

For $a = b$ we obtain

$$s(P)\, U(a) \approxeq \left(s(PQ) + s(P\bar{Q})\right) U(a)$$

As A contains at least two elements, this relation is an equality and

12.5.7 $s(P) = s(PQ) + s(P\bar{Q})$; therefore also the relation (**) is an equality. U_P is increasing and thus $s(P) > O$.

12.5.8 **Corollary:** For all $Q \in \mathscr{E}$ and all $a, b \in A$:

$$U(a \circ_Q b) = s(Q)\, U(a) + (1 - s(Q))\, U(b).$$

We may interpret the term $s(Q)$ occurring in 12.5.8 as subjective probability of the event Q. This interpretation is strongly supported by the following

12.5.9 **Theorem:**

(i) $\quad s(Q) \geqq 0$, for all $Q \in \mathscr{E}$,

(ii) $s(P \cup Q) = s(P) + s(Q)$ for all $P, Q \in \mathscr{E}$ such that $P \cap Q = O$,

(iii) $s(E) = 1$.

We remark that the question for conditions yielding σ-additivity will not be discussed here.

Proof: (iii) see 12.5.5.

(ii) Replacing P by $P \cup Q$ and Q by $\bar{Q}$ in 12.5.7 we obtain $s(P \cup Q) = s(P \cap \bar{Q}) + s(Q)$. Together with 12.5.7 this yields:

12.5.10 $s(P \cap Q) + s(P \cup Q) = s(P) + s(Q)$.

Therefore, if $P \cap Q = O$, 12.5.10 reduces to assertion (ii), the so-called *addition-theorem* for disjoint events.

(i) As the functions U and U_R $(R \in \mathscr{E})$ are constant or increasing (12.4.3), the assertion follows from 12.5.4.

12.5.11 **Proposition:** $P \subset Q$ implies $s(P) \leqq s(Q)$.

Proof: 12.5.9 (i) and 12.5.9 (ii) together imply $s(P) \leqq s(P) + s(Q \cap \bar{P}) = s(Q)$.

In accordance with the interpretation of $s(Q)$ as subjective probability of the event $Q \in \mathscr{E}$ the term $s(P \cap Q) / s(P)$ occurring in 12.5.6 is to be interpreted as the subjective probability of the event $Q|P \in \mathscr{E}|P$. Introducing the symbol $s(Q|P)$ for this probability we obtain the common formula

12.5.12 $s(Q|P) = s(Q \cap P) / s(P)$.

Going back to the definition of independence by 12.5.1 we obtain from 12.5.6 and 12.5.12 a characterization of independence in terms of subjective probability, namely

12.5.13 **Theorem:** Q is independent of P iff $s(Q|P) = s(Q|\bar{P})$.

12.5.14 **Multiplication - Theorem for Independent Events:** The event $Q \in \mathscr{E}$ is independent of the event $P \in \mathscr{E}'$ iff $s(Q \cap P) = s(Q)\, s(P)$.

Hence independence is a symmetric property.

Proof: Using (12.5.9 ii) we obtain

$$\frac{s(Q \cap P)}{s(P)} = \frac{s(Q \cap \bar{P})}{s(\bar{P})} \quad \text{iff} \quad s(Q \cap P) + \frac{s(Q \cap P)}{s(P)} s(\bar{P}) = s(Q)$$

iff $s(Q \cap P)\big(s(P) + s(\bar{P})\big) = s(Q)\, s(P)$ iff $s(Q \cap P) = s(Q)\, s(P)$.

12.6 The MORGENSTERN — VON NEUMANN Approach

In this section it will be shown that the approach outlined in sections 12.1 – 12.4 may be considered as a generalization of the MORGENSTERN – VON NEUMANN approach in so far as subjective probabilities are not tight to objective probabilities, and it is not necessary to have events with a continuous range of probabilities available. Our assumption that A is connected is implicitely contained (see theorem 12.6.11) in the following assumptions of MORGENSTERN – VON NEUMANN:

Let A be an ordered set. Assume:

12.6.1 To each $\alpha \in (0, 1)$ there exists an operation, say α, assigning to each pair $a, b \in A$ an element $a \alpha b \in A$.

12.6.2 For all $\alpha \in (0, 1)$ and all $a, b \in A$: $a < b$ implies $a < a\alpha b < b$ ((1953), axioms 3:B:a and 3:B:b).

12.6.3 For all $\alpha \in (0, 1)$ and all $a \in A$: $a\alpha a = a$.

12.6.4 For all $\alpha \in (0, 1)$ and all $a, b \in A$: $a\alpha b = b\,(1-\alpha)\,a$ ((1953), axiom 3:C:a).

12.6.5 For all $a, b, c \in A$ with (i) $a < c < b$ or (ii) $b < c < a$ there exist real numbers $\alpha, \beta \in (0, 1)$ such that $a\alpha b < c < a\beta b$ ((1953), axioms 3:B:c and 3:B:d).

12.6.6 For all $\alpha, \beta \in (0, 1)$ and all $a, b \in A$: $(a\alpha b)\,\beta b = a\alpha\beta b$ ((1953), axiom 3:C:b).

Axiom 12.6.3 is not given explicitely by MORGENSTERN – VON NEUMANN. It is, however, included implicitely in the interpretation they give to their system of axioms.

In these axioms MORGENSTERN and VON NEUMANN implicitly assume that (i) the wagers are based on events having an objective probability α, (ii) the evaluation of such wagers depends on the objective probability α only. Therefore all wagers based on events with identical objective probabilities are to be regarded as equal if the corresponding outcomes are equal. Moreover, 12.6.6 implicitly requires that the events α, β occurring in compound wagers are independent.

From axioms 12.6.1 – 12.6.6 we can now deduce the following lemmata on MORGENSTERN – VON NEUMANN wagers.

12.6.7 Lemma: For all $\alpha, \beta \in (0, 1)$ with $\alpha < \beta$: $a \leqq b$ implies $a\alpha b \geqq a\beta b$.

Proof: (i) $a < b$: For all $\alpha, \beta \in (0, 1)$ with $\alpha < \beta$ there exists $\gamma \in (0, 1)$ such that $\alpha = \gamma\beta$. From 12.6.5 we obtain $a\beta b < b$ and from this by 12.6.2: $a\beta b < (a\beta b)\gamma b$. Hence together with 12.6.6 we obtain $a\beta b < a\beta\gamma b$ and $a\beta b < a\alpha b$.

(ii) $a > b$: is reduced to (i) by 12.6.4.

(iii) $a = b$: is an immediate consequence of 12.6.3

12.6.8 Lemma: For all $\alpha, \beta \in (0, 1)$ and all $a, b \in A$: $a\alpha(a\beta b) = a(\alpha+\beta-\alpha\beta)b$.

Proof: Follows immediately from 12.6.6 and 12.6.4.

12.6.9 Theorem: The map $\alpha \to a\alpha b$ is continuous for all $a, b \in A$.

Proof: We will show that for all $c \in A$ the set $A_0 := \{\alpha \in (0, 1) : a\alpha b > c\}$ is open. By 12.6.4 we may assume that $a \leqq b$. If $c \geqq b$ or $c \leqq a$, we have $A_0 = \emptyset$ or $(0, 1)$. If $a < c < b$ we obtain from 12.6.7 that for all $\alpha \in A_0$ and all $\beta \in \bar{A}_0$ we have $\alpha < \beta$. If we assume that there exists a greatest element $\alpha_0 \in A_0$, then $c < a\alpha_0 b$. Using $a < c$ we obtain from 12.6.5 that there exists $\beta \in (0, 1)$ such that $c < a\beta(a\alpha_0 b)$. Hence by 12.6.8: $c < a(\alpha_0 + \beta(1-\alpha_0))b$. As $\alpha_0 < 1$, this contradicts the assumption that α_0 is the greatest element of A_0.

12.6.9 implies that the map of the interval (0, 1) into A defined by $\alpha \to a\alpha b$ is continuous. Both, monotony (established by 12.6.7) and continuity as well as 12.6.3–12.6.8 are preserved if this map is extended for $\alpha = 0$ and $\alpha = 1$ by defining $a0b = b$, $a1b = a$ for all $a, b \in A$.

12.6.10 Theorem: For all $a, b, c \in A$ with $a \leqq c \leqq b$, there exists $\gamma \in [0, 1]$, such that $a\gamma b = c$. In case $a \neq b$, γ is uniquely determined.

Proof: Follows immediately from 12.6.7 and 12.6.9 if we apply the intermediate value theorem 3.6.13 to the map $\alpha \to a\alpha b$.

12.6.11 Theorem: A is connected in its interval topology.

Proof: Let $A_1, A_2 \subset A$ be two nonempty open sets with $A_1 \cap A_2 = \emptyset$, $A_1 \cup A_2 = A$. Let $a \in A_1$ and $b \in A_2$ be arbitrary. Then also the sets $A_1^* = \{a\alpha b : \alpha \in [0, 1]\} \cap A_1$ and $A_2^* = \{a\alpha b : \alpha \in [0, 1]\} \cap A_2$ are open in the induced topology of $\{a\alpha b : \alpha \in [0, 1]\}$. A_1^* and A_2^* are nonempty sets with $A_1^* \cap A_2^* = \emptyset$ and $A_1^* \cup A_2^* = \{a\alpha b : \alpha \in [0, 1]\}$. This is, however, a contradiction since $\{a\alpha b : \alpha \in [0, 1]\}$ is the picture of $[0, 1]$ under the continuous map $\alpha \to a\alpha b$ and hence connected.

12.6.12 Proposition: For all $\alpha \in (0, 1)$ and all $a, b, c \in A$: $b \leqq c$ implies $a\alpha b \leqq a\alpha c$.

Proof: In the case $b = c$ the assertion becomes equivalent to 12.6.1. As the cases by $b < c$ and $b > c$ are analogous, we will only prove the assertion for $b < c$.

(i) $a < b < c$: By 12.6.10 there exists $\gamma \in (0, 1)$ such that $b = a\gamma c$. 12.6.4 and 12.6.6 together imply that $a\alpha(a\gamma c) = a\gamma(a\alpha c)$. As $a\alpha b = a\alpha(a\gamma c)$ and $a\gamma(a\alpha c) < a\alpha c$ by 12.6.2 we obtain $a\alpha b < a\alpha c$.

(ii) $b \leqq a \leqq c$: The assertion follows immediately from 12.6.2 and 12.6.3.

(iii) $b < c < a$: 12.6.10 implies that there exists $\gamma \in (0, 1)$ such that $c = a\gamma b$. Hence, by 12.6.1, 12.6.4 and 12.6.6 we obtain $a\alpha c = a\alpha(a\gamma b) = a\gamma(a\alpha b) > a\alpha b$.

12.6.13 **Lemma:** For all $\alpha, \beta \in [0, 1]$ and all $a, b, c \in A$ we have

$$(a\alpha b)\beta c = a\alpha\beta\left(b\frac{\beta(1-\alpha)}{1-\alpha\beta}c\right).$$

Proof: We assume that a, b, c are different elements and that $\alpha \neq 0,1$ and $\beta \neq 0,1$; otherwise the assertion follows immediatly from 12.6.4, 12.6.6 and 12.6.8. These three rules will be used frequently in the following.

a) If c lies between a and b ($a < c < b$ or $b < c < a$) there exist $\xi \in (0,1)$ with $c = a\,\xi\,b$ (12.6.10) and either
(i) $\gamma \in [0,1)$ with $a\,\gamma\,c = a\,\alpha\,b$, or
(ii) $\gamma \in (0,1]$ with $c\,\gamma\,b = a\,\alpha\,b$.

For (i), $a\,\alpha\,b = a\,\gamma\,c = a\,\gamma(a\,\xi\,b) = a\,(\gamma + \xi - \gamma\xi)$ and thus by 12.6.7

$$\xi = \frac{\alpha - \gamma}{1 - \gamma}.$$

Hence

$$(a\alpha b)\beta c = (a\gamma c)\beta c = a\beta\gamma c = a\beta\gamma\left(b\frac{1-\alpha}{1-\gamma}a\right) = b\frac{(1-\alpha)(1-\beta\gamma)}{(1-\gamma)}a.$$

On the other hand,

$$a\alpha\beta\left(b\frac{\beta(1-\alpha)}{1-\alpha\beta}c\right) = a\alpha\beta\left[b\frac{\beta(1-\alpha)}{1-\alpha\beta}\left(b\frac{1-\alpha}{1-\gamma}a\right)\right]$$
$$= b\frac{(1-\alpha)(1-\beta\gamma)}{(1-\gamma)}a$$

whence the assertion follows.

For (ii), $a\,\alpha\,b = c\,\gamma\,b = (a\,\xi\,b)\,\gamma\,b = a\,\xi\,\gamma\,b$ and thus $\xi = \dfrac{\alpha}{\gamma}$.

Hence

$$(a\alpha b)\beta c = (c\gamma b)\beta c = b(1-\gamma)\beta c$$
$$= b(1-\gamma)\beta\left(a\frac{\alpha}{\gamma}b\right) = a\left(\frac{\alpha(1-\beta)}{\gamma} + \alpha\beta\right)b.$$

On the other hand

$$a\alpha\beta\left(b\frac{\beta(1-\alpha)}{1-\alpha\beta}c\right)=a\alpha\beta\left[b\frac{\beta(1-\alpha)}{1-\alpha\beta}\left(a\frac{\alpha}{\gamma}b\right)\right]=a\left(\frac{\alpha(1-\beta)}{\gamma}+\alpha\beta\right)b$$

whence the assertion follows.

b) If c does not lie between a and b ($c < \min(a, b)$ or $c > \max(a, b)$) then either

(i) a lies between b and c, and thus there exist ξ and $\gamma \in (0,1)$ such that $a = c\,\xi\,b$ and $a\,\alpha\,b = c\,\gamma\,b$, or

(ii) b lies between a and c, and thus there exist ξ and $\gamma \in (0,1)$ such that $b = a\,\xi\,c$ and $a\,\alpha\,b = a\,\gamma\,c$.

For (i), $c\,\gamma\,b = a\,\alpha\,b = (c\,\xi\,b)\,\alpha\,b = c\,\alpha\,\xi\,b$ whence $\xi = \dfrac{\gamma}{\alpha}$.

$$(a\,\alpha\,b)\,\beta\,c = (c\,\gamma\,b)\,\beta\,c = b\,\beta\,(1-\gamma)\,c.$$

If $\zeta = \dfrac{\alpha}{\gamma}\dfrac{1-\beta}{1-\alpha\beta} \leqq 1$ we obtain, on the other hand,

$$a\,\alpha\,\beta\left(b\frac{\beta(1-\alpha)}{1-\alpha\beta}c\right) = (c\,\xi\,b)\,\alpha\,\beta\,((c\,\xi\,b)\,\zeta\,b) =$$
$$= (c\,\xi\,b)\,(\alpha\beta+\zeta-\alpha\beta\zeta)\,b = b\,(1-\xi\,(\alpha\beta+\zeta-\alpha\beta\zeta))\,c = b\,\beta\,(1-\gamma)\,c.$$

If $\zeta > 1$, then $0 < \eta = \dfrac{\gamma\zeta-\gamma}{\alpha-\gamma} \leqq 1$ and, as $\eta+\xi-\eta\xi = 1-\dfrac{\beta(1-\alpha)}{1-\alpha\beta}$,

$$a\,\alpha\,\beta\left(b\frac{\beta(1-\alpha)}{1-\alpha\beta}c\right) = (c\,\xi\,b)\,\alpha\,\beta\,(c\,\eta\,(c\,\xi\,b)) =$$
$$= (c\,\xi\,b)\,(\alpha\,\beta+1-\eta-\alpha\,\beta\,(1-\eta))\,c =$$
$$= b\,((1-\xi)\,(\alpha\,\beta+1-\eta-\alpha\,\beta\,(1-\eta)))\,c = b\,\beta\,(1-\gamma)\,c$$

whence the assertion follows.

For (ii), $a\,\gamma\,c = a\,\alpha\,b = a\,\alpha\,(a\,\xi\,c) = a\,(\alpha+\xi-\alpha\xi)\,c$ and thus $\xi = \dfrac{\gamma-\alpha}{1-\alpha}$.

$$(a\,\alpha\,b)\,\beta\,c = (a\,\gamma\,c)\,\beta\,c = a\,\beta\,\gamma\,c.$$

On the other hand,

$$a\,\alpha\,\beta\left(b\frac{\beta(1-\alpha)}{1-\alpha\beta}c\right) = a\,\alpha\,\beta\left((a\,\xi\,c)\,\frac{\beta(1-\alpha)}{1-\alpha\beta}c\right) =$$
$$= a\,\alpha\,\beta\left(a\frac{\beta(\gamma-\alpha)}{1-\alpha\beta}c\right) =$$
$$= a\left(\alpha\,\beta+\frac{\beta(\gamma-\alpha)}{1-\alpha\beta}-\alpha\,\beta\frac{\beta(\gamma-\alpha)}{1-\alpha\beta}\right)c = a\,\beta\,\gamma\,c.$$

12.6.14 **Theorem:** For all $\alpha, \beta \in [0, 1]$ and all $a, b, c \in A$ we have

$$(a\alpha b)\,\beta\,(c\alpha d) = (a\beta c)\,\alpha\,(b\beta d).$$

Proof: By repeated application of 12.6.13 and 12.6.5 we obtain

$$(a\alpha b)\,\beta\,(c\alpha d) = a\alpha\beta\left[(c\alpha d)\frac{1-\beta}{1-\alpha\beta}\,b\right] = a\alpha\beta\left[c\,\frac{\alpha(1-\beta)}{1-\alpha\beta}\,(b\beta d)\right]$$

$$= c\alpha(1-\beta)\left[(b\beta d)\frac{1-\alpha}{1-\alpha(1-\beta)}\,a\right]$$

$$= (b\beta d)(1-\alpha)(a\beta c) = (a\beta c)\,\alpha\,(b\beta d).$$

12.6.15 **Theorem:** For all $\alpha \in [0, 1]$ the map $(a, b) \to a\alpha b$ is continuous.

Proof: If $\alpha = 0$ or $\alpha = 1$ the assertion is trivial. If $\alpha \in (0, 1)$, the map $a \to a\alpha b$ is increasing by 12.6.12.

Let be $A_1 := \{x\varepsilon A : x\alpha b < c\}$. We have $a_1\alpha b < c \leqq a_2\alpha b$ if $a_1 \in A_1$ and $a_2 \in \bar{A}_1$. From 12.6.10 we conclude that there exists $\gamma \in [0, 1]$ such that $(a_1\alpha b)\,\gamma\,(a_2\alpha b) = c$. Hence by 12.6.14 and 12.6.3 we obtain $(a_1\alpha b)\,\gamma\,(a_2\alpha b) = (a_1\gamma a_2)\,\alpha\,(b\gamma b) = (a_1\gamma a_2)\,\alpha b$, i.e. there exists an element $(a_1\gamma a_2) \in A$ such that $(a_1\gamma a_2)\,\alpha b = c$. Now by 12.6.12 we obtain $\{x\varepsilon A : x\alpha b < c\} = \{x\varepsilon A : x\alpha b < (a_1\gamma a_2)\,\alpha b\} = \{x\varepsilon A : x < a_1\gamma a_2\}$. As this is an open set the map $a \to a\alpha b$ is continuous. Similarly, we show that $b \to a\alpha b$ is increasing and continuous. Hence the assertion follows from (3.7.11).

12.6.16 **Theorem:** The operations $(a, b) \to a\alpha b$, $\alpha \in [0, 1]$, have the properties stated in 12.2.12, 12.3.2 and 12.3.3.

Proof: Extending the map $\alpha \to a\alpha b$ by $0 \to b$ and $1 \to a$, we obtain:

12.2.12 (i): 12.6.2. (ii): by definition of the map $a1b$. (iii): 12.6.12 and 12.6.4. (iv): 12.6.15. (v): 12.6.4. (vi): $a\alpha b = a\beta b$ for at least one pair a, b is equivalent to $\alpha = \beta$ (12.6.7). 12.3.2: 12.6.14. 12.3.3: 12.6.6.

Because of Theorem 12.6.16 we can apply the representation theory developed in section 12.5 to obtain a subjective probability, say $s(\alpha)$, pertaining to events with objective probabilities α. Moreover, we are able to show that for MORGENSTERN–VON NEUMANN wagers subjective and objective probabilities are necessarily identical:

12.6.17 **Theorem:** If a respresentation

$$U(a\alpha b) = s(\alpha)\,U(a) + (1 - s(\alpha))\,U(b)$$

exists and if U is increasing, then $s(\alpha) = \alpha$ for all $\alpha \in [0, 1]$.

Proof: From 12.6.4 we obtain

$$s(\alpha)\,U(a) + (1 - s(\alpha))\,U(b) = U(a\alpha b) = U(b\,(1-\alpha)\,a)$$
$$= s(1-\alpha)\,U(b) + (1 - s(1-\alpha))\,U(a).$$

Hence

12.6.18 $s(1-\alpha) = 1 - s(\alpha)$ for all $\alpha \in [0, 1]$.

Furthermore, 12.6.6 implies

$$\begin{aligned} s(\alpha\beta)\, U(a) + (1 - s(\alpha\beta))\, U(b) &= U(a\alpha\beta b) = U((a\alpha b)\,\beta b) \\ &= s(\beta)\, U(a\alpha b) + (1 - s(\beta))\, U(b) \\ &= s(\beta)\,[s(\alpha)\, U(a) + (1 - s(\alpha))\, U(b)] \\ &\quad + (1 - s(\beta))\, U(b) \\ &= s(\alpha)\, s(\beta)\, U(a) + (1 - s(\alpha)\, s(\beta))\, U(b). \end{aligned}$$

Hence

12.6.19 $s(\alpha\beta) = s(\alpha)\, s(\beta)$ for all $\alpha, \beta \in [0, 1]$.

From 12.6.18 we obtain $s(1/2) = 1/2$. Substituting $\alpha = 1/2$, $\beta = 0$ in 12.6.19, we obtain $s(0) = 0$. Moreover, for $\alpha < \beta$ and $a > b$ 12.6.7 implies

$$s(\alpha)\, U(a) + (1 - s(\alpha))\, U(b) < s(\beta)\, U(a) + (1 - s(\beta))\, U(b)$$

and thus

$$s(\alpha)\, (U(a) - U(b)) < s(\beta)\, (U(a) - U(b));$$

by the monotony of U we obtain $s(\alpha) < s(\beta)$. Hence (see Aczél (1961, p 44ff)) 12.6.19 implies $s(\alpha) = \alpha$.

12.6.20 **Corollary:** If axioms 12.6.1 – 12.6.6 are fulfilled there exists a representation $U(a\alpha b) = \alpha U(a) + (1 - \alpha)\, U(b)$ for all $a, b \in A, \alpha \in [0, 1]$.

Proof: Follows immediately from 12.6.16, 12.5.8 and 12.6.17.

12.7 Concluding Remarks

The theory of measuring utility and subjective probability developed here is based on a set of axioms. These axioms are to be considered as normative principles defining the concept of rational behavior rather than as a description of actual behavior.

Starting from these axioms, we obtain as a mathematical theorem that there exist two functions, U (defined on the domain A) and s (defined on the domain $\mathscr{E}$), such that

$$U(xPy) = s(P)\, U(x) + (1 - s(P))\, U(y).$$

The interpretation of U and s as *utility* and *subjective probability*, respectively, is strongly suggested by the fact that U is strictly increasing and s

has all the properties usually required for probabilities. Therefore, rational behavior in situations involving risk can be described by means of utility and subjective probability. The "rational person" behaves as if he would evaluate situations involving risk according to their expected utility (the expectation being based on subjective probabilities).

We want to stress that the subjective probabilities are means for describing rational behavior. Nothing more! They cannot be used as estimates of the objective probability of an event, or the credibility of a statement, or for the corroboration of a theory.

The result that rational behavior can be described by means of expectation might suggest that this theory is of relevance only for decisions related to events which are repeated independently a great number of times. This is not the case. The theory is exclusively designed to deal with unique events. (It can be applied to a combination of n independent repetitions by considering the combined wager based on an event with 2^n possible outcomes).

As shown in 12.6 this approach can be considered as a generalisation of the MORGENSTERN–VON NEUMANN approach, in so far as our assumptions are less restrictive than those made by MORGENSTERN–VON NEUMANN. The essential relaxations are: allowing for divergence between objective and subjective probability, and not requiring the range of probabilities to be connected. Nevertheless there exists a relationship between subjective probability and objective probability for those events where objective probabilities are associated with, if we assume that subjective probability is uniquely determined by objective probability and if in addition objectively independent events are also subjectively independent. Under these conditions subjective probability is equal to objective probability. Hence in this case subjective probability would merely be an extension of the concept of probability to events for which no objective probability exists.

The utility concept developed by MORGENSTERN–VON NEUMANN was criticized on account of their assumption that the objective probabilities (in the sense of the frequency interpretation) are relevant for the evaluation of wagers. This attitude is, for example, taken by SUPPES and WINET (1955): "The interaction between probability and utility makes it difficult to make unequivocal measurements of either one or the other. The recent MOSTELLER and NOGEE experiments (1951) may be interpreted as measuring utility if objective probabilities are assumed or as measuring subjective probabilities if utility is assumed linear in money."

There is an obvious way out of this dilemma: to determine one of the two scales independently and to use the evaluation of wagers for the determination of the other scale. (See e.g. Davidson and Suppes (1956) and Anscombe and Aumann (1963)).

In his outstanding contribution, Savage (1954) develops first a measure of subjective (personal) probability, and determines utility afterwards. The main difference to our approach is Savage's assumption that there exists a great number of events of small probability (corresponding, roughly speaking, to the Morgenstern–von Neumann assumption of a connected range of probabilities).

More closely related to our approach is that of Ramsey, who determines utility by using events of subjective probability 1/2 only. After having determined a utility scale in this way, he defines subjective probability (degree of belief) for arbitrary events and shows that it has the usual properties. The approach taken here eliminates the special role of events of subjective probability 1/2. It furthermore renders scales for utility and subjective probability simultaneously. Starting from results obtained in Pfanzagl (1959a and b) this theory was developed in Pfanzagl (1967). This chapter is essentially an adaptation of the latter paper to the framework of this book. A forthcoming paper of Baumann will weaken the solvability condition of 12.5.2.

References

ACZÉL, J.: Ein Eindeutigkeitssatz in der Theorie der Funktionalgleichungen und einige ihrer Anwendungen. Acta Math. Acad. Scient. Hung., 15, 1964, 355—362.

— —: Lectures on functional equations and their applications. Academic Press, New York and London, 1966.

ACZÉL, J., D. Ž. DJOKOVIĆ and J. PFANZAGL: On the uniqueness of scales derived from canonical representations. Metrika, 16, 1970, 1—8.

ACZÉL, J., G. PICKERT and R. RADO: Nomogramme, Gewebe und Quasigruppen. Mathematica, 2, 1960, 5—24.

ADAMS, E. W.: Elements of a theory of inexact measurement. Philos. Science, 32. 1965, 205—228.

— —: On the nature and purpose of measurement. Tech. Rep., 4, 1966.

ADAMS, E. W. and R. F. FAGOT: A model of riskless choice. Behav. Sci., 4, 1959, 1—10.

ADAMS, E. W., R. F. FAGOT and R. E. ROBINSON: Invariance, meaningfulness and appropriate statistics. Tech. Rep., 1, 1964.

— —: A theory of appropriate statistics. Psychometrika. 30, 1965 (a), 99—127.

— —: On the empirical status of axioms in theories of fundamental measurement. Tech. Rep., 3, 1965 (b).

ALLAIS, M.: Le comportement de l'homme rationnel devant le risque: Critique des postulats et axiomes de l'école Americaine. Econometrica, 21, 1953, 503—546.

ANSCOMBE, F. J. and R. J. AUMANN: A definition of subjective probability. Ann. Math. Statist., 34, 1963, 199—205.

BECKER, G. M., M. H. DEGROOT and J. MARSCHAK: Probabilities of choice among very similar objects: An experiment to decide between two models. Behav. Sci., 8, 1963, 306—311.

BEHREND, E. A.: A Contribution to the theory of magnitudes and the foundation of analysis. Math. Z., 63, 1956, 345—362.

BIRNBAUM, A.: Some latent trait models and their use in inferring an examinee's ability. See LORD and NOVICK. Part 5.

BJÖRKMAN, M.: An experimental comparison between the method of ratio estimation and pair comparisons. Rep. Psychol. Lab. Univ. Stockholm, 71, 1959.

BLOCK, H. D., and J. MARSCHAK: Contributions to probability and statistics, edd. I. Olkin and others, Stanford Univ. Press, Stanford. 1960, 89—132.

BRADLEY, R. A.: Rank analysis of incomplete block designs. II. Additional tables for the method of paired comparisons. Biometrika 41, 1954, 502—537 (a).

BRADLEY, R. A.: Incomplete block rank analysis: on the appropriateness of the model for a method of paired comparisons. Biometrics, 10, 1954, 375—390 (b).

——: Rank analysis of incomplete block designs. III. Some large-sample results on estimation and power for a method of paired comparisons. Biometrika, 42, 1955, 450—470.

BRADLEY, R. A. and M. E. TERRY: The rank analysis of incomplete block designs. Biometrika, 39, 1952, 324—345.

CAMPBELL, N. R.: Physics: The elements. Cambridge, 1920, republished as: Foundations of Science, Dover Publications, New York, 1957.

——: An account of the principles of measurement and calculation. Longmans and Green, London, 1928.

CAMPBELL, N. R. and B. P. DADDING: The measurement of light. Philos. Mag., Ser. 6, 44, 1922, 577—590.

CANTOR, G.: Beiträge zur Begründung der transfiniten Mengenlehre. Math. Ann., 46, 1895, 481—512.

CHURCHER, B. G.: A loudness scale for industrial noise measurements. J. Acoust. Soc. Am., 6, 1935, 216—226.

CLARKE, R. F.: Constant-ratio rules for confusion matrices in speech communication. J. Acoust. Soc. Am., 29, 1957, 715—720.

COOMBS, C. H.: A theory of data. Wiley, New York, 1964.

COOMBS, C. H. and R. C. KAO: Nonmetric factor analysis. Engng. Res. Bull., 38, Univ. Michigan Press, Ann Arbor, 1955.

COPELAND, A. H., SR.: Probabilities, observations and predictions. Proc. 3rd Berkeley Symposium, II, 41—47.

DAVIDSON, D. and J. MARSHAK: Experimental tests of stochastic decision theory in: Measurement: Definitions and theories, edd. C. W. CHURCHMAN and P. RATOOSH, Wiley, New York, 1959, 233—269.

DAVIDSON, D. and P. SUPPES: A finistic axiomatization of subjective probability and utility. Econometrica, 24, 1956, 264—275.

DEBREU, G.: Representation of a preference ordering by a numerical function, in: Decision Processes, edd. R. M. THRALL, C. H. COOMBS and R. L. DAVIS, New York, 1954, 159—166.

——: Topological methods in cardinal utility theory, in: Mathematical methods in the social sciences, edd. K. J. ARROW, S. KARLIN and P. SUPPES, Stanford Univ. Press, Stanford, California, 1960, 16—26 (a).

——: Review of R. D. LUCE: Individual choice behavior. Amer. Econ. Rev., 50, 1960, 186—188 (b).

EISLER, H.: On the problem of category scales in psychophysics. Rep. Psychol. Lab. Univ. Stockholm, 107, 1962.

EKMAN, G.: Measurement of moral judgments: A comparison of scaling methods. Perceptual and Motor Skills, 15, 1962, 3—9.

EKMAN, G. and T. KÜNNAPAS: Scales of aesthetic value. Perceptual and Motor Skills, 14, 1962, 19—26 (a).

——: Measurement of aesthetic value by "direct" and "indirect" methods. Scand. J. Psychol., 3, 1962, 33—39 (b).

ELLSBERG, D.: Risk, ambiguity and the SAVAGE axioms. Quart. Econ., 75, 1961, 643—669.

FECHNER, G. T.: Elemente der Psychophysik. Leipzig 1860.

FISHBURN, P. C.: Utility theory. Management Science, 14, 1968, 335—378.

— —: Utility theory for decision making. Wiley, New York, 1970.

FISHER, I.: The making of index numbers. Houghten Mafflin Co, Boston and New York, 1923.

FRISCH, R.: The problem of index numbers. Econometrica, 1936, 1—38.

FUCHS, L.: On mean systems. Acta Math. Acad. Scient. Hung., 1, 1950, 303—320.

GAGE, F. H.: The measurability of auditory sensations. Proc. Royal Soc., 116b, 1934, 103—119.

GARNER, W. R.: A technique and a scale for loudness measurement. J. Acoust. Soc. Am., 26, 1954, 73—88.

GUILFORD, J. P.: Scale values derived from the method of choices. Psychometrika, 2, 1937, 139—150.

GULLIKSEN, H.: A generalization of THURSTONE's learning function. Psychometrika, 18, 1953, 297—307.

HAUSNER, M.: Multidimensional utilities. Decision processes, edd. R. M. THRALL, C. H. COOMBS, H. L. DAVIS, Wiley, New York, 1954, 167—180.

HELMHOLTZ, H. V.: Zählen und Messen, erkenntnistheoretisch betrachtet; in: Philosophische Aufsätze EDUARD ZELLER gewidmet, Leipzig, 1887, translated by C. L. BRYAN: "Counting and Measuring", New York, 1930.

HEMPEL, C. G.: Fundamentals of concept formation in empirical science. Int. Enc. Unified Science, 2, no. 7, Univ. Chicago Press. 1952.

HEVNER, K.: An empirical study of three psychophysical methods. J. Gen. Psychol., 4, 1930, 191—212.

HÖLDER, O.: Die Axiome der Quantität und die Lehre vom Maß. Berichte der Sächsischen Gesellschaft der Wissenschaften, mathem. phys. Klasse, 53, 1901, 1—64.

HOFMANN, K. H.: Zur mathematischen Theorie des Messens. Rozprawy Matematyczne XXXII, Warszawa, 1963.

HOSSZÚ, M.: Nonsymmetric means. Publ. Math. Debrecen, 6, 1959, 1—9.

— —: Note on commutable mappings. Publ. Math. Debrecen, 9, 1962, 105—106.

JUDD, D. B.: Saturation scale for yellow colors. J. Opt. Soc. Am., 23, 1933, 35—40.

KELLEY, J. L.: General topology. van Nostrand, New York, 1955.

KRANTZ, D. H.: Conjoint measurement: The LUCE-TUKEY axiomatization and some extensions. J. Math. Psychol., 1, 1964, 248—278.

KRUSKAL, J. B.: Multidimensional scaling by optimizing goodness of fit to a nonmetric hypothesis. Psychometrika, 29, 1964, 1—27 (a).

— —: Non-metric multidimensional scaling: A numerical method. Psychometrika, 29, 1964, 115—229 (b).

KÜNNAPAS, T., G. MÄLHAMMAR and O. SVENSON: Multidimensional ratio scaling and multidimensional similarity of simple geometric figures. Scand. J. Psychol., 5, 1964, 249—256.

LAZARSFELD, P. F. and N. W. Henry: Latent structure analysis. Houghton—Misslin, Boston, 1968.

LEVINE, M.: Transformations that render curves parallel. J. Math. Psychol., 7, 1970. In press.

——: Transformations that render curves similar and linearly related random variables. J. Math. Psychol., 7, 1970. In press.

LOEVINGER, J.: The technique of homogeneous tests compared with some aspects of "scale analysis" and factor analysis. Psychol. Bull., 45, 1948, 507—530.

LORD, F. M. and R. NOVICK: Statistical theories of mental test scores. Addison-Wesley, Reading, 1968.

LORENZ, C.: Untersuchungen über die Auffassung von Tondistanzen. Philosophische Studien, 6, 1890, 26—103.

LUCE, R. D.: Individual choice behavior. A theoretical analysis. Wiley, New York, 1959.

——: A generalization of a theorem of dimensional analysis. J. Math. Psychol., 1, 1964, 278—284.

——: Two extensions of conjoint measurement. J. Math. Psychol., 3, 1966, 348—370.

LUCE, R. D. and W. EDWARDS: The derivation of subjective scales from just noticeable differences. Psychol. Rev., 65, 1958, 222—237.

LUCE, R. D. and E. GALANTER: Psychophysical scaling, in: Handbook Math. Psychol., Vol. I, edd. R. D. LUCE, R. R. BUSH and E. GALANTER, Wiley, New York and London, 1963, 191—307.

LUCE, R. D. and J. W. TUKEY: Simultaneous conjoint measurement: A new type of fundamental measurement. J. Math. Psychol., 1, 1964, 1—27.

MACDONALD, P. A. and D. M. ROBERTSON: Psychophysical law III. Philos. Mag., Ser. 7, 10, 1930, 1063—1073.

MARKOWITZ, H. M.: Portfolio Selection. Wiley, New York, London, Sidney, 1959.

MENGER, K.: Mensuration and other mathematical connections of observable material, in: Measurement: Definitions and theories, edd. C. W. CHURCHMAN and P. RATOOSH, Wiley, New York, 1959, 97—128.

MESSICK, S. J.: An empirical evaluation of multidimensional successive intervals. Psychometrika, 21, 1956, 367—375.

MOSTELLER, F.: A theory of scalogram analysis, using noncumulative types of items: A new approach to THURSTONE's method of scaling attitudes. Rep. no. 9, Lab. Soc. Rel., Harvard University, 1949.

MOSTELLER, F. and P. NOGEE: An experimental measurement of utility. J. Pol. Econ., 59, 1951, 371—404.

MOTZKIN, T.: Beiträge zur Theorie der linearen Ungleichungen. Dissertation, Basel, 1936.

MÜNSTERBERG, H.: Vergleichung von Tondistanzen. Münsterbergs Beiträge zur experimentellen Psychologie, 4, 1892, 147—177.

VON NEUMANN, J. and O. MORGENSTERN: The theory of games and economic behavior. Princeton Univ. Press, Princeton, 3rd edition, 1953.

NEWMAN, E. B., J. VOLKMANN and S. S. STEVENS: On the method of bisection and its relation to a loudness scale. Amer. J. Psychol., 49, 1937, 134—137.

PENDERGRASS, R. N. and R. A. BRADLEY: Ranking in triple comparisons, in: Contributions to probability and statistics, edd. I. OLKIN et al., Stanford Univ. Press, 1960, 331—351.

PFANZAGL, J.: A general theory of measurement—Applications to utility. Naval Res. Logist. Quart., 6, 1959 283—294 (a).

——: Die axiomatischen Grundlagen einer allgemeinen Theorie des Messens. Schriftenreihe Statist. Inst. Univ. Wien, Vol. 1, Physica-Verlag, Würzburg, 1959 (b).

——: Über die stochastische Fundierung des psychophysischen Gesetzes. Biometrische Zeitschrift, 4, 1962, 1—14.

——: Subjective probability derived from the MORGENSTERN—VON NEUMANN utility concept, in: Essays in Mathematical Economics, edd. M. SHUBIK, Princeton Univ. Press, 1967, 237—251

PLATEAU, M. H.: Sur la mesure des sensations physique, et sur la loi qui lie l'intensité de ses sensations á l'intensité de la cause excitante. Bull. des Acad. Roy. Belg., 33, 1872, 376—388.

PRATT, C. C.: Bisection of tonal intervals smaller than an octave. J. Exp. Psychol., 6, 1923, 211—222.

RAMSEY, F. P.: The foundation of mathematics and other logical essays. Harcourt, Brace and Co., New York, 1931.

RASCH, G.: Probabilistic models for some intelligence and attainement tests. Nielson Lydiche, Copenhagen, 1960.

ROBINSON, A.: Introduction to model theory and to the metamathematics of algebra. North-Holland Publ. Comp., Amsterdam, 1965.

ROSS, S.: Logical foundations of psychological measurement. A study in the philosophy of science. Munksgoord, Copenhagen, 1964.

SAMUELSON, P. A.: Probability, utility and the independence axiom. Econometrica, 20, 1952, 670—678.

SAVAGE, L. J.: The foundations of statistics. Wiley, New York, 1954.

SCOTT, D. and P. SUPPES: Foundational aspects of theories of measurement. J. Symb. Logic, 23, 1958, 113—128.

SHEPARD, R. N.: The analysis of proximities: Multidimensional scaling with an unknown distance function. Psychometrika, 27, 1962, I 125—139, II 219—246.

——: Approximation to uniform gradients of generalization by monotone transformation of scale, in: Stimulus Generalization, edd. D. J. MOSTOFSKY, Stanford Univ. Press, 1965, 94—110.

STEVENS, J. C.: Stimulus spacing and the judgment of loudness. J. Exp. Psychol., 56, 1958, 246—250.

Stevens, S. S. : Mathematics, measurement and psychophysics, in: Handbook Exp. Psychol., New York, 1951, 1—49.

— —: On the averaging of data. Science, 121, 1955, 113—116.

— —: On the psychophysical law. Psychol. Rev., 64, 1957, 153—181.

— —: Cross-modality validation of subjective scales. J. Exp. Psychol.,57, 1959, 201—209.

— —: The surprising simplicity of sensory metrics. American Psychologist, 1962, 29—39.

Stevens, S. S. and E. H. Galanter: Ratio scales and category scales for a dozen perceptual continua. J. Exp. Psychol., 54, 1957, 377—411.

Stevens, S. S. and J. Volkmann: The relation of pitch to frequency; a revised scale. Amer. J. Psychol., 53, 1940, 329—353.

Suppes, P. and M. Winet: An axiomatization of utility based on the notion of utility differences. Management Science, 1, 1955, 259—270.

Suppes, P. and J. L. Zinnes: Basic measurement theory, in: Handbook Math. Psychol., edd. R. D. Luce, R. R. Bush and E. Galanter, Wiley, New York, 1963, Vol. 1, 1—76.

Tarski, A.: Contributions to the theory of models. Indagationes Mathematicae, 16, 1954, 572—581.

Thorndike, E. L.: Handwriting. Teach. Coll. Rec., 11, 1910.

— —: The measurement of intelligence. Columbia University, Teachers College Bureau of Publ., New York, 1927.

Thurstone, L. L.: A method of scaling psychological and educational tests. J. Educ. Psychol., 16, 1925, 433—451.

— —: A law of comparative judgment. Psychol. Rev., 34, 1927, 273—286.

— —: Equally often noticed differences. J. Educ. Psychol., 18, 1927, 289—293(b).

— —: Method of paired comparisons for social values. J. Abnorm. & Soc. Psychol., 21, 1927, 384—400(c).

— —: The learning function. J. Gen. Psychol., 3, 1930, 469—493.

— —: Rankorder as a psychophysical method. J. Exp. Psychol., 14, 1931, 187 201.

Thurstone, L. L. and E. J. Chave: The measurement of attitude., Univ. Chicago Press, 1929.

Titchener, E. B.: Experimental psychology, Vol. II, New York, 1905.

Torgerson, W. S.: Theory and methods of scaling. New York, 1958.

— —: Distances and ratios in psychophysical scaling. Report 58-G-0014. Lincoln Lab., Inst. Tech., Massachusetts, 1960.

Tversky, A.: A general theory of polynomial conjoint measurement. J. Math. Psychol., 4, 1967, 1—20

Waugh, F. V.: The marginal utility of money in the United States from 1917 to 1921 and from 1922 to 1932. Econometrica, 3, 1935, 376—399.

Weitzenhoffer, A. M.: Mathematical structures and psychological measurements. Psychometrika, 16, 1951, 387—406.

Zermelo, E.: Die Berechnung der Turnierergebnisse als ein Maximumproblem der Wahrscheinlichkeitsrechnung. Math. Z., 29, 1929, 436—460.

Author Index

Subject Index

Notation Index